For A. Edgar Benton
Class of 1950

A great graduate of Colorado College. I greatly admired your work for Denver school integration in the 1960s.

Best wishes from
Robert D. Loevy
May 5, 2005

Colorado College:
A Place of Learning, 1874–1999

COLORADO COLLEGE:
A PLACE OF LEARNING
1874 – 1999

by

Robert D. Loevy

The 125th Anniversary of Colorado College

COLORADO COLLEGE
1999

Colorado College, Colorado Springs, CO 80903

Published 1999

Printed in the United States of America

ISBN 0-935052-32-1

TABLE OF CONTENTS

AUTHOR'S PREFACE

This book was written to be read in conjunction with two other books. The first is Charlie Brown Hershey's *Colorado College: 1874–1949*, which is a detailed history of the founding and the first 75 years of Colorado College. The second is J. Juan Reid's *Colorado College: The First Century, 1874–1974*, which chronologically reviews the first 100 years at Colorado College with particularly fine treatment of student life on campus.

This book covers the first 125 years of Colorado College history, but with a view toward relating the story of the College to the history of the state of Colorado and the history of the city of Colorado Springs. This book also is distinguished from its two predecessors in that one-half of this book is concentrated on the 25 years from 1974 to 1999–years that have not previously been chronicled by a Colorado College history writer.

To keep things simple and uncomplicated, this book refers to individual members of the faculty by the title "professor." The author is well aware that most faculty members at Colorado College come in three ranks–assistant professor, associate professor, and the so-called "full" professor. In everyday usage, however, almost all members of the faculty are addressed as "professor," and this book follows that custom.

By 1999 Colorado College has become large enough in size that it is not possible to mention, in one book covering 125 years, every faculty member, administrator, and student who contributed to the life of the College. Those faculty members, administrators, and students who were mentioned by name in this historical account might best be regarded as typical examples of a much larger number of people who have served the College well and done many meritorious things.

Special thanks are due to the following: Professor of Economics Mike Bird and Alumni Director Diane Benninghoff, who co-chaired the celebration of Colorado College's 125th Anniversary; two former presidents of the College–Louis Benezet and Gresham Riley–who each gave an entire working day to be bombarded with questions; current President Kathryn Mohrman, who was unusually helpful with an hours-long interview and a lengthy memorandum on issues of concern at the College; Dean of the College Timothy Fuller, who strongly supported this project, intellectually and administratively, from its inception; and Virginia Kiefer, the Archivist at Colorado College, who was most skilled and helpful at providing key historical documents and photographs from the College's past. Special thanks also go to my brother, Walton T. Loevy, who proofread and critiqued the final draft of the manuscript.

This is the first annotated book on Colorado College history to be published. It identifies many subjects in the College's past that are worthy of further careful research and writing. I found learning and writing about the College's rich history to be a most enjoyable form of academic endeavor. I heartily recommend it to others.

Robert D. Loevy
Colorado Springs, Colorado
July 1, 1998

CHAPTER 1

William Jackson Palmer and Thomas Nelson Haskell:

"In the Beginning . . ."

Few colleges or universities can attribute their reason for being to a mountain, but Colorado College can.

It was at the foot of a very large mountain that a very adventurous man first got the idea to build a very cultivated city and equip it with a very fine college or university.

The mountain is Pike's Peak, the 14,110 foot snowcapped tower of granite that rises out of the high prairies that roll westward from the Mississippi and Missouri river valleys.

A towering and distinctive sentinel, Pike's Peak is the eastern-most of the many peaks in the Rocky Mountain chain that are 14,000 feet high or higher. Its unique ability to loom on the western horizon where no other mountains are visible made it a notable landmark and viewable goal for those heading west across the prairies toward the Rocky Mountains.

The first Europeans to claim ownership of Pike's Peak and the surrounding real estate were the Spaniards. They explored much of what is now the southwestern United States, but they concentrated their settlement efforts in the Rio Grande valley in what later became the Albuquerque and Santa Fe sections of northern New Mexico.

In 1800 the Spaniards traded the vast land area that included Pike's Peak to the French in return for a kingdom in Italy. In 1803 the French sold that same land to the United States. This giant addition to the territory of the United States, negotiated and executed under President Thomas Jefferson, became known as the Louisiana Purchase.

It was President Jefferson who sent U.S. Army Lieutenant Zebulon Montgomery Pike to explore the southern part of the Louisiana Purchase. The famed Lewis and Clark expedition was dispatched to explore the northern part. Zebulon Pike advanced up the Arkansas River in 1806 and soon spied the great landmark mountain looming to the northwest. He and his men spent two and a half days trying to climb the challenging peak. Heavy snows and their light clothing eventually forced them to give up.

But Zebulon Pike was the first official emissary of the United States to write a description of the great mountain and try to reach its summit. As a result, those who came to the region after Pike called the mountain Pike's Peak.

Fourteen years later, in 1820, a party of three men, led by scientist Edwin James, succeeded in climbing the mountain.

The next important visitor to the region was William Green Russell. In 1858 he and his two brothers, Oliver and Levi, set out from Georgia to look for gold in the Rocky Mountains. The three brothers collected a sizable party of men and prospected their way up the Arkansas River valley to the foot of Pike's Peak.

They found no gold near the mighty mountain, so they moved northward and crossed the divide between the Arkansas River and the South Platte River. They then worked their way down the South Platte valley. At a point close to where Cherry Creek flows into the South Platte River, the Russell party panned out several hundred dollars worth of gold.

That simple feat made Pike's Peak the most famous mountain in the United States.

Word of the Russell gold discovery spread rapidly throughout the rest of the nation. There was an economic depression at the time, so large numbers of men raced westward to see if they could find mineral riches in the South Platte valley. This great population movement was named the Pike's Peak Gold Rush, because the prominent mountain seventy miles to the south was the distinguishing feature of this primitive and lightly inhabited land. Would-be miners painted the words "Pike's Peak or

Bust" on their covered wagons to inspire them during their long and dangerous journey to the goldfields.

The initial gold strike made by the Russell party quickly played out, but subsequent large and lucrative strikes were made at places that came to be known as Central City, Idaho Springs, and Boulder. As the population rush to the region accelerated, a "supply town" was founded at the confluence of the South Platte River and Cherry Creek, near the spot where the Russells first found gold. This rapidly-growing city was named Denver, for General James W. Denver, the territorial Governor of Kansas. At that time Pike's Peak and the surrounding gold prospecting country were in the western end of Kansas Territory.

This great gold rush did have an effect on the immediate Pike's Peak region. Gold discoveries were made in South Park, the great mountain valley that lay to the west of the Peak. One route to this particular goldfield went up Ute Pass, a tortuous mountain trail that started at the eastern foot of Pike's Peak and then led westward past the north side of the great mountain. A small village named Colorado City grew up at the base of the Ute Pass trail and survived economically by feeding and outfitting would-be miners bound for the South Park diggings.[1]

This little city, Colorado City, took its name from the gigantic and spectacular red rock formations located nearby. Colorado is the Spanish word for "ruddy colored."

As the gold rush increased in intensity, the population growth in Denver became substantial, and soon the many residents of that brand-new city began wondering if they wanted to be governed from a place as far away as Topeka, the capital of Kansas Territory. They concluded they did not. They petitioned the U.S. Congress to separate the goldfields of western Kansas Territory into a new territory, with a view to this territory someday becoming a state.

The firing on Fort Sumter in South Carolina provided Congress with the impetus to act. The South seceded from the Union, thereby precipi-

---

[1]South Park became famous for placer mining, finding gold by mechanically processing the gravel in river and stream beds. Even in the latter half of the 20th Century, the remains of large placer mining machines could be seen rotting and rusting away in river beds in South Park west of Colorado Springs.

tating the Civil War. As a result of southern senators and representatives leaving the nation's capital for their home states, northerners came to dominate both the U.S. Senate and the U.S. House of Representatives. In 1861 Kansas was admitted to the Union as a free state—no human slavery allowed—and the Pike's Peak area was admitted as a free territory.

The new territory was created by drawing a big square box around the city of Denver. The result was a territory shaped like a rectangle that measured 400 miles east to west and 300 miles north to south. Pike's Peak, like Denver, was situated more or less in the middle of this vast new governmental unit. Eventually Denver was chosen to be the capital city. As for a name, the new territory was called Colorado, the same Spanish word that had been used to describe the sensational red rocks at the foot of Pike's Peak.

Things were happening very fast. Less than three years had passed from the discovery of gold by the William Green Russell party to the official creation of the Territory of Colorado.

And then, almost as quickly as it had boomed, the Pike's Peak Gold Rush went bust. By 1864 the gold-bearing ores were beginning to play out in Colorado, and the new gold being found was mixed with other elements from which the gold could not easily be separated. In April of 1864 the price of the major Colorado gold stocks spiraled downward. It was the first step in Colorado developing its world-famous "Boom and Bust" reputation.

The gold mining industry began to revive in 1868. Nathaniel P. Hill, a Professor of Chemistry at Brown University in Providence, Rhode Island, discovered a profitable way to refine pure gold from gold ore. The state's first gold smelter was constructed at Black Hawk, near the great Central City gold mines, and Colorado's mineral-dependent economy staged a healthy comeback.[2]

---

[2]For the history of Colorado, see Carl Ubbelohde, Maxine Benson, and Duane A. Smith, *A Colorado History*, 7th ed. (Boulder, CO: Pruett Publishing, 1995). Also see Marshall Sprague, *Colorado: A History* (New York, NY: Norton, 1984). Carl Abbott, Stephen J. Leonard, and David McComb, *Colorado: A History Of The Centennial State*, 3rd ed. (Niwot, CO: University Press of Colorado, 1994). For a summary history of Colorado, see "A Sociopolitical History of Colorado" in Thomas E. Cronin and Robert D. Loevy, *Colorado Politics And Government: Governing The Centennial State* (Lincoln, NE: University of Nebraska Press, 1993), 31–53.

Enter General Palmer

One year later, in late July of 1869, a former Union cavalry officer, General William Jackson Palmer, was traveling through southern Colorado. At the time he was supervising the construction of a railroad line from Kansas City to Denver. General Palmer described the scene as his stagecoach approached Pike's Peak from the southeast:

"Just before sunset we came in sight of the mountains, Pike's Peak, Spanish Peaks and the Greenhorn Range. A thunderstorm came on and the clouds threw themselves into grand and fantastic shapes, blending with the mountain peaks so as scarcely to be distinguishable. Riding as usual on top of the coach I got wet, but what of that? One can't behold the Rocky Mountains in a storm every day."[3]

As General Palmer's coach approached Colorado City later that night, he tried to sleep but was awakened by bright moonlight. "I found the magnificent Pike's Peak towering immediately above," Palmer noted, "topped with a little snow. I could not sleep any more with all the splendid panorama of mountains gradually unrolling itself, as the moon faded and the sun began to rise. . . . I sat up and drank in, along with purest mountain air, the full exhilaration of that early morning ride."

That day, July 27, 1869, General Palmer breakfasted in the spectacular red rocks near Colorado City. Even at that early date the area was known as the Garden of the Gods. He "freshened up by a preliminary bath" in the nearby waters of Fountain Creek. He found the area "enticing," noted its suitability to become a "famous resort," and concluded that "the scenery is even finer south of Denver than north of it."[4]

It was at this moment that General Palmer decided to build a home in the eastern foothills of Pike's Peak, next to the Garden of the Gods, and locate a new city on a low, broad mesa top nearby. The city was to be Colorado Springs, and part and parcel of "Palmer's Dream" for that new city was the idea that it should contain a college or university.

---

[3]Letter, William Jackson Palmer to Queen Mellen, 26 July 1869, quoted from John S. Fisher, *A Builder Of The West: The Life Of General William Jackson Palmer* (Caldwell, ID: Caxton Printers, 1939), 161.

[4]Letter, William Jackson Palmer to Queen Mellen, 28 July 1869, quoted from Fisher, *A Builder Of The West*, 162.

Thus one reason Colorado College came to be was that a great man, General William Jackson Palmer, was swept away by the incredible scenery surrounding a high mountain, Pike's Peak, and resolved to build there a city that included what he hoped would be a foremost institution of higher learning.

General Palmer was not a man whose resolutions could be taken lightly. Within less than five years of his inspiring visit to Pike's Peak and the Garden of the Gods, both the city—Colorado Springs—and the institution of higher learning—Colorado College—were reality.

THE EARLY LIFE OF GENERAL PALMER

William Jackson Palmer was born on September 17, 1836, on a farm at Kinsale, near Leipsic, in Kent County, Delaware. He was of English, Dutch, and German origin, but it was believed that his English ancestors had come to the United States with William Penn, the Quaker founder of Philadelphia and Pennsylvania.[5]

When William Palmer was five-years-old, his mother and father left Delaware and moved to Philadelphia. Palmer grew up in a house at 513 High Street in Germantown, a section of northwest Philadelphia. The young Palmer thus became a city-dweller from Philadelphia rather than a farmer's child from rural Delaware.

He went to the Friends' School and the Zane Street Grammar School in Philadelphia and attended Boys' High School. He did not go to a college or university, which seems strange for a man who, later in life, wanted his new city to include an institution of higher learning. What he did become was a self-made "Philadelphia aristocrat," a man who was "enormously persistent to achieve his own ends, which had to do with a dream of building around him a neat, trim, happy, sensible world."[6]

At the age of 17 William Palmer went to work on a civil engineering crew in the railroad industry, surveying and locating railroad lines in the Allegheny Mountains of western Pennsylvania. At that time railroads

---

[5]For a detailed account of William Jackson Palmer's life, see Fisher, *A Builder Of The West.*

[6]Marshall Sprague, *Newport In The Rockies: The Life And Good Times Of Colorado Springs*, Centennial ed. (Chicago, IL: Sage Books, 1971), 16.

William Jackson Palmer
He selected the location for Colorado College and made major financial contributions for its support.

were expanding westward and were just pushing over the Appalachian Mountains into the Midwest. Palmer devoted the remainder of his working life to conceiving, financing, and building a variety of railroad projects. He received an insider's education in how to run a railroad by serving several years as the private secretary to J. Edgar Thomson, the famous builder and President of the Pennsylvania Railroad.

During this period Palmer spent eight months in England and France, observing the latest in railroad facilities and operations and, in his spare time, visiting museums and other cultural landmarks. This visit to the Old World helped to develop the aura of sophistication and the appreciation of education and culture that marked his later life.

WILLIAM PALMER IN THE CIVIL WAR

The Civil War intervened dramatically in William Palmer's railroading career. Although a good Pennsylvania Quaker, Palmer put aside the pacifism of his religious faith and opted to join the fight to abolish human slavery. He sought and won a Captain's commission in the Union Army and proceeded to recruit and train a cavalry regiment of hand-picked young Pennsylvanians. Leading his cavalrymen on horseback, General Palmer fought at the Battle of Antietam Creek in Maryland, the bloodiest single day in the Civil War. Palmer and his men reconnoitered Confederate troop movements at Antietam and, following a long hard ride up the towpath of the Chesapeake and Ohio Canal along the Potomac River, destroyed a Confederate pontoon bridge.[7]

Palmer and his men fought in a variety of other engagements throughout the upper South. In his most famous military effort, Palmer chased Confederate President Jefferson Davis down the Appalachian Mountains to Georgia, where the Southern leader was finally captured by Union cavalry from Michigan.

By the end of the Civil War, William Palmer had attained the rank of Brigadier General. He was formally addressed as "General Palmer" for the

[7]Fisher, *A Builder Of The West*, 87. For detailed accounts of General Palmer's actions in the Civil War, see Charles E. Kirk, ed., *History of the Fifteenth Pennsylvania Volunteer Cavalry* (Philadelphia, PA: 1906). Also see Samuel P. Bates, *History of Pennsylvania Volunteers, 1861–1865* (Harrisburg, PA: B. Singerly, State Printer, 1869–71), 902–910. Suzanne C. Wilson, *Column South, with the 15th Pennsylvania Cavalry. . . .* (Flagstaff, AZ: J.F. Colton, 1960).

remainder of his life. He returned to civilian pursuits and reentered the railroad industry. But in 1866, the action in railroad building had shifted from the Appalachian Mountains to the vast, undeveloped prairies west of the Missouri River. Palmer left the East, moved to the West, and was hired to help build the Kansas Pacific Railroad westward from Kansas City.

QUEEN PALMER

In the spring of 1869 William Palmer was riding on a railroad train heading east from St. Louis, Missouri, when he met Queen Mellen, a 19-year-old woman from New York. He fell instantly in love with her, became her most ardent suitor, and within weeks they were engaged to be married.

It was just a few months later, in July of 1869, that Palmer paid his historic first visit to Pike's Peak and visualized his new city of Colorado Springs. When he fantasized about building a home in one of the canyons close by the Garden of the Gods, his fantasy included the young and elegant Queen living in that home with him as his wife. He wrote to his betrothed: "I somehow fancied that an exploration of the dancing little tributaries of [Monument Creek] or [Fountain Creek] might disclose somewhere up near to where they come leaping with delight from the cavernous wall of the Rocky Mountains, perhaps some charming spot that might be made a future home."[8]

THE DENVER AND RIO GRANDE RAILROAD

Things came together quickly for William Jackson Palmer. The Kansas Pacific Railroad line was completed from Kansas City to Denver, and Palmer began to dream of a major railroad project of his own. He would build a line south from Denver that would pass just a few miles east of the Garden of the Gods. This line would continue southward down to and beyond Pueblo and then cross the Sangre de Cristo Mountains into the Rio Grande Valley. The wealthy owners of the vast ranch lands south of the Sangre de Cristos would help finance the railroad, because when the tracks reached their area the value of their landholdings would quadruple in value.

---

[8]Letter, William Jackson Palmer to Queen Mellen, 28 July 1869, quoted from Fisher, *A Builder Of The West*, 162.

Palmer named this ambitious new venture the Denver and Rio Grande Railroad.[9]

But Palmer built his new railroad in a way that made him—and Colorado—famous in railroad history. He did not space the rails at four feet, eight and one-half inches apart, the so-called "standard gauge" which almost all the other railroads in the United States were using. Palmer laid his rails just three feet apart, thereby introducing "narrow gauge" railroading to the Colorado mountains and foothills. This "baby railroad," as it soon was called, was less expensive to construct and could more easily be built up steep mountain grades and around sharp mountain curves. Other railroaders followed Palmer's example and built narrow gauge tracks into the Rocky Mountains. Colorado soon became renowned for its many colorful and scenic narrow gauge lines.

And something else was unusual about William Palmer's new railroad. Most other railroad builders constructed their lines from one established city to another, seeking to do business with communities that already existed. Not General Palmer! He carefully built his railroad away from established cities and towns and then, along his railroad right-of-way, founded his own new communities. He was careful to own or control much of the land in the new cities and towns along his new railroad, and that way he made generous profits from the increased land values his railroad brought to his new communities. The Rio Grande railroad was "responsible for the creation of such towns as Alamosa, Garland City, and La Veta and for tripling the population of Pueblo in a year's time."[10]

The Founding of Colorado Springs

On November 7, 1870, William Jackson Palmer and Queen Mellen were married and sailed to Europe for their honeymoon. One month earlier,

---

[9]For a history of the Denver and Rio Grande Railroad, see Robert G. Athearn, *Rebel Of The Rockies: A History Of The Denver And Rio Grande Western Railroad* (New Haven, CT: Yale University Press, 1962). For a detailed account of the first ten years of the Denver and Rio Grande Railroad, see George L. Anderson, *General William J. Palmer: A Decade Of Colorado Railroad Building 1870–1880* (Colorado Springs, CO: Colorado College, 1936).

[10]Abbott, Leonard, and McComb, *Colorado: A History Of The Centennial State*, 3rd ed., 92.

Palmer had organized the Denver and Rio Grande Railroad so it could begin building its narrow gauge line south toward Palmer's new city of Colorado Springs. In 1871, just back from a lengthy wedding trip, Palmer formed the Colorado Springs Company to own all the land in his new city and sell it, at a profit of course, to new settlers.

Palmer hired a city planner, Robert A. Cameron, to lay out the streets, parks, and major public facilities of his new community. "My theory for this place," he told Cameron in a letter, "is that it should be made the most attractive place for homes in the West, a place for schools, colleges, science, first class newspapers, and everything that the above imply." This reference to "schools, colleges, science" was made in December of 1871 and is one of the first written records that General Palmer intended his new city to have a college or university.[11]

On July 31, 1871, the first stake was driven, at the corner of Cascade Avenue and Pike's Peak Avenue, to begin the building of Colorado Springs. The first train of the Denver and Rio Grande Railroad reached the new city on October 21 of that year, connecting it to the great cities of the Midwest and East. In 1872 the first Colorado Springs newspaper, *Out West*, began publishing. In 1873 Colorado Springs was designated the County Seat of El Paso County, Colorado Territory. And approximately one mile north of the first stake, on the west side of Cascade Avenue, 20 acres of land was set aside for a college or university.

An Entrepreneurial Philosophy

Thus it was that General Palmer's desire to build a new railroad in Colorado became linked with his love for Queen Mellen and his enchantment with the scenery at the eastern foot of Pike's Peak. He built the railroad to make money. He built the city to make even more money and to please his new wife. He included a college or university in his site plans because such an institution would help guarantee the financial success of Colorado Springs and, coincidentally, make his new hometown a more liveable and cultured community.

[11]General William Jackson Palmer, recalled in an article he wrote for the *Colorado Springs Gazette*, Carnival Edition, 3 August 1896. Reprinted August 1923 and August 1926.

It is important to keep in mind that General Palmer was a Quaker from Pennsylvania. He was a businessman first and a college or university founder second. He believed it was important for the individual to serve his or her own interests first. But Palmer also believed that, when serving his or her own interests, the individual would create wealth that would benefit his or her fellow men and women. To Palmer, the community was basically a place for the individual to be entrepreneurial and make money. But it was an important coincidental benefit that such activities also improved the community.

In a long letter to Queen Mellen written in January of 1870, Palmer outlined his early plans for building the Denver and Rio Grande Railroad. He described the money-making nature of the project, but he also wrote of seeing to it that there was "no distress among the workmen and their families," and that he would see that they had schools, bath-houses, libraries, and lectures available to them. He concluded with this telling line: "But my dream was not all of a new mode of making money, but of a model way of conjoining that with usefulness on a large scale, solving with it a good many vexed social problems."[12]

General Palmer was an organizer. "He made plans and picked henchmen to carry them out while he went off promoting something else."[13] Palmer planned to spend his time continuing to build the Denver and Rio Grande Railroad and founding many other cities and towns throughout Colorado, New Mexico, and Utah. He would give money, land, and moral support to his proposed institution of higher learning. But someone else would have to do the actual work of founding the college or university which Palmer wanted for his dream city of Colorado Springs.

The Minister and His Ailing Daughter

That man was Thomas Nelson Haskell. He was a Congregational minister who had moved his family to Colorado Territory in 1873 in hopes of restoring the health of his 14-year-old daughter, Florence Edwards Haskell. She

---

[12]Letter, William Jackson Palmer to Queen Mellen, 17 January 1870, quoted from Fisher, *A Builder Of The West*, 178.

[13]Sprague, *Newport In The Rockies*, 27.

was suffering from a lung disease. Many families came to Colorado at that time hoping that the cool and dry mountain air might cure a family member who had tuberculosis or some other pulmonary ailment.

General Palmer had let it be known that he wanted to talk with anyone who might be willing to found a college or university in Colorado Springs. Apparently "one sect was as good as another, if responsible and efficient." Around 1872 or 1873 the Order of the Jesuit Fathers considered the new city for the site of a Catholic college or university. The Jesuits were favorably impressed with Colorado Springs, but they finally selected Denver.[14]

In 1873 Thomas Haskell and his daughter Florence traveled to Colorado Springs to speak with General Palmer about founding a Congregational college. They met at Glen Eyrie, the large and luxurious home which, just as he said he would do, General Palmer was building for Queen Palmer in one of the beautiful canyons north of the Garden of the Gods.

Florence Haskell apparently was a precocious young woman who shared her father's love of learning. While at Glen Eyrie she saw eagles perched upon the rocky canyon walls and gliding through the sky. She suggested to her father that it would be most appropriate to found a college nearby, "where persons inclined to pulmonary disease might learn to soar as light of heart and free of wing as old Glen Eyrie's king of birds, whose flight above the clouds symbolized her aspiring faith and hope."[15]

Sadly, Florence Haskell died shortly thereafter. On October 29, 1873, her father presented to the Conference of Colorado Congregational Churches, meeting at Boulder, a proposal to establish a Christian college

---

[14]Edward Payson Tenney, *Looking Forward Into The Past* (Nahant, MA: Rumford Press, 1910), 65 note 1. Tenney was an early President of Colorado College. Also see James Hutchison Kerr, "The Pioneer Days Of Colorado College," *El Paso County Democrat*, Pioneer ed., December 1908. Kerr, one of the first professors at Colorado College, kept a series of scrap books on Colorado Springs and Colorado College history. This newspaper article can be found in Book I, 1–6, in the Colorado College Archives.

[15]Horace M. Hale, *Education In Colorado* (Denver, CO: News Printing Company, 1885), 96. Hale does not tell this story about Florence Edwards Haskell himself. It is included in an article on Colorado College inserted at the end of the book. The author of the article is not identified. There is a second reference to this story written by hand on the back of a drawing of Florence Edwards Haskell. It reads: "Florence Edwards Haskell, whose early death while longing for a college in this health-giving climate, inspired her father to start Colorado College." Drawing, Florence Edwards Haskell, Colorado College Archives.

FLORENCE EDWARDS HASKELL
AT 12; (1871)

'Florence Edwards Haskell, whose early death while longing for a college in this health-giving climate, inspired her father to start Colorado College.

Florence Edwards Haskell At Age 12
Shortly after her death from a lung ailment at age 14, her father, Thomas Nelson Haskell, sought to establish a college in Colorado Territory in her memory.

in Colorado. He wanted the new college to be his fatherly tribute to his deceased daughter's memory.

The Colorado Congregationalists enthusiastically accepted Haskell's proposal. The cities of Denver, Greeley, and Colorado Springs competed to have the institution located in their community. Haskell selected Colorado Springs following a meeting with local political and religious leaders at the home of Frank L. Rouse, located at the northwest corner of Cascade Avenue and Costilla Street.[16] The city won Haskell over by offering ten acres of land for the college campus, 70 acres of residential lots in the city that could be sold to raise money, and $10,000 cash. In addition, General Palmer had banned the sale of alcohol in his new city, and that made Colorado Springs appear particularly desirable to Reverend Haskell.

A Board of Trustees was appointed, and it gathered for its first formal meeting in Denver from February 3rd to February 5th, 1874. It drew up and approved a Charter for the new college dated February 4, 1874. That day thus was the day on which Colorado College came into existence as a proposed but finite legal entity.

The Charter was filed with the Territory of Colorado on February 9, 1874, and in El Paso County on February 17, 1874. The Board toyed for a while with naming the new institution "Colorado Springs College," but the corporate name finally adopted was "The Colorado College."

Haskell was appointed Solicitor of the new institution of higher learning with a salary of $3,000 per year plus expenses. He was to see to housing the new college, hiring its first faculty, and raising money to support it from East Coast benefactors.

Thomas Nelson Haskell thus is the *founder* of Colorado College. As for General Palmer, his role cannot be minimized, but he qualified more as the *locator* and *benefactor* of the College rather than its founder. William Jackson Palmer conceived of having a college in Colorado Springs, and he gave land and money for that college. But it was Thomas Nelson Haskell who actually organized the new institution and set it in operation. "Other men took part in the deliberations of committees and confer-

[16]Kerr, "The Pioneer Days Of Colorado College."

ences, and were constructively active in the early days of the College. The names of these men recur many times during the formative period and on into the period of its more substantial growth, but the name of Haskell is the pivot around which the ideas and actions of the first days moved."[17]

THE FOUNDER'S CREDENTIALS

Thomas Nelson Haskell was ably qualified to be the founder of Colorado College. He perfectly represented that complex intermixture of religion and education that led to the founding of a great many colleges and universities in the United States in the 19th Century.

Haskell described himself as an Ohio man, and that is what he was. Although he was born in Mina in Chautauqua County, New York, on January 20, 1826, his family moved to Ohio when he was very young. He attended preparatory school at Farmington Academy in Ohio and spent his freshman year in college at Miami University in Oxford, Ohio, northwest of Cincinnati. For his sophomore and junior years he attended Oberlin College in Oberlin, Ohio, near Cleveland. He came back to Miami University for his senior year, graduating in 1851.

Although it was called a university, Miami of Ohio in the early 1850s was mainly a small college combined with a preparatory school. There were 142 students in both the university and the preparatory school, and only 11 students in Thomas Haskell's senior class. He was listed in the 1851 catalog as T. Nelson Haskell from Sandusky City, Ohio. The university at that time was all men.[18] It was "a religious college" and said to be "the principal training ground of Presbyterian ministers in Ohio."[19]

But, when organizing Colorado College, Thomas Haskell seemed to be thinking more of Oberlin College as his model rather than Miami of Ohio. At a meeting on forming Colorado College held in Colorado Springs, Haskell said it was his intention to found a coeducational institu-

---

[17]Charlie Brown Hershey, *Colorado College: 1874–1949* (Colorado Springs, CO: Colorado College, 1952), 31.

[18]*Eighth Triennial Catalogue Of The Officers And Graduates Of Miami University, 1851* (Cincinnati, OH: T. Wrightson for the University, 1851), 30.

[19]Walter Havighurst, *The Miami Years, 1809–1984*, 175th Anniversary ed. (New York, NY: Putnam's, 1984), 103.

Thomas Nelson Haskell
He founded Colorado College and said it was to be patterned after Oberlin College in Ohio. Similar to Oberlin, Colorado College was to be open to both sexes and all races.

tion molded along the lines of Oberlin College.[20] That meant a college that was open to both sexes and all races. Oberlin was the first college in the United States to admit women students—on December 4, 1833—and from 1835 to 1900 was the major college or university in the northern United States that was educating African-Americans. "There were probably 25 African-Americans attending Oberlin College when Haskell was studying there from 1848 to 1850."[21]

During his undergraduate years at Oberlin, Haskell was the Principal of Wayne Academy, a preparatory school. In the year following his graduation from Miami University, he was the Principal of the high school in Sandusky. While there he organized the first statewide meeting of teachers ever held in Ohio.[22]

Following this brief foray into public school education, Haskell prepared for the ministry at Union Theological Seminary, a Presbyterian-oriented institution in New York City. He then went for one year to Andover Theological Seminary in Andover, Massachusetts, which was Congregationalist. He returned to Union Seminary to complete his religious training, getting his divinity degree in 1854.[23]

Haskell had one foot planted in the Congregational Church and the other foot in the Presbyterian Church. He served as Pastor of the Western Presbyterian Church in Washington, D.C., where he was ordained a Presbyterian minister in 1855. But he then moved to the Maverick Congregational Church in East Boston, where he served as Pastor. He was

---

[20]Louise Buckley, "The History Of Colorado College, 1874–1904," M.A. Thesis in History, Colorado College, 1935, 4. This thesis is annotated and is an excellent guide to original source material on the early history of the College, particularly newspaper articles from the *Colorado Springs Gazette*.

[21]Author's notes, telephone interview with Roland Baumann, Archivist, Oberlin College, 5 May 1998. For information on coeducation and African-American education at Oberlin in the mid–19th Century, see Robert S. Fletcher, *A History Of Oberlin College* (Oberlin, OH: Oberlin College, 1943), Volume I, 373–385, Volume II, 523–536.

[22]Thomas Nelson Haskell took an interest in public education in Colorado. He was a strong supporter of opening educational opportunities for Spanish-speaking persons in Colorado. He advocated teaching in the Spanish language in the public schools and hiring a Spanish-speaking Assistant Superintendent of Public Instruction for Colorado. See Hale, *Education In Colorado*, 32, 38–39, 47–48.

[23]*General Catalogue Of The Graduates And Former Students Of Miami University, 1809–1909* (University Archives, Miami University, Oxford, Ohio, 1909), 58. Much of the information on Thomas Nelson Haskell is from this source. Also see Hershey, *Colorado College, 1874–1949*, 31–32.

married to Ann Eliza Edwards, the daughter of Justin Edwards, the President of Andover Theological Seminary. Prior to her marriage to Thomas Haskell, Ann Eliza Edwards was the private secretary of Harriet Beecher Stowe, the anti-slavery author of *Uncle Tom's Cabin.*

It is necessary to emphasize at this point the central role which Andover Theological Seminary played in the founding and early history of Colorado College. The three biggest names in the creation and successful development of the College—Thomas Nelson Haskell, Edward Payson Tenney, and William Frederick Slocum—attended or took their divinity degrees from Andover Theological Seminary. The same was true of many of the early faculty of Colorado College. Producing graduates who were simultaneously equipped to be both ministers and educators was a major characteristic of Andover Theological Seminary in the mid–19th Century.[24]

Haskell became ill from overwork while serving his Congregational church in East Boston, so he took a therapeutic tour to Europe, Egypt, and Palestine. When he returned he became pastor of the First Presbyterian Church in East Boston.

It is important to note that, despite his Ohio upbringing and undergraduate education, Haskell spent a considerable amount of time in New England and made many important contacts there. He studied at Andover Theological Seminary for one year, married a New England woman closely associated with Andover Theological Seminary, and pastored both a Congregational and a Presbyterian church in East Boston. He thus came to know New England, its people, and its religious and educational traditions very well.

In 1866 Haskell briefly switched from religion to education. For three years he served as a Professor of Logic, Literature, and Political Economy at the University of Wisconsin in Madison. The broad sweep of his teaching assignment at Wisconsin, covering as it did subjects in Philosophy,

---

[24]Andover Theological Seminary subsequently combined with Newton Theological Seminary and moved to Newton, Massachusetts. In the late 1990s a number of the original buildings that Haskell, Tenney, and Slocum lived and studied in were part of the campus of Phillips Academy, a preparatory school in Andover. The cemetery adjacent to the original campus of Andover Theological Seminary contained the graves of many men who, similar to Haskell, Tenney, and Slocum, followed combined ministerial and education careers.

English, and Social Science, suggests that Haskell had been broadly educated in the liberal arts and could teach accordingly.

Following his three years at the University of Wisconsin, Haskell became pastor of the New England Church in Aurora, Illinois, a distant suburb of Chicago. While there he served on the Board of Trustees of Wheaton College in Wheaton, Illinois. It was in Illinois that his daughter Florence's lung disease worsened, thereby necessitating the family's move to Colorado.

THE CONGREGATIONAL CONNECTION

Although Haskell had close ties to both the Presbyterian and Congregational churches, it was the Congregational Church that dominated in his efforts to found Colorado College. As previously noted, it was the Colorado Congregational Conference which officially backed Haskell's early efforts in the field of higher education in Colorado and accepted his recommendation that the new College be located in Colorado Springs. Perhaps even more important, prominent and wealthy members of the Congregational Church in New England took an interest in Colorado College and sent their money and, in some cases, their children to this fledgling school in the Rocky Mountain West.

It was no surprise that the Congregational Church played a leading role in the founding of Colorado College. Scholars have identified more than 40 liberal arts colleges in the United States that were initially sponsored by the Congregationalists, those New England-based heirs of the Pilgrim-Puritan tradition. As happened at Colorado College, the Congregationalists tended to subsequently relinquish religious control over the institutions they founded. Among the better known colleges founded by Congregationalists were Yale, Dartmouth, Williams, Amherst, Bowdoin, Middlebury, Oberlin, Knox, Grinnell, and Carleton.

THE COLLEGE BEGINS

Haskell recommended that his brother-in-law, Jonathan Edwards of Dedham, Massachusetts, take charge of the new College and organize the first classes. The Board of Trustees appointed Edwards to this task. Jonathan Edwards had an educational background that was similar to most of the early leaders of Colorado College. He prepared at Phillips Academy in Andover, attended college at Yale in New Haven, Connecticut, and studied for the ministry at Andover Theological Seminary. Before coming to Colorado Springs, he had been a successful minister at parishes in both New England and New York.

On May 6, 1874, the first classes met at Colorado College. Jonathan Edwards ran the College and did most of the teaching himself. During that first session in the spring of 1874, all the students were in the preparatory department. It was a common practice at that time, when there were so few preparatory schools and public high schools, for colleges and universities to include a preparatory department where students were given the educational background they needed to do college and university level work.

These first classes were held in a two-story brick building called the Wanless Block. It was located at the northwest corner of Pike's Peak Avenue and Tejon Street, which later became the site of the First National Bank building, subsequently Bank One.

The College was coeducational from the moment of its inception. There were 25 students in that first session of classes, 13 men and 12 women. There also was a woman on the faculty. Miss Minna Knapp, of Germany, helped Jonathan Edwards with his instructional duties by teaching both German and Music.[25] Other women faculty members during the early years of the College were Minnie S. Mackenzie, Instructor in English, and Georgia B. Gaylord, Instructor in Music.

It was decided to build a permanent structure for the College beginning with the first classes in the fall of 1874. A wood frame structure consisting of three rooms was constructed in the 300 block of North Tejon Street, just north of the Cumberland Presbyterian Church. The new building was located across from Acacia Park, an entire city block set aside by the founders of Colorado Springs for park and recreational activities. The men students went there to play ball. Acacia Park thus was the first informal athletic field of Colorado College.

---

[25]Jonathan Edwards, Report to the Board of Trustees of Colorado College, June 30, 1874.

1874

Colorado College.

THE first term of the Preparatory Department of **Colorado College** will open at Colorado Springs, Wednesday, May 6, 1874, and continue ten weeks.

The object of this department is to give students, of both sexes, a thorough drill in the rudiments of English and Classical Education, and thus fit them for either college or business.

Classes suited to the age and advancement of all who may apply, will be formed.*

Rev. Jonathan Edwards, of Mass., who has been elected by the Board of Trustees as Principal of this Department, is highly recommended as a practical, efficient educator. He will be assisted by competent and experienced teachers.

Rooms well adapted to the purpose have been secured, and will be fitted up in the best and most approved manner.

Arrangements have been made by which boarding can be secured in private families and otherwise, at reasonable rates.

Tuition, - - $10.00 to $20.00 - - per Term,

According to the Studies Pursued.

For further particulars address, until May 1st, Rev. J. M. Sturtevant, or J. E. Ayers, of Denver, Col., and after May 1st,

REV. JONATHAN EDWARDS,
Colorado Springs.

*Instruction will be given to under graduates, in College studies, if desired.

Getting Started

This printed announcement of the opening of Colorado College circulated prior to the holding of the first classes on May 6, 1874.

This first College building cost $1,500 to put up. An additional $200 was provided for furnishings. This smallish wooden structure was the only building Colorado College had for the next six years, from the summer of 1874 until the building that became Cutler Hall was ready for occupancy in 1880 on the permanent College grounds several blocks to the north.[26]

HASKELL RESIGNS

That same fall of 1874, the Board of Trustees began inquiring of Thomas Nelson Haskell as to how his fund-raising activities were progressing. He reported that he had $17,000 in subscriptions, but the actual money was difficult to collect due to the economic recession that slowed the United States economy from 1873 to 1875. The business situation was so dire in the nation and in Colorado Springs that Professor James Hutchison Kerr later wrote a pamphlet about it. He noted: "Even here in Colorado Springs one could not go upon the street without being compelled to listen to one of these imps of despair asserting that Colorado Springs . . . had no financial basis and never could have; that it was the wild scheme of reckless speculators originated for the sole purpose of hoodwinking and swindling honest men and women."[27]

Then there was another problem. A plague of grasshoppers hit Colorado Springs in August of 1874, causing an agricultural depression in the immediate region.[28] On September 10, 1874, in light of his inability to raise substantial and badly needed funds for the College, Thomas Haskell resigned as Solicitor.

Thomas Nelson Haskell truly was the founder of Colorado College, but his active participation in the day-to-day work of the new institution actually was quite brief. He had been Solicitor for a period of only six

---

[26]One of the first professors at the College, James Hutchison Kerr, called for erecting a tablet to commemorate this first home of Colorado College. He wrote: "When a permanent building is erected upon this lot, the writer hopes that a tablet may be permanently placed in front of the same, saying: On this desert lot was erected the first home for Colorado College. . . . Occupied first Sept. 9, 1874." Kerr, "The Pioneer Days Of Colorado College."

[27]James Hutchison Kerr, "When Colorado College Was Not In Flower," 24 October 1904, 5. This pamphlet can be found in the Kerr scrap books, Book I, 11.

[28]A photograph showed grasshoppers piled four feet deep within two blocks of Tejon Street and Pike's Peak Avenue. See Kerr, "The Pioneer Days Of Colorado College."

months. During that time, however, he did get the College started and left behind him a going educational institution.

He remained a member of the Board of Trustees until 1878. He lived the rest of his life in Denver, serving for several years as Custodian of the Colorado State Library. He composed a number of popular hymns and songs, and he wrote extensively on such topics as "Lives and Wives of the Presidents" and "The Negro Problem."[29]

Thomas Nelson Haskell passed away on September 9, 1906. He lived long enough to see the small college he founded become a thriving and successful educational institution.

EDWARDS DEPARTS

Jonathan Edwards continued to run the College during the 1874–1875 academic year. He simultaneously served as the first Pastor of the First Congregational Church in Colorado Springs.[30] He resigned both positions early in 1875 to become the Pastor of a church in Wellesley Hills, Massachusetts. He remained there until he passed away in 1894. He would have been the first President of Colorado College, but he refused the title when the Board of Trustees offered it to him.[31]

JAMES G. DOUGHERTY

Jonathan Edwards was succeeded as head of the College by the Reverend James G. Dougherty of Wyandotte, Kansas. Similar to Edwards, Dougherty was from New England and spent his life as both a clergyman and an educator. He had the now-familiar educational pedigree of early leaders of Colorado College—preparatory school (Phillips Andover), a good liberal arts college (Brown University in Providence, Rhode Island), and religious training (Andover Theological Seminary). His ministerial

---

[29]*General Catalogue Of The Graduates And Former Students Of Miami University, 1809–1909*, Miami University Archives. According to a note on the back of a photograph in the Colorado College Archives, Thomas Nelson Haskell's home in Denver was located at 1643 Sherman Avenue.

[30]For a history of the First Congregational Church in Colorado Springs, see Mary Elizabeth Burgess and Wanetta W. Draper, *The First Congregational Church of Colorado Springs, Colorado: The First One Hundred Years, 1874–1974* (Colorado Springs, CO: First Congregational Church, 1974).

[31]Kerr, "The Pioneer Days Of Colorado College."

work was concentrated in the Midwest and West at Congregational churches in Missouri, Colorado, and Kansas.

James G. Dougherty was never officially appointed President of Colorado College, but he was often referred to as the President in the minutes of Board of Trustees meetings. There has been considerable discussion over the years over whether or not he actually deserves to be called the first President of Colorado College.[32]

The small wooden building on Tejon Street bustled with activity during the 1875–1876 academic year. Dougherty greatly improved the image of the College by publishing the first catalog.[33] There was a strong bias toward scientific courses, but a classical curriculum was offered as well. The College, as distinct from the preparatory school, had an enrollment of 17 students, all listed as freshmen. Most of the students were from Colorado Springs, but there were six students from other cities in Colorado, four from outside Colorado Territory, and one student from a foreign country—Canada.

In the winter of 1875–1876, Dougherty traveled to the East Coast to raise money for the College. His solicitations were largely unsuccessful due to the continuing depressed state of the national economy. The day he was trying to raise money in Providence and Newport, Rhode Island, there was a major bank failure in that state. When the College's Board of Trustees learned of the meager results of Dougherty's fund-raising efforts, the Board called for the College to suspend instruction during the spring of 1876 and declared that a "vacation be taken till the time for opening of the Fall Term." When Dougherty learned of the Board's action, he resigned his position as the head of the College.[34]

---

[32] "Daugherty . . . was elected first President of Colorado College," Kerr, "The Pioneer Days Of Colorado College." "He is regarded as the first President of Colorado College." Hershey, *Colorado College, 1874–1949*, 40. "Dougherty accepted on condition that he be named President of the College." J. Juan Reid, *Colorado College: The First Century, 1874–1974* (Colorado Springs, CO: Colorado College, 1979), 12. "But the first real President was Edward P. Tenney. . . ." Sprague, *Newport In The Rockies*, 274. Sprague was strongly influenced when writing about Colorado College by Robert M. Ormes, a Professor of English at Colorado College and the son of Manley D. Ormes, the Librarian at the College from 1904 to 1929. The author favors the Ormes-Sprague preference for Edward P. Tenney as the first President of Colorado College.

[33] *Catalogue Of The Officers And Students*, Colorado College, 1874–1875.

[34] For a description of James G. Dougherty's year as President of Colorado College, see James G. Dougherty, "The Beginnings Of Colorado College," *Colorado College Bulletin*, February 1975, 10–15.

A TENUOUS BEGINNING

Colorado College ended the 1875–1876 academic year on March 31, 1876. College classes did not resume until the following fall. During this period of quiet and inactivity, a large contingent of Ute Indians passed through Colorado Springs on their way to a buffalo hunt on the eastern plains of Colorado. They camped out on the vacant fields at the north end of the city that had been designated for a college or university campus.[35]

But elsewhere important things were happening. The Territory of Colorado became the State of Colorado on August 1, 1876. Because the year 1876 marked the 100th anniversary of the Declaration of Independence in 1776, Colorado took the nickname of "The Centennial State." Achieving statehood gave a big boost to the citizens of Colorado, serving to convince many a doubter that the place really did have a bright and promising future.

And General Palmer continued to build his Denver and Rio Grande Railroad. As prospectors found more and more valuable minerals in the Colorado mountains, however, Palmer became less concerned with serving the Rio Grande valley and more interested in building his narrow gauge lines into the Rocky Mountains to reach the latest gold and silver strikes. Real money was being made as the Denver and Rio Grande hauled heavy mining machinery and supplies into the newest mining camps and then transported gold and silver ore to the major smelters in the state for refining. Palmer was particularly bold and successful at this practice. "It was a railroad with a master prospector at the helm, one that followed the miner and his burro, bound for where they were headed, looking for the same thing, wherever it was."[36]

One should not judge too harshly the tenuous and uncertain early days of Colorado College. Although neither Thomas Nelson Haskell, nor Jonathan Edwards, nor James G. Dougherty was with the College for an extended period of time, each of the three men did his necessary work and did it well. The "vacation" taken in the spring and summer of 1876

---

[35]Reid, *Colorado College: The First Century, 1874–1949*, 15.

[36]Athearn, *Rebel Of The Rockies*, 101.

was only that—an extended vacation—because the Board of Trustees fully intended that the College should resume its work in the fall of 1876. "Colorado College has had an uninterrupted period of service to higher education in the Rocky Mountain region and to the nation from the time of its beginning in the spring of 1874."[37]

---

[37]Hershey, *Colorado College, 1874–1949*, 44.

CHAPTER 2

Edward Payson Tenney:

The Advocate of "The New West"

The first order of business at Colorado College in the spring and summer of 1876 was to find a President. As was to be expected, the Board of Trustees turned to New England and the ministry of the Congregational Church to find a new leader. The man selected was Edward Payson Tenney, Pastor at the First Congregational Church in Ashland, Massachusetts, a small town southwest of Boston. The Trustees made it very clear to Tenney that it would be his job to raise the necessary funds to pay the expenses of operating the College.

Tenney was the son of a clergyman. He was born in 1835 on a farm in Concord, New Hampshire. His education fit the familiar pattern—Pembroke Academy, Dartmouth College, and Bangor and Andover theological seminaries. As a young man he went to California, where he worked unsuccessfully to establish an educational institution called the College of California. He returned to New England, then came out to Colorado to pastor the Congregational church in Central City, the great gold mining camp in the Rocky Mountains west of Denver. While in Central City, Tenney founded, but only on paper, a college called the Rocky Mountain Institute, which was to be built on the high ground midway between Colorado Springs and Denver.[1]

---

[1]Twenty years after his departure from Colorado College and Colorado Springs, Tenney wrote a book, a first-person memoir, on his life and thoughts. In the book Tenney contended that the Rocky Mountain Institute "was not only the herald but the forerunner of [Colorado] College." He also said the Rocky Mountain Institute was to be based "upon the Oberlin Colony plan." Tenney, *Looking Forward Into The Past*, 41, 49–51, 53, 58.

Tenney thus combined familiarity with the West with a great zeal to found a college in the West. By chance, an acquaintance of Tenney's, the Reverend F. B. Perkins of Wellesley Hills, Massachusetts, visited Colorado Springs and attended a "College prayer-meeting." Upon learning that Colorado College needed a President, and knowing of Tenney's great interest in the West, Perkins suggested Tenney as the ideal man for the job.

Tenney was "summering" in Manchester-by-the-Sea, Massachusetts, on the Cape Anne coast northeast of Boston, when he received a letter inviting him to become the President of Colorado College. He immediately took the letter and retreated deep into the Cape Anne woodlands, thinking the matter over and praying for divine guidance near "a great bowlder." He later argued that the rock, where he decided to take the challenge and come to Colorado College, was "related to Colorado College as Plymouth Rock is related to our national life."

Tenney next discussed the matter with Henry Cutler, a Massachusetts philanthropist, at Cutler's home in Ashland. Cutler and a group of other Massachusetts men, all members of the Congregational church, agreed to provide the money to get Colorado College operating again under Tenney's leadership.[2]

In addition, Tenney persuaded the American College and Education Society, headquartered in Boston, to put Colorado College on its list of approved institutions. The Society supported colleges and universities in the West by raising money for them. The association between Colorado College and the American College and Education Society, begun by Tenney in 1877, was both a long and a fruitful one. During one eight year period the Society raised in excess of $60,000 for Colorado College.[3]

---

[2]Tenney's recruitment to Colorado College, and his recruitment of Henry Cutler and other Massachusetts benefactors, is related in detail in Tenney, *Looking Forward Into The Past*, 66–72.

[3]For a description of the work of the American College and Education Society, see E. P. Tenney, *The New West: As Related To The Christian College*, 3rd ed. (Cambridge, MA: Riverside Press, 1878), 69–71. The Society, similar to Colorado College, was founded by Congregationalists but went about its work in a non-sectarian fashion. "Though its funds and its students are drawn chiefly from Congregational sources, there has never been a year since its origin that it has not had upon its lists young men of other denominations–Baptists, Methodists, Presbyterians, German Reformed, Lutherans, etc." Paper published by the Secretary of the Society in the *Congregationalist*, 6 February 1878, quoted from Tenney, *The New West*, 76. Among the prominent New Englanders who supported

Tenney claimed that Henry Cutler and his New England friends "saved the College from extinction." He stated: "By the timely gifts of a few men in Massachusetts, who were also praying for the coming of a divine kingdom, new life was put into the work."[4] Tenney said the College would hold "in grateful remembrance the names of Henry Cutler of Ashland, Alvan A. Sweet and Samuel Crooks of Hopkinton, Deacon James G. Buttrick of Lowell, Deacon B. T. Thompson of South Framington, and Mr. E. H. Cutler of Wilbraham, the men who believed in the College, and paid cash down upon their faith. . . ."[5]

According to Tenney, events taking place in Massachusetts were as vital to the revival of Colorado College as those taking place in Colorado. He concluded: "So true it was that in the identical years, 1870–1875, in which General Palmer, Professor Haskell and President Dougherty were making ready in Colorado for the College that was to be, the Moral Governor of the Universe, who sees the end from the beginning was, in these self-same years, in the Old Bay State [Massachusetts], preparing the minds of the chief actors [Cutler and other benefactors] for what they were to do for opening up the College work in the autumn of 1876."[6]

THE NEW WEST

In an effort to promote both Colorado College and the newly developing region it served, Tenney wrote and published a small book entitled *The New West.* The document was simultaneously inspirational and filled with geographical boosterism. Tenney defined the "New West" as the general Rocky Mountain region. It included Idaho, Montana, and Wyoming on the north, Nevada, Utah, and Colorado in the center, and Arizona and New Mexico

---

fund-raising for Colorado College was Mark Hopkins, the well-known President of Williams College in Williamstown, Massachusetts. Hopkins said of Colorado College: "It seems to me that no Western institution has stronger claims upon the sympathy and support of the philanthropist, the statesman, and the Christian." Quoted from an 1883 fund-raising circular entitled "Colorado College" in the Colorado College Archives.

[4]Tenney, *The New West*, 72.

[5]Edward Payson Tenney, *Report To The American College And Education Society*, 1877.

[6]This quote occurs at the end of a long discourse on the character of the early Massachusetts benefactors of Colorado College in which the individual benefactors are not identified by name. Tenney, *Looking Forward Into The Past*, 59–63.

Edward Payson Tenney
The 2nd President of Colorado College, he built the College's first building (Cutler Hall) on the permanent campus north of downtown Colorado Springs.

on the south. Colorado—and Colorado College—were beneficially located in the middle of this lightly populated area, blessed with what Tenney claimed was a most promising future. He repeatedly pointed out that this region comprised one third of the land area of the United States.

It was the "New West" because it was developing after both the prairie states, such as Kansas and Nebraska, and the West Coast states, such as Oregon and California. Tenney saw this Rocky Mountain region as both the last frontier and the last opportunity to found educational institutions to promote religiosity and morality on that frontier.

Similar to many persons of a strong religious persuasion, Tenney saw religious significance in all events, both good and bad. He saw the lust for material wealth—particularly gold and silver—as Heaven's way of luring new residents to unpopulated areas. "The passion for mining," he wrote in *The New West*, "is the instrument of Providence in transferring populations to new seats of empire."[7]

Tenney saw the mission of Colorado College as providing well-educated citizens for his New West. He wrote: "An enlightened patriotism will plant the Christian college in the New West, and, through its manifold influences, elevate all the people. . . . May we not anticipate an honorable future for a literary institution, established as a fountain of Christian influence and intellectual power, in this enchanting spot?"[8]

But if religion was the motivating force, Tenney argued, the College should not be a sectarian institution. "It must be free from ecclesiastical control," he noted. "If it becomes the mere tool of a sect, it will never rise to the highest rank."[9]

Amazingly for his time, Tenney took an inclusive view of those who would be served by Colorado College. "Is it not then essential to plant the Christian College in the New West," he argued, "to develop the common school system among Mormons, Mexicans, Indians, and the heterogeneous border population?"[10]

---

[7]Tenney, *The New West*, 9.

[8]Tenney, *The New West*, 5, 14.

[9]Tenney, *The New West*, 47.

[10]Tenney, *The New West*, 33.

And Tenney saw the influence of the College as permanent and enduring. "Although individual teachers and graduates fall like leaves," he opined, "the College will endure and prove a perpetual power. . . . Through its unending roll-call of students [it will] bestow a benediction upon the shining shores of far-off seas in distant ages."[11]

Tenney also gave subtle arguments as to why successful businessmen and industrialists should contribute their hard-earned money to this new College in the New West. "If it is wise to clothe and feed America," he explained, "it is Christian wisdom to use a part of the money made in the business for endowing the educated men of America with the thoughts of God."[12]

With an unusually clear vision of the future, Tenney saw Colorado College as a good place from which to study the anthropology and archeology of the Native Americans of the southwestern United States. He noted: "We must reckon it as one of the peculiar privileges of the location, to train men to investigate Indian philology in connection with the work of aiding Indian civilization."[13] He also saw the merits of the region for studying Geology. "The great plains and mountain regions of western America offer today the most attractive resort in the world to the student of Geology. Colorado College is surrounded by the most remarkable formations on the continent."[14]

Edward Payson Tenney's *The New West* was a significant literary effort. It revealed clearly the religious fervor of the founders of Colorado College. It identified their origins in the Congregational church, but it made clear the determination of the College's founders to create a nonsectarian institution. And it included non-Protestant groups, such as Hispanics, Native Americans, and Mormons, in those residents of the New West who were to benefit from the leadership and guidance of the College's educated graduates. In succeeding years, Colorado College very

---

[11]Tenney, *The New West*, 22, 24.

[12]Tenney, *The New West*, 30.

[13]Tenney, *The New West*, 53.

[14]Tenney, *The New West*, 90.

much became the inspired, non-sectarian, leadership-oriented, and inclusive institution that Tenney described in *The New West* in the late 1870s.[15]

Tenney viewed the American West as a liberating and improving influence on persons from the northern and eastern United States. In an address given at the First Congregational Church in Colorado Springs in 1882, Tenney opined: "One of the best of God's creatures is the Yankee enlarged by coming west!"[16]

THE FIRST PERMANENT BUILDING

Edward Payson Tenney's greatest contribution to Colorado College was to raise the funds and see to the construction of the College's first permanent building on the designated campus area at the north end of Colorado Springs. At first this building was called simply The College. Then for a brief period it was known as Palmer Hall. For most of its history, however, the first permanent building has been known as Cutler Hall, named for Henry Cutler, the generous New England benefactor of Colorado College.

General William Jackson Palmer selected the site for the building, choosing a spot on the west side of Cascade Avenue where the ground began to slope downward toward Monument Creek. The front of the building faced to the east, but the structure had western windows with beautiful views of Pike's Peak and the surrounding foothills. The building was constructed of trachyte stone, grey in color, mined near Castle Rock, Colorado. Cutler Hall began an early tradition of building major Colorado College structures with stone rather than brick.

On July 4, 1877, General Palmer ceremoniously took a shovel and broke ground for the new building. In a speech given at this optimistic moment in the history of the College, he said: "My friends, in breaking this ground, let us set apart and forever devote it to the purpose of

---

[15]At least one of President Tenney's contemporaries thought highly of *The New West*. James Hutchison Kerr wrote: "For advertising purposes these pamphlets have not to this day been surpassed." Kerr, "The Pioneer Days Of Colorado College."

[16]Burgess and Draper, *The First Congregational Church Of Colorado Springs, Colorado*, 17.

education, in the most unsectarian ways, to the discovery and inculcation of truth."[17]

The central part of the building was completed in 1880. The major windows were slightly pointed at the top, giving the building a Boston Gothic look. An ornate tower with a belfry, somewhat Venetian in appearance, was the distinguishing feature of the structure.[18] A large bell in the belfry rang at 8:30 A.M. to call the students to class. President Tenney later noted: "The design of the building was spoken of as so attractive that it would maintain itself in comparison with College halls in later years."[19]

General Palmer contributed the money to add the one-story-high north and south wings, which were completed in 1882. Originally these wings were to include large bays (facing north and south) and dormer windows on the roof, but the high extra cost caused these features to be eliminated. Tenney also planned a large addition on the west side of the building that would serve as an amphitheater, probably intended for chapel services, dramatic productions, and large lecture classes. Again, due to lack of money, this addition was never constructed.[20]

A triple ceremony was held on May 31, 1882. The new building was dedicated, Edward Payson Tenney was formally inaugurated as the President of Colorado College, and Parker Sedgwick Halleck and Frederick Wells Tuckerman received their degrees as the first two graduates of the College.[21] An important tradition was begun when, following the ceremony, President and Mrs. Tenney held a reception in honor of the new graduates and their families and friends.

---

[17]Hershey, *Colorado College, 1874–1949*, 136.

[18]Sprague, *Newport In The Rockies*, 277.

[19]Tenney, *Looking Forward Into The Past*, 176 note 1.

[20]The proposed bays, dormer windows, and the proposed amphitheater can be seen in line drawings in Tenney, *The New West*, 24, 106. Also see Tenney, *Looking Forward Into The Past*, 180 note 1.

[21]Tenney's inauguration as President was delayed by his own determination to achieve solid accomplishments at the College first. "But I decided to have no installation till we should have one permanent building erected, and have a College class to graduate." Tenney, *Looking Forward Into The Past*, 70.

College Building as seen from Cascade Avenue.

College Building, as seen from the Railway.

Discarded Features

The original plan for Cutler Hall included bays and dormer windows on the north and south wings (top). The rear of the building was to have an auditorium with a semi-circular design (bottom). Both drawings from Tenney, The New West, *24, 106.*

The First Residence Hall

President Tenney also saw to the construction of the College's first residence hall. The wood structure was three stories high and had a long front porch, high dormer windows, and an off-center cupola on the roof. It was built at the northeast corner of Cascade Avenue and Columbia Street, four blocks north of the main campus. The dormitory was for women students and paid for by Tenney himself. He referred to it as the Columbian clubhouse.[22]

Prior to the construction of this dormitory, all out-of-town students boarded with local families in Colorado Springs. About the same time the Columbian clubhouse opened for women, President Tenney acquired an existing structure, Hooper House, and used it as a residence hall for men.

Sadly, on New Years Day 1884, the Columbian clubhouse burned to the ground.[23] The men students responded to this tragedy by organizing the Colorado College Hose Company to fight any future fires in the campus area. The student firemen had a small firehouse, complete with a large alarm bell mounted on a high wooden tower, located on the northwest corner of Nevada Avenue and Cache La Poudre Street.

The First President's House

In July of 1883 President Tenney and his family moved into a new house. Tenney paid for this large and comfortable stone structure with his own money. It was built about 1,000 yards north of the main College building that subsequently became Cutler Hall. It became the official residence of the College's presidents for the next fifty years.[24] The President's House was torn down in the early 1950s to permit the construction of Loomis Hall, a large women's dormitory.

---

[22]Tenney, *Looking Forward Into The Past*, 167 note 1.

[23]The College lost women students after the fire because it no longer could provide low cost room and board. *Colorado Springs Gazette*, 3 June 1888.

[24]When Tenney left the Colorado College presidency in 1884, the structure temporarily became a privately-owned residence. The College purchased it in 1888 to use as the President's House.

A Strong Faculty

President Tenney hired a talented and committed faculty for his College in the New West. Two important ones were Frank Herbert Loud, who taught Mathematics, Physics, and Astronomy, and William Strieby, who taught Mineralogy and Metallurgy. Given the prevalence of gold and silver mining in Colorado, many students wanted to major in science with an emphasis on Mineralogy and Metallurgy. Colorado College is believed to have carried on "the first continuous, systematic work in Mining and Metallurgy organized in the Rocky Mountains."[25]

Another well-known professor during the Tenney era was John Hutchison Kerr, a successful mining engineer and entrepreneur who taught Mining and Metallurgy at the College from time to time. Kerr built a beautiful brick home at the northwest corner of Platte Avenue and Tejon Street that later became a leading social club in Colorado Springs—the El Paso Club.

The social sciences were not neglected. George Nathaniel Marden was hired to teach History, Political Science, and Metaphysics. And women continued to play an important role on the faculty. Emma Bump was an instructor in French and English language and literature.

An Ambitious Program

Edward Payson Tenney was a man of imagination and charitable ambition who sought to enhance Colorado College in every way possible. He promoted the idea of offering graduate work in Theology at the College, the program to be called the New West Theological Seminary. The idea looked good on paper and was supported by the Board of Trustees, but Tenney was unable to raise the required funds and recruit a sufficient number of graduate theological students. The graduate school in Theology had to be abandoned.

Another idea of Tenney's was to found a number of preparatory schools around the Rocky Mountain West that would feed students into Colorado College. Such schools were established in Albuquerque, Las

[25]Kerr, "The Pioneer Days Of Colorado College."

Vegas, and Santa Fe, New Mexico, as well as in Trinidad and Leadville, Colorado. Another successful school was set up in Salt Lake City, Utah. These schools were supported by Colorado College until the communities in which they were located were able to operate and finance them.[26]

But President Tenney's most courageous venture was to buy extensive landholdings in Colorado Springs as future investments for the College. Tenney believed that General Palmer's little city would continue to grow and that the College would benefit greatly from the increase in the value of the lands he was purchasing. One tract was located north of the College campus and comprised much of what later became the North End residential area. Harkening back to his New England roots, Tenney named the area New Massachusetts.[27]

Another tract of land purchased by President Tenney was in North Cheyenne Canyon southwest of Colorado Springs. Tenney named it Colorado College Park and charged a 25 cent toll to those wishing to see and hike in it. This unusually beautiful canyon and foothill property eventually became a Colorado Springs city park.

In order to finance his land investments for the College, Tenney borrowed money in Boston, with Henry Cutler's help, at 12 percent interest. Unfortunately, land in Colorado Springs did not sell as rapidly in the early 1880s as Tenney had hoped. He jeopardized his health as he worked harder and harder trying to keep his various land schemes adequately financed. In the spring of 1884 the entire speculation collapsed, and Tenney was asked to resign as President of Colorado College. When he refused to do so, the Board of Trustees declared the President's office "vacated."

THE TENNEY YEARS EVALUATED

Edward Payson Tenney left Colorado Springs under a cloud of suspicion and failure. A number of the faculty at the College turned against him

[26]For a lengthy and complicated account of Tenney's efforts to promulgate Christian education in the New West, see Tenney, *Looking Forward Into The Past*, 97–161. Also see Kerr, "The Pioneer Days Of Colorado College."

[27]Sprague, *Newport In The Rockies*, 275.

because of his failed real estate ventures. He was accused of confusing the College's finances with his own personal financial affairs. Tenney returned to New England, dejected over the bad fortune that ended his presidency and made uncertain his grandiose plans for Colorado College.[28] He carried on ministerial and literary work in colorful New England settings such as Manchester-by-the-Sea, the Monadnock country, the White Mountain plateau, and near Ascutney and Moosilauke on the Connecticut River.[29]

Tenney passed away in 1916.[30] Similar to Thomas Nelson Haskell, Tenney lived long enough to see the College he helped to start become, as he had faith it would, one of the premier educational institutions of his beloved New West. In the end, he was delighted that Colorado College eventually thrived following his departure. He wrote: "To me there is nothing more beautiful than that the College has succeeded by other means than mine."[31]

In retrospect, the financial cards do appear to have been stacked against Tenney. Colorado Springs grew nicely during the late 1870s, reaching a population of more than 4,000 persons by the time of the 1880 census. But the early 1880s saw very little population growth in Colorado Springs. The city had only a few more people in 1884 than it had in 1880. Trying as he was to build a local real estate empire for the College in the early 1880s, Tenney was doomed by the lackluster growth of Colorado Springs at that time.

Part of the problem was that the 1880s were the great decade of silver mining in Colorado, and none of the silver mines were near Colorado Springs. The big silver strikes were in places like Georgetown and Leadville, both of which were better connected by road and rail to

---

[28]Kerr, "The Pioneer Days Of Colorado College." Also see Buckley, "The History of Colorado College, 1874–1904," 65.

[29]Tenney, *Looking Forward Into The Past*, 219.

[30]Tenney died on 24 July 1916 at 16 Greystone Park in Lynn, Massachusetts. He was buried in Manchester-By-The-Sea, Massachusetts. "E. P. Tenney, Second President Of Colorado College, Died During Summer: Planned Efficient Land Scheme For C.C.," *Tiger*, 22 September 1916, 1.

[31]Tenney, *Looking Forward Into The Past*, 221.

Denver and Pueblo.[32] The fabulous rise of silver mining in Colorado during the early 1880s made Denver and Pueblo thriving cities but largely left out Colorado Springs.

Tenney also faced the problem that General Palmer was concentrating his time and effort on his railroad projects rather than on Colorado Springs and Colorado College. In 1883 Palmer lost financial control of the Denver and Rio Grande Railroad and resigned as President. He continued, however, to control the Rio Grande Western, a railroad that ran across eastern Utah and connected the western end of the Denver and Rio Grande Railroad to Salt Lake City. In addition, Palmer was planning, surveying, and building an extensive narrow gauge railroad system in the nation of Mexico. "Meantime the founders of [Colorado Springs] were absorbed in railway enterprises of incredible difficulty," Tenney later wrote, "so much so as to give little thought or money to the College."[33]

But President Tenney accomplished much for Colorado College. He built the College's first permanent building, eventually named Cutler Hall, and created a structure of grace and beauty that has become the very symbol of Colorado College. He hired a strong faculty and recruited students for them to teach. In one year during Tenney's eight years as President, enrollment in the College and its preparatory program reached a high of 132 students.

Tenney increased the library at the College to 6,000 volumes. He fenced the campus and began landscaping it by planting large numbers of trees. During the Tenney presidency the men students organized an athletic association and fielded a football team that played games against teams from Colorado Springs. Most of all, Tenney recruited wealthy contributors from New England who gave the money that first made Colorado College a going educational enterprise.

One faculty member who changed his mind and ended up admiring Tenney for his financial efforts on behalf of the College was James Hutchison Kerr, who taught Mining and Metallurgy during Tenney's ad-

---

[32]Colorado Springs experienced a mini-boom when silver was first discovered in Leadville in 1876. There was a rush of miners and mule teams hauling supplies through Colorado City and up Ute Pass to Leadville. The first railroads to reach Leadville, however, originated in Pueblo and Denver. Fisher, *A Builder Of The West*, 250–251.

[33]Tenney, *Looking Forward Into The Past*, 75 note 2.

ministration. In a newspaper article written long after Tenney had left Colorado Springs and moved back to New England, Kerr said his further investigations of the situation had convinced him that Tenney was completely honest, had only the best interests of the College at heart in his real estate transactions, and had been seriously misjudged and falsely blamed by his faculty and Board of Trustees. "Had Mr. Tenney's scheme been carried out as he had outlined," Kerr finally concluded, "Colorado College would be today one of the richest colleges in America."[34]

And Tenney spoke up in his own defense. The reason he mixed the College's financial affairs with his own, he argued, was that he could get credit when the College could not. "During six years not a dollar could be had for ordinary current College expenses without my individual agreement to pay it," Tenney explained. "During these six years, the College corporation could get no money, either West or East, without my name on the note. And when College property was acquired . . . [it] was acquired upon . . . my direct financial liability for large amounts of money."[35]

A number of scholars and writers eventually came to the conclusion that Tenney was a positive and effective force in the history of Colorado College. Some typical evaluations: "A just appreciation of [President Tenney's] work is only now beginning to be formed, as misconceptions long current have been removed, and the conditions which he had to meet have been more correctly appraised. . . ."[36] "Tenney was a good President who saw Colorado College through its feeble infancy until it was too strong to die of malnutrition."[37] "It was during Tenney's administration that the roots of the College penetrated to great depths and its flower and fruitage became generally recognized."[38]

---

[34]Kerr, "The Pioneer Days Of Colorado College." Tenney quoted Kerr's newspaper article extensively in his own defense of his activities at Colorado College. See Tenney, *Looking Forward Into The Past*, 202–204.

[35]Tenney, *Looking Forward Into The Past*, 168–169.

[36]Appeal Letter on the Occasion of Mr. and Mrs. Tenney's 50th Wedding Anniversary, undated, signed by the President and members of the faculty of Colorado College, Colorado College Archives.

[37]Sprague, *Newport In The Rockies*, 275.

[38]Hershey, *Colorado College, 1874–1949*, 50.

A PERIOD OF PROFESSORIAL RULE

From 1884 to 1888 Colorado College lacked a President and was governed by the faculty that Tenney had hired. Professor George N. Marden became the financial agent and took on the task of keeping eastern contributors, so carefully recruited by Tenney, financially supporting the College. Professor William Strieby directed the instructional program and attended to a variety of administrative tasks, such as collecting tuition and paying small bills.

During this period the Board of Trustees struggled to straighten out and pay down the debts which former President Tenney had undertaken in his efforts to finance the College. There was serious debate of a proposal to sell off the four-square blocks east of Cascade Avenue that later became the site of Palmer Hall, Shove Chapel, and other major College buildings. That proposal was dropped, however, and the Board elected to sell instead the large land area north and west of the campus which Tenney had proposed to develop as New Massachusetts.

But some progress was made at the College. A student speech and debating team, known as the Oratorical Society, traveled to Boulder, Colorado, and engaged a University of Colorado team in an oratorical contest. The campus was wired for electrical service, and an electric bell system soon was calling students to and from their classes. The Colorado Springs Water Company laid a pipeline to the main College building (Cutler Hall), and soon a "faucet" and a "water closet" were functioning there.

The men's football team played and defeated a University of Denver team by a score of 12 to 0. The game took place in Colorado Springs on April 12, 1885. It was the first intercollegiate football game played west of the Mississippi River. Some of the luster of this great athletic victory was lost when it was revealed that five non-students had played as "ringers" for the Colorado College team.

Despite these positive events, the overall condition of Colorado College declined during this period with no President on the job. In the fall of 1885 only six of the fifty-five students were in the College program. In a subsequent report to the Board of Trustees, Professor Strieby noted that enrollments were declining and the teaching staff was growing restless. In a memoir of his years at Colorado College, Professor James Hutchison Kerr described some of the more difficult days. "You are all undoubtedly aware," Kerr wrote, "that Colorado College was a very puny, sickly child. A number of times we thought she was breathing her last; and no one except those who rocked the crib by day and walked the floor by night, has any definite idea of the amount of New England paregoric and soothing syrup, that was necessary to relieve her dear little colicky frame."[39]

Two men would come along and change all that.

One was a Congregational minister from the East Coast who agreed to accept the presidency of Colorado College under these challenging conditions. His name was William Frederick Slocum.

The other was a ne'er do well cowboy walking across a meadow near a mountain town southwest of Pike's Peak known as Cripple Creek. His name was Bob Womack.

---

[39]James Hutchison Kerr, "Colorado College: After Dinner Paper," 12 June 1907, 4. This pamphlet can be found in the Kerr scrap books, Book I, 13.

CHAPTER 3

WILLIAM FREDERICK SLOCUM:
THE "BUILDER" PRESIDENT

On one of his fund-raising trips to the East Coast, Professor George N. Marden stopped in Baltimore, Maryland, and visited the First Congregational Church. There he met the Pastor, the Reverend William Frederick Slocum, and the two men formed an immediate and warm acquaintance. They came to know each other well enough that Professor Marden stayed as a guest in Pastor Slocum's Baltimore home. Upon returning to Colorado Springs, Professor Marden placed Slocum's name before the Board of Trustees as a promising possibility for President of Colorado College.

The Board inquired of a number of well-known persons on the East Coast and found that Professor Marden's high opinion of Slocum was widely shared. Among his endorsers was John Greenleaf Whittier, the celebrated American poet. The Board offered Reverend Slocum the job of President at a salary of $3,000 per year. Slocum accepted, and he and his wife, Mary Montgomery Slocum, came out to Colorado Springs to see what could be done to revive and reenergize Colorado College.

William Frederick Slocum was born on July 29, 1851, in Grafton, Massachusetts, a small town west of Boston near Worcester. His more distant ancestors were Quakers from Rhode Island, but his parents were Congregationalists from Massachusetts. His father was a lawyer, as were two of his brothers. His father was a Deacon in the Congregational Church and went to Sunday services regularly, so William Frederick Slocum naturally gravitated to the Congregational Church when he chose the ministry as his life's calling.

AMHERST, ANDOVER, AND AMESBURY

Slocum and his brothers all attended Amherst College in Amherst, Massachusetts. In the early 1870s Amherst College was the very embodiment of what later became known as the small liberal arts college. The central building on the campus, Johnson Chapel, sat on a high hill overlooking the village green and the prim houses of the town of Amherst. Johnson Chapel, similar to the other major buildings at Amherst College, was built of red brick with white wooden trim. This chapel, equipped with a high clock tower, was surrounded on both sides and behind by a quadrangle of dormitories and other campus buildings.

In one of those dormitories, East College, the young William Slocum developed a reputation as a "reader" because of his habit of studying his books late into the night.[1] One story reported that he became so engaged in his reading one night that he was still hard at it when bright sunlight penetrated his dormitory window the next morning. When not with his books, Slocum participated in a literary society at Amherst and was a leading debater. In his spare time he enjoyed hiking the nearby hills and searching out places of historical interest in the Connecticut River valley.[2]

Following his graduation from Amherst College in 1874, Slocum spent a year traveling in England and Europe. He developed a particular interest in educational institutions in Germany. Upon his return to the United States, he went to Andover Theological Seminary to prepare for the ministry. For two years he pursued his religious studies with an emphasis on the church and its relationship to solving social problems. Upon graduating from Andover, Slocum became the Pastor of the Congregational Church in Amesbury, Massachusetts, a classic New England mill town afflicted with many of the social and economic problems that Slocum had been studying.

---

[1]The East College which Slocum lived and studied in was torn down, but a similar building with the same name was erected at the same location. In the late 1990s Johnson Chapel stood on the Amherst campus in the same form that Slocum knew it as an undergraduate.

[2]For a description of Amherst College at the time William F. Slocum was a student there, see Claude Moore Fuess, *Amherst: The Story Of A New England College* (Boston, MA: Little, Brown, and Company, 1935), 149–207. In 1914, while he was President of Colorado College, Slocum was elected the first President of the Amherst Alumni Council, which had just been formed. Fuess, *Amherst*, 345.

While attending Andover Theological Seminary, William Slocum made the acquaintance of Mary Goodale Montgomery. She was a young woman teaching at Abbott Academy, a preparatory school for women located across the road from the Seminary.[3] Their friendship continued after Slocum took up his ministerial duties in Amesbury. On July 29, 1881, William Slocum's 30th birthday, they were married.

Mary Slocum joined her husband in ministering to the social needs of the Amesbury community. Working conditions were highly unsatisfactory in the large red brick factory buildings that characterized Amesbury and so many other 19th Century New England industrial towns.[4] William Slocum never abandoned the moralistic concern for the social and economic health of the working classes that he first exhibited at Amesbury.

THE JOHNS HOPKINS CONNECTION

Successful ministers often move from small town parishes to larger congregations in big cities. William Slocum made such a move in 1883, when he became Pastor of the First Congregational Church in Baltimore. The church was located in a historic part of Baltimore near Mount Vernon Place, a cross-shaped public park with a tall, shaft-like monument topped by a statue of George Washington, the first President of the United States. Close by Slocum's church were the early buildings of Johns Hopkins University, which had been founded in 1876, only seven years earlier, with a $3 million gift from Johns Hopkins, a successful Baltimore merchant.

At that time Johns Hopkins University lacked a campus of the traditional sort with broad grassy lawns and picturesque stone or brick buildings. The University was housed in a number of row houses grouped around the intersection of Howard and Centre streets in downtown Baltimore. Because many of the students attended services at Slocum's First Congregational Church, Hopkins President Daniel Coit Gilman began to refer to it unofficially as the "University Church." Slocum's pas-

[3]Phillips Academy, originally a men's preparatory school, merged with Abbott Academy and became coeducational. The Abbott name was dropped. The Abbott campus still existed in the late 1990s but some of it was being converted to non-educational uses.

[4]The red brick factory buildings of Amesbury still stood in the late 1990s. Many of them had been preserved and turned to other uses as part of an industrial historical park.

toral work with the students and faculty at Hopkins resulted in President Gilman granting Slocum the free use of the University's library for Slocum's own studies.

Although now in a much different setting, William Slocum continued the social ministry that he first took up in Amesbury. He joined with President Gilman of Johns Hopkins and other Baltimore civic leaders in organizing the Associated Charities, a unified charity appeal to support local social services. Slocum also showed concern for the needs of African-Americans. He spoke to a student intellectual society at Johns Hopkins on the topic of education for Negroes in the South.[5]

During his five years in Baltimore, William Slocum was thoroughly exposed to higher education in the United States as represented by Johns Hopkins University and its President, Daniel Coit Gilman. When the call came to become President of Colorado College, Slocum knew what he was getting into and also knew he had a love and a talent for academic life. "At the age of thirty-seven he cast his lot with the College, and from that time forth, for almost a third of a century, the story of William Frederick Slocum and the story of Colorado College are one story."[6]

FIRST EFFORTS

When they arrived in Colorado Springs in the fall of 1888, William and Mary Slocum found Colorado College in dire straits. There was but one College building—the building later known as Cutler Hall. There were fewer than 50 students in both the College and the preparatory division. There were only four faculty members, three men and one woman. The woman, Eloise Wickard, taught History and English in the preparatory school.

President Slocum made some immediate changes. The College calendar had consisted of three unequal terms. Slocum instituted the standard two-semester calendar found at many other colleges and universities. As for the preparatory school, Slocum separated it from the College and

---

[5]Hugh Hawkins, *Pioneer: A History Of The Johns Hopkins University, 1874–1889* (Ithaca, NY: Cornell University Press, 1960), 279.

[6]Hershey, *Colorado College, 1874–1949*, 64.

William Frederick Slocum
A Congregationalist minister from New England, Slocum served as President of Colorado College for 29 years (1888 to 1917). This photo dates from the earlier years of his presidency.

named it Cutler Academy, in honor of Henry Cutler, the College's early and longtime benefactor. To provide housing for himself and his wife, the new President had the College buy Edward Tenney's former house located to the north of Cutler Hall. Although the College owned the structure, Slocum had to raise the $2,000 down payment himself and personally guarantee the $6,000 mortgage.

Slocum became the religious and moral leader of Colorado College as well as its President. He became famous among the students for his Friday morning chapel sermons, which were called "Ethicals." He referred to the "higher plane" so frequently that it became a campus saying and inside joke to the students. Clearly, William Frederick Slocum intended to continue at Colorado College the New England moralism that had characterized and inspired his predecessors at the institution.[7]

Although Slocum's contract with the College did not require him to raise funds, he sized up the financial situation and soon set out on a 6,000 mile trip to the East to raise money for a new men's residence hall.

HAGERMAN HALL

Slocum's fund-raising, combined with the continuing work of George Marden, garnered sufficient funds to begin the construction of a substantial and permanent dormitory for men. The large stone building was three stories high and included electricity, indoor plumbing, and a dining room for men students in the basement. It was located at the northwest corner of Cascade Avenue and Cache La Poudre Street.

The project ran out of money and the third floor could not be completed. Two members of the Board of Trustees, James J. Hagerman and William S. Jackson, eventually supplied the funds to finish the structure. Jackson insisted that the new dormitory be named Hagerman Hall in honor of Hagerman's substantial contribution.

The former head of the Milwaukee Iron Company, James John Hagerman amassed a substantial fortune in the iron ore and steel business. He came down with a bad case of consumption and, late in 1884,

[7]For a full discussion of President Slocum's religious and educational ideas, see Hershey, *Colorado College, 1874–1949*, 69–76.

HAGERMAN HALL

This dormitory for men was the first building at Colorado College constructed with pink peachblow sandstone and Romanesque architecture. It was located at the northwest corner of Cascade Avenue and Cache La Poudre Street. It was torn down in the 1950s.

moved to Colorado Springs in hopes the high altitude and dry climate would cure him. Finding the city pretty much dead economically, Hagerman decided to liven things up by raising the money to build a standard gauge railroad westward from Colorado Springs.

The new line, named the Colorado Midland Railway, went up Ute Pass and across South Park to the silver mines in Leadville. It then tunneled under the Continental Divide to reach the silver mines at Aspen. Going almost straight across the Rocky Mountains, "the Colorado Midland was an epic effort to defy the laws of gravity."[8]

Hagerman did more than give money to Colorado College. When he learned the College was building a new men's dormitory, Hagerman used his power as a Trustee of the College to convince President Slocum to build the new residence hall with pink "peachblow" sandstone from a quarry owned by Hagerman and served by the Colorado Midland Railway. Slocum had originally intended for Hagerman Hall to be built out of grey Castle Rock stone in order to match the stone used in the first College building, later named Cutler Hall. Slocum soon "fell in love with peachblow stone" and used it in the construction of three more College buildings, including the present-day Palmer Hall.

Boston Gothic architecture was appropriate for the grey stone used to build Cutler Hall. It was not appropriate at all when building with pink stone. For that reason Hagerman Hall was designed in a Romanesque style, with some arched windows and a large Roman arch over the front door. It started a trend in Romanesque architecture for pink sandstone buildings at Colorado College.[9]

At the dedication ceremonies for Hagerman Hall, President Slocum praised the Trustees of the College for the manner in which they had pushed for the funding and construction of the building. A little later in the ceremonies, one of the speakers noted that "it was President Slocum, not the Trustees, who did the pushing."[10]

---

[8]Sprague, *Newport In The Rockies*, 106. For a detailed account of Hagerman's life, see John J. Lipsey, *The Lives of James John Hagerman: Builder Of The Colorado Midland Railway* (Denver, CO: Golden Bell Press, 1968).

[9]Sprague, *Newport In The Rockies*, 277–278.

[10]Buckley, *The History Of Colorado College, 1874–1904*, 28.

Professor Frank Herbert Loud established a weather station on the third floor of Hagerman Hall which was operated by Colorado College students. The weather station later was incorporated into the United States Weather Bureau and, with students reading the instruments and keeping the records, served the city of Colorado Springs for 60 years.

The railroad-building efforts of James J. Hagerman, coupled with other venturesome local investments such as constructing the Pike's Peak Cog Railroad, revived the Colorado Springs economy in the late 1880s. The population grew from 4,500 persons in 1884, the year that President Tenney was forced out of office, to 11,200 persons in 1890. The opening of Hagerman Hall in 1889 symbolized the economic revival of Colorado Springs as well as the financial rejuvenation of Colorado College.[11]

The Central Heating Plant

By late 1889 the College had two buildings—Cutler Hall and Hagerman Hall. The Trustees determined that the time had come to construct a central heating plant. A boiler room was built behind Cutler Hall and steam lines carried heat to Cutler Hall and Hagerman Hall through underground tunnels. The heating plant had high smokestacks which became something of a landmark at the western end of the campus. As additional buildings were constructed at the College, they were connected to and heated from this central facility.

Montgomery Hall

Mary Slocum, the wife of President Slocum, organized the women of Colorado College and Colorado Springs into a formal group called the Woman's Educational Society (WES). The first project undertaken by the WES was to plan and raise the money for a "cottage" for women

[11]It was interesting that William S. Jackson insisted that the new men's dormitory be named after James J. Hagerman. When General Palmer lost control of the Denver and Rio Grande Railroad in 1883, William S. Jackson became the receiver and then the President of the line. Jackson's Denver and Rio Grande competed strenuously with Hagerman's Colorado Midland to see which line could reach the silver mines at Aspen first. Jackson's Rio Grande won the race but only got to Aspen six weeks ahead of the Midland. It is notable that two men who competed so avidly as railroad builders cooperated so completely in getting a dormitory for men, Hagerman Hall, built at Colorado College. See Sprague, *Newport In The Rockies*, 104–108.

Mary Montgomery Slocum
The wife of College President William Frederick Slocum, Mary Slocum founded the Women's Educational Society (WES) at Colorado College and oversaw the fund-raising and design of Montgomery Hall.

Montgomery Hall

The first residence hall for women students built on the main campus at Colorado College, Montgomery Hall had this simple appearance when it opened in the early 1890s. The upper floors and the front porch were extensively rebuilt in the late 1930s.

students. This new residence hall was called a "cottage" because the Society intended to make it as warm and comfortable a residence hall for women as possible. The "cottage" system for housing women students had been developed at Smith College, a women's college in Northampton, Massachusetts.

The WES not only collected the necessary funds for constructing the new dormitory but also furnished and decorated the building for its first inhabitants.[12] The fund-raising drive was helped along by a $5,000 contribution from Mrs. J. J. Hagerman, the wife of the College trustee who contributed so much of the money for Hagerman Hall.

The new women's dormitory was named Montgomery Hall in honor of a sister of Mrs. Slocum's who had recently died. Montgomery was Mrs. Slocum's maiden name. The construction was of Castle Rock Lava, a grey stone similar in appearance to that used in the building of Cutler Hall. The first floor included a living room, a small infirmary, and a kitchen and pantry.[13]

Montgomery Hall was located to the north of the main academic building (Cutler Hall) but set a few feet further to the west. After Montgomery Hall opened in 1891, the College, like so many other institutions of higher learning, had a "row" of major buildings, although there was a considerable distance between the three buildings. Hagerman Hall, the dormitory for men, was on the south. The main academic building (Cutler Hall) was in the middle. Montgomery Hall, the dormitory for women, was to the north.

ROBERT WOMACK

Although the 1858–1859 Pike's Peak Gold Rush to Colorado produced plenty of gold, virtually none of that precious metal was found on the slopes of Pike's Peak. Many a prospector tried to find gold on America's most prominent mountain, but every digging and test hole turned up

[12]For a history of the Women's Educational Society at Colorado College, see Barbara M. Arnest, Editor, *A Quiet Work: One Hundred Years Of The WES* (Colorado Springs, CO: Women's Educational Society, 1990).

[13]Buckley, *The History Of Colorado College, 1874–1904*, 29–33.

nothing. As a result, most of the "high country" around Pike's Peak was used to graze cattle.

For years a man named Robert Womack had divided his time between herding cattle for wealthy ranch owners in the area and digging for precious metals. He was considered a "dreamer" for continuing to prospect in such an unlikely location.

Late in the year 1890, however, Bob Womack dug out some ore samples. He found them southwest of Pike's Peak near a small stream called Cripple Creek. The nearest major community was Colorado Springs, so Womack hurried down to the Springs and had his ore samples assayed. They turned out to contain real gold.[14]

At first Bob Womack had great difficulty convincing people he had made a significant discovery. But other prospectors went up to Cripple Creek and also found substantial quantities of the precious metal. By May of 1891 a small gold rush was under way. It did not stay small very long. In 1892 over $500,000 in gold was mined. In 1893 output soared to $2 million. In 1896 more than $7 million in gold came out of the ground near Pike's Peak. Eventually the region produced the largest mining profits ever generated in Colorado. Cripple Creek ended up being the biggest precious metals bonanza in the state's history.[15]

And it all began just two years after William Frederick Slocum came to Colorado Springs and took over the presidency of Colorado College.

CRIPPLE CREEK AND COLORADO SPRINGS

Cripple Creek was located at more than 10,000 feet of altitude and rapidly turned into a rough, roaring, bawdy mining camp. Colorado Springs was only about 40 miles away by road, so many of the men who rushed to the area to make money from Cripple Creek gold elected to build their homes and locate their families in the Springs. The result was a gold-inspired pop-

---

[14]For Bob Womack's life and efforts to find gold in Cripple Creek, see *Men Of Note Affiliated With Mining And Mining Interests In The Cripple Creek District* (no publisher cited, 1905), 3–5. Book available in Colorado College Archives.

[15]Ubbelohde, Benson, and Smith, *A Colorado History*, 201–205.

ulation boom in Colorado Springs. Ready and waiting to educate the older children of all these new residents was Colorado College.

The impact of the Cripple Creek gold discovery on Colorado Springs was significant. By 1894 there were three stock exchanges in town specializing in Cripple Creek gold mining stocks. One of them, the Colorado Springs Mining Exchange, soon was trading "more shares than any other exchange in the world." Astute Colorado Springs businessmen ended up owning the more productive mines. During the decade of the 1890s bank deposits in Colorado Springs multiplied nine times.

The city's population doubled from 1890 to 1900. A total of 420 mining companies located their offices in downtown Colorado Springs along Tejon Street. A number of the newly wealthy bought lots and built large mansions on the land just to the north of Colorado College. That area, some of which had been part of President Tenney's New Massachusetts development, became known as the North End. During the 1890s the number of millionaires residing in the North End jumped from three to over fifty.[16]

Many people made big money at Cripple Creek, but one person who did not was Bob Womack. He sold his diggings up at Cripple Creek for a relatively small amount of money shortly after he found the first gold there. Bob Womack ended up with more fame than fortune for his efforts.

A GOLDEN AGE

The discovery of gold at Cripple Creek ushered in a Golden Age for Colorado College, both educationally and financially. "The College campus seemed to come alive in the early 1890s as enrollment increased steadily."[17] A men's literary society, the Apollonian Club, was organized in 1890. A similar intellectual club for women, the Minerva Society, was formed the following year. The students wrote and published a magazine, the *Colorado Collegian*, which reported the latest campus news events and included student literary compositions.

---

[16]Sprague, *Newport In The Rockies*, 166–168.

[17]Reid, *Colorado College: The First Century, 1874–1974*, 43–44.

Intercollegiate oratorical contests had become important events in Colorado by the early 1890s. Apparently Colorado College students were skilled at giving effective and entertaining speeches. The Oratorical Society won the state oratorical contest in both 1892 and 1893. Oratorical contests were as popular as intercollegiate athletics, with student supporters wearing college colors and insignia and cheering thunderously from the audience. In 1892 a special train was chartered to take 150 Colorado College students and other local supporters to the state oratorical finals in Denver.

In 1891 the students at the College raised the money to build a small men's gymnasium. It was a one-story wooden frame structure located west of Cutler Hall. It contained gymnastic equipment and also served as a dressing room for the College football and baseball teams. Along with the other major institutions of higher learning in Colorado, including the University of Colorado at Boulder and the Colorado School of Mines at Golden, Colorado College helped to form the Colorado Intercollegiate Athletic Association. Teams competed in men's football, baseball, and track.

Colorado College graduated the largest graduation class in its brief history in 1893. A total of five seniors received their diplomas at commencement exercises in the Colorado Springs Opera House. One of those graduating seniors was a foreign student—Taizo Nakashima of Japan. Two years later, in 1895, Nettie Carey and Elizabeth Powell became the first two women students to earn degrees from Colorado College.

But what really made the 1890s the beginning of a Golden Age at Colorado College was the wealth which Cripple Creek millionaires began to lavish on the College. The contributions came slowly at first, but later on Cripple Creek money flowed to the College in considerable amounts. Men such as James Burns, Albert Carlton, Irving Howbert, William Lennox, Spencer Penrose, Eugene Shove, and Charles Tutt, Sr., contributed to both the College endowment and the building program. In later years the names of a number of these men could be found on major buildings at the College.[18]

[18]The major buildings named for Cripple Creek millionaires were Lennox House (the first student union), Shove Chapel, Tutt Library, and Tutt Alumni House. El Pomar Sports Center was named for a charitable foundation set up by the Penrose and Tutt families. James Burns contributed money to build spectator stands for the football field.

Former President Edward Payson Tenney uncannily predicted the effect which Cripple Creek gold would have on Colorado College. In 1878, twelve years before Bob Womack first discovered great treasure on the southwest slopes of Pike's Peak, Tenney wrote: "Consecrated gold from the Colorado mountains will enlarge and beautify her Christian college [Colorado College]."[19]

COBURN LIBRARY

But the influx of new money from Cripple Creek did not diminish the importance of the New England connection at Colorado College. In 1892 Nathan Parker Coburn, of Newton, Massachusetts, made a $50,000 gift to the College to pay for a new library. Newton was another one of those small towns located west of Boston, the area in which so many Colorado College benefactors lived. It also was significant that Nathan Coburn was a childhood friend of William Frederick Slocum.

When he contacted Nathan Coburn on behalf of the College, President Slocum at first intended only to ask for money for new books. At the last minute, however, Slocum decided to be courageous and ask Coburn for enough money to build the entire library building. Coburn agreed to it, and President Slocum was very pleased he had decided to ask for the larger amount of money.

The new structure was located on the northeast corner of Cascade Avenue and Cache La Poudre Street. It was the first College building to be erected on the four-block-square area east of Cascade Avenue.

As for building material and architecture for the new library, President Slocum decided to follow the patterns set by Hagerman Hall directly across the street. Coburn Library was built in the Romanesque style with pink peachblow sandstone from western Colorado. Its most distinguishing architectural feature was large arched windows. The new building also sported a red tile roof, a covered entrance on the Cache La Poudre Street side, and interior woodwork of solid red oak.

Coburn Library had the atmosphere of sumptuous intellectualism often associated with major buildings at New England colleges and uni-

[19]Tenney, *The New West*, 87.

Coburn Library

N. P. Coburn, a childhood friend of President William F. Slocum, contributed the money to build the College's first library building. It stood at the northeast corner of Cascade Avenue and Cache La Poudre Street. It was torn down in the 1960s.

versities. The structure was designed with galleries and alcoves which soon contained marble busts of Antinous and Dante and metal casts of Hermes of Praxiteles and Mercie's "David." A full-length cast statue of the Winged Victory of Samothrace presided over the main hall. The lower level was equipped with pews so it could be used for daily chapel services, College assemblies, and lectures. President Slocum located his offices on the main floor.[20]

Coburn Library and its collection of books and its study spaces were made available to the people of Colorado Springs as well as to the students and faculty of Colorado College. It marked the beginning of the College, to as great an extent as is reasonable, sharing its major facilities with the local community. Colorado Springs returned the compliment by providing athletic venues and large assembly spaces for Colorado College events.

THE FIRST CHALLENGE FUND

In 1893 a wealthy Chicago real estate man offered to contribute $50,000 to Colorado College if the College would raise a matching $150,000 on its own. Dr. D. K. Pearsons had been a school teacher, a medical doctor, and an Illinois farmer before making a fortune buying and selling property in Chicago. He spent the later years of his life making gifts to colleges and universities he believed were doing exceptional work. Apparently President Slocum's efforts at the College impressed Pearsons, because Pearsons said he gave the money because he "liked that young man who was doing things out there in Colorado."

President Slocum recruited everyone he could—trustees, students, citizens of Colorado Springs, traditional New England benefactors—in his efforts to raise the $150,000 needed to secure Pearsons's $50,000. The College met the goal on December 31, 1896, thereby gaining a total of $200,000 from the "Pearsons Fund." In the ensuing celebration, the men students pulled President Slocum around downtown Colorado Springs in a buggy. An onlooker described the scene:

---

[20]Reid, *Colorado College: The First Century, 1874–1974*, 45.

"The center of interest was President Slocum, trying not to look too unhappy, seated in a high run-a-bout, drawn by students who were in cap and gown, and clasping to him a large money bag (made, I heard afterwards, of one of Mrs. Slocum's sofa pillows) with $150,000 on it in large figures. . . . I said, 'How amusing!'"[21]

"AMERICA THE BEAUTIFUL"

In 1893 Katherine Lee Bates, a Professor of English at Wellesley College in Massachusetts, came to Colorado Springs for a summer visit. She was teaching in the Colorado Summer School of Science, Philosophy, and Languages. This summer program was sponsored by a number of colleges and universities in Colorado and was held at Colorado College.

During her sojourn in Colorado Springs, Katherine Lee Bates took a two-day wagon trip to the top of Pike's Peak. She was so inspired by the view that, upon her return to her quarters at the Antlers Hotel, she wrote a poem entitled "America The Beautiful."

The poem was published in the *Congregationalist*, a nationally circulated magazine of the Congregational Church. Later the words were set to an existing musical piece. The patriotic song that resulted was so popular that a number of unsuccessful efforts were made to make it the national anthem.

"America The Beautiful" used such images as "spacious skies," "amber waves of grain," and "purple mountain majesties above the fruited plain." These images confirmed the Pike's Peak and Colorado origins of the song. If it ever wishes to do so, Colorado College can call itself "The 'America The Beautiful' College."[22]

---

[21]The onlooker was Ruth Loomis, prior to her employment as the first Dean of Women at Colorado College. She was visiting Colorado Springs while taking a year off from her teaching duties at Vassar College. Letter, Ruth Loomis to Mr. Ormes, 25 February 1928, Colorado College Archives.

[22]In 1981 Mike Bird, a Professor of Economics at Colorado College, was serving on the Colorado Springs City Council and had been elected the City's Vice Mayor. Acting on a suggestion from the author, Mike Bird introduced and got adopted a City Council resolution that designated Colorado Springs as "The 'America The Beautiful' City."

Wolcott Observatory

In the spring of 1894 a small astronomical observatory was constructed down the hillside to the west of Hagerman Hall, the new men's dormitory. It was named Wolcott Observatory for Henry R. Wolcott, of Denver, who gave $3,000 to build the observatory and also contributed a fine telescope for the dome-shaped observation room on the second floor. The building was square-shaped with a large Romanesque arch over the front entrance. On the first floor was a lecture hall, a photographic laboratory, and a faculty office.

Professor Loud taught the Astronomy courses, and one evening a week he held open house at the observatory so that people from Colorado Springs could come study the planets and the stars. "The College authorities were very anxious that the townspeople feel free to use the College facilities at all times."[23]

The Cripple Creek Miners Strike

In the early 1890s the miners at Cripple Creek, who were unionized in the Western Federation of Miners, went on strike for an eight-hour day and a wage of $3 per day. They seized all the large gold mines and shut them down, much to the consternation of the wealthy mine owners and stockholders, many of whom lived in Colorado Springs. The sheriff of El Paso County gathered a posse of 1,200 instant deputies in Colorado Springs and prepared to physically fight the striking miners for control of the mines.[24]

The mine owners turned to Colorado College President William F. Slocum for help. After all, Slocum was the man who had worked to better the lives of factory workers in Amesbury, Massachusetts, and helped to form the Associated Charities in Baltimore, Maryland. President Slocum fearlessly walked through the picket lines at Cripple Creek in an effort to arrange an acceptable settlement with the armed and angry strikers. His

---

[23]Buckley, *The History Of Colorado College, 1874–1904*, 37–38.

[24]At that time Cripple Creek was in El Paso County. The city became part of newly-created Teller County in 1899.

Wolcott Observatory

This small astronomical observatory was constructed on Cache La Poudre Street to the west of Hagerman Hall. It was located in the general area where El Pomar Sports Center was later built.

efforts were rewarded when the striking miners agreed to peacefully negotiate their differences with the mine owners.

Slocum then was asked to address the striking miners, many of whom were armed and had been drinking whiskey to get their courage up for the anticipated battle with the El Paso County deputies. Despite these challenging conditions, Slocum spoke forcefully to the miners, urging them to negotiate with the mine owners in good faith and to obey the laws of the state of Colorado.

The Governor of Colorado, Davis H. Waite, was a member of the Populist Party and refused to use the state militia against the striking miners. In an effort to settle the strike, Governor Waite met with the mine owners in the main academic building (Cutler Hall) at Colorado College. President Slocum called the meeting to order and presided. No solution to the strike acceptable to the mine owners could be worked out, and an angry mob formed in front of the building yelling threats and taunts against the Governor. After dark Governor Waite had to quietly slip out the back door of the building and sneak down the railroad tracks to the railroad station in order to get safely out of town.

The strike was eventually settled. The miners received their eight-hour day and their $3 daily wage. President Slocum came out of the encounter with a reputation for personal physical courage and possessing good skills as a peacemaker.[25]

The Cripple Creek Fire

President Slocum was not the only member of the Colorado College community to do good works at Cripple Creek. In April of 1896 a fire started in a dance hall and rapidly spread throughout the gold camp. Before the conflagration was over, 5,000 people were without shelter and food to eat. A major effort was made in Colorado Springs to find blankets

---

[25]Hershey, *Colorado College, 1874–1949*, 85–86. Also see Sprague, *Newport In The Rockies*, 168–170, 276. Ubbelohde, Benson, and Smith, *A Colorado History*, 220–221. For a detailed account of the entire 130-day strike, see B. M. Rastall, *The Cripple Creek Strike Of 1893* (Colorado Springs, CO: Colorado College, 1905). President Slocum's efforts are related on 22–24, 27.

and food supplies to help relieve the suffering. Classes were cancelled at Colorado College so the students could canvass nearby residential areas for food, clothing, firewood, and anything else that might help the burned-out miners and their families in Cripple Creek.[26]

The Cross of Gold

The silver mines of Colorado were so productive that, throughout the 1880s and early 1890s, the price of silver declined rapidly. As a result, many silver mines closed, the miners were thrown out of work, and once thriving "silver queens," such as the city of Leadville, began to turn into ghost towns. A movement grew in Colorado to revive the silver mining industry by having the U.S. Government arbitrarily set the price of silver at one-sixteenth of the price of gold.

This movement to fix the price of silver gained its greatest political strength at the 1896 National Convention of the Democratic Party. The Democratic nominee for President of the United States, William Jennings Bryan, joined the silver crusade and, in one of the most famous speeches in U.S. political history, pledged to save the nation from crucifixion upon "the cross of gold." Bryan's Republican opponent, William McKinley, committed his candidacy to keeping the United States on just one monetary standard—the gold standard—and continuing to let the market determine the price of silver.

Colorado College and Colorado Springs could not escape this great struggle over silver, even though the economy of Colorado Springs was based firmly on Cripple Creek gold. The idea was very strongly about all over Colorado that the state's economy could not survive if the U.S. Government did not fix the price of silver at a profitable level.[27]

As it turned out, the Republican candidate, William McKinley, won the 1896 presidential election. The U.S. Government did not support the price of silver, and the days of silver mining in Colorado ended abruptly

---

[26]Sprague, *Newport In The Rockies*, 173–174.

[27]For a brief account of the silver struggle in Colorado, see Cronin and Loevy, *Colorado Politics And Government*, 60–63. For a more detailed version, see Ubbelohde, Benson, and Smith, *A Colorado History*, 208–212, 222–225.

as the price of silver dropped so low there was no profit to be made mining it. Colorado voted solidly for William Jennings Bryan, but this last ditch political effort to save the silver mining industry was in vain.

William McKinley's election to the U.S. presidency turned out to be good news for Colorado College. Some observers had estimated that, if Bryan had won the election and fixed the price of silver, the value of the gold mines at Cripple Creek would have been cut in half.[28] But with silver eliminated as a competitor to be the monetary standard in the United States, the gold in the ground at Cripple Creek retained its value. Gold production at Cripple Creek increased after 1896 rather than diminishing.

In summary, as a result of the 1896 U.S. presidential election, gold continued to be mined in Cripple Creek, fortunes continued to be made from that gold by mine owners and investors in Colorado Springs, and a significant portion of those gold profits continued to be contributed to Colorado College. The silver "depression" that hit the rest of Colorado did not have a major effect on Colorado Springs and Colorado College. It became clear that the Golden Age that had characterized Colorado College in the 1890s was going to last into the early 1900s, and perhaps beyond.

TICKNOR HALL

Enrollments at Colorado College continued to rise throughout the 1890s, and by the end of the decade the College had 216 students. The number of women students far exceeded the accommodations available in Montgomery Hall. The College used two residential houses close to the campus for women's dormitories. One was located in the 1300 block of North Weber Street. The second, called East Hall, stood at 930 North Weber Street. The western part of the Plaza Hotel, at the southwest corner of Tejon Street and Cache La Poudre Street, was used temporarily for women students and called South Hall.

---

[28]Sprague, *Newport In The Rockies*, 174. Sprague, describing Winfield Scott Stratton, a famous Cripple Creek millionaire, wrote: "If Bryan should be elected, he [Bryan] would resume silver coinage at the old silver-gold ratio of sixteen to one, which would cut Stratton's gold fortune in half, in effect."

Faculty Baseball Team

The Colorado College faculty baseball team posed on the front steps of Montgomery Hall prior to playing a game against the 1896 senior class. President Slocum is standing at the far left.

In 1897 the College received an anonymous gift of $5,000, later increased to $10,000, to construct a new residence hall for women. The building was located between Montgomery Hall and Cutler Hall, but it was set back so that, taking advantage of the slope of the ground, well-lighted and ventilated rooms could be used on the basement floor. The building material was Ute Pass Green Stone. The brownish color of the stone contrasted with the grey of Cutler and Montgomery halls and the peachblow pink of Hagerman and Coburn halls.

The completion of this new dormitory tripled the living space for women on the Colorado College campus. From Cascade Avenue the new women's dormitory appeared to be the same size as Montgomery Hall, but a large west wing, not visible from in front, made it a much larger building. The design emphasized the social as well as the residential needs of the women students. A club-recreation room was included with a separate entrance on the south side of the building. There also was a room for storing bicycles, given that bicycling was one of the favorite pastimes of students in that era. On the main floor there were parlors and reception rooms where the women students could entertain visitors. There was a dining room seating 40 to 50 women.

The 1890s were the Victorian era, and the College treated the students in a Victorian manner. The men took their meals in Hagerman Hall. The women ate in the new women's dormitory and Montgomery Hall. There also were separate exercise and club facilities for the two sexes.

The new women's residence hall was completed in 1898. Five years later, in 1903, it was revealed that the building was the gift of a young woman named Elizabeth Cheney. A resident of Wellesley, Massachusetts, Elizabeth Cheney had come to Colorado Springs because of her health. The structure was named Ticknor Hall in honor of Anna Ticknor, of Boston, who was a close friend and adviser to Elizabeth Cheney. The following account was given of how Elizabeth Cheney came to give Ticknor Hall to Colorado College:

"Miss Cheney had watched [President] Slocum's taxing work on the Pearsons Fund in addition to all the other things he was doing. [She] put an envelope into his hand one day, . . . and he found that it was a check for $5,000. He did not hesitate long. That evening he and Mrs. Slocum went over to . . . tell . . . [the women students of their plan to build another] building for them on the campus. When [President Slocum] told Miss Cheney, she said, 'I'll make it $10,000.' When [President Slocum] showed her the plans of what afterward became Ticknor [Hall], she said, 'Build it, and I will pay for it.' [Miss Cheney] was then in her early twenties, and it seemed best to her mother and herself that no announcement of her gift should be made."[29]

Ruth Loomis

Following the completion of Ticknor Hall, the College hired Ruth Loomis to become the first Dean of Women. Miss Loomis, as she was addressed by the students, attended Vassar College in Poughkeepsie, New York, graduating in 1885. She taught English for nine years at Vassar before coming to Colorado College. She was the first full-time administrative appointee at the College, taking office in 1897.

Although Ruth Loomis worked full time as a Dean, she was treated and regarded as a member of the faculty. Her most important contribution was to bring to a small western college the sophistication, gentility, and sense of proper behavior typified by an eastern college for women such as Vassar. "In effect, she maintained a college for women in a coeducational institution."[30]

Ruth Loomis became a living symbol of how a Victorian woman should act. She was noted for imparting "sterling integrity" to her charges and elevating "the ideals of . . . young women."[31] A woman member of the class of 1906 said of her: "Dean Loomis felt it was important to give [the women students] a polish along with strict moral standards. Dignity marked Dean Loomis's bearing; even her laughter was subdued and lady-like and her taffeta lined skirts swished in quiet elegance as she moved down the stairs. . . . She knew all the proper requirements for proper young women, and lest we forget, a list of reminders was tacked inside our closet doors."[32]

---

[29]Letter, Ruth Loomis to Mr. Ormes, 25 February 1928, Colorado College Archives.

[30]Hershey, *Colorado College, 1874–1949*, 163.

[31]Student testimony to Miss Ruth Loomis upon her retirement in 1917, quoted in Hershey, *Colorado College, 1874–1949*, 163–164.

[32]Mabel Barbee Lee, class of 1906, quoted in Reid, *Colorado College: The First Century, 1874–1974*, 49–50.

RUTH LOOMIS
The first full-time administrator hired at Colorado College, Ruth Loomis was the Dean of Women during the 1890s and the early 20th Century. She was credited with maintaining "a college for women in a coeducational institution."

A GROWING FACULTY

As the student body grew in size through the 1890s, President Slocum hired additional faculty members. Slocum himself taught Philosophy and Ethics, aiming his courses at students in their junior and senior year. In hiring new faculty, Slocum sought to find young and brilliant teachers who also were outstanding in their academic field. "The faculty that President Slocum did succeed in bringing to Colorado College gave to the institution a name among the best colleges and universities in the land. Some of the faculty had international reputations as scholars, and they were men of strong personalities that were an inspiration to the students."[33]

President Slocum recruited a number of his new faculty members from the large group of people who moved to Colorado Springs to seek a high-altitude cure for lung disease. One of them was Florian Cajori, a native of Switzerland who came to the United States at the age of 16. Cajori began his studies at Johns Hopkins University in Baltimore. He subsequently earned his B.S. and M.S. degrees from the University of Wisconsin and his Ph.D. from Tulane University in New Orleans, Louisiana. When Cajori moved to Colorado Springs to improve his health, Slocum quickly recruited him to teach Mathematics and Physics at Colorado College.

When Professor Cajori read about Wilhelm Roentgen's X-ray experiments in Germany, he took his advanced Physics class to the laboratory. There they carried out the first successful X-ray experiments west of the Mississippi River.[34] It was typical of the emerging style and manner of Colorado College that Florian Cajori involved his students in his pioneering X-ray research.

Another celebrated Slocum hire was Professor Moses Clement Gile. He went to preparatory school at Phillips Academy in Andover and then attended Brown University, where he received both his B.A. and M.A. degrees. Gile began studying for the ministry at Andover Theological Seminary, but financial stringency forced him to begin teaching at Phillips Academy in Andover. He subsequently taught Greek at the University of Chicago before moving to Colorado Springs to recover from a pulmonary

---

[33]Buckley, *The History Of Colorado College, 1874–1904*, 103.

[34]Reid, *Colorado College: The First Century, 1874–1974*, 47.

ailment. President Slocum hired him to teach Latin and Greek. Moses Gile was one of the most popular teachers at the College from 1892 until he passed away in 1916.

The numerous faculty members hired by President William Frederick Slocum were an outstanding lot, many of them characterized by a commitment to disciplined research and writing as well as a devotion to teaching. One scholar looked back and described them as the "first . . . distinguished faculty" of Colorado College.[35]

Creating an Administrative Staff

By the mid–1890s the faculty numbered more than 20. This required President Slocum to begin hiring full-time administrators to help him run the College. It was Slocum who began the practice, long honored at Colorado College, of customarily hiring academic deans from the existing faculty. The first Dean was William Montague Hall, a graduate of Yale University, who came to the College to teach Political Science.

Slocum also hired Edward S. Parsons, who subsequently became a Vice President and then Dean of Colorado College. Similar to Slocum, Parsons was an Amherst graduate, earning both a B.A. and an M.A. at Amherst and a Bachelor of Divinity at Yale. He served a brief period as a minister in Greeley, Colorado, before coming to Colorado College to teach English.

Throughout most of his career at the College, Edward Parsons was known and addressed as Dean Parsons. He established a reputation for being a skilled executive and taking a sympathetic and understanding approach when working with students. Through the middle years of William Frederick Slocum's presidency, Dean Parsons was Slocum's most loyal and supportive lieutenant. In 1894 Parsons turned down a lucrative offer from another college because of his admiration for President Slocum and all that Slocum was accomplishing at Colorado College.[36]

---

[35]Hershey, *Colorado College, 1874–1949*, 155–156. Hershey wrote detailed descriptions of a number of the faculty members hired by President Slocum. See 155–170. Also see Buckley, *The History Of Colorado College, 1874–1904*, 103–113.

[36]Buckley, *The History Of Colorado College, 1874–1904*, 107–108. Also see Hershey, *Colorado College, 1874–1949*, 162–163.

Other administrative posts appointed by President Slocum included the Superintendent of Buildings and Grounds, the Librarian, and the Treasurer. Arthur Baylis was named to direct Buildings and Grounds in 1900 and held the post for 42 years. Manley Ormes, a Congregational minister, took charge of the Library in 1904 and served 25 years. William W. Postlethwaite was appointed Treasurer in 1911 and was on the job for 30 years.

By and large all the other administrative functions, such as raising money, issuing press announcements, and distributing student aid, were handled by President Slocum. That was in addition to teaching his Philosophy courses and leading daily chapel services.

And President Slocum sometimes had to fulfill the most routine of functions. On a Sunday morning in September in the late 1890s, the temperature dropped unusually low and the dormitories became uncomfortably frigid. Dean of Women Ruth Loomis was worrying about how cold the students were when suddenly the heat came on in Montgomery Hall. "As I looked out," Miss Loomis recalled, "there was President Slocum going back to his house from the boiler house, his hat a little back on his head, and holding his hands as if they were more grimy than they really were. Afraid that the [students] might take cold, he had opened the boiler house and started the fire himself. At that time of year there was no fireman in the boiler house. Indeed, it was many years before we could afford to keep a man [there] all the time."[37]

Washburn Field

In 1898 it was decided that Colorado College needed an athletic field in order to stimulate more student interest in physical development and intercollegiate competition. The natural amphitheater created by the hill behind Cutler Hall was chosen as the location for the new field. The ground was leveled and smoothed to provide a football field, a baseball diamond, and a circular running track.

[37]Letter, Ruth Loomis to Mr. Ormes, 25 February 1928, Colorado College Archives.

The new athletic field was dedicated at the start of a baseball game between Colorado College and the Colorado School of Mines on April 7, 1898. President Slocum performed the traditional symbolic ritual of pitching the first ball. The Colorado College team won the game over Mines by a score of 12 to 10, en route to winning the Colorado Intercollegiate Athletic Association baseball championship three years in a row.

One of the speakers at the dedication was Reverend Philip Washburn of Grace Episcopal Church in Colorado Springs. Washburn was an avid supporter of Colorado College sports. Following his death later in the year, the students and faculty voted to name the new athletic field for Reverend Washburn. An archway was erected over the entrance to the field that bore the name "Washburn Field."

The new athletic field came with a grandstand seating 600 persons. In 1900 James Burns, one of the first Cripple Creek millionaires to contribute to the College, gave the money to build an additional grandstand for 800 persons. There was no trouble filling all those seats with spectators. In 1899 and 1900 the Colorado College football team was undefeated, winning the state championship both years. In 1900 Colorado College won its football game with the University of Colorado by a score of 53 to 0. Top quality intercollegiate men's athletic teams had become a major part of the Colorado College scene.

PERKINS HALL

Willard B. Perkins was an architect who had come to Colorado Springs for his health and subsequently became one of the leading architects in the region. When he passed away in 1897, he stipulated in his will that Colorado College should receive the sum of $24,000. Some of the money was designated for scholarships, but a large portion was given as a building fund to be used as the Board of Trustees saw fit.

During the previous three years President Slocum had overseen the creation of both a Department of Music and a Department of Fine Arts at Colorado College. The two programs had proven popular with the students, so a combined Music and Fine Arts building seemed to be the best thing to do with the Willard B. Perkins bequest. Two Cripple Creek millionaires,

Perkins Hall

Constructed just to the east of Coburn Library, the first floor of Perkins Hall had an auditorium with a large pipe organ. On the second floor were classrooms, offices, practice rooms, and studio space for the Music and Art departments. Perkins Hall was torn down in the 1960s.

Winfield Scott Stratton and James Burns, joined a number of other contributors in making additional gifts to the Perkins Hall building fund.[38]

The new building was located immediately to the east of Coburn Library and faced on Cache La Poudre Street. Similar to Coburn Library, it was constructed of pink peachblow sandstone in a Romanesque architectural style. It was two stories high, with classrooms, art studios, and music practice rooms on the second floor. The major feature of the building, a 600-seat assembly hall, was located on the first floor. The assembly hall was equipped with a pipe organ contributed by Elizabeth Cheney, the same youthful benefactor of the College who gave the money for Ticknor Hall.

A NATIONALLY-PROMINENT PRESIDENT

By the year 1900 William Frederick Slocum's strenuous efforts and readily visible accomplishments as President of Colorado College had lifted him to national prominence. His photograph and his name constituted the entire front cover of the February 22, 1900, issue of the *Congregationalist*, the national magazine of the Congregational Church. The accompanying article lauded Slocum for his commitment to "the best traditions of New England learning and culture" and for succeeding in a situation where "any other than a man of vision would have utterly failed." The praise for Slocum was soaring, even for the Victorian Age. "Men around him have again and again learned from him to attempt courageously the right even when it seemed the impossible."

The article went on to cite President Slocum for his good business sense and administrative skills as well as his commitment to public service. It concluded with a prayer for his continued service as the head of Colorado College. "Long may he be spared to develop the institution which owes, in great measure, its marvelous growth and its wide influence to his energy, tact, wisdom and character."[39]

---

[38]The Willard B. Perkins who contributed much of the money to construct Perkins Hall should not be confused with Charles Eliot Perkins, an executive of the Chicago, Burlington, and Quincy Railroad who purchased the Garden of the Gods. Charles Eliot Perkins influenced his heirs to give the Garden of the Gods to the city of Colorado Springs for a public park.

[39]"President Slocum," *Congregationalist*, 22 February 1900, 259. This article was found in the archives at Andover-Newton Theological Seminary in Newton, Massachusetts.

In 1903 President Slocum was invited to be the Southworth lecturer at Andover Theological Seminary. He gave a series of talks on the subject of "The Moral and Religious Evolution of the West." According to the *Congregationalist*, Slocum traced the various migrations to the West and the educational movements that resulted. It was assumed that many of the young divinity students to whom he was speaking would follow his example and become either church pastors or college teachers and administrators on the nation's western frontier. "The West," Slocum was quoted as saying, "demands today as never before that its clergymen should be men of breadth, scholarship, intensity of moral conviction, and possessed of the deepest personal religious experience."[40]

General Palmer Retires

In 1901 General William Jackson Palmer began to sell his remaining railroad interests and thereby ended his business career as "a builder of the West." He had been very financially successful. He sold the Rio Grande Western railroad, his line across eastern Utah, to the Denver and Rio Grande Railroad for $6 million. He unloaded his remaining railroad properties in Mexico for another $500,000. These monies, combined with Palmer's extensive real estate assets, gave him a personal fortune of $9 million and an income of $360,000 per year.[41]

This was a major development for both Colorado Springs and Colorado College. The good General, now relieved of his entrepreneurial responsibilities, was able to devote more of his time—and his fortune—to his city and his College.[42] This process began when General Palmer purchased the land, paid for the landscaping, and gave the city Monument Valley Park. Since Monument Creek ran along the western edge of the Colorado College campus, Monument Valley Park beautified the College as well as the city.

---

[40]"President Slocum's Lectures At Andover," *Congregationalist*, 25 April 1903, 581. This article was found in the archives at Andover-Newton Theological Seminary in Newton, Massachusetts.

[41]Sprague, *Newport In The Rockies*, 148. Also see Fisher, *A Builder Of The West*, 279, 302–303.

[42]Reid, *Colorado College: The First Century, 1874–1974*, 71.

CAMPUS PLAN
This theoretical conception of the campus, drawn about 1900, shows Palmer Hall facing on Cascade Avenue. All the buildings, including the College Chapel, were to be constructed of pink peach-blow sandstone with Romanesque architecture.

The portion of the park that immediately adjoined the campus had a number of trees and rustic benches. It was next to the women's dormitories, so it became a favorite spot for men and women students to get together and enjoy each other's company. Ruth Loomis, the Dean of Women, declared this area off-limits for women students at night. The area was nicknamed "The Jungle," and there were occasional references in student publications to "night jungling."[43]

PALMER HALL

From the earliest days of its founding Colorado College had a strong offering of science courses. Classical studies were never neglected, but pioneer science professors such as James Hutchison Kerr and William Strieby saw to it there was high quality instruction in all the major scientific fields.

---

[43] Reid, *Colorado College: The First Century, 1874–1974*, 68.

As the College grew in size throughout the 1890s, however, it became increasingly difficult to find the needed space for science classrooms and well-equipped laboratories.

As the 19th Century came to an end, President Slocum increased his determination to see that Colorado College became a leading educational institution. The rapid growth in the student body and the faculty during the 1890s had already brought the College a significant reputation. But Slocum wanted to do more. He wanted to establish science programs that would compare favorably with the best colleges and universities in the nation. The first step, and the most necessary step, to accomplish this goal would be to raise the money to build a new science building.[44]

The new building was designed to include science laboratories, lecture halls, and the College administrative offices. It was to be larger in size and sturdier in construction than any previous building on the campus. In short, it was to perform the dual function of increasing the space available for the sciences while at the same time symbolizing the recent growth in the size and reputation of Colorado College.

---

[44]Buckley, *The History Of Colorado College*, 44–45.

The construction cost of the new science facility was $270,000. It had a steel frame and concrete floors overlaid with a terrazzo finish. The major interior walls were of red brick. The building was three stories high, with the first story called the basement and the top two stories called the first and second floor. Additional space was available in a sub-basement and a third-floor attic. The administrative offices of the College were moved into the new building.

President Slocum had been granted a leave of absence for the 1901–1902 academic year. While he and Mary Slocum were away from the campus, Dean Edward Parsons served as Acting President. Parsons apparently had difficulty securing the proper-sized pink peachblow sandstone to build the new science building. He told the Board of Trustees in June of 1902 that he had been forced by necessity to order Greenlee stone instead.

When President Slocum returned from his year away, he was not happy with the decision to construct the new science building with Greenlee stone. He envisioned a building that would match Hagerman, Coburn, and Perkins halls by having Romanesque architecture and exterior walls of pink peachblow sandstone. Hurried changes were made, and the necessary pink peachblow sandstone was secured.[45] The Greenlee stone that had already arrived at the construction site was set aside for a future, as yet undetermined campus building project.[46]

The most interesting story about the new science building concerned its location. Originally it was slated to be built due north of Coburn and Perkins halls, but it was to be quite some distance away from those two buildings at the corner of Cascade Avenue and San Rafael Street. This plan was put on hold, however, when the streetcar company in Colorado Springs announced that it wanted to run its trolley tracks straight up Tejon Street right through the center of the Colorado College campus.

---

[45]President Slocum subsequently let it be known that he intended for all College buildings constructed east of Cascade Avenue to be built out of pink peachblow sandstone and have Romanesque architecture. For economic reasons, this plan of Slocum's was not carried out by his successors in the presidential office. "Colorado College," *Mecca* (no date), 7–11. See Photograph Files: Buildings—Campus Views—Collections, Colorado College Archives.

[46]Hershey, *Colorado College, 1874–1949*, 147. The Greenlee stone was subsequently used to build McGregor Hall, a women's dormitory. For another account of this story, see Letter, Ruth Loomis to Mr. Ormes, 25 February 1928, Colorado College Archives.

The streetcar company was owned by Winfield Scott Stratton, a carpenter who garnered instant millions by discovering and developing one of the first successful gold mines at Cripple Creek. Stratton, similar to many of the Cripple Creek millionaires, returned to Colorado Springs to spend his new fortune. He decided to purchase and improve the local trolley system. It would be very inconvenient, and expensive, to have his streetcars avoid the College campus by detouring from Tejon Street over to Nevada Avenue.

President Slocum was appalled at the thought of trolley cars clanging their way through what he had visualized as the green and grassy center of the campus. General Palmer joined him in opposing Stratton's plan, and the City Council sided with General Palmer and voted not to let the streetcar line bisect Colorado College. The tracks eventually were routed over to Nevada Avenue. The streetcars returned to Tejon Street once they were north of the College.

And then a mysterious event occurred. President Slocum announced at a Board of Trustees meeting that an anonymous donor had contributed $100,000 for the construction of the new science building. At the same meeting, at the suggestion of General Palmer, the location of the building was moved further to the east, exactly in the middle of where Tejon Street would be if it were ever extended, along with trolley tracks, through the campus. The Board of Trustees accepted the gift, and the new building began to rise at a spot that would physically block any future attempt to build a streetcar line through Colorado College.

There has been much speculation over the years that it was General Palmer who gave the $100,000 for the new science building, perhaps in an effort to get the building up more quickly and Tejon Street permanently blocked as soon as possible. But this is only speculation. The name of the anonymous donor has never been revealed.

And what about Winfield Scott Stratton, the owner of the streetcar company. There was a rumor that, prior to his streetcar argument with President Slocum, Stratton had included a large bequest for Colorado College in his will. When Stratton died, however, he left all his money for a home for orphans and elderly persons living in poverty. Many observers conjectured that Stratton would have left a considerable amount of money to Colorado College if his streetcar line had not been blocked with a massive pink stone building.

On February 23, 1904, elaborate dedication exercises were held for the new science building. The structure was officially named Palmer Hall, and General Palmer himself was present to receive an honorary LL.D. degree from the College. There was an academic procession from Perkins Hall, where the ceremonies began, to the front steps of Palmer Hall, where President Slocum made a short speech and said a prayer of dedication. Fifty colleges and universities sent official representatives to this grand and reverent occasion.

Palmer Hall was highly praised for both its attractiveness and utility as an educational structure. Fifty years after the building was completed, a close observer of Colorado College wrote: "It is one of the finest college buildings among liberal arts colleges in the United States. Its lines are remarkably well-drawn to give it, at the same time, the effect of enduring mass and pleasing elevations. Within, it serves well both the student and the teacher in their scientific as well as their more general academic pursuits."[47]

The completion of Palmer Hall was a major symbolic event in the history of Colorado College. The building was considerably larger than any building previously constructed. Its cost was a full six times higher than any other structure on the campus. The building was pleasing in appearance, and its great mass indicated that the builders of the College planned for their institution to be around for many years to come. By its very presence, Palmer Hall announced that Colorado College had made its mark as a successful institution of higher learning in the western United States.[48]

THE MUSEUM IN PALMER HALL

From the first days of the College the professors began gathering geological and biological specimens to aid in teaching the students. Friends of the College donated mineral and paleontological collections. By the time of the dedication of Palmer Hall in 1904, the College had a sufficient number of these materials to open a museum on the second floor of the new building.

---

[47]Hershey, *Colorado College, 1874–1949*, 148–149.

[48]For a description of the optimistic atmosphere at Colorado College at the time Palmer Hall was constructed, see Judith Reid Finley, *Time Capsule 1900: Colorado Springs A Century Ago* (Colorado Springs, CO: Pastwords Publications, 1998), 86–90.

A PINNACLE MOMENT

Dedication ceremonies for Palmer Hall were held on February 23, 1904. Both the large size and the high cost of Palmer Hall symbolized the emergence of Colorado College as one of the finest small liberal arts colleges in the United States.

The museum was a large, high-ceilinged room with tall arched windows. It included a natural history collection with a large number of stuffed animals and birds. The most interesting exhibit was the skeleton of a giant whale, which hung from the ceiling and stretched over much of the length of the room.

This natural history collection had been given to the College by Cripple Creek millionaire Winfield Scott Stratton. He made the donation in 1900, just one year before he and President Slocum quarreled over Stratton's streetcars crossing the Colorado College campus.

MAJORS AND ADVISORS

The academic program was changing in the early 1900s. It began to evolve into what could be called the conventional academic program of leading United States colleges and universities in the 20th Century. All students were required to choose a major field in which they concentrated their studies in the junior and senior year. Each student was assigned a faculty advisor and encouraged to work closely with that particular faculty member in developing the student's own personalized academic schedule. Courses were calibrated in semester hours, with the average course providing three semester hours of credit. The semester hours system made it possible to easily convert Colorado College credits into academic credits at other colleges and universities—and vice versa.

Also at the beginning of the 20th Century, Colorado College began a long but not too serious flirtation with graduate and professional school education. A Masters degree program was organized for many of the major academic fields. Professor Florian Cajori established a School of Engineering which offered Bachelor degrees in electrical, mining, and civil engineering. After General Palmer gave the College 10,000 acres of forest land at the top of Ute Pass, a Forestry School was instituted. It was the fifth forestry school to be created in the United States and the only one with its own private forest to use as a living laboratory.

MCGREGOR HALL

Student enrollment at the College continued to grow during the early 1900s. President Slocum and the Board of Trustees once again needed to find comfortable and safe housing for additional women students. The problem was compounded by the fact that the College's lease on the west wing of the Plaza Hotel had expired. The women students who lived in that facility, known as South Hall, would soon need other accommodations.

It was decided to build a third women's dormitory to go with Montgomery and Ticknor halls. President Slocum noted that the rental fees paid by the women students in the new dormitory could be used to help pay for the project. The College would build the new structure partly on gifts but also partly with a loan.

The new residence hall was constructed down the hill and a considerable distance west of Ticknor Hall. It was four stories high, had sixty bedrooms, and included a women's gymnasium in the basement. The Greenlee sandstone originally intended for Palmer Hall was used to complete this new dormitory. It was named McGregor Hall in honor of Miss Marion McGregor Noyes, who taught Latin and Philosophy and was President Slocum's assistant in the Philosophy Department from 1891 to 1897. It was she who solicited a number of the major contributions for the new residence hall. McGregor was Professor Noyes's mother's family name.[49]

Together with Montgomery Hall and Ticknor Hall, the new McGregor Hall formed the beginning of a residential quadrangle. Shortly after McGregor Hall opened, people began referring to the three dormitories as the Women's Quadrangle. The sport of tennis was so popular at the beginning of the 20th Century that the large area in the center of the Women's Quadrangle was filled with tennis courts.

A MAJOR ENDOWMENT DRIVE

Palmer Hall, the new science building, and McGregor Hall, the new women's residence hall, were completed and added to the building inventory of the College at roughly the same time. In his short speech at the dedication of Palmer Hall, President Slocum indicated that he and the College were finished with the building program for a while. "The science hall is completed," Slocum said. "I have no other building in mind at pre-

---

[49]Marion McGregor Noyes was a popular member of the campus community in the 1890s. See Letter, Ruth Loomis to Mr. Ormes, 25 February 1928, Colorado College Archives.

sent, and my every effort from now on will be to secure the endowment necessary to carrying on the work of Colorado College."[50]

Slocum was as good as his word. Late in 1904 he personally took charge of a $500,000 endowment fund drive. That was a very ambitious figure for the time, but Slocum had said earlier that the College would not be safe for the future unless $1 million could be added to the treasury.[51] Even Slocum himself recognized the magnitude of the task. He said later: "This seemed an insurmountable undertaking, and to many it was hopeless from the start."[52]

It was a measure of the increasing prominence of the College that one of the nation's leading philanthropists, and a leading philanthropic organization, contributed to this fund drive. Multi-millionaire steel baron Andrew Carnegie gave $50,000. The General Education Board, with the support of the Rockefeller Foundation, also contributed $50,000. At the local level, Charles M. McNeil, a Cripple Creek gold mining millionaire, put in $25,000. "As usual, General Palmer was the largest individual contributor to the campaign with a gift of $100,000."[53]

The $500,000 endowment fund drive was $60,000 short of its goal when President Slocum launched a final effort in the Colorado Springs community. The $60,000 was raised in only 15 days with $12,000 to spare. President Slocum had kept his pledge, stated at the dedication of Palmer Hall, to make enlarging the endowment his next major task at the College.

BEMIS HALL

Also at the dedication of Palmer Hall in 1904, President Slocum had said that he had "no other building in mind at present. . . ." He may have meant that when he said it, but it was not in the nature of President Slocum to rest on his laurels or let his College vegetate. In 1908 Colorado

---

[50]Buckley, *The History Of Colorado College, 1874–1904*, 50.

[51]Buckley, *The History Of Colorado College, 1874–1904*, 72.

[52]Hershey, *Colorado College, 1874–1949*, 123.

[53]Reid, *Colorado College: The First Century, 1874–1974*, 65.

College began building a fourth dormitory for women, Bemis Hall, in between and south of Ticknor and McGregor halls.

Similar to Palmer Hall, this new building was sufficiently large and endowed with luxury features to symbolize the new, higher status of Colorado College. A spacious dining room with a high-vaulted ceiling enabled all the women students to take their meals in one place. A small theater for dramatic productions was installed in the basement.

Bemis Hall was named for Judson M. Bemis, a leading manufacturer of paper and cloth bags. General Palmer joined Bemis in providing the major funding for the new building. The first three stories were constructed of grey stone in an Old English architectural style, with half-timbered walls and dormer windows at the fourth floor level. A large stone porch ran the full length of the front of the building.

But the most important feature of Bemis Hall was a large common room, known as Bemis Lounge. It had a big fireplace, was furnished with comfortable sofas and chairs, had large windows looking out on the Women's Quadrangle, and was sizeable enough to be used as a campus social center for receptions, informal lectures, and panel discussions. "Bemis Hall has cast its refining influence over the women students and over the whole College.... Trustees, faculty members, students and friends of the College have met within its walls for the finest of the fine arts [-] friendly and gracious associations."[54]

THE RISE OF FRATERNITIES

Throughout the 1890s and early 1900s, the College was only building dormitories for women. There was a good reason for this gender-based policy. Respectable Victorian parents would not send their daughters to Colorado College unless there was safe and well-supervised housing and meals for them.

The only men's dormitory was Hagerman Hall, which opened in 1889. When the number of men students began to exceed the capacity of

---

[54]Hershey, *Colorado College, 1874–1949*, 149. According to Ruth Loomis, the architect of Bemis Hall promised he would make Bemis Lounge "look like the Council Chamber of the Doge's Palace in Venice." Letter, Ruth Loomis to Mr. Ormes, 25 February 1928, Colorado College Archives.

Hagerman Hall, the College left these additional men no choice but to arrange their own housing and meals in the general community of Colorado Springs. It was not long before these off-campus men began organizing themselves into coherent social units that provided them with much-needed housing and meal service.

Thus did the fraternity system, and that venerable institution the fraternity "house," come to Colorado College. This same process took place at many other colleges and universities throughout the nation. In fact, it can be argued that the prominent institutions of higher education in the United States inadvertantly created the fraternity system by not building more men's dormitories and thereby providing decent housing and meals for their men students.

Kappa Sigma was installed at Colorado College in 1904. The following year Sigma Chi was organized. Next came Phi Gamma Delta, Phi Delta Theta, and Beta Theta Pi. The fraternity houses obtained by these organizations quickly became the locale of a goodly portion of the social life at the College. The fraternities held dances, threw parties, and organized hikes and picnics in local parks.

RACIAL INTEGRATION

In 1905 Colorado College became the first college or university in Colorado to have a racially integrated athletic team. Two African-Americans, Fred Roberts and Charles Jackson, played on the football team, which was undefeated that year. The Boulderado Hotel in Boulder, Colorado, refused to provide overnight accommodations for these two Black players during an "away" game at the University of Colorado. John Richards, the football coach at Colorado College, protested this act of racial discrimination by refusing to let the team stay at the Boulderado Hotel. Coach Richards had the team, White and Black members alike, stay overnight in Denver instead.[55]

---

[55]Reid, *Colorado College: The First Century, 1874–1974*, 73, 241.

THE DEATH OF GENERAL PALMER

By the early years of the 20th Century General Palmer had become the revered and admired patriarch of both Colorado Springs and Colorado College. In 1906 the good General, ever modest and opposed to ostentation, reluctantly acceded to President Slocum's request that Palmer's portrait be hung on the west wall of the grand stairway in the main entrance to Palmer Hall. The portrait was painted in England by a well-known German-born British artist, Sir Hubert Von Herkomer.[56] It presented Palmer in a familiar pose—dressed in his horseback riding outfit, with a stylish green vest, and with his hands holding his horseback riding crop behind his back.

Later in 1906 a great tragedy befell General Palmer. He was horseback riding with two of his three daughters at his home at Glen Eyrie when he fell off a small cow pony and broke his neck. For the remainder of his life he was totally paralyzed from the neck down and had to be carried by servants from place to place. He stayed as active as possible, however, being driven about Colorado Springs in a white steam-powered automobile and even making one last trip to England and the European mainland.

But his condition steadily deteriorated. Early in the afternoon of March 13, 1909, General Palmer passed away quietly in his sleep. The Colorado College student newspaper, the *Tiger*, reported that College President William Frederick Slocum was at the General's bedside, along with other friends and family members, at the moment William Jackson Palmer breathed his last.[57]

General Palmer's remains were cremated and buried at Evergreen Cemetery, the city-owned graveyard in Colorado Springs. A simple memorial service was held for the General in the auditorium of Perkins Hall at Colorado College. Edward S. Parsons, the Dean of the College,

---

[56]The original copy of the portrait hung for years in the lobby of the Antlers Hotel in downtown Colorado Springs. When that building was replaced in the early 1960s, the original copy was moved to the Board of Trustees room in Armstrong Hall at Colorado College. General Palmer liked the original of the portrait so much he asked the artist to paint two copies, one of which was displayed in Palmer Hall at Colorado College and the other in the auditorium of the Colorado School for the Deaf and Blind in Colorado Springs. Sprague, *Newport In The Rockies*, 155, 155 note 2.

[57]"Death Of General Palmer," *Tiger*, 19 March 1909, 1.

opened the service by reading an appropriate passage from the Bible. Among the speakers at the Memorial Service were Irving W. Howbert, a longtime Trustee of the College, and President Slocum. Following the service, the public was invited to walk over to Palmer Hall and see the oil painting of General Palmer hanging above the main stairs.

In his remarks at the Perkins Hall memorial service, President Slocum lauded the General for his social and community accomplishments. President Slocum also challenged his listeners to reflect in their lives the values and accomplishments that characterized General Palmer's life.

"His death marks an era in the history of the state," Slocum said. "Who is to take his place? Who is to take up his work and carry it on to its fruition? There may be no one person who can do what he has done; but there are those in our city who, by uniting for the betterment of the social and moral condition, can bring things to pass which will count for just as much in the new era as the things which he has done counted for in the past."

"He has placed a sacred trust in the keeping of this College," Slocum continued. "What are we to do with it? What he has done for us is for the purpose of helping us to live our lives nobly and do our work well in our state and in the life of the community. Only the future can tell whether we are to be worthy of all he has been and all that he has done."[58]

On the day of the General Palmer's burial, his ashes were carried out to Evergreen Cemetery in a horse drawn carriage. President Slocum, Dean Parsons, and the College faculty walked solemnly behind, followed by the General's family, friends, and many citizens of Colorado Springs. More than 150 men students at the College showed their respect by walking on both sides of the carriage. Special cars were hired to bring the women students at the College to the grave site. The College also provided a large floral wreath.

Following a brief religious ceremony, a small black casket containing General Palmer's ashes was lowered into its final resting place by College President William F. Slocum and Colonel D. C. Dodge, a friend of General Palmer's from his railroading days.[59]

---

[58]"Address By President Slocum," *Tiger*, 19 March 1909, 7.

[59]"Tribute To First Citizen," *Tiger*, 19 March 1909, 1.

More than 3,000 residents of Colorado Springs attended these final services for the city's great founder and benefactor. "He was buried under the pines and evergreens of Colorado: beyond them, across the town, stood up the great Peak and the range of mountains which had lifted his heart from the first hour when he saw them, new and remote and lovely, forty years [earlier]."[60]

COSSITT HALL

President Slocum was well aware of the poor facilities that had been made available to men students at Colorado College. The one men's dormitory, Hagerman Hall, only housed a small percentage of the male student body. As for athletics, there was only that small wooden frame building located to the west of Hagerman Hall. It served as little more than an exercise room with rough and rustic locker facilities for the men's sports teams.

In 1913 a relative of President Slocum, Mrs. A. D. Juilliard, gave $100,000 to the College to build a social and athletic center for the men students. The old wooden gymnasium was torn down and in its place began to rise a major building that included a full-size gymnasium with a basketball court. There were also locker and shower facilities. The most interesting feature of the new structure was an outdoor amphitheater which could also be used as a small exercise yard. It was designed for gymnastic exercises, outdoor dramatic productions, sports pep rallies, etc.

As for social life, the new building included a large lounge area that could also be used for informal group meetings. At the west end of the building, with a spectacular view of Pike's Peak, was a men's dining hall and the accompanying kitchen facilities. Similar to Bemis Hall for the women students, this new building was designed to provide an attractive and comfortable environment for student social and intellectual activities.

As soon as the dining facilities in the new structure were open and operating, the College ordered the fraternities to stop serving meals. All the men on campus except those who lived in Colorado Springs were expected to eat all their meals in the new dining hall, which had a capacity

---

[60]Fisher, *A Builder Of The West*, 318–319. Also see Sprague, *Newport In The Rockies*, 165. Reid, *Colorado College: The First Century, 1874–1974*, 71–72.

of 200 persons per meal. Note that men and women students were not allowed to dine together on a regular basis. The women students continued to eat their meals in the women's dormitories, primarily Bemis Hall.

Mrs. Juilliard named the building in honor of her father, Frederick H. Cossitt. It was built of a grey stone that closely matched both Cutler Hall and Bemis Hall. The architecture was Greek-and-Roman with something of a military look. The College Seal, with the motto "Scientia et Disciplina" clearly visible, was inscribed in the eastern wall of the building above the main door.

The lounge area in Cossitt Hall got off to a controversial start. The faculty prohibited card playing and smoking, and the men students staged the first organized protest in the College's history to let the faculty know what they thought of such restrictions. A board composed of faculty members, alumni, and students was set up to govern Cossitt Hall, and the board quickly rescinded the rules against smoking and card playing. In addition, a pool table was installed in a lower-floor room located underneath the lounge area.

A MISSIONARY IN INDIA

During the late 19th and early 20th Centuries, college and university students with a strong religious interest were motivated to participate in overseas missionary work. An example was Dr. Mary R. Noble, Colorado College class of 1896, who completed her medical training in the United States and then spent five years as an instructor in the Ludhiana Women's Medical College in the Punjab in India. At that time Ludhiana was the only Christian medical college for women in India.

Dr. Noble returned to Colorado College for a visit in the spring of 1909. In addition to lecturing on her experiences in India, she conducted a mission class for the students at the College which met every Wednesday evening in Bemis Hall.[61]

THE END OF THE GOLDEN AGE

In June of 1913 the College celebrated William Frederick Slocum's 25th year as President. The festivities, which lasted for five days, coincided with

[61]"Alumni Notes," *Tiger*, 19 March 1909, 6.

the 1913 commencement exercises. The major event was an academic procession from Palmer Hall to the Burns Theater, a vaudeville theater located in downtown Colorado Springs near the corner of Cascade and Pike's Peak avenues. The distance from Palmer Hall to the Burns Theater was eleven city blocks. Representatives of 60 institutions of higher learning, all dressed in full academic regalia, joined the faculty and the graduating seniors in marching in President Slocum's honor.

The most gratifying event for President Slocum must have been the unveiling of a full-length portrait of him, dressed in his academic robes, painted by John White Alexander. The portrait eventually was hung on the eastern wall of the grand staircase in the main entrance to Palmer Hall, exactly opposite the portrait of General Palmer. The images of the two men—they had worked together for two decades to build Colorado College—would face each other, in a place of honor, for decades to come.

But trouble was brewing for President Slocum and the manner in which he was operating the College. A growing number of faculty members were displeased with their lack of participation in the governing process at the institution. Slocum maintained almost complete control over financial decisions and unilaterally set faculty salaries. Furthermore, Slocum transferred money from one account to another as needed without paying particular attention to the uses for which particular funds were designated. Some faculty members opposed this financial sleight-of-hand, despite the fact that independent audits showed no irregularities and all of Slocum's financial transactions were approved by the Board of Trustees.

What was happening was that the faculty was beginning to demand a much larger role in the academic governance of Colorado College. This process was taking place at other institutions of higher learning as well. The person who came to symbolize this faculty demand for more faculty power was Dean Edward S. Parsons. Although he had long expressed great admiration for President Slocum, and at one time had turned down other job offers to continue working with Slocum, Dean Parsons took the lead in publicly criticizing Slocum and demanding the faculty be given a larger role in decision-making at the College.

The battle was a crucial and bitter one. By 1915 President Slocum was a holdover from the late 19th Century days of the great capitalists, men who single-handedly made great fortunes and achieved great things.

Edward S. Parsons
Dean of the College during the Slocum years, Parsons led the effort to gain more faculty control over academic policies at Colorado College.

Such men did not waste time worrying about people's feelings and conscientiously consulting the views of others. The great success of Colorado College under President Slocum's leadership was ready justification for the individualistic way he had centered control of the College's affairs in his own person. "It was hardly a case of 'the end justifies the means,' but a conviction that the end sought must not be lost sight of in too many conferences and committee meetings concerned largely with what he considered the lesser details of the grand project."[62]

But Dean Parsons and the rebellious faculty members he led had their arguments as well. President Slocum himself had hired an energetic and competent faculty, and it was only natural that such a skilled crew would want to help captain the College ship. Also the College was much larger, with an enrollment of over 700 students, and such an enlarged and improved institution no longer was appropriate for "one-man rule." Furthermore, advancing years of age had robbed Slocum of the mental quickness he needed to govern what had become a more complicated and complex institution.

In the midst of this situation of sharp personal conflict and grave institutional turmoil, questions were suddenly raised about President Slocum's personal morals. "As is usual in instances of this nature, rumor begat rumor and adverse comments were met with denials."[63] The known details were these. Two women on the administrative support staff told Dean Parsons that President Slocum had "made improper and immoral advances toward them."[64] Instead of taking these charges directly to the Board of Trustees, Dean Parsons shared them with three faculty members who were critical of Slocum. Shortly thereafter rumors about President Slocum's personal conduct were circulating widely throughout the College and the community of Colorado Springs. Clearly Dean Parsons's faculty allies had decided to use these unadjudicated and unproven charges to personally discredit President Slocum in the most damaging way possible.

---

[62]Hershey, *Colorado College, 1874–1949*, 91.

[63]Hershey, *Colorado College, 1874–1949*, 92.

[64]Reid, *Colorado College: The First Century, 1874–1974*, 82. Reid was the only writer on Colorado College history to give this much detail about the charges against President Slocum.

This carefully constructed and very effective rumor-mongering campaign against President Slocum presented the College Board of Trustees with a difficult set of options. "In reviewing these more personal criticisms of the President, the Trustees, although persuaded that all such charges rested on rumor and hearsay rather than on convincing proof, felt that their general discussion in the community and the effect of such discussion on both the President and the College could not be ignored."[65]

The Board asked William Frederick Slocum, in view of his advancing years, to withdraw from the active administration of the College and prepare to retire. This Slocum agreed to do, spending the 1916–1917 academic year on the East Coast raising funds for the College to complete a major endowment drive.[66] Slocum returned in June 1917 and presided over the commencement exercises, giving the baccalaureate address, receiving an honorary Doctor of Laws degree, and then becoming President Emeritus of Colorado College.

When it became known among the student body that President Slocum was leaving the campus to raise money on the East Coast, and that his presidency officially would end shortly thereafter, there was a large gathering in Perkins Hall to honor President and Mrs. Slocum for their contributions to Colorado College. Slocum was presented with a gold watch, and Mrs. Slocum was given a seed pearl pin.[67] Then, the next day, the entire student body went with the Slocums to the railroad station to see them off. It was a send-off more frequently associated with a winning sports team rather than a departing President.[68]

But William Frederick Slocum was not the only person to depart from Colorado College at this particular moment. The Board of Trustees was displeased with the manner in which Dean Edward S. Parsons had han-

---

[65]Hershey, *Colorado College, 1874–1929*, 92.

[66]"W. F. Slocum Resigns From C.C. Presidency: Goes East Soon In Interests Of Endowment Fund," *Tiger*, 15 September 1916, 1. Also see "Last Ethical Was Delivered By Prexy This Morning: Chooses 'The Colorado College To Be' For Subject," *Tiger*, 5 October 1916, 1.

[67]"President Slocum Leaves Tonight For East To Complete Endowment," *Tiger*, 10 October 1916, 1. Also see "We're Behind You, Prexy!" *Tiger*, 10 October 1916, 2.

[68]"Students Gave The Slocums Big Send-Off Tuesday Night: Marched To The Station Where Many Cheers Were Given," *Tiger*, 13 October 1916, 1.

dled the morals accusations against President Slocum, particularly the fact that rumors were spread in the community before the Board of Trustees was officially informed of the problem. Dean Parsons was asked to resign and, when he refused to do so, he was dismissed from the College's employment. He subsequently served 17 years as the President of Marietta College in Marietta, Ohio.[68a]

But, in his own way, Dean Edward S. Parsons was an important influence on the future development of Colorado College. The battle he inaugurated for greater faculty influence in the governance of the College was eventually won by the faculty. More and more of the major decisions, particularly concerning the academic and instructional aspects of the institution, were made in faculty meeting rather than unilaterally in the President's office. Even the process of setting faculty salaries came to be initiated by the faculty, even though the final figure setting was done by the President and the Board of Trustees. Despite the controversial nature of his departure, Edward S. Parsons left a significant mark and laid the groundwork for important changes at Colorado College.[69]

PRESIDENT SLOCUM EVALUATED

William Frederick Slocum was the giant personage in the early history of Colorado College. He took a failing institution of some 50 students and, 30 years later, left behind a financially sound College with more than 500 students and an endowment of over $2.5 million. He built what can be called the Slocum Campus, a collection of 10 major buildings, all constructed of stone, many of which, even in the year 1999, were thought to constitute the most attractive buildings on the campus.[70] And for 37 years,

[68a]For material on Edward S. Parsons at Marietta College, see Arthur G. Birch, *A Pioneer College: The Story Of Marietta* (privately printed, 1935), 278–281. Vernon E. "Dan" McGrew, *". . . In The Various Branches of Useful Knowledge:" Marietta College, 1935–1989* (Marietta, OH: Marietta College, 1994.

[69]The author joined the faculty at Colorado College in 1968 after teaching at Goucher College and Johns Hopkins University in Baltimore. One of the first things the author noted about Colorado College was the considerable amount of decision-making power vested in the College faculty.

[70]The ten major buildings, in rough order of completion, were Hagerman Hall, Montgomery Hall, Coburn Library, Wolcott Observatory, Ticknor Hall, Perkins Hall, Palmer Hall, McGregor Hall, Bemis Hall, and Cossitt Hall. The Slocum-built buildings that survived to 1999 were Montgomery Hall, Ticknor Hall, Palmer Hall, McGregor Hall, Bemis Hall, and Cossitt Hall.

from 1917 until the post-World War II year of 1954, the Slocum Campus remained essentially as Slocum had built it. Only Shove Chapel was added in 1931, and former President Slocum had a part to play in the design and development of that building as well.[71]

President Slocum strongly supported the athletic program at Colorado College. He oversaw the construction of Washburn Field for men's intercollegiate football and baseball. He also provided the College's first athletic facilities for women when a gymnasium for women was constructed in the basement of McGregor Hall. Cossitt Hall, with its indoor basketball court and outdoor exercise gymnasium, demonstrated Slocum's heavy commitment to having a first-rate athletic program at the College.[72]

Slocum's personal reputation as a leader in higher education in the United States was substantial. He was offered the presidencies of Oberlin College and the University of Illinois but declined them to complete his mission at Colorado College. He was awarded honorary degrees by Allegheny College, Amherst College (his alma mater), Beloit College, the University of Colorado, Harvard University, Illinois College, and the University of Nebraska. And Slocum continued the personal charitable activities that had characterized his life in Amesbury, Massachusetts, and Baltimore, Maryland. He helped to organize the Colorado State Board of Charities, and he served on the Colorado State Board of Pardons.

Slocum's efforts and influence brought many honors to Colorado College. In 1904 the College was one of four institutions in the western United States to be selected for a chapter of Phi Beta Kappa, the national scholastic honor society. The other three were all large universities—the University of California, the University of Colorado, and Stanford University. In 1911 Harvard University selected Colorado College as one

---

[71]President Emeritus Slocum, living in Newton, Massachusetts, apparently was consulted about the new Chapel and recommended C. W. Walker, a Boston architect, to draw up plans for conducting a national competition to select an architect. Hershey, *Colorado College, 1874–1949*, 102.

[72]President Slocum saw a definite relationship between a winning football team and his ability to raise money for the College. See Hershey, *Colorado College, 1874–1949*, 85. Dean Edward Parsons described President Slocum's passion for victorious athletic teams but noted that the College wanted an athletic program in which many students, and not just those with great athletic skills, participated. See "Colorado College," *Mecca* (no date), 7–11, Photograph Files: Buildings—Campus Views—Collections, Colorado College Archives.

William Frederick Slocum
The great "builder" President of Colorado College, Slocum raised the money and supervised the construction of ten major buildings. This photo dates from the later years of his presidency.

of four liberal arts colleges with which Harvard would annually exchange professors. The other participants in this famous Harvard faculty exchange were Beloit, Grinnell, and Knox colleges.

In the latter years of Slocum's presidency, President A. Lawrence Lowell of Harvard University described Colorado College as "among the four best colleges in America."[73] David Starr Jordan, President of Stanford University, said in a newspaper interview in 1908: "I have had many opportunities to judge of the standing and character of Colorado College, and in my opinion, it is an ideal college, with a ranking equal to the best in the country, such as Amherst and Williams in the East. In the Middle West, Knox and Iowa College [Grinnell] are in the same category. [Colorado College] is the best college in the West, and in some respects it is better fitted than eastern colleges, in that it has better equipment for the number of students. . . ."[74]

William Frederick Slocum deserves to have his name listed with the other giants of American higher education. He ranks with Mark Hopkins, the great teacher and President of Williams College in the mid–19th Century, and Daniel Coit Gilman, the outstanding founder-President of Johns Hopkins University in the late 19th Century. Slocum compares with his contemporary and friend, J. W. Main, the early 20th Century builder-President of Grinnell College.[75]

Perhaps the saddest aspect of the unsavory events surrounding Slocum's departure from Colorado College was that the unadjudicated rumors about him have made partisans of the College somewhat hesitant about rendering to Slocum the high praise that he most certainly merits. This is true despite the fact that, in 1920, an investigating committee of "eminent collegians" completely exonerated Slocum of the morals charges against him.[76]

---

[73]"A Reward For Service," *Tiger*, 15 September 1916, 2.

[74]*Colorado Springs Gazette*, 6 June 1908, quoted in "Colorado College (Special Announcement): New Residence Hall," Photograph Files: Buildings—Campus Views—Collections, Colorado College Archives.

[75]For the reaction of contemporary college and university presidents to Slocum's resignation, see "Prexy Receives Many Notes Praising Work: Prominent Educators Express Regrets At Resignation," *Tiger*, 26 September 1916, 1.

[76]A local Colorado Springs newspaper reported: "The findings expressed are that the charges are not sustained, that the former President is an innocent man who has been grievously wronged, and that the evidence does not justify any reflection on his character. . . ." *Colorado Springs Gazette*, 7 April 1920.

The reasons for Slocum's great success were obvious. He skillfully maintained and expanded the New England connections that were first carefully established by Thomas Nelson Haskell and Edward Payson Tenney. To these New England contributors he was able to add the gifts of the newly-wealthy Cripple Creek millionaires. Slocum found a good friend and staunch ally in William Jackson Palmer, particularly when the General increased his interest in and gifts to the College as, over the years, he sold his various railroad interests. In addition, Slocum benefited from the fact that the last two decades of the 19th Century were years of growth and prosperity for many of the liberal arts colleges throughout the nation. The discovery that a liberal arts education was good preparation for a business or professional career sent college enrollments upward as the 1800s drew to a close.

As Slocum gave up the presidency of Colorado College and moved away from the city of Colorado Springs, an era was ending in Colorado. Just as it had refused to subsidize the silver industry, the United States Government in the early 20th Century declined to fix or stabilize the price of gold. The price of this most precious of metals gradually fell so low that there was no profit in digging it out of the ground.[77] Cripple Creek and the other gold camps in Colorado slowly turned into ghost towns, with the result that economic activity in Colorado Springs and Denver significantly slowed down. The great silver and gold mining years in Colorado were over, and both Colorado and Colorado College were going to become quieter places as a result.

William and Mary Slocum moved to Massachusetts and lived their final years in the Boston-area town of Newton. William Slocum returned to the Colorado College campus only twice. One time was to attend the inauguration of a subsequent President of the College, Charles Mierow, in 1925. Slocum's second visit was one of considerable honor. He gave the major speech at the dedication of General Palmer's equestrian statue, placed at the intersection of Nevada and Platte avenues, in 1929.[78]

---

[77]Cronin and Loevy, *Colorado Politics And Government*, 62–63.

[78]William F. Slocum was an active participant in the effort to erect a statue of William Jackson Palmer. He served as the head of the original group of men and women that formed a memorial association for the General. "Memorial Statue To General Palmer Will Be Erected," *Colorado Springs Gazette and Telegraph*, Annual Edition, 1925.

The Slocum Campus

This photograph shows the Colorado College campus of the 1930s and 1940s. Every major building except Cutler Hall and Shove Chapel was constructed during the 29 years of the Slocum presidency—1888 to 1917. Slocum deserves some of the credit for Shove Chapel because he helped with the process of securing the architect.

In his retirement years, Slocum gave sermons and speeches at many places on the East Coast. Mary Slocum passed away in 1933. President Emeritus Slocum died in 1934.

The departure of William Frederick Slocum from Colorado College marked the end of an important era at the College—the era when students at small liberal arts colleges were taught a curriculum based on a combination of Christian morality and classical literature. This approach to a college education was widespread in the United States at the close of the 19th Century. With his weekly "Ethicals" in compulsory chapel, President Slocum urged his students and his faculty toward such lofty goals as respect for the sacred, love and benevolence for other human beings, moderation in both business and social affairs, and the constant development of individual worth.

But by 1917 times were changing in American higher education. Scientific discipline was progressively replacing Christian moralism and classical thought as the underlying spirit of the better small colleges as well as the great universities. Slocum's struggles at the end of his presidency can be viewed as an old partisan of moralistic and classical education warring with younger members of his faculty committed to a disciplined scientific search for truth. Moralism and a classical emphasis lost their primary position at Colorado College when Slocum departed.[79]

To the very end, one of the most significant things about William Frederick Slocum was the high opinion that his contemporaries had of him and the College which he had done so much to help create. Irving Howbert, who served on the Board of Trustees from 1880 to 1922, made a typical comment: "The first eight years of my connection with the Board were ones of anxiety and discouragement, but the growth and development of the College that followed under the administration of President Slocum made service on it a great pleasure."[80]

---

[79]For a discussion of the decline of moral and classical education and its replacement by principles of rigid scientific scholarship, see Dennis O'Brien, "The Disappearing Moral Curriculum," *Key Reporter*, Summer 1997, 1.

[80]Irving Howbert, *Memories Of A Lifetime In The Pike's Peak Region* (Glorieta, NM: Rio Grande Press, 1970), 290. This book was first published in 1925 by Louis V. Boling Books, Corpus Christi, TX.

Even more lavish praise came from Charlie Brown Hershey, author of the first published history of Colorado College: "But Slocum lives on. The institution which is his 'lengthened shadow' is a monument to his dreams and to his plans and energy for bringing them to reality. His high place among the great prophets of American higher education is secure, for it rests on ideals nobly conceived and skillfully set in material and spiritual values."[81]

[81]Hershey, *Colorado College, 1874–1929*, 94.

CHAPTER 4

DUNIWAY—MIEROW—DAVIES:
THE QUIET YEARS

The 1920s and 1930s were quiet years in Colorado. The gold and silver mining had ended, "most of the booming mining towns were ghost towns, and the 'roaring and bawdy' life of the mining era was mainly a treasured memory." The Colorado lifestyle, long associated with a "frontier spirit" and a "mining camp mentality," had become similar to that found in the remainder of the United States. Most Coloradans worked on farms on the Eastern Plains, or herded cattle on the Western Slope, or were factory and office workers in Denver and Pueblo. An increasing number of the state's residents were making a living by lodging, feeding, and entertaining the growing number of tourists coming to Colorado and the scenic Rocky Mountains by automobile.[1]

During the more than two decades from 1917 to 1941, the population of Colorado grew only slightly. The spectacular population increases of the gold and silver mining eras were a thing of the past. Colorado became a stable and conventional place, with both a falling birthrate and declining opportunities for employment. Only three cities in the entire state—Denver, Pueblo, and Colorado Springs—had more than 25,000 residents.[2]

---

[1]Cronin and Loevy, *Colorado Politics And Government*, 49.

[2]Ubbelohde, Benson, and Smith, *A Colorado History*, 310–311. Duane Smith, a Professor of History at Fort Lewis College in Durango, Colorado, gave a lecture at Colorado College on Colorado history that the author attended. The author recalled Smith saying: "The 1920s were the decade when the citizens of Colorado became just like the citizens of all the other states in the United States."

If not a quiet place during the years 1917 to 1941, Colorado College was an unusually stable place. Throughout most of that period the student enrollment at the College remained in a narrow range between 500 and 700 students.[3] Only one major new building, Shove Chapel, was added to the campus. Although there were periodic changes and improvements to the curriculum and the calendar of the College, no additional graduate or professional programs were added. In fact, throughout the period, what few graduate programs the College had, such as the School of Forestry and the Engineering School, were progressively eliminated.

When the United States entered World War II in 1941, Colorado College was much the same place it had been in 1917, when William Frederick Slocum's presidency ended. The College very much looked like the same place, the physical characteristics of the campus having changed hardly at all. The 1920s and 1930s were two decades when Colorado College devoted almost all of its attention to the fundamental purpose for which it was designed—giving a good liberal arts education to a selected group of talented and motivated young men and women.

Because the population of the state of Colorado grew so slowly during this period, the College mainly had to rely on the other states in the United States to provide it with students. It was during this period that Edward Payson Tenney's and William Frederick Slocum's efforts to build a national reputation for Colorado College paid off. Year in and year out during the 1920s and 1930s, only about 10 percent of the students at Colorado College came from the state of Colorado. Because of its lack of population growth and lackluster economy, the state of Colorado gave little support—in terms of student enrollments—to the College that bore its name.[4]

Three men held the presidency of Colorado College from 1917 to 1948. They were Clyde Augustus Duniway (1917–1924), Charles Christopher Mierow (1924–1934), and Thurston Jynkins Davies (1934–1948). These

---

[3]Hershey, *Colorado College, 1874–1949*, 110.

[4]Louis T. Benezet, President of Colorado College from 1955 to 1963, argued that the lack of an in-state population base from which to recruit students was the major source of the nagging enrollment and financial problems at Colorado College during the 1920s and 1930s. Author's notes, interview with Louis T. Benezet, President of Colorado College 1955–1963, Mill Valley California, 18 March 1998.

three presidents brought the College through World War I, the Roaring Twenties, the Great Depression, and World War II. Although this was not a period of spectacular progress for the College, as had occurred under President Slocum, it was a period when students were successfully recruited, a competent faculty was hired, classes met, grades were given, seniors graduated, and the physical plant was kept in good condition. In other words, from 1917 to 1947, these three presidents fought to preserve, under sometimes quite trying conditions, the nationally significant College that had been bequeathed to them by Thomas Nelson Haskell, Edward Payson Tenney, and, most especially, William Frederick Slocum.

CLYDE AUGUSTUS DUNIWAY

When the time came to choose a successor to President Slocum, the College broke with tradition and chose a man who was not a Congregational minister and had not been born in New England. Clyde Augustus Duniway was a native of Oregon who had headed east to get his B.A. at Cornell University in Ithaca, New York, and his Ph.D. at Harvard University in Boston, Massachusetts. His academic fields were History and Political Science. Duniway returned to the West to teach History for a number of years at Stanford University in Palo Alto, California.

In 1908 Duniway became the President of the University of Montana. After four years, he then became President of the University of Wyoming. After five years at Wyoming, in 1917, he accepted the presidency of Colorado College.

Duniway thus was a professional educator. He was the first President of Colorado College to come to the office with previous experience in the presidential office at another institution. His appointment marked the formal ending of direct Congregationalist and Christian influences in the administration of Colorado College.

One of the major tasks facing President Duniway was to rebuild the faculty and administration of the College. A considerable number of professors and administrators had retired or resigned when President Slocum departed. For instance, Ruth Loomis resigned as Dean of Women in 1917 and re-

Clyde Augustus Duniway
He succeeded William F. Slocum as President and guided Colorado College through World War I and the early years of the "Roaring Twenties."

turned to the East Coast. Professor of Physics Florian Cajori departed from the College in 1918 and took a job at the University of California. President Duniway appointed 26 faculty members who remained at the College for ten years or more. Particularly notable among them were W. Lewis Abbott in Economics and Sociology, Edith Bramhall in Political Science, Ralph Gilmore in Biology, and Charlie Brown Hershey in Education.

World War I

Shortly before President Duniway took office, on April 6, 1917, the United States entered World War I. Enrollment declined by more than 100 as a large number of men students went into military service. In January 1918 the College instituted a compulsory military training program for all the male students, and an Army Signal Corps service school was set up at the College to train radio operators. Hagerman Hall and Cossitt Gymnasium were converted into military barracks, Cossitt dining room became a military mess hall, Washburn Field was used as a drill field, and trenches were dug on the campus near Nevada Avenue to provide training in trench warfare. Straw-filled dummies were set up so that male students could practice bayoneting the enemy.

In the fall of 1918 an influenza epidemic swept the United States, and Colorado College was not spared. Eight of the young men in the Army radio school died in one month, and a young instructor in Physics, William W. Crawford, also succumbed to the disease. The College was quarantined by the local Health Department, classes were suspended, and Ticknor Hall was converted into an infirmary for the large numbers of ailing military personnel.

This turmoil began to end on November 11, 1918, when the Armistice was signed that ended World War I. The influenza quarantine at Colorado College was lifted on December 13, 1918, and classes quickly resumed. The College had made a significant contribution to the World War I war effort. More than 500 men had received radio training at the College, and more than 350 of them had served overseas in Europe.

Faculty Improvements

President Duniway did much to improve working conditions for the faculty. The College joined in the formation of the Teachers Insurance and Annuity Association (TIAA), a national pension system for college and university professors to which both the faculty member and the College contributed. Most important, TIAA retirement funds were portable. Faculty leaving Colorado College could take their accumulated benefits with them to jobs at other educational institutions. This increased a faculty member's sense of retirement security in an age when faculty moved quite frequently from one institution to another.

With President Duniway's support, a faculty "Committee-On-Committees" was created to speak and act for the faculty in the governance of the College. This committee was elected by the faculty and was given the power to appoint the members of all the other faculty committees.

Under President Duniway a tenure policy was adopted which gave individual faculty members virtually permanent job security once they had demonstrated their abilities as skilled teachers. The faculty also was given a powerful voice in the appointment and promotion of faculty members.

Social Changes

In 1918 Spencer Penrose, one of the Cripple Creek gold mine millionaires, built a large and luxurious hotel to the southwest of Colorado Springs at the foot of Cheyenne Mountain. Known as the Broadmoor, this new hotel had a large ballroom that soon became the preferred site for formal dances at Colorado College. The fox trot was the latest dance step, and bands at College dances began to play the loud new jazz music that was coming into fashion. "A new dance, 'the shimmy,' was banned as being immoral, and 'cheek to cheek' dancing was disapproved as being improper."[5]

Campus Discord

The Duniway presidency was not a peaceful one. A number of faculty members were angry with Duniway for not opposing forcefully the termination of

---

[5]Reid, *Colorado College: The First Century, 1874–1974*, 90.

Dean Edward S. Parsons. The students, beginning to reflect the values of the Roaring Twenties, strongly criticized Duniway's strict maintenance of College rules, such as those prohibiting women students from going on dates on Sundays. The situation badly deteriorated when President Duniway fired a popular and winning athletic coach for using profane language on the athletic field.

Soon the students were holding protest rallies and shouting: "Do Away With Duniway!" In a combined prank and protest, unknown individuals removed the large stuffed animals from the Palmer Hall museum and distributed them about the campus. A live cow was found one morning in Palmer Hall. Someone released a large quantity of hydrogen sulfide in Perkins Hall. The pungent rotten-egg smell caused morning chapel services to be suspended.[6]

The antagonism between the students at the College and President Duniway overflowed the campus and began to affect alumni relations. When the executive committee of the Colorado College Alumni Association raised questions about the leadership of the institution, Duniway announced his intention to resign as of June 1924. The Board of Trustees granted him a leave of absence at full pay for the 1923–1924 academic year in an effort to smooth his exit from the College. He completed his professional academic career as a highly respected Professor of History at Carleton College in Northfield, Minnesota.

Clyde Augustus Duniway had come to Colorado College at an exceedingly difficult time. Both the faculty and the student body were demanding more freedom and more power. Duniway made major concessions, particularly to the faculty, but even more concessions were demanded, especially by the student body. To his credit, President Duniway successfully steered the College through World War I and the influenza epidemic, and he began the process of making Colorado College, for faculty and students alike, a more democratic place.

---

[6]For a more detailed description of campus life during President Duniway's time at Colorado College, see Reid, *Colorado College: The First Century, 1874–1974*, 85–97.

CHARLES CHRISTOPHER MIEROW

Duniway's successor was Charles Christopher Mierow, a Professor of Classical Languages and Literature at Colorado College. Mierow was the first President of the College to be chosen from the institution's own faculty and administration. He had served on a number of key faculty committees and was respected for his cordial and friendly working relationships with both the students and the faculty.

Mierow was born in New York City. He spent seven years at Princeton University in New Jersey, earning his B.A. degree in 1905 and his Ph.D. in 1908. He taught one year at Phillips Academy in Andover, Massachusetts, and seven years at Princeton before coming to Colorado College in 1916. He was hired by William Frederick Slocum, the President at that time, to replace the legendary Professor of Classics, Moses Clement Gile, who had passed away in 1916.

The Mierow administration lasted for ten years, from 1924 to 1934. It thus embraced both the later, prosperous years of the Roaring Twenties and the early, poverty-stricken years of the Great Depression. Mierow guided the College through both periods with considerable accomplishment and success.

ROARING TWENTIES SOCIAL LIFE

The rigid rules that governed the dormitory lives of Colorado College women were sorely tested during the 1920s. Prohibition had made the hip flask a significant part of College life, and "hot jazz" provided the musical background for young women who were demanding more freedom and self-expression. The Dean of Women at Colorado College during the 1920s was Mabel Barbee Lee, a graduate of the class of 1906. It became Dean Lee's responsibility to adjust the social rules of the College to meet the changing standards and values of the 1920s.[7]

One Saturday night after Colorado College had won an important football game, a large group of male students snake danced their way into the Women's Quadrangle and advanced up to the front door of Bemis

---

[7]For the impact of the 1920s on student social life, see Reid, *Colorado College: The First Century, 1894–1994*, 104–107, 114–117.

CHARLES CHRISTOPHER MIEROW
The first President of Colorado College to be recruited from the College faculty, Mierow worked hard to see that the College survived financially during the grim first years of the Great Depression.

Hall, the largest women's dormitory at that time. The men students demanded to be let into Bemis in order to dance with the women students. The women had responded to the sound of the approaching males by climbing out on the window ledges and roofs of the three women's residence halls and clapping their hands in unison for the snake dancers.

Dean Lee realized that Bemis Hall could not possibly hold all the men and women students who would want to join in such an impromptu College dance. "How would you like it," she said to the men students, "if the girls came out, instead, and danced with you on the lawn?" The men accepted this inspired compromise. Six "lumbering athletes" carried the Bemis Hall piano out into the center of the quadrangle. A bonfire was used to light the festivities. Dean Lee recalled: "Immediately the place came alive with swinging, swaying boys and girls. I walked over and stood by the bonfire. The 'No Parking' signs . . . crackled merrily in the flames as if glad to come at last to a useful end. The moon was high above old Cutler, like a ball that had just been kicked for a goal. The crowd hailed it with lusty songs."

This particular after-hours outdoor dance was not the only instance of high jinks taking place in the Women's Quadrangle during the 1920s. A late Sunday night tradition was the Fraternity Serenade, when the various fraternities would try to outdo each other providing entertainment for the women students. The men would stealthily creep into the quad with their kettle drums, saxophones, and other instruments for loud music making. The women students would gather on Bemis porch and at the windows of the dorms to watch and hear the fraternity men perform. Often Dean Lee could hear the sounds of feminine feet dancing to the music on the flat roof of Bemis Lounge. Occasionally, despite the dark night, the Dean of Women could see the faces of female students who had crept down the dormitory fire escapes to join the male students out in the quadrangle. The festivities lasted for as long as an hour, with skyrockets, red flares, hula dancing, and blues singing all part of the show.[8]

[8]Mabel Barbee Lee, "Stormy Young Rebels," *Denver Post*, Empire Magazine, 30 December 1951, 8–9.

SHOVE CHAPEL

Eugene P. Shove was a Cripple Creek millionaire who was on the Board of Trustees of Colorado College. In 1930 he donated a chapel to the College in memory of his English clergymen ancestors. The new building was located at the Nevada Avenue end of the campus, exactly opposite and facing Cutler Hall. Once again Romanesque architecture was chosen, but this time it was of the Norman variety rather than the more florid type from southern France and Italy.

Shove Chapel was not built of pink peachblow sandstone (to match Hagerman, Coburn, Perkins, and Palmer halls) because the price of that particular stone had become prohibitively expensive, particularly given that it was the early years of the Great Depression. Bedford stone was hauled in from Indiana, thereby saving $20,000.

The building was designed by John Gray, an architect from Pueblo, Colorado, and cost $350,000 to construct. Architect Gray modeled the new chapel after Winchester Cathedral in England, and the chimes and the deep-toned bell in the chapel clock tower were cast in Croyden, England. The chapel was equipped with a fine organ and many beautiful stained glass windows.[9]

THE FINE ARTS CENTER

Alice Bemis Taylor, whose maiden name was on Bemis Hall, contributed a large amount of money to build a major new art museum in Colorado Springs. The site selected was just south of the College campus on West Dale Street. Although the art museum was a completely separate institution from Colorado College, art courses and studio space in the museum were made available to the College students by agreement. The new museum, completed in 1936, was called the Colorado Springs Fine Arts Center, was art-deco in design, and included a comfortable theater that, from time to time, was used for Colorado College dramatic productions.

---

[9]Hershey, *Colorado College, 1874–1949*, 101–102, 150–151. Reid, *Colorado College: The First Century, 1874–1974*, 111. Sprague, *Newport In The Rockies*, 279. Also see Timothy Fuller, *This Glorious And Transcendant Place* (Colorado Springs, CO: Colorado College, 1981).

TWO BRONZE MONUMENTS

In 1929 a bronze bas-relief of General Palmer was installed on the west wall of the main staircase in Palmer Hall. It was located just below the painting of General Palmer in his horseback riding clothes. The bronze monument described the General's many accomplishments, including that he "founded" Colorado Springs and "fostered" Colorado College. The bas-relief of the good General was the work of sculptress Evelyn Beatrice Longman Batchelder.

Similar castings of this monument were placed in railroad stations in Denver, Salt Lake City, and Mexico City, Mexico. Another was placed in the wall of another Palmer Hall, this one located at the Hampton Institute in Virginia, a college for African-Americans which General Palmer had supported financially.[10]

A second bronze casting appeared on the campus in 1931. This was the Earle Flagpole, which included four bronze tigers facing outward from the base of a 75-foot flagpole. It was located in the large grass and tree-covered area to the east of Cossitt Hall and Cutler Hall. This monument was given by Mrs. Augusta Swart-Earle in memory of her husband and was designed by Stephen Beames of Evanston, Illinois. The Earle Flagpole quickly established itself as a good location to hold outdoor rallies and protest demonstrations.

THE WILM AFFAIR

The issue of academic freedom came to the forefront at Colorado College in 1930. Professor E. C. Wilm included the theories of agnostic philosophers in his classes in modern philosophy. Word of this reached the Colorado Springs Ministerial Alliance, which demanded a report from the College on Wilm's teaching. In a letter to the Ministerial Alliance, President Mierow wrote to the effect that "Wilm was an agnostic who lost no opportunity to scoff at religion." Apparently pleasing the local ministry was more important than staunchly defending Wilm's freedom to teach, because at the close of the 1930–1931 academic year Professor

[10]Fisher, *A Builder Of The West*, 321–322.

Wilm was given a leave of absence with two-thirds severance pay and never reinstated.[11]

THE NEW COLORADO COLLEGE PLAN

During the 1930–1931 school year, two outside consultants were brought to the College to study the academic program and make recommendations for improvement. Dr. Henry Suzzallo, Chairman of the Carnegie Foundation, and Dr. Samuel P. Capen, President of the University of Buffalo in New York, worked with the faculty at Colorado College to devise what came to be known as "The New Colorado College Plan."

The cornerstone of this new program was to clearly divide the academic program into three divisions. There was established a School of Letters and Fine Arts, a School of Social Sciences, and a School of Natural Sciences. Each school was governed by an executive committee elected by each school's faculty members. In subsequent years the three schools came to be called the Humanities Division, the Social Science Division, and the Natural Science Division, but the basic tripartite structure endured. It was significant that this reform widely dispersed governance of the academic program throughout the College faculty.

Required courses for the degree, such as Latin, English, and foreign languages, were made optional under this new academic plan. Degree requirements were made more general in nature, and during freshman and sophomore year students were encouraged to take a wide variety of courses in the arts and sciences. For junior and senior year, students were to choose an academic major in the Humanities, the Social Sciences, or the Natural Sciences.

Another provision of "The New Colorado College Plan" included liberalizing entrance requirements and creating a Committee on Admissions to exercise flexibility and judgement in deciding which students would be admitted to Colorado College. Given that college and university applications throughout the United States dropped during the early years of the Great Depression, easing up on the entrance require-

---

[11]Reid, *Colorado College: The First Century, 1874–1974*, 110–111.

ments to Colorado College in the early 1930s probably was a good idea for financial as well as flexibility reasons.

The new plan discontinued the old semester hour system for granting course credit and installed a course system. A "full load" for each student became four courses per semester, and a course could meet either three or four classroom hours per week. The new plan also required each graduating senior to take and pass a comprehensive examination in his or her major field. The examination often required the student to present an oral defense of the written portion of the exam. Preparing for and taking "orals" became the bane of many a prospective graduate of Colorado College.

The social life at the College was scrutinized by the two consultants. Upon their recommendation, the four women's literary societies were reorganized as sororities. This gave women students as well as men the right to join national college and university social associations. The women students were not allowed to live in their sorority houses, however, as men were allowed to live in their fraternity lodges. The women were to use their sorority houses only as places for intellectual and social activities. The transformations from literary societies to sororities were: Minerva to Delta Gamma, Contemporary to Kappa Alpha Theta, Hypatia to Kappa Kappa Gamma, and Zetalethian to Gamma Phi Beta.

"The New Colorado College Plan" became the basis for the academic program at the College for the ensuing 40 years. Its basic provisions were not altered in a major way until the implementation of the Block Plan in the fall of 1970. Similar to much of what was happening at Colorado College in the 1920s and 1930s, the new plan provided for greater flexibility and wider dispersal of decision-making, both for the students and the faculty.

ATHLETIC ACCOMPLISHMENT

The 1920s and the 1930s were years of men's athletic glory at Colorado College. By handing out full-tuition, room, and board scholarships, the College was able to recruit quality athletes and compete on an equal basis with much larger institutions such as the University of Colorado at Boulder and Colorado State University at Fort Collins.

By the late 1920s the spectator stands at Washburn Field had become much too small for the crowds of people wanting to watch Colorado College football games. Edmund C. van Diest, a Colorado Springs businessman who had worked with General Palmer on a variety of projects, took personal charge of raising the money and planning a 9,000 seat stadium for Washburn Field. The new facility, with wooden stands on both sides of the playing field, was named Van Diest Stadium. It included a grass playing surface in place of the hard dirt surface previously used.

The most outstanding Colorado College athlete of that time was Earl "Dutch" Clark, who played quarterback on the football team from 1927 to 1929. Clark was born in Fowler, Colorado, and graduated from Central High School in Pueblo, Colorado. At Colorado College he was the high scorer in the Rocky Mountain Conference in each of his three years of varsity football. In 1928 he became the first all-American football player in the history of the state of Colorado. He went on to a distinguished professional football career with the Detroit Lions, and he was chosen a charter member of the National Football League Hall of Fame.[12]

PRESIDENT MIEROW DEPARTS

By March of 1933 the Great Depression was taking its toll at Colorado College. The stock market crash in November of 1929 greatly reduced the income from the endowment. Out-of-town student enrollments dropped so precipitously that Montgomery, Ticknor, and McGregor halls were closed and the dining service suspended in Cossitt Hall. To meet current expenses, the College was forced to spend $215,000 of the endowment. Faculty salaries were cut 20 percent beginning with the 1933 fall semester.

The unrelenting financial pressures on the College bore down heavily on President Mierow. He also had to deal with personal tragedy when his oldest daughter, Barbara, met death in the waters of Lake Erie. The Board of Trustees offered President Mierow a leave of absence during the 1933–1934 academic year, during which time Charlie Brown Hershey,

---

[12]Gary Street, *A History Of Colorado College Football*, publication available at the Colorado College Book Store, 36–42.

the Dean of the College, served as Acting President. Mierow spent his year leave of absence residing and studying in Rome with his wife and younger daughter Dorothy. While in Rome he elected to resign from the presidency effective in June of 1934, but he returned to the College to preside at the 1934 commencement exercises.

President Mierow succeeded in restoring a degree of normalcy to Colorado College following the controversial end to Slocum's presidency and the turbulent years under President Duniway. He ably led the College during the boom years of the late 1920s, and he began the process of seeing to it that the College survived the Great Depression. After leaving Colorado College, Charles Christopher Mierow returned to teaching and served 16 years as a Professor of Biography at Carleton College in Northfield, Minnesota.

THURSTON JYNKINS DAVIES

Clyde Augustus Duniway and Charles Christopher Mierow came to the presidency of Colorado College from the college and university classroom. Both had put in considerable time teaching as well as serving as administrators. When it came time to find a successor to President Mierow, the Board of Trustees of Colorado College opted for Thurston Jynkins Davies, a man whose experience was concentrated in educational administration, at the preparatory school level as well as the college and university level.

Thurston Davies was born in Tennessee, but he went to preparatory school at the Penn Charter School in Philadelphia, Pennsylvania. He graduated from Princeton University in 1916 and shortly thereafter served with distinction as a First Lieutenant in the United States Marine Corps during World War I. He fought in the Belleau Wood and Argonne campaigns, receiving two medals for gallantry, the Croix de Guerre and the Silver Star, and two Purple Hearts for being wounded.

Upon leaving the military service, Davies taught for a number of years at Gilman, an elite men's preparatory school in Baltimore, Maryland. He next took a job at the Nichols School, a men's preparatory school in Buffalo, New York. It was at Nichols that Thurston Davies began his career as an educational administrator, eventually becoming Headmaster.

Thurston Jynkins Davies
Noted for his promotional and public relations skills, President Davies led the College back to high enrollments and economic solvency during the late 1930s and early 1940s.

In 1929 Davies made the jump from the preparatory school to the college and university level. He became Secretary of the Graduate Council at Princeton University, his alma mater, and in that job demonstrated great skill in promoting and publicizing the academic needs and goals of the institution. Davies accepted the presidency of Colorado College in 1934.

Thurston Davies could be characterized as the "public relations" President of Colorado College. "He met people easily and his enthusiasm for the interests he represented was contagious. The language of schools and colleges was familiar to him, but he was not pedantic in using it. He made friends easily among educators and business and professional people. . . ."[13]

AN ECONOMIC REVIVAL

The effects of President Davies's promotional efforts on behalf of the College soon became evident. In the 1938–1939 academic year enrollment surged past 700 students and continued rising until the advent of World War II. Although the lingering effects of the Great Depression made fund-raising difficult in the mid–1930s, by the late 1930s a substantial increase in private gifts began to put the College back on a sound and secure financial footing.

The best measure of the revival of the College's economic prospects was the reopening of the three women's dormitories that were closed in the early days of the Depression. McGregor Hall reopened in 1934, Ticknor Hall in 1936, and Montgomery Hall in 1937. Montgomery Hall, the oldest of the women's dormitories, was rehabilitated and refurnished prior to its reopening. The roof, the third floor, and the front porch were completely rebuilt, giving the building an Old English look somewhat similar to Bemis Hall.[14]

Although no new major buildings were constructed during Thurston Davies's presidency, a somewhat hidden form of physical expansion was taking place at Colorado College. The Davies administration began an

---

[13]Hershey, *Colorado College, 1874–1949*, 111.

[14]For a brief history of Montgomery Hall, see Barbara Arnest, "Montgomery Hall's 100th Anniversary Also Celebrates National Historical Dedication," *Catalyst*, 19 April 1991, 9.

accelerated program of buying up the large and attractive homes immediately adjacent to the campus. These structures, many of them sporting a picturesque Victorian architectural style, were then converted to College uses such as dormitories, faculty offices, and classroom space. This process of acquiring houses and other properties surrounding the campus was labeled "The Growth That Nobody Saw."[15]

Notable acquisitions included Hamlin House, at 1122 Wood Avenue, which was used for a women's dormitory and faculty apartments. Also significant was Hayes House, at the southwest corner of Cascade Avenue and Cache La Poudre Street, which became faculty offices and classrooms, primarily for the Humanities. Lennox House, located on North Nevada Avenue, functioned over the years as a student activities center, a fraternity house (Beta Theta Pi), and a residence hall.

At the end of President Davies's first year in office, on Memorial Day 1935, heavy rains in the Pike's Peak region caused a destructive flood to roar down Monument Creek past the College. The raging waters destroyed the section of the park west of the campus that was nicknamed "The Jungle." Instead of restoring that portion of the park, the City of Colorado Springs gave the land to Colorado College. Funds provided by Trustee P. B. Stewart were used to turn the area into a baseball diamond and practice football field. The new athletic field was named Stewart Field, and it later became the men's and women's varsity soccer field.

As enrollment at the College increased in the late 1930s, there was a growing need in Coburn Library for more shelf and study space. A small addition was built on the north side of Coburn with four levels of stacks capable of holding 60,000 books. There also were 35 study carrels where students could do heavy-duty reading or write major research papers.

CREATION OF EL POMAR FOUNDATION

In the late 1930s Colorado College began to receive additional financial benefits from the Cripple Creek gold boom. Spencer Penrose and Charles Leaming Tutt, Sr., two adventurous young men from Philadelphia, made

---

[15]Lloyd Worner oral history, 5 February 1985, 67. This and other oral histories can be found in the Colorado College Archives Oral History Project, conducted by Judith Reid Finley.

millions from various gold mining properties during the Cripple Creek glory days. The two then settled down to live with their families in Colorado Springs. More money subsequently was made from successful investments in Utah copper mines.

In 1937 Spencer Penrose, who had a wife but no children, set up El Pomar Foundation to disperse his considerable fortune for charitable purposes. Although money from the Foundation was given to many educational institutions, Colorado College was one of the main beneficiaries. Over the ensuing years El Pomar Foundation financially supported College athletic teams, contributed to the College's endowment, and provided money for new buildings. After Spencer Penrose passed away in 1939, the heirs of Charles Leaming Tutt, Sr., played a major role in the successful administration and continued financial viability of El Pomar Foundation.

MEN'S ICE HOCKEY

The Broadmoor Hotel in 1938 decided to convert its indoor horseback riding arena into an ice rink. Shortly thereafter a men's ice hockey team was organized at Colorado College. It was not very long before this team was playing major college and university opponents from across the nation and drawing capacity crowds to the new Ice Palace, subsequently renamed the Broadmoor World Arena. The College was able to support such a first rate men's ice hockey program by providing athletic scholarships, many of them going to promising young players from Canada.

The Colorado College men's ice hockey team had more good years than bad over its first two decades, and two instances of national success stand out. In 1950, and again in 1957, Colorado College won the National Collegiate Athletic Association (NCAA) men's ice hockey championship. Both national crowns were won on Colorado College's home ice at the Broadmoor World Arena, where the NCAA men's ice hockey championships were held throughout the 1950s.

WORLD WAR II AT COLORADO COLLEGE

In 1939 enrollment at Colorado College exceeded 800 students for the first time in the College's history. Sadly, the psychological momentum that was building on the campus during the late 1930s began to be blunted by the growing threat to the United States of involvement in World War II. After the Japanese attack on Pearl Harbor on December 7, 1941, winning the war replaced educational excellence as the primary goal of Colorado College.

Men students began to disappear from the campus as they volunteered or were drafted into military service. Many of the younger male faculty members also went off to fight the enemy. President Davies, with his World War I military experience, volunteered to go back into the Marine Corps. His offer was accepted, and he was assigned to Washington, D.C., to command the Marine Corps V–12 training programs on college and university campuses across the nation.[16] For the remainder of the war, Dean of the College Charlie Brown Hershey served as the Acting President of Colorado College.

The College was designated as a training center for the Navy-Marine V–12 program. The young men received military training while simultaneously taking college-level courses at Colorado College. Once again Washburn Field became a military drill field.[17] At the same time, in the center of the main campus, women students were helping to plant "Victory Gardens" to grow vegetables to help with the "war effort."

A total of 52 Colorado College men lost their lives in World War II. One of them was Bert Stiles, who completed his quota of bombing missions in the United States Air Force and then volunteered for fighter pilot duty. He was killed when his P–51 fighter plane was shot down over Germany.[18]

By the time World War II ended in 1945, almost 2,000 Navy-Marine trainees had participated in the V–12 program at Colorado College. A number of them came back to the College after the war and resumed their education under the G.I. Bill, a U.S. Government program that helped pay for World War II veterans to get a college education. As a re-

---

[16]James G. Schneider, *The Navy V–12 Program: Leadership For A Lifetime* (Boston, MA: Houghton-Mifflin, 1987), 136–137.

[17]Schneider, *The Navy V–12 Program*, 265, 534.

[18]For a recollection about Bert Stiles, see Worner oral history, 28 January 1985, 20. Also see Reid, *Colorado College: The First Century, 1874–1974*, 150–151.

sult of this great influx of veterans, student enrollment hit a new high of 1,250 students in the fall semester of 1946.

THURSTON DAVIES MOVES ON

Thurston Jynkins Davies returned to Colorado College after World War II and resumed his duties as President. But the war had weakened the man, and a serious illness in his family led to a serious illness of his own. The tribulations of heavy involvement in World War II had left Thurston Davies with a severe alcohol problem.[19] In December of 1947 the Board of Trustees gave Davies a leave of absence due to a "deep seated chest infection," and five months later Davies resigned as President of Colorado College. He subsequently recovered his health, however, and held a number of important public relations and promotional positions before dying of cancer at the age of 67 in 1961.

The Davies years were important ones at Colorado College. He infused the institution with a feeling of confidence and a spirit of progress that the College badly needed in the latter days of the Great Depression. The many private residences that were purchased by the College during the Davies administration stand as an enduring monument to Thurston Jynkins Davies. Some of these structures remained in full use by the College. Others were torn down to provide sites for major new buildings.

President Davies took command of an underfinanced and struggling institution in 1934. Fourteen years later, in 1948, he left to his successors a Colorado College characterized by high student enrollments and financial solvency.

---

[19]Worner oral history, 28 January 1985, 25–26.

CHAPTER 5

GILL—BENEZET—WORNER:
IN THE AFTERMATH OF WORLD WAR II

By the year 1999 it was clear that there had been two major events in the history of the state of Colorado.

The first major event was the discovery of gold and silver and the great mining bonanza which it produced in the latter years of the 19th Century.

The second major event was World War II.

In the all-out effort to win the war, the United States rapidly expanded its military and industrial capacity. Partly because of Colorado's inland location far from both oceans, the state was selected as the site for a considerable number of U.S. Government military bases and industrial plants. Most of these new government facilities were located at the foot of the Front Range of the Rocky Mountains.

In Denver the national government built the Denver Arms Plant, a large ammunition factory making cartridges, fuses, and shells. On open land northeast of Denver was constructed the Rocky Mountain Arsenal, a major chemical warfare facility. At Lowry Air Base, located to the east of downtown Denver, the Army Air Corps trained pilots. Denver also was the site of a major Medical Depot and Fitzsimmons General Hospital, where military personnel were sent to recuperate from their war wounds.

And there was plenty of World War II activity 70 miles south of Denver in Colorado Springs. Camp Carson, which was subsequently expanded and named Fort Carson, became a major Army training base, particularly for tanks and other forms of mechanized warfare. Peterson

Air Field, located to the east of Colorado Springs, trained Army Air Corps bomber crews.

Even the city of Pueblo, located 40 miles south of Colorado Springs, became the site of a World War II facility. A major Ordinance Depot was built and operated there.

One effect of all this World War II activity in Colorado was to expose thousands of war workers and military service personnel to the beneficial climate and the great recreational opportunities in the state. Many people sent to Colorado during World War II discovered the sunny skies and cool dry air and found it all much to their liking. Weekends and vacation days spent hiking and skiing in the nearby Rocky Mountains made the area even more attractive. After World War II ended, substantial numbers of these wartime temporary residents moved back to Colorado, thereby rapidly increasing the state's population.

The Cold War between the United States and the Soviet Union helped to sustain this post–World War II population boom in Colorado. Rocky Flats, a major nuclear weapons facility, was constructed northwest of Denver. In Colorado Springs the United States Air Force (formerly the Army Air Corps) dug deep into the solid rock of Cheyenne Mountain to build the North American Aerospace Defense Command (NORAD). Fort Carson continued in its role as a major Army training center. And the newly-created United States Air Force Academy, a military college for training Air Force officers, was located on a brand new campus in the foothills to the northwest of Colorado Springs.

During World War II the U.S. Army trained its ski troops at Camp Hale high in the Rocky Mountains near the old silver mining town of Leadville, Colorado. Many of these ski troopers noted the ease and pleasure of skiing on the deep powder snow of the Colorado Rockies. Some of them returned to Colorado after the war to develop major ski facilities and ski communities at picturesque places such as Aspen and Vail. Colorado became closely associated in the national consciousness with good skiing, and that caused even more people to move to the state.

By the mid–1950s Colorado was experiencing a population boom that rivaled that of the gold and silver mining era. Along with the former military personnel and the war-plant workers came other new Coloradans who planned to make money in real estate, shopping center construction, and similar consumer-related businesses. "Colorado was once again attracting prospectors, but these new prospectors were coming with blueprints for housing developments and shopping centers rather than picks and shovels."[1]

The great population growth that hit Colorado during and after World War II had definite effects on Colorado College. As the population of the state increased markedly, so did the available pool of young men and women from within the state who might want to attend Colorado College. This was particularly true in the Denver suburbs, where large numbers of brand new homes were rapidly being filled with well-to-do families. These were exactly the kind of families that would be interested in sending their children to a good liberal arts college. Close by—but far enough from Denver that the students were going "away" from home—was Colorado College in Colorado Springs.

WILLIAM HANSON GILL

When health concerns led Thurston Davies to resign from the presidency of Colorado College, the Board of Trustees turned to William Hanson Gill, a retired U.S. Army Major General who had commanded Fort Carson during the early days of World War II. General Gill, as he was often called, served a brief period as Acting President and then, in the fall of 1948, was appointed permanent President.

General Gill was a native of Virginia. He attended the Virginia Military Institute (VMI) in Lexington, Virginia, and graduated in 1907. He joined the U.S. Army in 1912 and was awarded the Silver Star for his bravery while fighting in the Meuse-Argonne offensive in France in World War I. Following the Armistice, Gill stayed in the Army and became a professional soldier.

William Gill's military career also was partly an educational career. He served tours of duty teaching at the Army Command and General Staff School as well as the Army War College. For two years he was a

---

[1]Cronin and Loevy, *Colorado Politics And Government*, 49–51. Also see Ubbelohde, Benson, and Smith, *A Colorado History*, 321–329.

William Hanson Gill
The first post-World War II President of Colorado College, Gill strongly defended academic freedom when critics said pro-Marxist and pro-Soviet ideas were being taught at the College.

Professor of Military Tactics in the Reserve Officer Training Corps (ROTC) at the University of California at Berkeley. He thus came to know the world of college and university teaching as well as he knew the principles of military organization and command.

One of William Gill's students at the Army Command and General Staff School was Dwight D. Eisenhower, who later commanded United States and other Allied forces in Europe during World War II and was President of the United States during the 1950s.

Shortly after World War II began, William Gill was named the Commanding General of the 89th Infantry Division stationed at Fort Carson near Colorado Springs. Early in 1943 he was transferred to the Pacific where he served under General Douglas MacArthur as Commander of the 32nd (Red Arrow) Infantry Division. He led his soldiers through major campaigns to conquer and hold New Guinea and the Philippine Islands. At the conclusion of hostilities he was awarded the Distinguished Service Cross, Distinguished Service Medal, Silver Star, Legion of Merit, and Bronze Star.

General Gill retired from the Army in 1946 and moved to Colorado Springs, where he renewed the business connections and personal friendships he had made while commanding Fort Carson early in the war. The Board of Trustees, having observed firsthand his ability to guide and develop a major organization, quickly came to regard him as a qualified successor to President Davies.

In many ways, a former Army General was just what Colorado College needed as President in the late 1940s. Four out of five of the men students were World War II veterans, as were a number of the faculty. Some major changes would be needed to put the College back on a civilian footing, particularly in view of the post-World War II surge in student enrollments. Who better than an Army General to firmly take command in such a challenging situation?

But there was one small side effect with having a former military commander as President of the College. In moments of excitement or concern, General Gill often referred to the students as "civilians."[2]

---

[2]Worner oral history, 28 January 1985, 28.

THE COMMUNIST THREAT

By 1948 there was considerable concern that agents of the Soviet Union and their domestic sympathizers were trying to infiltrate educational institutions in the United States and preach a philosophy of world communist revolution. In this highly charged political environment, two residents of Colorado Springs conducted a survey of the books in Coburn Library and found that many of them discussed the history and ideas of Karl Marx and other leading communist thinkers. The two residents immediately sent a letter to the *Colorado Springs Gazette Telegraph* charging that the College was teaching communism to its students.

President Gill responded to these charges with a letter to the *Gazette Telegraph* that firmly defended academic freedom and the ability of Colorado College students to make their own judgements about various philosophical points of view. "I have seen no evidence of communism or any other 'ism' among the students at Colorado College," Gill wrote. "I have the greatest confidence in our students and their ability as mature persons to evaluate ideas and philosophies. . . . While I am at Colorado College the faculty and executive departments of the College will teach and administer Colorado College as intended by its founders."

One year later there was an attempt by a congressional committee in Washington, D.C., to search for communists at Colorado College. The Committee on Unamerican Activities of the U.S. House of Representatives requested that 103 colleges and universities across the nation, including Colorado College, send a list of textbooks and readings used in Social Science and American Literature courses. A number of Colorado College faculty members protested this action, and President Gill turned down the Unamerican Activities Committee's request most explicitly and firmly. "Colorado College is a private, independent college," Gill wired the Committee. "We are not about to send you or any other agency of the government the information you requested concerning textbooks and collateral readings."[3]

During this same period, Professor of History Lloyd Edson Worner was teaching a course at Colorado College on Soviet government and pol-

---

[3]Reid, *Colorado College: The First Century, 1874–1974*, 167–169.

itics and had assigned a book written by Frederick Schumann of Williams College in Massachusetts. Schumann had been attacked by various communist hunters as being overly tolerant of communist and Soviet ideas. The book was entitled *Soviet Politics At Home And Abroad* and had a red cover with a communist "hammer-and-sickle" on it. The fact that such a book was required reading for a course at the College further inflamed the institution's anti-communist critics.

The cause of the anti-communists against Colorado College was severely weakened, however, when Professor Worner revealed that Frederick Schumann's book on Soviet politics and government also was on a recommended reading list for the Army cadets at the United States Military Academy at West Point.[4]

Still another incident highlighted President Gill's commitment to academic freedom. When the faculty voted to install a voluntary Reserve Officers Training Corps (ROTC) program at Colorado College, only one member of the faculty voted against it. President Gill looked at him and asked, "Couldn't you make it unanimous?" The faculty member, Professor George McCue of the English Department, looked back at Gill and said, "President Gill, I just can't."

When the meeting ended and the faculty were leaving, a number of faculty members gathered around Professor McCue and questioned him about his lone vote. When President Gill walked by and overheard some of the conversation, he turned and said: "Look! Professor McCue . . . stood up for what he believed in, and that I respect, and I want to hear *no more* of that!"[5]

General Gill's strong defense of academic freedom at Colorado College became one of the most notable events of his presidency. Some had thought that, because he was a former military commander, he might support some of the more brazen anti-communist tactics of the time. He proved himself every inch a committed educator when he stood up for

[4]Worner oral history, 28 January 1985, 30–31. The author attended Williams College in the mid–1950s and took many of Frederick Schumann's courses and read his International Relations text book. Although Schumann's campus nickname at Williams was "Red Fred," his writings took a "power politics" position rather than a "pro-communist" line.

[5]Worner oral history, 28 January 1985, 27.

complete freedom to teach and learn at Colorado College.[6] Gill also compensated for the somewhat sorry record of the College administration almost 20 years earlier when it failed to boldly defend Professor E. C. Wilm's right to teach about agnosticism.

THE HONOR SYSTEM

During his student days at Virginia Military Institute (VMI), President Gill had studied, taken tests, and written papers under an academic Honor System. There were no faculty proctors checking on student honesty during examinations at VMI, and written work handed in by students was automatically assumed to be the student's own work.

President Gill decided to implement a similar Honor System at Colorado College. He selected a young Professor of History, Lloyd Edson Worner, to be the faculty member in charge of the new program. Worner studied under the Honor System for two years while an undergraduate student at Washington and Lee University in Lexington, Virginia.

An incremental approach was taken at Colorado College. In the spring of 1948 only twelve classes were taught under the Honor System. That experiment worked, so 37 more classes were added to the Honor System during the 1948–1949 academic year. Eventually, effective in the fall of 1950, the faculty voted to put all classes at Colorado College into the Honor System. Students were bound by an Honor Code, and a student Honor Council was created to supervise the new system and investigate alleged infractions.[7]

AMERICAN ASSOCIATION OF UNIVERSITY PROFESSORS

During William Gill's presidency a group of Colorado College professors organized a faculty chapter of the American Association of University Professors (AAUP). Leading this drive to create an organized voice for the faculty were some of the College's leading teacher-scholars, such as

---

[6]For a lengthy and rambling account of President Gill's struggles with anti-communist witch hunters, see Worner oral history, 28 January 1985, 29–37.

[7]Reid, *Colorado College: The First Century, 1874–1974*, 173. Also see Worner oral history, 28 January 1985, 40–45.

Harvey Carter, George McCue, Nat Wollman, Frank Krutzke, Clyde Holbrook, and Howard Olson. Professor of History Lloyd Worner became the amateur statistician for the AAUP chapter, diligently typing up detailed charts and graphs that compared faculty salaries at Colorado College with those at similar small liberal arts colleges.

A number of professors, administrators, and members of the Board of Trustees disapproved of the faculty organizing something that looked a great deal like a labor union. But President Gill supported and encouraged the fledgling AAUP chapter at Colorado College. He allowed the AAUP to make specific recommendations for faculty salary increases, and then he appointed a faculty Salary Committee to review the AAUP recommendations and formally present them to the College administration. In some instances the same faculty members who were on the AAUP committee also sat on the faculty Salary Committee.

Professor of History Lloyd Worner later described the formation of the faculty Salary Committee this way: "We ended up with . . . an AAUP committee on salaries and fringe benefits, and on policies with regard to faculty personnel problems. And then General Gill would declare a faculty committee. It was the same committee. As he said, we just simply took a hat of AAUP off and he called it a faculty committee. And that was much more acceptable at the time."[8]

Allowing the AAUP chapter to initiate faculty salary recommendations became an established and enduring procedure at Colorado College. It was one more step in the on-going practice of encouraging more faculty involvement in the administrative decision-making process at the College.

SLOCUM HALL

By the fall of 1954 there were 1,027 students at Colorado College. The steady population growth in Colorado was having an effect, as was the College's growing reputation nationally. The student body came from 45 states. The women students not only filled the four women's dormitories but spilled over into seven former private residences owned by the College.

---

[8]Worner oral history, 5 February 1985, 61–62.

The time had come for new building construction at Colorado College. With the help of a $600,000 U.S. Government loan, a new men's dormitory was constructed at the northwest corner of Nevada Avenue and Cache La Poudre Street. The building was three stories high, provided housing for 160 men students, and had a comfortable lounge and two large classrooms. There were two wings, but the structure was designed so that additional wings could be added in the future. The new men's dormitory was named Slocum Hall in honor of William Frederick Slocum, the renowned former President of the College.

Slocum Hall was the first new building erected on campus since Shove Chapel was completed 23 years earlier in 1931. Slocum Hall also was the first new dormitory since Bemis Hall was finished 46 years earlier in 1908. In addition, Slocum Hall was the first major dormitory constructed on the east side rather than the west side of Cascade Avenue.

A major change was made in building design at Colorado College when Slocum Hall was constructed. For the first time in the College's history, a major building was built of brick rather than stone. From an aesthetic point of view, this was a loss, because stone buildings are thought by many observers to have a great aura of permanence and high quality. Looking at the situation realistically, however, the cost of stone had become prohibitively expensive, and the College could get a great deal more for its money by building with brick.[9]

But it is important to note the color of brick selected for Slocum Hall. A mixture of red, brown, and dark gray bricks was used. From a distance, this mixture of brick colors produced a color that was similar to the dark pink of pink peachblow sandstone, the stone used in constructing Palmer Hall. Major new brick buildings erected at the College after Slocum Hall all were built with this mixture of red, brown, and dark gray bricks. This created a subtle campus-wide design consistency and gave these new brick buildings at least some relationship to Palmer Hall.

In arranging for the construction of Slocum Hall, President Gill initiated a great post-World War II building boom at Colorado College. In

---

[9]In Great Britain colleges and universities with stone buildings were considered more prestigious than those with brick buildings. It was not thought as beneficial to be "a graduate of a brick college."

the closing year of his presidency, William Gill oversaw the design and financing of a new residence hall for women (Loomis Hall) and enlarged dining facilities (Taylor Dining Hall). Gill's successors in the College's presidential office were quick to carry on the physical expansion of the campus that Gill had so competently begun.

PRESIDENT GILL RETIRES

In the spring of 1955 William Gill became the first President of Colorado College to voluntarily retire from the job. He was 69-years-old. He had successfully completed the task of bringing the College into the post-World War II world. Furthermore, student enrollments at the College were strong, the institution's finances were in sound condition, and the reputation of the College had been significantly improved. With optimism high and even greater success appearing to lie just ahead, William Hanson Gill stepped down and turned the presidential office over to a much younger successor.

William Gill lived the remainder of his life in Colorado Springs. He was 89-years-old when he passed away on January 17, 1976. Services were held for him in Shove Chapel, and he was buried at Evergreen Cemetery in Colorado Springs. He had proven to be as competent and successful a President of Colorado College as he was a military commander.

LOUIS TOMLINSON BENEZET

The next President of Colorado College was Louis Tomlinson Benezet, a man who had spent almost his entire life preparing to be a college and university administrator. He brought a rare combination of scholarship and professional educational administrative experience to the President's office at the College.

Lou Benezet, as he was called, was born June 29, 1915, in LaCrosse, Wisconsin. His father was a school superintendent, and the family moved frequently as the father advanced from job to job. But Louis Benezet spent most of his youth in Manchester, New Hampshire, and thus acquired many of the attitudes and ideals associated with New England. He went to college at Dartmouth College in Hanover, New Hampshire, where he ran on the track team, made Phi Beta Kappa, and graduated in 1936 with a B.A. in Psychology.

After two years of teaching at the Hill School in Pottstown, Pennsylvania, Benezet moved on to Reed College in Oregon, where he taught Psychology part time and earned a Masters degree. His Masters thesis was a study of the measurable differences between those persons who are "scientific types" and those who are "verbal types."

At this point in his academic career, Louis Benezet decided to take some advice from his father. "My father said the greatest lack in this nation was the number of persons qualified to be college presidents," Benezet explained. "He told me to learn about colleges and what they teach. I therefore began a scholarly study of what it takes to lead a small college."

Louis Benezet won a fellowship at Columbia University Teachers College to study for a Ph.D. in Higher Education. His doctoral dissertation was a study of three liberal arts colleges—Bard, Bennington, and Sarah Lawrence—and what those institutions were doing to educate their students. Louis Benezet borrowed $700 from his father to pay to get his dissertation published.[10] He received his Ph.D. in 1942 shortly after the beginning of World War II.

Following one year at Knox College as Assistant Professor of Psychology and Assistant Director of Admissions, Louis Benezet was commissioned an officer in the U.S. Navy. His military career became mainly an educational experience as he organized classes and correspondence courses for Navy personnel stationed in the southwest Pacific. His base of operations was Brisbane, Australia. When World War II ended, Benezet took charge of the night school and other extension programs at Syracuse University in upstate New York.

Night schools and extension schools were particularly busy in the late 1940s because of the large number of World War II veterans going to colleges and universities on the G.I. Bill. "My career grew with the G.I. boom," Benezet said. "My big break came when the Chancellor of Syracuse University asked me if he could have some of my time to work

[10]Louis T. Benezet, *General Education In The Progressive College* (New York, NY: Arno Press, 1971). Benezet's dissertation was originally published by the Columbia University Teachers College in 1943.

as his assistant. I said, 'Why don't you take all of my time?'" Becoming the Assistant to the Chancellor of Syracuse University moved Benezet firmly into college and university administration.

In 1948 Louis Benezet was named the President of Allegheny College in Meadville, Pennsylvania. He was only 32-years-old at the time. One of the first things he noticed about Allegheny College was that it had a strong regional base with most of the students coming from the Pittsburgh, Pennsylvania, and Cleveland, Ohio, areas. "Allegheny was provincial," Benezet noted. "When I came to Colorado College, I found it much less provincial than Allegheny, with students coming from many more states and more distant parts of the nation."

Benezet instituted two major reforms at Allegheny College. One reform was to revamp the curriculum, putting in more "core" courses that every student had to take, creating senior seminars to "stretch the seniors' thinking," and providing for "Leadership Lectures" so students could learn directly from important and successful business and labor leaders.

The second reform by Benezet was to embark on a major building program. There had been no new buildings constructed at Allegheny, College since before World War II. In the seven years he was President at Allegheny, Louis Benezet saw to the construction of a classroom building, a dormitory, and an athletic field house. The classroom building was Quigley Hall (1953), the dormitory was Baldwin Hall (1953), and the athletic building was David Mead Field House (1954).

THE MOVE TO COLORADO COLLEGE

In 1955 Louis Benezet accepted the presidency of Colorado College. "I've never been stuck in any particular geography," Benezet said. "Colorado College had a tradition of excellent teaching, and it had a good record for sending its students to graduate and professional schools. Furthermore, Colorado College had the ambiance that comes from being located in Colorado Springs. The beneficial environment has a great deal to do with Colorado College's attractiveness to students, faculty members—and administrators."

Benezet also saw something in Colorado College that former-President Edward Payson Tenney had seen. "Colorado College is the only good liberal arts college in over one-third of the land area of the United States," Benezet said.[11] The new President also was familiar with the prestigious position of the College back when William Slocum was President. Benezet often remarked that he wanted to get Colorado College back to the reputation it had at the turn of the 20th Century.[12]

But Louis Benezet found some problems when he arrived at Colorado College to embark on his second small college presidency. "The campus was in terrible shape," he said. "Things looked shabby. At least I thought things looked shabby. The College had had a series of presidents who knew nothing about modern techniques of financing an institution of higher learning. The entire operation was dangerously underfinanced."

Louis Benezet set to work to change the situation. He hired Robert Brossman, an expert on fund-raising and educational promotion, to be Vice President for Development. "I had to have someone to sell the place," Benezet said about Brossman. The new President also hired Robert Broughton to be Vice President and Business Manager. "I had to have someone who could do double-entry bookkeeping," Benezet quipped.

But President Benezet's biggest concern was the deteriorated state of the physical plant. He made an extra effort to hire Richard A. Kendrick, the physical plant manager at the University of New Mexico in Albuquerque. In order to get Kendrick, Benezet made the decision to pay his physical plant manager a higher salary than he was paying the Dean of the College. Apparently the high salary was worth the money. "Richard Kendrick took the campus over and treated it like it was his own child," Benezet said.[13]

BUILDING A COLORADO BASE

One of the major changes instituted by President Benezet was to increase the number of students coming to Colorado College from the state of

---

[11]All Benezet quotes from author's notes, interview with Louis T. Benezet, President of Colorado College 1955–1963, Mill Valley, California, 18 March 1998.

[12]Worner oral history, 5 February 1985, 65.

[13]Author's notes, interview with Louis Benezet, 18 March 1998. For details on the high salary paid to Richard Kendrick, see Worner oral history, 5 February 1985, 67–68.

Louis Tomlinson Benezet
President of the College during the late 1950s and early 1960s, Benezet presided over a building boom that included Rastall Center, Olin Hall, Schlessman Pool, Honnen Ice Rink, and Tutt Library.

Colorado. Benezet was the first President of the College to take note of the large post-World War II population boom in Colorado and try to take advantage of it. Benezet told the Board of Trustees: "I believe that Colorado College has the brightest future of any small liberal arts college in the country, *if* we capitalize on our . . . unique region. The spirit around us breeds optimism. We live in an age and in a region where the economy is expanding at almost a bursting rate."[14]

The obvious way to act on such a statement was to recruit more students from Colorado. "Students in a college's own state should know the college and want to go there," Benezet explained. "During my tenure in the President's office, Colorado College changed from having 10 percent of the students from Colorado to having 30 percent from within the state. I told the Admissions Office to effect that."[15]

Knowing how strongly the Pittsburgh and Cleveland areas had provided students to Allegheny College, Benezet decided to have the rapidly-growing Denver region do the same thing for Colorado College.

HIGHER ADMISSION STANDARDS

Another change instituted by President Benezet was to raise admission standards. He concluded that the College was admitting too many applicants, thereby filling up with mediocre students and students who could not get into any other college or university. "I told the Admissions Office to start turning weak applicants down," Benezet said. "The number of students at the College dropped at first, but the word got around, and the quality of the student body began to go up."

President Benezet also raised tuition in an effort to improve the prestige of the College. "I believed we needed to charge more for a superior product," Benezet explained. "I went to the Trustees and said: 'Gentlemen, we are underselling this College!'"

---

[14]Reid, *Colorado College: The First Century, 1874–1974*, 196.

[15]Author's notes, interview with Louis Benezet, 18 March 1998. When the author came to Colorado College in 1968, one of the first things he was told by then-President Lloyd Worner was that the College had greatly improved its student body because of the larger number of high quality students coming from the state of Colorado.

Another change instituted under Louis Benezet was the elimination of the compulsory chapel requirement. Sunday services were still held at Shove Chapel, but students attended them on a voluntary basis.

NO GRADUATE SCHOOL

At one point President Benezet's expansionary plans for Colorado College went a little too far. He began talking about creating a graduate school at the College. Shortly thereafter a small group of faculty members marched into his office and gave him three reasons why Colorado College should not become a university: (1) The College was a fine undergraduate college and should not dilute its efforts trying to become a graduate school. (2) Starting at such a late date and with relative meager resources, Colorado College could expect to become only a mediocre graduate school. (3) This faculty had hired on at Colorado College to teach undergraduates and *not* to administer a graduate school.

President Benezet listened to this representative sample of his faculty and dropped all thought of Colorado College becoming a university. The proposal was never brought up again.[16]

THE BENEZET "BUILDING BOOM"

Louis Benezet launched Colorado College on an ambitious program of adding new buildings to the campus. The first major project was to construct a new heating plant. The boilers in the old plant behind Cutler Hall were so rusted and dilapidated that the rebuilding project was undertaken in something of an emergency atmosphere. The new plant was moved slightly west and south of the old plant and located to the west of Cossitt Hall. The skyline view at the western end of the campus changed as the tall smoke stacks on the old heating plant were torn down and replaced by much lower stacks on the new facility.

The previous President of the College, William Gill, had built Slocum Hall for men and initiated the construction of Loomis Hall for women. President Benezet embellished Gill's work by adding a west wing on to Loomis Hall while it was still under construction. Benezet also expanded

---

[16]Glenn Brooks oral history, 14 February 1996, 57.

Slocum Hall by adding a west wing to that building as well. Loomis Hall, of course, was named for Ruth Loomis, the legendary Dean of Women at the College during the Slocum years.

To make room for Loomis Hall, the old President's House, built by President Tenney in 1882, had to be torn down. A new President's House was purchased at 1210 Wood Avenue, just north of Uintah Street. President Benezet, his wife Mildred, and their four young and active children were the first residents of this attractive addition to the campus.

In an effort to improve the "shabby" look of the campus, Benezet had the old men's dormitory, Hagerman Hall, torn down. Thus the first College building to have Romanesque architecture and peachblow sandstone walls was dismantled and removed. "Hagerman Hall had become a flea bag," Benezet said. "It was infested with rats. The old hall's dilapidated look was dragging the College down."[17]

About the same time Hagerman Hall was torn down, the dining room for men students in Cossitt Hall was closed. Men students who were not dining at a fraternity house were directed to eat with the women students in Taylor Dining Room, the new dining facility added on to Bemis Hall, the main women's residence hall. For the first time in its history, Colorado College permitted men and women students to dine together on a regular basis in a coeducational dining hall.

Taylor Dining Hall was named for Alice Bemis Taylor. She was the daughter of Judson M. Bemis, the man who had given a significant portion of the money for Bemis Hall. Because it was attached to Bemis Hall, Taylor Dining Hall was built of stone to match the stone construction of Bemis Hall. It was, however, the last College building to be built of stone, at least through the year 1999.

A new student union was constructed on the former site of Hagerman Hall. A student planning committee helped to define the uses in the building that would best serve the interests and needs of the student body. The new student union included a large coeducational dining hall, a snack bar known as "The Hub," meeting rooms, and offices for student activities such as the student newspaper and the yearbook. The building was financed partly by a U.S. Government loan. It was named Rastall

---

[17]Author's notes, interview with Louis Benezet, 18 March 1998.

Center for Benjamin Rastall, Class of 1901, who was a longtime member of the Board of Trustees. Similar to Slocum Hall and Loomis Hall, Rastall Center was built of red, brown, and dark gray brick.

The Olin Foundation contributed $1.5 million to Colorado College to help pay for the construction of a new science building. Olin Hall of Science was built east of Palmer Hall and north of Shove Chapel. In addition to laboratories and classrooms, the new four-stories-high science building had an attractive "pod" on its west side that included a large lecture hall downstairs and a comfortable lounge area upstairs. The lounge area was enclosed by large plate glass windows that "brought the outdoors indoors" by giving marvelous views of the grass, trees, and shrubbery at the east end of the campus.

During Louis Benezet's presidency, Colorado College withdrew from the Rocky Mountain Athletic Conference (RMAC) and, except for men's ice hockey, stopped awarding athletic scholarships. The College could no longer compete athletically with large universities such as the University of Colorado at Boulder and Colorado State University at Fort Collins. Having decided to de-emphasize sports, the College faced the problem of how best to attract non-scholarship athletes. "In order to attract amateur athletes," President Benezet said, "we had to have a more attractive athletic plant."[18]

The result was the construction of a large swimming pool, Schlessman Pool, and a skating rink, Honnen Rink. The skating rink hosted intramural ice hockey, which subsequently became a women's as well as a men's intramural sport. Honnen Rink also served as a practice rink for the men's ice hockey team, although the team continued to play its home games at the Broadmoor World Arena at the Broadmoor Hotel.

The new swimming pool was named for the family of Gerald Schlessman, Class of 1917, and the new ice hockey rink was named for the family of Edward Honnen, Class of 1921. Both were successful businessmen who gave many years to serving as members of the Board of Trustees of Colorado College.

Because of the new de-emphasis of sports, particularly men's football, there was little need for the large wooden stands on both sides of the foot-

---

[18]Author's notes, interview with Louis Benezet, 18 March 1998.

ball field that had been called Van Diest Stadium. These stands were dismantled and replaced by a smaller section of spectator seats located on the hillside east of the field.

In an effort to provide better housing for men students, three new fraternity houses were built north of Palmer Hall. The two-story modern-design buildings included dining rooms, lounges, and large recreation rooms in the basement. Two of the new fraternity houses were built of red brick and occupied by Phi Gamma Delta and Phi Delta Theta. The third was built of a dark gray brick and became the home of Kappa Sigma.

By the early 1960s Coburn Library was much too small in size to house the books required for a growing Colorado College. A new library was constructed at the southeast corner of Cascade Avenue and San Rafael Street, on the approximate spot where Palmer Hall originally was going to be located before it was moved to block the Tejon Street streetcar line. The new building was named Tutt Library for Charles Leaming Tutt, Jr., a strong supporter of the College and President of El Pomar Foundation. He was the son of Charles Leaming Tutt, Sr., who, along with Spencer Penrose, made millions in Cripple Creek gold.

The new trend toward brick at Colorado College was interrupted briefly by Tutt Library. This new building was all plate glass on the first floor and constructed of cast concrete slab on the second and third floors. The highlight of the building was a light and airy atrium that served as a study lounge for the students. In one of the more memorable days in Colorado College history, the student body joined en masse in the volunteer effort to transport all of the College's books from Coburn Library to Tutt Library.[19]

Louis Benezet's presidency was significant not only for the large number of new buildings constructed but also for the rapidity with which they were built. Although President Gill had initiated Colorado College's post-World War II building boom, it was President Benezet who really got the bulldozers digging and the bricklayers working. It was a period of physical expansion in the College's history previously rivaled only by the

---

[19]Reid, *Colorado College: The First Century, 1874–1974*, 228. Reid argued that "the era of togetherness" at Colorado College ended in 1962 on that famous day when the books were transferred from Coburn to Tutt. Six years later, however, when the author arrived at Colorado College, he was impressed by the extent to which a spirit of togetherness still characterized the College.

large number of buildings erected under President Slocum at the turn of the 20th Century.

Academic Progress

And President Benezet's time at Colorado College was characterized by academic progress as well as new buildings. First year students who received high grades in college-level courses taken their senior year in high school were given Colorado College credit for those courses. This eliminated the need for incoming students to retake at Colorado College the same courses they took in high school.

A Selected Student Program was set up for highly qualified first year students. These students took seminar classes that emphasized classroom discussions rather than sitting and listening to lectures. A new academic calendar was adopted which scheduled the entire first semester prior to Christmas vacation. This calendar caused the academic year to begin earlier, in late August and early September, but it eliminated having the last month of first semester occur after Christmas vacation.

Soon there were definite signs that the College was making academic progress. During the 1962–1963 academic year there were 1,209 students, the highest enrollment to that date in the College's history. Scholarship aid had been granted to 295 of those students, and 179 others were awarded student loans. There were 31 recipients of the Boettcher Scholarship, a prestigious merit scholarship given to outstanding students from the state of Colorado.[20] Max Power, a Political Science major, was chosen for a Rhodes Scholarship. He was Colorado College's first Rhodes Scholar in 25 years.

And there was increasing interest in improving international relations. The Summer Crossroads Program brought 40 to 70 foreign students to Colorado College each summer to participate in "exit" discussions before returning to their home countries. These foreign students had been studying at colleges and universities throughout the United States. They came

---

[20]Boettcher Scholarships are awarded by the Boettcher Foundation to high school graduates in Colorado. The scholarships can be used at any institution of higher learning in Colorado. The choice is made by the scholarship recipient. It has always been a mark of prestige and success for a college or university in Colorado to have been selected by a large number of Boettcher scholars and have them studying on campus.

to Colorado College for one week to talk among themselves and with faculty mentors about their experiences in and impressions of the United States. Summer Crossroads students lived with families in the Colorado Springs community. For many of these foreign students, it was their only "home stay" while in the United States.[21]

Benezet Moves On

In the spring of 1963 Louis Benezet announced that he was leaving Colorado College to become the President of the Claremont Graduate School in Claremont, California. He had often said that college and university administrations should change frequently, thereby infusing new ideas and new energies into these institutions. After serving as President of the Claremont Graduate School for seven years, Benezet became the President of the State University of New York at Albany (SUNY Albany). He later held an administrative post at the University of New York at Stonybrook (SUNY Stonybrook) on Long Island. He retired in Mill Valley, California, a suburb of San Francisco.

The Benezet era at Colorado College was remembered for the spirit which the young President had brought to the campus. The dynamic building program and the academic changes seemed to give everyone the feeling that things were happening at the College and real progress was being made.

Above all Louis Benezet saw the rapid population growth in post-World War II Colorado and moved to exploit it on behalf of Colorado College. The students attending colleges and universities in the 1950s were born in the depths of the Great Depression, and birth rates for that generation were low as a result. Despite the small applicant pools produced by these "Depression babies" in the late 1950s and early 1960s, Louis Benezet succeeded in expanding the enrollment at Colorado College by 10 percent. The new emphasis on recruiting students in Colorado contributed greatly to that steady increase in enrollment at a difficult time.

---

[21]Mike Bird, memo to author, 6 May, 1998. Bird, Professor of Economics at Colorado College, helped to direct the Summer Crossroads program for a number of years. Also see Reid, *Colorado College: The First Century, 1874–1974*, 206.

Students as well as faculty were aware of President Benezet's great contributions. The 1963 yearbook labeled Benezet's years in the presidency as the "Colorado College Renaissance 1955–1963." A lengthy citation included these thoughts: "Dr. Benezet's vision has given Colorado College a pervasive spirit of dynamism and growth. In a sense, all of us at Colorado College have been pioneers and builders, too. For Louis Benezet's vision has become an indelible part of the College community."[22]

Lloyd Edson Worner

Colorado College did not have to search very hard to find a qualified successor to out-going President Louis Benezet. The Dean of the College throughout the eight years of the Benezet administration was Lloyd Worner, and it was to Worner that the College turned when the need for a new President arose.

Worner was a graduate of Colorado College, Class of 1942. He was the first graduate of the College ever to be chosen as President of the College.

Lloyd Edson Worner, Jr., was from Missouri. He grew up in a middle-class home at 714 Woodlawn Street in the quiet little town of Mexico, Missouri. His most notable characteristic, even as an adult, was his slow Missouri drawl. His predecessor as President of Colorado College, Louis Benezet, liked to point out that Worner had "the quickest mind and the slowest speech" of anyone Benezet had ever known.[23]

Virtually no one ever addressed Worner by his given name of Lloyd. He preferred to be called Lew, a nickname created from his initials, L. E. W.

Lew Worner went to high school at Missouri Military Academy, a well-known military school located just a few blocks away from his home in Mexico, Missouri. He wore a military uniform to class every day, marched in parade with his fellow students to lunch, and was a member of the school drill team, the Fusileers. He played varsity football, basketball, and tennis. He was a Missouri State Interscholastic Finalist in golf.

---

[22]Reid, *Colorado College: The First Century, 1874–1974*, 231.

[23]Author's notes, interview with Louis Benezet, 18 March 1998.

His senior year he was President of the "M" Club (varsity athletes) and Vice President of the Dramateers (acting club). He also was the Captain of his dormitory—Company D.[24]

Lew Worner thus gained early in life the intellectual, mental, and physical discipline that is an integral part of military school training. He learned the art of effective command. But he also demonstrated at Missouri Military Academy a penchant to do things his own way. His disciplinary record for his high school years included demerits for "ditching class," "wearing slippers at mess," "throwing erasers," "eating in class," and "no hat uptown."[25]

Worner began his college career at Washington and Lee University in Lexington, Virginia. He was forced to withdraw at the end of his sophomore year when he badly injured his back in a varsity lacrosse game. It took two years for Worner to regain his health, after which he transferred to Colorado College to complete his undergraduate education. He played on the golf team, was elected President of the Beta Theta Pi fraternity, and also was elected President of the student body. The student newspaper, the *Tiger*, complimented Worner for the "unique morale" that his leadership imparted to his fellow students at Colorado College.[26]

Lew Worner was something of a campus character during his undergraduate days at Colorado College. He owned a collie dog named Patty, who was often with him but also more-or-less had the free run of the campus. Several times, when Lew Worner failed to attend Professor Edith Bramhall's class in International Relations, Worner's dog Patty came to the class just as if it was she and not Lew Worner who was taking the course. Apparently it really amused Professor Bramhall that the dog showed up for class even when Lew Worner did not.[27]

---

[24]*Missouri Military Academy 1935–1936*, a combined catalog and yearbook, Missouri Military Academy, Mexico, Missouri.

[25]File on Lloyd Edson Worner, Jr., Class of 1936, Student Files, Missouri Military Academy, Mexico, Missouri.

[26]Reid, *Colorado College: The First Century, 1874–1974*, 123.

[27]Worner oral history, 28 January 1985, 14–15.

Morale was high on the Colorado College campus when Worner was a student in the early 1940s. World War II had not yet begun, and the College had survived the Great Depression and had an enrollment of 800 students. In speaking of the time, Lew Worner often quoted one of his classmates, Joel Husted, who pointed out that the College did not have a counseling center, and did not have much of an infirmary, but it did have one thing. "We all thought it was about the finest place in the world we could be," Worner quoted Husted as saying.[28]

At the end of his senior year at Colorado College, Lew Worner was offered graduate fellowships in History at both Princeton University and Duke University. The President of Colorado College at that time was Thurston Davies, a Princeton graduate, and President Davies convinced Worner to go to Princeton rather than Duke. One of Worner's History professors at Colorado College, George Anderson, asked Worner why he wanted to go to graduate school in History. "Because," Lew Worner replied, "I want to do just what you are doing!"[29]

After one year of graduate study at Princeton, Lew Worner transferred to the University of Missouri at Columbia. He wanted to be closer to his family home in Missouri and to incorporate more teaching into his graduate school training. He took a number of Political Science courses in addition to his graduate program in History. He received an M.A. from Missouri in 1944 and a Ph.D. in 1946. His doctoral dissertation was a study of the life and career of Herbert Spencer Hadley, a leading Missouri politician of the early 20th Century who supported progressive reforms.[30]

While at Missouri, Lew Worner met his future wife, Mary, in the University library. They married in 1945, and she helped to support the two of them by working as a nurse in the medical center at the University. One day in the spring of 1946 Lew Worner received a telephone call from

---

[28]Worner oral history, 28 January 1985, 11.

[29]Worner oral history, 28 January 1985, 22.

[30]"Program Of The Final Examination For The Degree Of Doctor of Philosophy of Lloyd Edson Worner, Jr.," University of Missouri, 25 July 1946, located in the File on Lloyd Edson Worner, Class of 1936, Student Files, Missouri Military Academy, Mexico, Missouri. Also see Worner oral history, 28 January 1985, 23.

Colorado College President Thurston Davies offering him a position at his undergraduate alma mater teaching both History and Political Science.

"I had said I would come," Worner recalled, and Mary said, 'Well, that's nice.' And she said, 'What rank, and what salary?'" Only then did Lew Worner realize he had accepted a teaching job at Colorado College without thinking to find out either the rank or the salary. As it turned out, his $2,500 starting salary at Colorado College was $300 less than his $2,800 salary as a graduate student at Missouri.

"I never regretted it for a minute," Worner said in his rambling way, "because I wanted to come back. There was something—these things are hard to describe. It's not [just] the region, or the mountains, or the buildings around here. There's just something about a college that gets to you in a different way. This did . . . At Princeton I used to look out and the clouds to the west would look a little like the [Rocky] mountains, and oh, boy, that [Colorado] climate and all. . . . So I was real happy to come back here."[31]

FREEDOM AND AUTHORITY

Lew Worner joined with two of his colleagues—Professor of Philosophy Glenn Gray and Professor of English George McCue—to start the General Studies program at Colorado College. They created a new course entitled *Freedom and Authority*, which was taught by all three professors and took an interdisciplinary approach to discussing and solving problems. By having two or three professors teaching at the same time, students could observe not only the different ways of viewing subject matter but also were exposed to a variety of teaching styles. The course became popular at the College and was famous for producing lively intellectual arguments, many of them between the team-teaching professors.[32]

The course *Freedom and Authority* turned out to be a durable invention. It started out as a course for senior year, with experienced students coming together to discuss the perennially important question of how personal liberty could, or should, be limited by public law. Students had to

---

[31]Worner oral history, 28 January 1985, 24–25.

[32]For a lengthy description of the creation and early days of the *Freedom and Authority* course at Colorado College, see Worner oral history, 28 January 1985, 48–52.

apply to get into the course, and only the more qualified applicants were accepted. As a result, a certain amount of intellectual prestige came to be associated with taking *Freedom and Authority*.

The course became so well known that, on Alumni Homecoming weekend, a special session of the course often was held so that returning alumni could once again enjoy this intense, discussion-oriented classroom experience. Professors who had taught the course in previous years taught the Alumni Homecoming sessions, so alumni often got to be back in the *Freedom and Authority* classroom with some of their original *Freedom and Authority* professors.

This interesting and exciting course evolved over the years and adapted to changing intellectual climates and differing academic needs. In the late 1990s *Freedom and Authority* was still being taught at Colorado College, only it had become an introductory, interdisciplinary course in Western intellectual thought.

WORNER PROMOTED TO DEAN

In March of 1955 Lew Worner received what might best be described as a "battlefield promotion" to Dean of the College. The previous Dean departed in the middle of the academic year. President William Gill called Worner to come over to the President's office. "The Dean's chair is going to be vacant," President Gill said. "I want you to go up and sit in it and be Acting Dean until President Benezet comes. I don't know whether he'll want you, [or] whether you'll like the job, but I hope you'll do this."

Lew Worner accepted this "on-the-spot" assignment. As it turned out, Worner proved to be a skilled and competent Acting Dean. When President Benezet arrived on campus in the fall of 1955, he appointed Lew Worner the permanent Dean of the College. Worner held the post the entire time of Benezet's presidency. "It turned out [Benezet and I] were very compatible," Lew Worner explained. "[We] shared a lot of things. It was a wonderful eight years with him."[33]

---

[33]Worner oral history, 28 January 1985, 56–58.

TEACHING VS. BEING DEAN

When Lew Worner took over the Dean's office at Colorado College in 1955, he had to relinquish his teaching duties. A young Professor of History, William Hochman, took over Worner's *Freedom and Authority* course. Worner had been out of the classroom for about two weeks, and already missed getting to teach, when he encountered some of his former *Freedom and Authority* students and stopped to chat with them. "Oh, gee, sir, we really miss you," Worner recalled the students saying, and that made the new Dean feel very good. But later in the conversation the students said, "Boy! That Hochman is *really* terrific!" Lew Worner said he knew then what he was losing by leaving the classroom. When he got back to his office, Worner said he "just kicked the desk."[34]

PRESIDENT WORNER

On April 29, 1963, it was announced at faculty meeting that Lloyd Edson (Lew) Worner had been appointed the next President of Colorado College. Out-going President Louis Benezet had strongly supported Worner to be his successor.[35] On receiving the news, the faculty gave Worner a warm and enthusiastic welcome. "A deafening, standing ovation swept the 110 person faculty as Armin B. Barney, Chairman of the Colorado College Board of Trustees, named Dean Worner to fill the President's shoes."[36]

When Lew Worner was offered the presidency of Colorado College, he decided to talk things over with one of his most influential mentors on the faculty—Political Science Professor Edith Bramhall.

"I think you're a good teacher and you *could* be a passable scholar," Worner said Bramhall told him. Then she added: "I'm going to be very blunt. It's not that you aren't . . . reasonably intelligent and all. [But] you do not have that cutting type of intelligence that would want to make a career of lonely study and books and scholarship. . . . You just would not like that." Worner said Edith Bramhall then smiled at him and put a lit-

[34]Worner oral history, 28 January 1985, 58.

[35]Worner oral history, 5 February 1985, 102.

[36]Unidentified newspaper paragraph, 30 April 1963, File on Lloyd Edson Worner, Jr., Class of 1936, Missouri Military Academy, Mexico, Missouri.

Lloyd Edson (Lew) Worner
The President of Colorado College for 18 years, Worner (left) was photographed talking to students during the early years of his presidency.

tle sarcasm into her final words of advice. "Although you may not be the *brightest* person in the world," she concluded, "I think you like to work with people. I think you'd be—perhaps—a good administrator. And I think you ought to take the job."[37]

Lew Worner took the job. At that moment in his life, he had become virtually the personification of Colorado College. He had been an undergraduate student at the College and President of the student body. After being away only four years in graduate school, he had returned to the College as a professor. During his teaching days, he helped to implement the Honor System and co-founded one of the College's most popular and durable courses, *Freedom and Authority*. He had served eight years as Dean of the College under one of its most popular and progressive presidents—Louis Benezet. In fact, the argument could be made that one of the reasons for Benezet's great success at Colorado College was that he had Lew Worner backing him up in the Dean's office.

THE BUILDING BOOM CONTINUED

The building boom inaugurated at Colorado College by presidents Gill and Benezet continued unabated under President Worner. In November of 1964 the new Boettcher Health Center was opened and dedicated. This thoroughly modern college infirmary had an innovative circular design which permitted nurses to observe and serve more patients. The nurses' station was located in the center of the building with the patient beds fanning out in the outer part of the circle. The new infirmary was located on Cascade Avenue just east of Loomis Hall.

With the benefit of a $2.25 million grant from the Olin Foundation, the College began the construction of a new Humanities building. Sadly, to make room for this new building, two of the College's lovely examples of Romanesque architecture had to be torn down. The beautiful peachblow sandstone walls of Coburn Library and Perkins Hall were dismantled and hauled away. The destruction of these two buildings, coupled with the earlier razing of Hagerman Hall, left Palmer Hall as the only re-

---

[37]Worner oral history, 5 February 1985, 102–103.

maining example of a Romanesque, peachblow sandstone building at Colorado College.

The new Humanities building was named Armstrong Hall in honor of Willis R. Armstrong, Class of 1899, who served on the College's Board of Trustees for 53 years. The building was three stories high. It was constructed of the now-familiar red, brown, and dark gray brick and had white cement trim. Included was an 800-seat indoor auditorium. The west end of the new edifice contained offices for the College administration and a plush executive meeting room. On the third floor was an audio-visual room, Armstrong 300, which was designed for showing films and photographic slides to classes and other small groups.

One of the major characteristics of Armstrong Hall was its size. It was longer and wider than Palmer Hall, which made it the largest structure on campus in terms of ground space occupied. It was representative of a post-World War II trend at colleges and universities in the United States to build very large dormitories and immense academic buildings.

In the fall of 1965 enrollment at Colorado College reached another all-time high with 1,483 students taking classes. The large number of children born immediately after World War II were beginning to go to college, and the result was the World War II Baby Boom at colleges and universities throughout the United States. Colorado College was being hit with both an increased number of students from Colorado as well as Baby Boomers from throughout the nation.

To accommodate this growing influx of students to the College, ground was broken at the southwest corner of Nevada Avenue and Uintah Street to construct a new dormitory for men. Similar to Armstrong Hall, the building was quite large. Its red, brown, and dark gray brick walls towered upward four stories into the sky. The new residence hall was U-shaped in design and provided a variety of accommodations for men students. Because of its gigantic dimensions, the students at the College quickly nicknamed the building "Superdorm." It was formally named Mathias Hall, for H. Edwin Mathias, a popular Dean of Men who died suddenly of a heart attack at the time the new dormitory was completed.

Meeting with the Dean
In the mid-1960s this group of students met with Kenneth Curran (far right), the Dean of the College and a Professor of Economics. The meeting was held in Olin Hall lounge.

AN ERA OF PROTEST

The mid–1960s were years of student protest on college and university campuses throughout the United States. One of the major areas of student concern was the continued existence of racial segregation, particularly in the southern United States. This volatile issue was intensely dramatized on national television in the spring of 1965 when Alabama state police violently attacked protest marchers demonstrating for minority voting rights in Selma, Alabama. To show their disapproval of the actions of the Alabama authorities, over 500 Colorado College students and faculty members marched down Tejon Street carrying signs and shouting slogans of protest.

The students also protested the College's newly-instituted rule that all students must live in on-campus housing. The College had sought to fill its new dormitories, particularly Mathias Hall, by requiring that all students live in one of the College residence halls. Following a large protest demonstration in front of Armstrong Hall and extended negotiations, the Board of Trustees agreed to allow seniors and students over the age of 21 to live off-campus. At the same time, the requirement that women students return to their dorms by a certain hour each night was removed for senior women and women students over the age of 21.

During the 1965–1966 academic year the United States greatly increased the number of American military personnel stationed in the embattled nation of South Vietnam. A Vietnam Study Group was formed on campus to organize lectures and panel discussions on the various issues raised by this rapidly-escalating war. Those opposed to U.S. involvement in the Vietnam conflict staged weekly vigils at the Earle Flagpole. There also were anti-Vietnam War protest marches to Fort Carson and peace demonstrations in Acacia Park.

ACADEMIC CHANGE

There were a number of changes in the academic program during Lew Worner's first years as President. Three new academic majors were created at the College—an Anthropology major, a Drama major, and an interdisciplinary Natural Science major. The faculty voted to give students the option of taking courses Pass-Fail rather than for the traditional A-B-

C-D-F grades. For a number of years, Montgomery Hall was designated the official French House at the College and only the French language was to be spoken there. To properly mark the event, the tricolored flag of France was raised over this women's residence hall.

Applications for admission continued to increase, so a Summer Matriculation Program was instituted in the summer of 1967. Colorado College had operated a Summer Session since 1935, and the new Summer Matriculation Program took advantage of the existing Summer Session course offerings. A selected group of students, called "Summer Starts," began their career at Colorado College by attending Summer Session prior to the start of freshman year. These students were not allowed to attend the College during the fall semester but were allowed to return for the following spring semester. In effect, Summer Starts filled student spaces at the College that became vacant when fall semester students flunked out or transferred out of the College.

A particularly pioneering and adventurous new program was the Ford Independent Study Program (FISP), which permitted a selected group of 26 students to design their own college education. The program was modeled after the tutorial system used at Oxford University in England. Working closely with a faculty adviser, FISP students set their own schedule for attending classes, writing papers, attending outside lectures and panel discussions, etc. These independent scholars could attend regular classes if they wished, but they were not required to do so. The program was directed by Professor of Political Science J. Douglas Mertz.

Another exciting and adventurous academic experiment in the mid–1960s was the Adviser Plan. A student in this highly-selective program was allowed to take any program of courses the student pleased. There was no necessity either to select a major or meet any other College course requirements. The only limitation on the student's freedom was that the course schedule selected had to be approved by the student's faculty adviser.

By the spring of 1968, things were going well at Colorado College. Although it was an age of student protest, the administration and the student body were on speaking terms with each other and able to work most of the problems out through negotiations that eventually led to workable agreements. Creative academic programs such as the Selected Student Program, the Ford Independent Study Program (FISP), and the Adviser Plan gave an aura of academic experimentation and progress to the campus. The accelerated building program over the previous 14 years had created an expanded and well-equipped physical plant.

But even more experimentation leading to progress lay ahead for Colorado College. In the fall of 1968 the College turned its attention to revising its academic calendar. The end result would be one of the most distinguishing modern features of Colorado College—the Block Plan.

CHAPTER 6

THE ADVENT OF THE BLOCK PLAN

Fred Sondermann, Professor of Political Science, was chairman of a key faculty committee in the spring of 1968. The committee discussed the upcoming Centennial of the College in 1974, and the idea was expressed that the College should do something more than just hold a celebration in honor of 100 years of existence. There should be some sort of major review of the College's program.

Professor Sondermann subsequently spoke with the College President, Lloyd Edson (Lew) Worner. Sondermann made the point that the 1974 College Centennial offered the opportunity to develop plans and ideas for moving the College forward. Sondermann then suggested that a comprehensive review of the calendar and the curriculum might be in order. Worner recalled Sondermann saying: "Look—wouldn't it be great at the Centennial, instead of having a bunch of . . . distinguished speakers, and talking about the great things of the College, and its past, and . . . the traditional thing, wouldn't it be good if we could be off and running about what we are doing as we go into the [21st] Century?"

President Worner liked the idea presented by Professor Sondermann on behalf of his faculty committee. "That really hit me hard," Worner later commented. The very next day, upon returning to his office, Worner appointed Professor Glenn Brooks, a member of the Political Science Department, to undertake a comprehensive review of the College's entire program—academic, athletic, social, etc. Professor Brooks was given the purposely vague title of Faculty Assistant to the President, but his mission was crystal clear. He was to study the College in depth, and make recommendations for infusing the College with the latest ideas and innovations in American college education. Worner's final words to Brooks were: "Let's see what we can come up with?"

The word quickly spread across the campus about Professor Brooks and his challenging new assignment. About a week later, Professor Sondermann ran into President Worner and told him: "You know, this is a great place. One of the things you learn around here is don't open your mouth and suggest something, because it may be acted on the next day!"[1]

It is interesting to speculate on these early stages of the process by which the Block Plan was developed at Colorado College. The initial idea—to have the Centennial of the College result in meaningful change at the College—originated in a faculty committee. This idea was then effectively presented to the President of the College, and the President promptly acted on it. The idea thus rose out of the general academic community at the College rather than being imposed from the top administrative levels downward, or coming from a report by a visiting consultant. It was a further indication that all levels at the College were infused with an innovative and pioneering academic spirit.

THE STUDY BEGINS

Glenn Brooks was a logical choice to head up a major study of the academic, athletic, and social programs at Colorado College. Brooks was born in August of 1931 in Kerrville, a small city in the hill country of central Texas west of Austin and northwest of San Antonio. After earning his B.A. and M.A. degrees at the University of Texas in Austin, Brooks received his Ph.D. degree in Political Science from the Johns Hopkins University in Baltimore, Maryland. In his final years at Johns Hopkins, Brooks participated in a major study of management practices in colleges and universities throughout the United States.

Brooks long had been a supporter of the core values of a liberal arts education. Having lived "a very provincial life" growing up in Texas, he found the "world of knowledge" opened up to him when he got to the University of Texas. On his application to graduate school he described

[1]Sondermann and Worner quotes from Worner oral history, 5 February 1985, 141. Also see Brooks oral history, 14 February 1996, 14–15.

himself as "a generalist looking for a place to generalize." He developed a credo of "Back To Fundamentals." He became convinced that human beings spent too much time on the "immediate and transient" things in life and thus did not have adequate time for "the enduring things."[2]

Glenn Brooks joined the Colorado College faculty in 1960, the same year he received his Ph.D. from Johns Hopkins. His special field within Political Science was Public Administration, so he was a student of the design and effective management of large organizations.

Instead of setting up a special committee to study the College, Glenn Brooks decided to have the College community function as "a committee of the whole." As many different people and groups as possible were brought into the study process, and the standing faculty committees and existing student organizations were recruited to do much of the fact gathering, thinking, and solution proposing. Brooks explained:

"What we did, and Lew Worner embraced this idea, was to make use of different committees, and different groups according to what kind of a thing we were taking a look at. So the faculty Academic Program Committee got involved in a department-by-department review of what [the departments] needed. And we put a pretty positive spin on it. What do you need to do a better job?"

Glenn Brooks made it very clear that the research and study that led to the Block Plan was undertaken in a very upbeat and positive atmosphere. "There was no atmosphere of crisis," Brooks said. "There was no atmosphere of financial or educational or ideological decay or anything of that sort. There was no interest in changing our fundamental direction. . . . The emphasis was on how to do a better job of traditional arts and sciences."

As more information poured into Glenn Brooks about academic and extra-curricular life at the College, there were some eye-opening discoveries. A study of dormitory life revealed that noise had become a more-or-less constant problem, so much so that responsible students could no longer study in the dorms. Brooks noted: "Nobody had understood the effects of the stereo system on life in Loomis Hall, or anywhere else [on campus]."

---

[2]Shelley Mueller, "The Private Policies Of Dr. Glenn Brooks," *Catalyst*, 19 September 1975, 3.

It quickly became clear to Professor Brooks that the conventional two-semester calendar had the effect of forcing faculty and students to "jump from one place to another" and "do too many things." The end result was that people "felt pulled apart." But Brooks found no criticism of what was being taught at Colorado College. There was widespread general approval of the content of the curriculum. It was the manner in which the courses were being presented to the students, and not the content of the courses, that was being brought into question.[3]

President Worner was watching this process closely and later summed up the manner in which it was developing: "Glenn literally just went into the dormitories, into the faculty. He spent a lot of time talking with people, and more and more it just seemed that our resources weren't being as wisely used, we thought, as they might be. We were thinking of . . . faculty energy and time. And Glenn found a good many people, when they thought about it, didn't much like the idea of the 50-minute periods and the three-periods-a-week, and the bell ringing. And some days you wished you could leave at the end of 20 minutes, and other days you'd want to go until noon. . . . And Glenn came up with the basic elements of [a new] scheme, which primarily were to aim at smaller classes, more writing, more discussion, and to do away with clock-watching."[4]

PROFESSOR SHEARN'S COMMENT

But perhaps the defining moment of the entire review process came in a comment to Glenn Brooks from Professor Don Shearn of the Psychology Department. According to Brooks, Shearn at one point said to him: "Why don't you just give me 15 students and let me work with them." Shearn made it clear that he was tired of going from class-to-class during the week and having to deal with 150 to 200 students throughout a 12 or 13-week semester. Shortly after this conversation with Don Shearn, Glenn Brooks started using the term "Unified Learning" when talking about the academic future of Colorado College.[5]

---

[3]All Brooks quotes from Brooks oral history, 14 February 1996, 15–17.

[4]Worner oral history, 5 February 1985, 141–142.

[5]In his oral history interview, Glenn Brooks twice referred to his conversation with Professor Shearn as being a very important point in the genesis of the Block Plan idea. Brooks also gave credit

The rough outlines of the Block Plan took shape rapidly. In only four months, from September to December of 1968, Glenn Brooks was able to gather his information and start making concrete proposals. Brooks explained: "These ideas just began to take shape so quickly, and were drawn from faculty and students in a genuine way. This was not a put-up job. Nobody came into this with any idea even that we were going to have a fairly major change in the structure of the academic program. Yet the ideas started flowing in."[6]

Glenn Brooks was doing more than just survey the faculty and students at Colorado College. He read the book *Effective Executives*, by Peter Drucker, which took the position that successful executives made the best use of their time by blocking their time. Brooks gathered materials on the latest teaching strategies in medical schools, where future physicians were taking six straight weeks of psychiatry, and twelve straight weeks in surgery, etc. Brooks found that progressive law schools were teaching only torts for a defined period, and then only contracts.[7]

By the spring of 1969, the Block Plan was clearly defined. Students would take only one course for three-and-one half weeks, and professors would teach only one course for three-and-one-half weeks. The academic year would consist of nine of these three-and-one-half week blocks, with four blocks in the fall semester (prior to Winter Break) and five blocks in the second semester (after Winter Break).[8] How often and how long a class would meet was left to each professor's personal judgement.

---

to Wilson Gately, Professor of Mathematics, for helping in a less clearly defined way to give structure to the Block Plan. Brooks said: "And Bill Gateley in the Math Department, ever the good technical analyst that he was, began to draw little pictures of how you could put things in boxes. . . ." Brooks oral history, 14 February 1996, 17.

[6]Brooks oral history, 14 February 1996, 18.

[7]Brooks oral history, 14 February 1996, 18. Worner oral history, 5 February 1985, 142–143.

[8]When first proposed and implemented, the Block Plan included an option where students could take two courses over three blocks. These courses were known as "ten-and-one-half week half-courses." Each half-course counted for one-and-one-half units of credit, so completing both half-courses resulted in three units of credit for three blocks of work. The half-courses proved highly unpopular with the students, so the half-course option was dropped when the Block Plan was only a few years old. The half-courses of the early 1970s should not be confused with the January Half-Block implemented in the early 1990s.

THE 25-STUDENT LIMIT

To make the promise of small classes a reality at Colorado College, a 25-student limit was proposed for each course taught under the Block Plan. This idea came from Professor Douglas W. Freed, a member of the Psychology Department, who wrote Glenn Brooks a memorandum to the effect that the College should make an effort to have class sizes reflect more closely the student/faculty ratio of approximately 13 students for each faculty member.[9]

Although the 25-student limit did not receive as much publicity or discussion as the idea of students taking only one course at a time, the 25-student limit was one of the key elements in the Block Plan. Liberal arts colleges such as Colorado College had long promised smaller classes but often delivered large lecture courses with more than 100 students just sitting and listening to a professor talk. The 25-student limit was designed to make small classes, with an emphasis on class discussion, a guaranteed reality at Colorado College.[10]

Suddenly the general review of the College's academic, athletic, and social programs, first suggested by Professor Sondermann, had turned into a radical proposal to completely overhaul the essential way the College conducted its academic business. Colorado College was the first college in the United States to propose adopting such an unusual and innovative academic program. Here was a plan to completely abandon the format, universally accepted throughout undergraduate American higher education, that students should take from three to five courses at a time, with different professors, over a 10 to 15 week term or semester. Glenn Brooks was proposing that Colorado College undertake academic pioneering in its most adventurous form.

The spring of 1969 found Professor Brooks going from academic department to academic department at the College, asking each department to try to mock up a new course schedule within the nine-block format of

---

[9]Douglas Freed, Psychology Department, Colorado College, memorandum to Glenn Brooks, 12 November 1968.

[10]The author long argued that the 25-student limit was as important a part of the Block Plan as dividing the academic year into nine equal blocks, but it was the change in the calendar that received all the publicity and discussion and not the 25-student limit.

the Block Plan. Brooks began with Political Science, his own department. If Brooks and his own departmental colleagues could not come up with a workable Block Plan course schedule for the department, then the Block Plan idea was pretty much doomed.

So late one afternoon, Glenn Brooks and the Political Science faculty gathered in the department seminar room in the northeast corner of the ground floor of Palmer Hall. Someone took a piece of chalk and divided the chalk board in the room into nine equal sections, and one-by-one the Political Science professors began putting their courses into the various blocks.

There was much erasing of the chalk board as the afternoon went on, and a great deal of transferring courses from one block to another. There also was a great deal of friendly wheeling-and-dealing, such as: "What if I move American Government from Block 4 to Block 1, and then you teach American Politics in Block 4. That way students can take both courses the same year."

By the end of the day a workable program of Political Science courses had been sketched out on the chalk board, and the members of the Political Science Department had seen for themselves that the proposed Block Plan could be made to meet the department's teaching needs. A tired but rewarded Glenn Brooks looked at the chalk board and said: "That's amazing. That's beautiful. It really will work!"[11]

THE LEISURE PROGRAM

Other details of the Block Plan were being filled in throughout the spring of 1969. It was decided that the academic day would end at 3 P.M., thus giving students a reserved block of time for athletics and extra-curricular activities. A Leisure Program would be created to develop interesting things for students to do both after classes ended at 3 P.M. and during the four-and-a-half day Block Break at the end of each block. Just as the Block Plan was designed to allow students and faculty to focus clearly on academic subjects for most of the day, it was also designed to allow stu-

[11]Recollection of the author.

dents and faculty to focus sharply on athletic and leisure time activities after 3 P.M.[12]

In a parallel effort to support the basic idea of the proposed Block Plan, Summer Session Dean Gilbert Johns organized two courses for the 1969 Summer Session on a modular basis. Students were to study only one subject for the eight weeks of Summer Session, and professors were to teach only one subject at a time. The two Block Plan-style Summer Session courses were the Ecology-Geology Institute, taught by professors Richard Beidleman of the Biology Department and William Fischer of the Geology Department, and the Urban Studies Institute, directed by Professor Robert Loevy of the Political Science Department.

GETTING THE PLAN APPROVED

As the 1969–1970 academic year got underway, Glenn Brooks began the process of getting faculty approval for his newly-minted Block Plan. Over the summer of 1969 Brooks issued three long memoranda to the faculty detailing the Block Plan and justifying its structure and procedures. The Block Plan was the subject of discussion at the 1969 Faculty Fall Conference, held before classes began at a camp up in the Rocky Mountains.

At the invitation of President Worner, Glenn Brooks gave the major address at the Fall Convocation, the traditional opening academic procession and gathering of faculty and students for the new academic year. Faculty felt obligated to "march" in the Fall Convocation, which meant that faculty members who were opposed to the Block Plan proposal had to sit quietly in Shove Chapel and listen to Glenn Brooks extol the plan's supposed benefits. There was no opportunity for dissenting and opposing views to be aired.

One faculty member who was particularly put-off by this one-sided presentation at the 1969 Fall Convocation was Professor Douglas Fox of

---

[12]An attempt was made to combine the Block Plan proposal with the 25-student limit and the Leisure Program proposal and call the entire program the Colorado College Plan. This nomenclature became the official policy of the College, but the term "Colorado College Plan" never really caught on with either the students or the faculty. In everyday use, all aspects of Glenn Brooks's many reforms were colloquially referred to as the Block Plan.

the Religion Department. Fox was a popular lecturer who had a devoted following among the students and who was highly respected by his professorial colleagues. Glenn Brooks had not intended to offend Professor Fox, but Brooks had used the word "draconian" in describing the old semester system then in use at Colorado College. Draconian referred to the rigid rules and regulations that had been imposed by an ancient ruler named Draco.

When Doug Fox returned to his office after the Fall Convocation was over, he wrote a "scathing" memorandum to Glenn Brooks accusing him of overstating the case for the Block Plan and misusing the venue of the Fall Convocation for propaganda purposes. Fox also criticized Brooks for "a terrible abuse of the word draconian." Rules and regulations are not, in themselves, bad things.[13]

AN ALTERNATIVE TO THE BLOCK PLAN

In the fall of 1969 four senior members of the faculty came forward with an alternative plan for the College calendar. It provided for some changes, but none so radical and daring as those in the proposed Block Plan. The four professors were Jane Cauvel and Glenn Gray of the Philosophy Department, Douglas Fox of the Religion Department, and J. Douglas Mertz of the Political Science Department. Rather than reject this competing proposal out-of-hand, Glenn Brooks worked with the four professors to bring their plan up to the same level of technical detail and intellectual sophistication that had been provided for the Block Plan. Although this alternative plan was later dropped, the fact that Glenn Brooks and the College administration considered it so carefully probably, in the long run, helped build faculty support for the Block Plan.[14]

---

[13]College faculty, particularly the Colorado College faculty, liked to argue with each other by exchanging memoranda on current issues facing the College. This particular memorandum from Doug Fox to Glenn Brooks is described in Brooks oral history, 14 February 1996, 21.

[14]Brooks oral history, 14 February 1996, 20. Philosophy Professor Glenn Gray later noted that he had been a "tooth and nail" opponent of the Block Plan, but he said the plan, once in operation, had worked much better than he anticipated. See Andrew Wolfson, "Capitalizing On Apathy: Panel Discusses Quality Of Life At CC," *Catalyst*, 13 May 1977, 1.

Throughout the early fall of 1969, the Colorado College faculty held a series of late afternoon faculty meetings at which the Block Plan was presented, described, and debated at length. Many of these meetings were held in the basement lounge of Loomis Hall, at that time a women's dormitory. Because the Block Plan proposal was long and complex, and because many respected members of the faculty had serious doubts about embarking on such a radical academic calendar, these meetings often began at 3:30 in the afternoon and lasted until 8 or 9 at night. President Worner had the laborious task of presiding at these lengthy discussions, dutifully giving every member of the faculty who wanted to participate in the debate a chance to do so. At the dinner hour a number of faculty members would give up and go home, but most would climb up the stairs to the Loomis Hall office, borrow the telephone, and tell their family members that, once again, they would be very late for dinner.[15]

Glenn Brooks was working hard at keeping detailed records on the development of the Block Plan and the subsequent debate over its adoption. At one of the faculty meetings prior to the final vote, Brooks decided to take a tape recorder and record some of the debate. Shortly after the faculty meeting was underway, one of the taller members of the faculty, Professor Paul Kutsche of the Anthropology Department, rose ominously out of his chair and, with a look of righteous indignation, said: "Is the faculty aware that Professor Brooks is tape recording this meeting?"

Glenn Brooks, who had never dreamed his tape recorder would offend anyone, was aghast. He later explained: "I just felt like a bowl of oatmeal at that point, because I instantly realized it was a big mistake. I had [the tape recorder] sitting right in front of me, propped up. I immediately turned it off. And destroyed the tape!"[16]

PRESIDENT WORNER SUPPORTED THE BLOCK PLAN

As the Colorado College Faculty moved closer to a final vote on the proposed Block Plan, President Worner publicly and forcefully threw his sup-

---

[15]Recollection of the author.

[16]Brooks oral history, 14 February 1996, 22.

port behind the adventurous new calendar. Worner was criticized by a number of persons closely associated with the College for taking such a biased stand, particularly by Barbara Arnest, who was the wife of Professor of Art Bernard Arnest and had done some research and writing about the College.

But Worner defended his decision to participate actively in the drive for final adoption of the Block Plan. "I came out absolutely 100 percent behind it," he said. Worner noted that he respected the views of those who wanted him to remain neutral, but he felt a responsibility to take a position when such a major decision faced the College community. "My view is that, at that point, I should have [supported the Block Plan], and if people disagree, they disagree. And you know, there was no threat hanging over anyone here, in spite of what some people always think!"[17]

Joining President Worner in giving strong support to the Block Plan proposal was George Drake, a faculty member in the History Department and the newly-appointed Dean of the College. Drake graduated from Grinnell College in Grinnell, Iowa, and then won a Rhodes Scholarship to Oxford University in England. George Drake studied under the tutorial system at Oxford, where one or two students studied with, talked with, and debated with just one professor. Drake thus was very comfortable with those aspects of the Block Plan, such as smaller classes and closer faculty-student communication, which resembled the Oxford tutorial system.[18]

THE VOTE ON THE BLOCK PLAN

Suddenly the time had come for the faculty to vote on Glenn Brooks's proposed Block Plan. A year-and-a-half of effort on Brooks's part would become either the official policy of the College or nothing more than a historical footnote. Prior to the faculty meeting, Glenn Brooks and George Drake, the Dean of the College, sat down and went over the en-

---

[17]Worner oral history, 5 February 1985, 142.

[18]It was President Worner who pointed out that George Drake, "with his Oxford experience, was *delighted* with the tutorial aspects of" the Block Plan. See Worner oral history, 5 February 1985, 149.

tire list of the faculty, carefully counting those they knew were for the plan, those they knew were against it, and making educated guesses about those who had not yet revealed their decisions. According to this final "whip count," the Block Plan was going to be adopted by a comfortable margin if not an overwhelming one.[19]

The faculty meeting was held on October 27, 1969. The room was packed for what everyone knew would be one of the most important faculty votes in the College's history. Final arguments, some of them exhibiting strong emotions, were made both for and against the Block Plan proposal. Then the tally was taken—and the Block Plan was adopted by a vote of 72 to 53. Fifty-eight percent of the faculty present and voting had supported taking this adventurous academic step.

A number of the faculty speeches opposing the Block Plan turned out to be as important—and as memorable—as many of those given in support. Robert Stabler, a senior professor in the Biology Department, opposed the plan but then said: "Well, let's let these young bucks do what they want to do. [Let's] give them a chance."

Right after the votes had been counted and the results announced, President Worner said to the faculty: "Well, what does this mean? What shall we do now?"

At that point a key comment and motion came from Ray Werner, Professor of Economics, a very outspoken opponent of the Block Plan. Professor Werner stood up and said: "Look, this has been discussed. We've been over it. Everyone's had plenty of time. I've been opposed to it. . . . I move that we make the decision unanimous."

There was an immediate second and an immediate voice vote on Professor Werner's motion for unanimity. It passed with only one or two faculty members unwilling to go along.[20]

---

[19]Brooks oral history, 14 February 1996, 22.

[20]Worner oral history, 5 February 1985, 144. Glenn Brooks recalled Ray Werner's motion for unanimous approval this way: "Mr. President, it's clear to me that this plan has the very substantial support of the faculty, and I move that we implement it." Brooks oral history, 14 February 1996, 22–23. Also see Reid, *Colorado College: The First Century, 1874–1974*, 270–273.

WHY WAS THE BLOCK PLAN ADOPTED?

There have been many explanations given and theories proposed as to why, in the fall of 1969, the Colorado College faculty was willing to vote decisively for such an innovative and radical change in the College calendar. Glenn Brooks speculated that it was the tenor of the times.

The spring, summer, and fall of 1968 had been one of the most violent and controversial periods in American history. The year began with the Viet Cong rebels in Vietnam launching a particularly bloody attack on United States military forces in that war-torn nation. As a result of escalating domestic controversy over the Vietnam War, U.S. President Lyndon Johnson announced in late March that he would not run for reelection to the White House, thereby setting off a battle for the Democratic nomination for president. In April of 1968 the nation's premier civil rights leader, the Reverend Martin Luther King, Jr., was shot to death by an assassin in Memphis, Tennessee. Shortly thereafter, in early June, U.S. Senator Robert Kennedy was gunned down in Los Angeles the night of his surprise victory in the Democratic Party presidential primary in California. Robert Kennedy died the next day.

In August of 1968, during the Democratic National Convention, there was a riot in the streets of Chicago when anti-Vietnam War protesters were attacked, or provoked an attack, by the Chicago Police. Many of the protesters who were beaten by the uniformed police officers in the Windy City were college and university students, and the event sparked a wave of rebelliousness and anti-establishment sentiment on college and university campuses across the nation. A Republican, Richard Nixon, was elected President of the United States in November of 1968. Nixon endeavored to reduce the role of U.S. military forces in the Vietnam War, but his ordering of frequent bombing raids on North Vietnam soon made him as unpopular on college campuses as his Democratic predecessor, Lyndon Johnson, had been.

Glenn Brooks, and a number of others, concluded that this tumultuous period in the nation's history and on college and university campuses set the stage for radical change to occur in a short period of time at Colorado College. The mood of the entire nation was to criticize and review institutions of all sorts—and to try to change them for the better. And there was a general feeling that change needed to occur *quickly*.

To Glenn Brooks, the unusual thing about the Block Plan process at Colorado College was that it united the campus at a time when so many other colleges and universities were the scene of demonstrations—some of them violent—against college and university administrations. Brooks explained:

"This was a collective operation. . . . Good Lord! . . . This was the time of . . . [riots at] Columbia [University] and [the University of California at] Berkeley. And [those] places were virtually falling apart."

"And we had radical students involved in working on this plan, as well as a lot of square students, because they had a sense that something was going to happen. And they liked that idea, and they were going in and testing these mock-up schedules and so on. And I'm not aware of any significant student resistance to the change."

"[It] brings us back once again to the point that this probably couldn't have happened if there hadn't been such an atmosphere of change, educational and cultural change, in society."[21]

But there was another explanation for why Colorado College developed and adopted this innovative academic calendar. This theory held that Colorado College had long been a place of educational and academic experimentation. It began with the pioneer spirit of the College's founder, William J. Palmer, who built a new railroad, a new city, and a new college in a new part of the country. It continued with an early President of Colorado College, Edward Payson Tenney, who wrote at length of the economic opportunities and educational challenges that lay ahead in a part of the nation he labeled the New West. This commitment to innovation and change also could be seen in a string of new ideas and new programs that were adopted at Colorado College in the early 20th Century. For instance, there was the faculty exchange with Harvard University in 1911 and the New Colorado College Plan in 1931.

---

[21]Brooks oral history, 14 February 1996, 23.

The late 1950s and early 1960s were intense periods of academic invention at Colorado College. The Selected Student Program took 25 highly-qualified first year students and enrolled them in seminar-style classes with heavy reading assignments and an emphasis on classroom discussions. The Adviser Plan allowed good students to take any courses they wanted to, free from the restrictions of College requirements and major requirements, as long as the program was approved by the student's faculty adviser. The Ford Independent Study Program (FISP) was even more daring and experimental, allowing students to pursue their college education however they wished, with no specific course requirements and the student's personal study plan worked out with a faculty adviser.

In short, Colorado College had been a place of academic innovation and experimentation—one might call it academic pioneering—throughout its entire existence and particularly in the 20-year period prior to the adoption of the Block Plan. Colorado College thus was *exactly* the place where a bold and revolutionary reform such as the Block Plan would have been expected to be developed and adopted.[22]

And the Block Plan proved to be a durable reform. A subsequent President of Colorado College, Gresham Riley, liked to point out that, of all the educational experiments that were undertaken by colleges and universities in the 1960s and 1970s, only a very few survived intact for a substantial period of time. One that did survive was the Block Plan at Colorado College.[23]

Dionysus '69

Just at the moment Glenn Brooks was developing a clear picture of his Block Plan reform proposal, the Colorado College campus was suddenly engulfed in one of the most controversial events in its history. The annual January Symposium in 1969 was on the subject of *Violence* in American life. The week-long program of speakers, movies, and panel

---

[22]Judith Reid Finley, who conducted the Oral History Project at Colorado College, mentioned this line of thinking in one of her interviews with President Worner. See Worner oral history, 5 February 1985, 100.

[23]Brooks oral history, 14 February 1996, 14.

discussions had been organized by Professor Alvin Boderman of the Sociology Department.

Among the speakers was Dick Gregory, an African-American comedian turned social activist who was famous for his jokes about Black-White relations in the United States. Gregory provoked a storm of criticism in the Colorado Springs community—or at least in the Colorado Springs newspapers—when he said that the "American flag moves me about as much as a pair of dirty drawers. To me the people under the flag are more important."

There were other controversial statements at the Symposium on *Violence* which stirred up the people and the press in Colorado Springs. Michael Klonsky and John Sundstrom, two leaders of SDS (Students for a Democratic Society), a radical-liberal national students' lobby, spiced their talk with swear words rarely heard from the podium at Colorado College. In his talk Klonsky advised his audience to "join us, get the hell out of the way, or fight us."[24]

A play, performed by a troupe of actors and actresses from New York City, was presented in Armstrong Theater as part of the Symposium. The play was entitled *Dionysus '69* and had gained a measure of fame on the East Coast because of having some "nude scenes." However, it was supposedly arranged that no nude scenes would be presented at Colorado College.

It did not turn out that way. Early in the first act several members of both sexes in the *Dionysus '69* company stripped off all their clothing. Not content to just perform nude on the stage, they ran out into the auditorium and then climbed over the audience, leaping and cavorting from row to row, balancing dangerously on the backs of the auditorium chairs. Students, faculty, and just-plain-citizens of Colorado Springs found themselves looking up at the genitalia of young men and women going by less than three feet from their eyes. A number of faculty members and their spouses had enjoyed a preperformance dinner with the *Dionysus '69* cast, little suspecting that they would be seeing a lot more of their dinner guests as the evening developed.[25]

---

[24]Gregory and Klonsky quotes from Reid, *Colorado College: The First Century, 1874–1974*, 262–264.

[25]Observation of the author—and his wife.

One member of the Colorado Springs community, City Councilmember Betty Krouse, claimed she tried to flee the auditorium when the nude scene began but for some reason could not get the auditorium door open. She later said she suspected members of the *Dionysus '69* company were somehow keeping the doors closed.[26]

The news media in Colorado Springs, and also in Denver, gave heavy coverage to the fact that there had been a nude scene presented at Colorado College, apparently with the official approval of Colorado College. The minister of one of the largest churches in Colorado Springs made a personal visit to President Worner to express his concern over the moral state of the College community. One infuriated observer of these events complained to the Olin Foundation, in Minneapolis, Minnesota, and implied that the Foundation should think a bit before giving any more money to Colorado College.[27]

The student body was as electrified by *Dionysus '69* as everyone else, but in a completely different way. The nude scenes, as well as some of the ideas in the play about personal freedom, fitted very well with much of the emerging student ideology of the late 1960s and early 1970s. The students also were impressed with the fact that their own College administration had brought them *Dionysus '69*. In addition, the College was adamantly defending the theatrical group's freedom to perform and express its ideas, no matter how unconventional. The students staged a nonviolent demonstration at the Earle Flagpole to show their support for the College and its stalwart defense of "Freedom of Expression." One of the major speakers at the demonstration was Richard Schechner, the director of *Dionysus '69*, who had attained star status among the more liberal students and faculty at Colorado College.

A number of observers noted that, at a time when so many students on so many campuses were demonstrating *against* their college or university administration, the students at Colorado College were demonstrating *for* their college administration. "It was really kind of funny," President Worner later commented, "but at the time it was really very encouraging."[28]

---

[26]Recollection of the author of a conversation with Betty Krouse, c. January 1969.

[27]Worner oral history, 5 February 1985, 111–112.

[28]Worner oral history, 5 February 1985, 113.

Of course the *Dionysus '69* company had put the College administration in a very difficult position. The show was *not* to be done in the nude, but then it was done in the nude anyway. This put President Worner and the College in the position of defending an action which had not been authorized by the College in the first place. But President Worner was firm on the point that defending "Freedom of Speech" and "Freedom of Expression" was more important than making excuses for the College.

During all the commotion over *Dionysus '69*, a motion was presented and seconded to the Board of Trustees that Alvin Boderman, the Director of the Symposium, be dismissed from the faculty, and that the College should make a public apology to the Colorado Springs community. President Worner recalled that, when the motion came before the Trustees, Russell Tutt, the Chairman of the Board, said: "This is a democratic board. We'll have discussion, but before the discussion I want to say one thing. If this motion passes, there will be two resignations in two seconds: the Chairman of your Board, and the President of your College." The motion failed.[29]

If one looked beyond the nude scenes in *Dionysus '69*, which caused the major part of the commotion, the 1969 Symposium on *Violence* had made a major contribution to intellectual life at Colorado College. There had been moderate and conservative speakers as well as radical-liberals, and there had been a number of panel discussions in which all sides of the political and social issues of the late 1960s had been fully discussed. Perhaps most important, the College had provided a platform for a challenging and provocative new point of view. This was the anti-establishment attitude of the Students for a Democratic Society, and other radical groups, that was coming into political and intellectual prominence at that time. The College simply was fulfilling its traditional role as a place of innovation and experimentation.

President Worner made the point that some of the fiercest critics of the 1969 Symposium on *Violence* later came to see it as an important intellectual and cultural event. Worner said: "It's interesting. Four or five years later, when everything was put in perspective, and people learned more, then some of the very people who had just been so upset were actually very

[29]Worner oral history, 5 February 1985, 112.

proud, saying they were there, and they saw the beginnings of the SDS [Students for a Democratic Society], and everything. They were saying that as though they were all in support of our being informed as to what was going on, which, of course, was not at all the way they felt at the time."[30]

VIETNAM WAR PROTESTS

Throughout the period that the Block Plan was being designed, debated, and adopted, there was perpetual discussion and commotion on the Colorado College campus over the war in Vietnam. As the number of United States military troops in that far-off conflict progressively increased, so did tensions on college campuses throughout the nation. At Colorado College, opposition to U.S. involvement in the war on the part of some faculty and many students was heightened when the Army ROTC (Reserve Officer Training Corps) refused to allow two College men to resign from the program in their senior year. The two students were compelled to honor their commitment to serve in the U.S. Army in return for the financial support and the academic credit earned in the ROTC program.

In 1968 a chapter of SDS (Students for a Democratic Society) was organized at the College. At that time SDS was devoting its major efforts to protesting the Vietnam War. The chapter at Colorado College held two anti-war marches from the campus to downtown Colorado Springs and staged two protest demonstrations at the entrance gate to Fort Carson, the large Army base in Colorado Springs.

In 1969 some faculty and a large number of Colorado College students joined with citizens from the local community in a candlelight march to the Colorado Springs Draft Board office. In an atmosphere of memorial as well as protest, the names of the more than 46,000 U.S. military personnel who had died in the Vietnam War up to that date were read aloud.

Faculty and student opposition to U.S. involvement in Vietnam reached great intensity in the spring of 1970 when President Richard Nixon ordered U.S. military forces to invade Cambodia, a small nation

---

[30]Worner oral history, 5 February 1985, 114.

adjacent to Vietnam. The situation was made even more volatile when, during the confusion of a violent campus protest at Kent State University in Ohio, four students were shot and killed by the Ohio National Guard.

As word spread across the campus about both the invasion of Cambodia and the shootings at Kent State, the students gathered for the customary protest meeting at the Earle Flagpole. President Worner met with them, and he convinced the faculty and student leaders of the protest not to stage a boycott of classes at Colorado College. The following day, there was a faculty and student anti-war rally held in the quadrangle north of Armstrong Hall, and this time disruption of classes was proposed. At that point President Worner announced that any student who used physical force or violence to prevent students from attending classes—or prevent faculty from teaching them—would be expelled from Colorado College. Not suspended, but expelled.

On the other hand, any student who did not want to go to class to protest the war, or who wanted to speak out or demonstrate in opposition to the war, was allowed to do so. President Worner then set aside May 8, 1970, as an optional day for class attendance during which a series of discussions were led by faculty on issues involved in the war. This form of protest, the so-called "teach-in," was widely used as an intellectually acceptable way of allowing students, faculty, and administrators to express their opinions and feelings about the Vietnam War.[31]

Palmer Hall was alive with faculty, students, and townspeople the day of the May 8, 1970, teach-in. The shocking events in Cambodia and at Kent State had disturbed the wider community as well as the College community. Although most of the classes and discussions were in opposition to the Vietnam War, there were one or two in which Nixon administration policy in southeast Asia was strongly defended.

Professor Robert Loevy, a member of the Political Science Department and an active Republican Party member in Colorado Springs, gave a spirited defense of U.S. policy in Vietnam, basing his arguments strongly on the idea that the southeast Asian war was an integral

---

[31]For a description of the many Vietnam War protests at Colorado College, see Reid, *Colorado College: The First Century, 1874–1974*, 254–257, 283.

part of U.S. efforts to contain the military expansion of the Soviet Union. After Loevy completed his talk, Professor Max Lanner of the Music Department came up to him and said: "At long last I have heard a reasonable and rational defense of United States policy in Vietnam and the recent invasion of Cambodia. I won't say that I agree or disagree with it, but at least I have been able to hear it."[32]

President Worner worked hard to focus campus opposition to the Vietnam War in a non-violent direction that provided for the expression and advocacy of multiple points of view. He was helped in this effort by the political and law enforcement leadership in Colorado Springs, which was willing to grant permits for parades and indulgently redirected traffic whenever faculty and student protesters blocked Cascade or Nevada Avenues for an anti-war demonstration.

The agreement with the city government was this: the Colorado Springs Police would allow the College administration to govern the campus during anti-war protests and demonstrations, but once the College called in the city police to restore order, the police would take firm control, enforce the law, and arrests, if necessary, would be made. Fortunately, President Worner never had to call the Colorado Springs police for anything more than redirecting traffic around streets closed for anti-war demonstrations. All this was occurring at a time when, at the University of Colorado at Boulder, anti-war demonstrations went out of control, there was considerable violence, the police had to be called in, and tear gas had to be used.[33]

In one instance that President Worner recalled, community support for Colorado College war protesters came from an unexpected source. During an anti-war parade in downtown Colorado Springs (for which the city government had issued a permit), a number of bystanders were condemning the students for openly opposing the war. These bystanders also suggested that protests should not be allowed while a military action was taking place. Mrs. Jeanne Crawford, the wife of an Army General who

---

[32]Recollection of the author.

[33]Worner oral history, 5 February 1985, 118–119.

had retired in Colorado Springs, turned to the bystanders, told them who she was and who her husband was, and said: "This sounds like Nazi Germany to me. You ought to be ashamed of yourselves!"[34]

BLOCKADING CASCADE AVENUE

President Worner said there were only two instances when faculty and student protests of the Vietnam War created major problems. One occurred when the city government blocked off Cascade Avenue during an anti-war demonstration. An ambulance, followed by a doctor in his private automobile, came speeding up Cascade Avenue, headed for Penrose Hospital. The ambulance had its siren on and was transporting a patient who had just suffered a heart attack. When the ambulance reached the southern edge of the campus, the ambulance driver screeched to a stop at the police barricade and asked for permission to drive straight up Cascade Avenue through the protesting faculty and students. The police officers on duty denied the request and made the ambulance, the patient, and the doctor drive the long way around the campus. Fortunately the patient recovered, but President Worner later expressed the view that the ambulance should have been allowed to proceed up Cascade Avenue through the anti-war demonstration.

The second anti-war demonstration that caused a problem again involved the closing of Cascade Avenue. The faculty and student protesters kept the street closed from early in the morning until late in the afternoon. At 5 P.M. President Worner received a telephone call from the Colorado Springs Police Chief, who said: "Now, it's 5, and people have had the whole day. We now want them to disband there and go, [but] there is a group there refusing to do it. Will you get on the bullhorn . . . and go over and see [what] you can do?"

In the time that it took President Worner to walk from his office in Armstrong Hall to the corner of Cascade Avenue and Cache La Poudre Street, the student leaders of the protest had agreed to end the demonstration and let traffic flow again through the campus. According to

[34]Worner oral history, 5 February 1985, 118.

Worner, the students were saying words to the effect of: "Look! We've done our job! We've had the day! Enough is enough." In making the decision to reopen the street at 5 P.M., Worner noted, the students overcame the arguments of a number of non-students present, some of them Colorado College faculty members, who wanted to provoke a confrontation with the police by keeping the street closed.[35]

POLITICAL CAMPAIGNING

There was one positive and enduring result from all the concern on campus following the invasion of Cambodia and the deaths at Kent State. The students at Colorado College, along with students at other colleges and universities across the nation, asked to be given academic credit for working in congressional election campaigns in the fall of 1970. The students believed they might best affect U.S. policy in Vietnam by supporting those candidates for the U.S. Senate and the U.S. House of Representatives who shared their views on the war issue.

The Block Plan was slated to go into effect in the fall of 1970, so there was an opportunity to respond to the students' request within the Block Plan format. Robert Loevy, a Professor of Political Science with an interest in experiential education, designed a one-block course entitled *Political Campaigning* which allowed a student to work full-time for three-and-one-half weeks in an election campaign of the student's choosing. The student could go anywhere in the nation to work in the election campaign. In order to earn a passing grade, the student was required to keep a daily journal of his or her "thoughts and conclusions" about that campaign in particular and United States politics in general. The course was adopted by the faculty at one of the last faculty meetings of the year. A sizeable number of students used the course to try to have an impact on the outcome of the 1970 congressional elections.

The course proved especially popular in the spring and fall of 1972, when more than 200 Colorado College students used it to work in George McGovern's presidential election campaign. A Democratic U.S. Senator

---

[35]President Worner's recollections of Vietnam War protests at Colorado College are from Worner oral history, 5 February 1985, 118–120.

from South Dakota, McGovern ran for president on a strong anti-war platform and received widespread support from college and university students across the nation. Thanks to the newly adopted Block Plan, Colorado College students made particularly valuable interns for the McGovern effort. They could work full-time for the three-and-a-half-week block and did not have to fit their work schedule around a semester-long class schedule. Furthermore, they could be sent anywhere in the nation to campaign because they were not tied to the Colorado College campus in Colorado Springs by other courses. Right off the bat, the Block Plan was demonstrating its freedom and versatility, and to people located far beyond the Colorado College campus.

The *Political Campaigning* course proved so popular that a companion course, *Governmental Participation*, was subsequently instituted. This course permitted students to go anywhere in the nation, but particularly to Washington, D.C., to work in a governmental office. Students earned a passing grade after they turned in a paper detailing and analyzing the work of that particular governmental office. Both *Political Campaigning* and *Governmental Participation* were still an active part of the Colorado College curriculum in the late 1990s.

OTHER CHANGES

The coming of the Block Plan, the ruckus over *Dionysus '69*, and protests against the Vietnam War were not the only signs of deep and enduring change at Colorado College in the late 1960s and early 1970s. In the spring of 1968, after a lengthy and hard-fought faculty debate, Saturday classes were eliminated. Then, in response to student demands, the College agreed to begin serving 3.2 beer to students over the age of 18 in the Hub snack bar in Rastall Center. President Worner had to take out a liquor license as the major proprietor of an establishment serving alcoholic beverages. That meant President Worner had to go downtown, have his photograph taken, and be fingerprinted. A copy of the liquor license, complete with President Worner's photograph (some jokingly called it his "mug shot"), was posted on the wall of the Hub.[36]

[36]Worner oral history, 5 February 1985, 121.

Honors-Credit-No Credit

In an effort to create a less grade-dominated academic atmosphere, the faculty adopted an Honors-Credit-No Credit grading system to replace the traditional A-B-C-D-F system. The only real effect of the change was to eliminate the B and the D grades, lumping all the students who performed at the B, C, and D level into the Credit category. The new grading system was an innovation at Colorado College but was not unique to the College. Many colleges and universities were experimenting with their grading systems, almost all of them moving in the direction of less strict grading, as the new Colorado College system did.

Alas, the Honors-Credit-No Credit grading system at Colorado College proved to be a disappointment. Senior year students applying to graduate school and professional school were at a particular disadvantage, because many graduate institutions simply converted the Credit grade to a C, thereby lowering the grade point average of any student who had earned a B in a course and only had a Credit recorded. Some of the more responsible graduate and professional schools tried to eliminate this unfairness by asking professors to convert a student's Credit grade into a B, C, or D grade. As more and more professors spent more and more time converting Credit grades into their "letter" equivalents, it became clear the Honors-Credit-No Credit grading system was hurting rather than helping.

After a couple of years the Colorado College faculty voted to go to an A-B-C-No Credit system with an optional PASS-No Credit system. At the start of taking a class, students were required to tell the Registrar if they were taking the course "for grades" or "Pass-No Credit." This new system ended the reporting difficulties with the graduate and professional schools and allowed those students who wanted to take *all* their courses "for grades" to do so. As it turned out, the vast majority of the students took most of their courses "for grades."

Coed Dormitories

Another major change in the late 1960s and early 1970s was the relaxation of the dormitory rules that had long been used to supervise social relationships between men and women students. Had there really been a time when young women could only visit with young men in the "date parlors" of the women's dormitories or on daytime and early evening walks around the campus? In 1969 residence hall policies at Colorado College were changed to permit students to entertain members of the opposite sex in their dormitory rooms. The prohibition against beer and liquor in the dormitories was lifted, thus only Colorado state statutes limited the right of students to drink alcoholic beverages in their rooms. Each residence hall was permitted to make and enforce its own social rules, with those halls that voted to do so being allowed to have both men and women residents. Mathias Hall, the large men's dormitory located at the northeastern corner of the campus, was the first dormitory to "go coed."[37] What would Miss Loomis have said?

EXIT THE *TIGER*—ENTER THE *CATALYST*

The rapid pace of change at Colorado College also extended to extracurricular activities. The editors of the *Tiger*, the student newspaper, were demanding more freedom to print whatever they wanted to, even if what they were printing was highly offensive to certain people or groups. This included everything from four-letter words to unorthodox religious ideas to anti-establishment political opinions. In some cases the things being printed were potentially libelous. In other instances the *Tiger* was introducing ideas and advocating positions with which the College administration did not wish to be associated.

An effort was made to preserve this new-found student "freedom of expression" but at the same time protect the College from libel suits and make clear that the opinions expressed in the *Tiger* were not the official views of the College. A new corporation, completely separate from the College, was formed to publish the student newspaper and a number of other student publications. Named Cutler Publications, this new corporation changed the name of the student newspaper to the *Catalyst*. After 70 years of continuous use at Colorado College, the *Tiger* name for the student newspaper was retired. Old timers at the College disliked seeing that traditional name dropped, but there was considerable determination to

---

[37]Reid, *Colorado College: The First Century, 1874–1974*, 261.

let the students, and not the faculty or administration, run the student newspaper the students' way.[38]

A Name Change?

Change was so completely in the air at Colorado College in the late 1960s and early 1970s that Glenn Brooks actually gave some thought to changing the name of the College. The main reason for proposing this particular idea was that so many other institutions of higher learning in Colorado were using the name Colorado. There was the University of Colorado at Boulder, Colorado State University, the University of Colorado at Colorado Springs, the University of Colorado at Denver, and several more. One option which Brooks considered was to adopt the name of Palmer College, for locator/benefactor General William Jackson Palmer. Like so many other ideas being kicked around at the time, the name change for the College was talked about but eventually discarded.[39]

Academic Computing

One of the biggest changes in the late 1960s and early 1970s was little noticed at the time. In the northeast corner of the glass-windowed lounge in Olin Hall, a teletype machine had been installed and hardwired to a single telephone line. Thus, in this simple manner, did the computer age come to the academic program at Colorado College.

The teletype was connected to a time-sharing computer owned and operated by General Electric. The computer supposedly was located in the city of Los Angeles. A time-sharing computer was one that served a large number of customers simultaneously, all of the customers being connected to the computer by telephone lines. Faculty and student users at Colorado College wrote their computer programs in the BASIC language, a new computer language specifically designed to use simple three-letter words, such as NEW for starting a new program, GET for getting

---

[38]The *Catalyst* distributed its first issue on September 11, 1969. See Reid, *Colorado College: The First Century, 1874–1974*, 264–265.

[39]Glenn Brooks proposed and discussed his name change idea in a number of conversations with the author and several other faculty members during the 1968–1970 period.

an old program, and RUN for running the existing program. These computer programs were typed into the teletype keyboard, transmitted to the time-sharing computer, and the results of the calculations were sent back and printed on roll paper by the teletype machine. If users wanted to make an electronic copy of a computer program or "store" some data, the teletype would "punch a copy" by putting holes in a narrow paper tape. The user could bring back the paper tape and "read in" the program and the data the next time he or she wanted to use the computer.

The two moving forces behind the introduction of computing at Colorado College were Wilson Gately, Professor of Mathematics, and Gary Bitter, also a member of the Math faculty. While at Colorado College, Gary Bitter wrote a handbook for students using time-sharing computers entitled *Basic For Beginners*. Other early computer users on the faculty were Werner Heim in the Biology Department, William Hochman in the History Department, and Robert Loevy in the Political Science Department. Professor Hochman wrote a number of computer programs in the BASIC language, and one of them, Bibliokeeper, was made commercially available to help students and scholars keep a bibliography on a given subject. Professor Loevy composed a number of computer simulations in Political Science, such as a bill going through Congress or a candidate running for the Democratic nomination for U.S. President, that later were distributed with a well-known American Government text book.[40]

The use of computers expanded rapidly at Colorado College. Soon there were additional teletype terminals installed in Olin Hall lounge, and entire classes were coming in to learn how to use the computer. The Math Department began teaching computer programming in the BASIC language as a credit course, and the Political Science Department offered a senior tutorial in the use of computers to solve governmental and political problems. The activity grew too large for Olin Hall lounge, so a small computing center, filled with more than ten teletype machines connected to a time-sharing computer, was opened on the second floor of Palmer Hall adjacent to the Math Department.

---

[40]Burns, Peltason, and Cronin, *Government By The People*, 14th ed. (Englewood Cliffs, N.J.: Prentice-Hall, 1990), Aviii.

The students of Colorado College quickly discovered how to use the new computers as entertainment devices. Particularly popular was a computer game that challenged the player to successfully land a rocket ship on the moon. If a player gave the retro-rockets too much fuel, or too little, the rocket ship crashed on the surface of the moon, leaving a large crater thoughtfully named in honor of the now deceased player.[41]

ASSOCIATED COLLEGES OF THE MIDWEST

In the fall of 1969 another enduring change took place at Colorado College. President Worner and Dean Drake decided to have the College join the ACM (Associated Colleges Of The Midwest). This consortium of liberal arts colleges had originally been founded as an athletic league, but it had come to offer a number of joint-academic programs, such as a study program in Costa Rica and an urban education program in Chicago. Colorado College did not join the athletic association run by the ACM but did decide to participate in the academic programs.

Joining the Associated Colleges of the Midwest greatly broadened the international offerings available to the students at Colorado College. The ACM added a number of interesting and exciting international programs in the period after Colorado College joined it, such as semester-long programs in India and Japan. There also was a semester program to study art and literature in London, England, and Florence, Italy. One of the most popular ACM programs with Colorado College students was the Urban Semester, which enabled students to live and study in working class neighborhoods in Chicago, Illinois, and personally observe the ethnic variety and economic disparities of a large United States city.[42]

WASHINGTON SEMESTER

In the fall of 1969 Glenn Brooks decided that the time had come for Colorado College to make a semester-long experience in Washington, D.C., available to its Political Science students. Brooks arranged for two

---

[41] Recollection of the author.

[42] The ACM colleges were Beloit, Carleton, Coe, Cornell, Grinnell, Knox, Lawrence, Macalester, Monmouth, Ripon, and St. Olaf. Colleges that joined after Colorado College included Lake Forest and the undergraduate college at the University of Chicago.

students, Timothy Marx and Barbara Snow, to attend the Washington Semester program at American University on a trial basis. Under the Washington Semester program, students from colleges and universities throughout the country came to the nation's capital to take courses, attend seminars, and intern in government and government-related offices. The students earned academic credit while at the same time getting a hands-on experience with government-in-action.

Timothy Marx and Barbara Snow brought back favorable reports on their Washington Semester experiences, particularly the internship programs. American University, Marx and Snow said, was able to place interns in congressional offices on Capitol Hill, at the White House, in lobbyist offices, and with the major television networks and well-known newspaper columnists. Based on Marx's and Snow's experience, Glenn Brooks recommended to the faculty that the Washington Semester be made a part of the Colorado College curriculum. Professor Robert Loevy of the Political Science Department was designated to advise the program. Over the years the Washington Semester became one of the most durable and popular off-campus programs at Colorado College.

Professor Loevy served more than 25 years as adviser to the Washington Semester program. Such lengthy service to the student body on the part of a Colorado College professor was not all that unusual. Professor of Economics William Barton served more than two decades as the College adviser to graduating students who were applying to law school and business school. "I loved the job," Barton said. "I got to spend a lot of time getting to know many of our brightest, most accomplished, and most promising students."[43]

EL POMAR SPORTS CENTER

The building spree that began at Colorado College following World War II continued unabated during the late 1960s and early 1970s. In the spring of 1969, El Pomar Foundation announced a gift to the College of

---

[43]Author's notes, interview with William Barton, Professor Emeritus of Economics at Colorado College, 23 June 1998.

$1.6 million to cover the cost of constructing a new sports center. The new building, to be built of brick, was located to the west of Honnen Ice Rink and Schlessman Pool. It included a large gymnasium with ample space for seating sports spectators. This filled a real need at Colorado College, because the existing gym was almost completely lacking in adequate spectator space. The new sports center also included a practice gymnasium and a reasonably large artificial turf area where College athletes could practice their skills in inclement weather.

In addition the new sports center introduced some new sports to the administrators, faculty, and students of Colorado College. The building included handball and squash courts, facilities that had not previously been available to the College community. The administrators and faculty seemed particularly taken with the handball facilities, with lunchtime often the favorite time for hard-fought handball contests. The project also included the construction of six tennis courts adjacent to the new building at the eastern edge of Monument Valley Park.

President Worner later commented that it was El Pomar Foundation's idea, and not his, to pay for the College's new sports center. Worner said the Foundation was very skilled at anticipating the needs of the College and proposing to pay for new academic programs and new buildings without first being asked by the College. "I'll tell you something most people will never believe," Worner said. "Through my years of working as Dean and as President . . . , I never once asked El Pomar . . . for anything. . . . It was my job to keep them well informed, and I would answer questions, but I never said, 'We need this and that.'"[44]

President Worner also pointed out that El Pomar Foundation timed the announcement of its gift to build the new sports center so as to mitigate the negative publicity that came to the College from the *Dionysus '69* performance. "That announcement coming at the time it did was no accident," Worner said with a chuckle.[45]

---

[44]Worner oral history, 5 February 1985, 75, 76.

[45]Worner oral history, 5 February 1985, 113.

THE BLOCK PLAN IMPLEMENTED

It was in this atmosphere of widespread and rapid change that Colorado College prepared to implement the newly-adopted Block Plan. During the spring of 1970, Professor Brooks headed up a temporary Planning Office to help prepare the campus for the fall 1970 shift to modular learning. A mock course registration was held to see how registration would work under the new system, and that helped get a number of "bugs" out of the process. Then registration was held "for real," and the first group of Colorado College students in history was signed up to take just one course at a time, usually with just one professor.

Computers were used to facilitate course registration under the Block Plan. The Registrar was James A. (Al) Johnson, who also was a Professor of Economics. Johnson devised a system of course registration where each student was assigned a fixed number of "points" that could then be used to "bid" on the courses the student most wanted to take. The students who bid the highest number of points on a particular course were given priority on getting into the course. It was the equivalent of "a free market in which all the participants had equal incomes (equal numbers of points to bid with)."[46]

This "point system" was particularly needed because of the 25-student limit per course that was an integral part of the Block Plan. For popular courses, the point system was designed to guarantee that the students who most wanted to take the course were the students who got into the course.

This "point system" required keeping track of and processing a vast amount of data. There was considerable speculation that, if Registrar Johnson had not devised a way of doing the Block Plan registration on a computer, the Block Plan might not have functioned successfully.

One of the major underlying ideas of the Block Plan was that each course would be taught in a "course room," and that the course room could be modified by the students and the professor to suit the particular course being taught. Thus a course room for an Art History course could

---

[46]Professor of Economics Mike Bird made this comparison of the Block Plan "point system" to "a free market with equal incomes." Mike Bird, memo to author, 6 May 1998.

be decorated with paintings and works of sculpture, or the course room for a course in American Politics could have the walls filled with maps showing United States voting trends.

Glenn Brooks regarded the "course room" concept as a very important facet of the Block Plan, and he and his Planning Office staff spent a great deal of time locating good course rooms in which classes could meet. To create a more relaxed and conversational atmosphere, a number of course rooms designated as seminar rooms were furnished with extra-comfortable sofas and chairs.

A number of faculty at Colorado College quickly took advantage of the unique scheduling opportunities offered by the Block Plan. An Anthropology class was scheduled to go on a three-week dig at an archeological site in southwest Colorado. Education students were slated to devote their entire day to student-teaching in Colorado Springs public schools. The Geology Department made plans to pile students and camping gear into buses and take its classes on one and two-week "rock chopping" trips into the Rocky Mountains.

And then, in September of 1970, it was the first day of the first Block One. Each student was to take nine blocks during the 1970–1971 academic year. Each faculty member was to teach nine blocks. In a time of widespread national discord and rapid change, one of the greatest academic experiments in Colorado College history was begun.

CHAPTER 7

At 100 Years

The Block Plan got off to an auspicious start at Colorado College. In the year that the new program was announced, admission applications jumped to 3,045, an increase of a thousand over the previous year. The exciting new calendar also attracted attention in academic donor circles. The Ford Foundation gave the College incentive funds totaling $150,000 to help meet the expenses of implementing the plan. At the end of the first year, 1970–71, an evaluation conducted by Associate Dean Max Taylor and a group of students revealed that 89 percent of the student body liked the new plan. A majority of the students supported continuing the Block Plan "without modification."[1]

The implementation of the Block Plan inspired additional academic innovations at the College. A group of faculty in the Humanities, the Social Sciences, and the Natural Sciences created a new course named *Renaissance Culture.* This course was three blocks long and sought to accomplish in the classroom what Renaissance scholars accomplished—an intellectual mixing of the classical thought of the Greeks and the Romans with modern thought.

The course was open only to entering students. There were two professors teaching in each of the three blocks, so before the course was over the students had been taught by a total of six professors. The emphasis was on team teaching with the students exposed to a multiplicity of ideas and a variety of teaching styles. A major reason for creating the *Renaissance Culture* course was to show the variety of intellectual and pedagogical purposes that could be served under the Block Plan.

---

[1]Reid, *Colorado College: The First Century, 1874–1974,* 273.

Among the faculty "founders" of the *Renaissance Culture* course were professors Timothy Fuller from the Political Science Department, Robert McJimsey from History, Joseph Pickle from Religion, Harvey Rabbin from Philosophy, Mark Stavig from English, James Trissel from Art, and Wilbur Wright from Physics. Also participating was Professor George Drake, of the History Department, who was the Dean of Colorado College when the Block Plan was adopted and implemented.[2]

THE IMMOBILIZED FACULTY

Almost at the very moment the Block Plan was instituted at Colorado College, there was a dramatic change in the economic mobility of the faculty. Prior to the early 1970s there had been a shortage of college teachers in the United States, and faculty members had been able to move from job to job—and institution to institution—with relative ease. A number of faculty members would gain tenure at a particular college or university and remain there for most of their teaching careers, but many others changed college teaching jobs frequently, more or less confident there would always be another job waiting for them at another campus.

The Baby Boom generation, the unusually large number of children born in the years following World War II, began going to graduate school in the late 1960s and earning M.A. and Ph.D. degrees. The result, by the early 1970s, was a rapidly increasing number of candidates for employment as faculty members at colleges and universities. The college-level "teacher shortage" of the early 1960s suddenly turned into a "teacher oversupply."

Colleges and universities did the logical thing. With a steady stream of inexpensive but well-trained graduate students pouring out of the nation's leading graduate universities, colleges and universities began filling all their vacancies with these new Ph.D.s (or almost Ph.D.s) rather than hire mid-career faculty from other institutions. The Baby Boom Ph.D.s cost less money than their older, experienced, middle-aged competitors, but they might be just as good as teachers or writers.

---

[2]*Renaissance Culture* proved to be a durable addition to the Colorado College curriculum. It was offered during the 1998–1999 academic year. It continued to count for three units of credit, have six professors teaching over the three blocks, and be open only to first year students.

The result was that colleges and universities, including Colorado College, suddenly had a tenured faculty that was *not* going to move on to other institutions. Faculty members with tenure in the early 1970s were suddenly "frozen in place," unlikely to get a job at any other institution of higher learning and thus planning to make a lifetime career of their present job.

This sudden change in the status of the faculty also could be viewed this way. Prior to the early 1970s Colorado College had a relatively small number of tenured faculty who devoted their entire teaching careers to Colorado College. After the early 1970s, almost every faculty member who achieved tenure planned to stay at the College "for life."

But there was a positive side to this phenomenon. The reduced mobility of the Colorado College faculty caused the faculty to become the most permanent and long-lasting group in the College community. Students came-and-went at the College, most graduating and moving on after the standard four years. The College President, and most other administrators, would likely serve between 10 and 20 years. But after 1970 most faculty members were putting in, or planned to put in, 30-year to 40-year teaching careers at the College. This gave the faculty a commitment to the College, and a long-term interest in the well-being of the College, that previously had not been so strong.

TENURE TRAUMA

The flip side of the loss of faculty mobility was the intense pressure placed on young Ph.D.s and Ph.D. candidates looking for jobs. Whereas previously the College had to struggle to attract strong faculty members, there was by the early 1970s an abundance of willing and qualified candidates for every faculty vacancy. By the end of the decade of the 1970s, there often were more than 100 applicants for any faculty position advertised by the College.

The result was intense pressure on the young scholars who got jobs at Colorado College to make tenure. The competition for college and university jobs was so severe that most of the young people with entry-level jobs believed they would never get another chance to teach at the college level if they did not get tenure at Colorado College. Those who did not get tenure would be forced back out into a "killer" job market, but they would be too old and too expensive to compete very well with the new Ph.D.s still coming out of the graduate schools.

George Drake, the Dean of Colorado College, became concerned about these pressures on the younger, untenured faculty members and decided to meet with them to give them some reassurance. The College would evaluate them fairly, Drake said, and many of them would earn permanent, tenured status on the faculty. But Dean Drake could not guarantee tenure to any particular young faculty member at the meeting, and the group began venting their frustrations with an impossibly competitive job market and the intense personal pressure that had put them under. They complained long and hard to a Dean who could do nothing specific to help them.

Prior to the meeting George Drake told some friends that he was "going into the lions' den with the young faculty on the tenure issue." After the somewhat rancorous and complaint-filled meeting was over, the word began spreading among the older faculty and administrators that Dean Drake had gone "into the lions' den with the young faculty" and had been "eaten alive."[3]

Another change was taking place in the status and role of the faculty at Colorado College. More of the faculty, particularly the younger faculty, had spouses who worked full-time outside the home. This put pressure on these faculty members to go home early in the day to help with child care and other household chores. As more of the faculty spent less time on campus, the faculty became less available to the students in the late afternoon and in the evenings. It became noticeable that, after 4 P.M., the College belonged mainly to the students. There no longer was a substantial faculty and administrative presence on campus except for the residence hall staff.[4]

WOMEN'S RIGHTS

Throughout the early 1970s increasing attention was paid to women's rights at Colorado College. As the decade began, the Admissions Office was pursuing a policy of accepting twice as many men as women into the College.

---

[3]Recollection of the author. Dean Drake held the meeting with untenured faculty in the early 1970s.

[4]Brooks oral history, 14 February 1996, 53.

More men than women were seeking a college education at that time, and even women students acknowledged that having twice as many men as women on the campus created a beneficial social situation for the women.

Ayuda, an activist women's rights group, was organized in the fall of 1971. This new student organization demanded that there be equal numbers of men and women in both the student body and on the faculty. The faculty Admissions Policy Committee gave a somewhat half-hearted response to this demand for an equal enrollment policy. The committee recommended that "an even balance of men and women students be sought, but not at the sacrifice of social, geographical and economic quality or the quality of special programs such as athletics, music and drama."[5]

The march of history was with Ayuda and not the faculty Admissions Policy Committee. Throughout the decades of the 1970s and the 1980s, the percentage of women in the student body progressively increased until, by the early 1990s, there were as many women students as men students at Colorado College.

Ayuda also demanded that the College provide free gynecological services for women students at the Boettcher Health Center. Ayuda said it wanted the College "to provide education necessary for insuring students against possible results of sex, i.e., venereal disease and/or pregnancy."[6]

At first the College reaffirmed its policy of referring women students to local Colorado Springs doctors for their sexual health needs, but eventually the policy was changed and an entire range of gynecological services were made available to women students at Boettcher. These services expanded over the ensuing years. Condoms were made readily available—to men students as well as women—and support groups were organized to help students deal with the problems, both mental and physical, of contracting venereal diseases such as herpes and chlamydia.[7]

---

[5]Reid, *Colorado College: The First Century, 1874–1974*, 278.

[6]Reid, *Colorado College: The First Century, 1874–1974*, 278.

[7]Kory Goldsmith and Shirin Day, "Gynecological Care To Begin; Baker, Langdon Start Nov. 29," *Catalyst*, 16 November 1979, 1. Annie Armstrong, "Health Center M.D. Explains S.T.D.s; Reynolds Concerned About V.D.," *Catalyst*, 7 February 1997, 3. For the full range of gynecological and sexual counseling services that were offered by the College in the late 1990s, see the *Boettcher Bulletin*, published by the Boettcher Health Center and the Student Health Advisory Committee, for the 1997–1998 academic year.

FROM "RULES" TO "SUPPORT GROUPS"

By this time it had become obvious that a major change was taking place in the way the College dealt with its students—both men and women. Prior to the late 1960s and the early 1970s, the College had sought to "protect" students with strict rules governing their personal and social behavior. Rules forbade students to have alcohol in the dorms, put men and women in separate dormitories with no visitation rights, and required women students to return to their dormitory rooms by a certain hour of the night. All of these rules and regulations were designed to prevent students from getting into damaging situations in the first place. They were based on the concept of "in loco parentis," that the College took the place of the students' parents in regulating behavior and preventing harmful consequences.

By allowing students—both men and women—to entertain members of the opposite sex in their dormitory rooms, the College began heading in a different direction. Instead of "protecting" its students, the College began adopting policies and programs that helped the students deal with the possible consequences of their newly liberated behavior. There were drug support groups for students with drug problems and alcohol support groups for students with alcohol problems. Eventually even "morning after" contraceptives became available at Boettcher to try and limit the effects of student behavior "after the fact."

Glenn Brooks lamented that the College had passed out of an age when "rules" were used to control student behavior and had entered an age when "support groups" had to be organized to help students deal with the consequences of their behavior. "I regret that we seem to need these kinds of counseling services and support groups and so on," Brooks said, "but I guess that's part of our new reality."[8]

THE WOMEN'S COMMISSION

As with so many student groups, the initial women's political organization, Ayuda, eventually faded from the campus scene. But the issue of equal rights for women did not fade. In 1973, in an effort to dramatize the

[8]Brooks oral history, 14 February 1996, 55.

lack of equal locker facilities for men and women in El Pomar Sports Center, a group of women invaded one of the men's locker rooms and staged a protest "shower-in."

In 1974 a Women's Commission, a more permanent group, was formed to represent women's rights and women's interests at Colorado College. One of the new group's goals was to see that there was more teaching about women and women's culture in the academic courses at the College. It was argued that "a feminist in every classroom" would encourage the professors to teach about the accomplishments—and ideas—of women as well as men.

Another goal of the Women's Commission was to support the existing Women's Studies program at the College and to develop a Women's Studies major. The Commission made it clear that the goal was to discover and record the literary and historical achievements of women, not, as some critics had charged, "create" such a literature and history. As a first step in that process, the Women's Commission prepared an extensive bibliography of books about women in every area of learning and distributed copies of it to every member of the faculty.

The Women's Commission eventually gained enough power to play a significant role in the important campus issues of faculty hiring and retention.[9]

GAY RIGHTS

An organization representing homosexual males, the Gay Liberation Front, sought recognition from the student government and asked to be allowed to hold meetings on campus. The student government, the Colorado College Campus Association (CCCA), recognized the new group, an action that was promptly vetoed by President Worner as not in the best interests of the College. Worner argued the major pressure to recognize the gay rights movement was coming from off campus and not from within the student body.

---

[9]Reid, *Colorado College: The First Century, 1874–1974*, 294. Vicki Ziegler, "Explanation Of Goals Of The Women's Commission," *Catalyst*, 25 January 1975, 5. Gail Bradney, "Women's Commission Strives To Improve Education At CC," *Catalyst*, 14 May 1976, 5.

This led to a major disagreement between the College President and the student government. The student leaders argued that recognition of a social and political movement was a matter "primarily of student concern." Then the American Civil Liberties Union became involved in the controversy, threatening to sue the College for trying to exclude the Gay Liberation Front from campus intellectual and political life. President Worner appointed an ad hoc faculty and student committee to study the problem. The committee recommended an end to all discrimination against the gay rights movement at Colorado College.

The following fall the student government sponsored and financed a mini-Symposium on homosexuality entitled *Same Sex Life Styles.* The cause of gay rights at Colorado College was strongly supported by Joe Simitian, the editor of the *Catalyst*, who used the student newspaper to give maximum coverage to gay movement issues. Three national leaders of the gay rights movement came to Colorado College to speak at the *Same Sex* mini-Symposium.[10]

CRIME PROBLEMS

Personal security issues were propelled to the forefront early in 1972 when a woman student, returning to her dormitory from a fraternity party, was abducted on San Rafael Street just north of Tutt Library. A non-student campus hanger-on, who was well-known to a number of faculty and students, overpowered the woman and locked her in the back of his homemade camping vehicle. He drove away with her, heading north on Nevada Avenue and then west on Uintah Street.

A member of the faculty, Professor of Philosophy Harvey Rabbin, witnessed the crime and immediately reported it to campus security officers. Because dormitory rules for women, with their "sign-in" and "sign-out" procedures, had recently been abolished at Colorado College, there was no way for the College administration to know who had been abducted or if the person was a Colorado College student. Twenty-four hours went by be-

[10]Reid, *Colorado College: The First Century, 1874–1974*, 278, 283–284. Also see Gail Bradney, "CC Woman Deals With Gay Life," *Catalyst*, 28 January 1977, 5. Penny Merritt, "Gay Students Discuss Their Experience; At Home And Here At C.C.," *Catalyst*, 16 May 1980, 7. Joanne Barker, "Is C.C. Hostile To Homosexuals," *Catalyst*, 17 January 1986, 5.

fore College officials could establish the name of the woman student who had been attacked and that she was, indeed, missing.

By then it was too late. The man drove to a remote spot on the Rampart Range Road and assaulted the woman in his camping vehicle. When she attempted to escape, he shot her with a rifle as she ran away. He left her to die in the bitter winter cold on Rampart Range Road, and she succumbed the next day from both the gunshot wound and exposure. The man was subsequently apprehended by the police, tried for the crime, and imprisoned.

The abduction and murder of a woman student sent shock waves through the Colorado College community. Reluctantly the College administration reviewed the noble concept of an "open campus" and began to make some compromises. Identification cards were issued to both the students and the faculty, and the new I.D. cards had to be shown when taking a book out of the library, using an athletic facility, entering a dormitory, etc. The campus security guards, previously provided by the Burns Detective Agency, were employed directly by the College and the number of guards increased.[11]

A major information campaign was launched to try to make faculty, students, and staff more aware of crime and security issues. Women students were encouraged to wear whistles around their necks—and to be certain to blow their whistles loudly in any situation where they sensed possible danger.[12] The College eventually created a new post, Administrative Assistant To The Dean For Security Education, and put that person to work full-time sensitizing everyone in the College community to be on guard against criminals.[13]

---

[11]Jennifer Morgan, "Safety Sargents Suggest Security For Saving Stuff," *Catalyst*, 14 February 1975, 2. Anne Reifenberg, "Lee Parks: CC's Rocky Mountain Steve McGarrett," *Catalyst*, 10 October 1975, 3.

[12]Photograph: "Hear The Whistles Blow!" *Catalyst*, 17 January 1975, 3. "Buy And Use A Whistle," *Catalyst*, 24 January 1975, 4.

[13]Gregg E. Easterbrook, "Amid Confusion, Controversy: Dwigans Appointed To Security Education Post," *Catalyst*, 21 November 1975, 1. The first Administrative Assistant To The Dean For Security Education was Donna Dwigans, a recent graduate of the College.

The fraternities set up an on-call escort service for women students for the hours of darkness from dusk to dawn. A woman student needing to move about the campus after dark could call a telephone extension and a male escort would be sent over to walk with her as she made her way from one building to another. A number of women students refused to use the escort service, preferring to rely on self-defense techniques or take their chances.

There even were accusations, never substantiated, that the fraternity men were using the escort service as a convenient way "to meet girls." The nighttime escort service apparently worked well for a considerable number of women students, however, because it became a permanent and durable part of the Colorado College scene. In subsequent years a variety of men's organizations on campus joined the fraternity men in providing escorts.[14]

DRUG ISSUES

A different kind of crime problem presented itself to the College administration in the form of student use of mind-altering drugs, particularly marijuana. In the fall of 1972 five students were charged with using marijuana in Mathias Hall. They were given the choice of voluntary temporary withdrawal from the College or facing disciplinary charges that could result in permanent expulsion. Many students, with strong editorial support from the *Catalyst*, made known their opposition to state and national drug laws and opposed the College administration's support of those drug laws. A special issue of the *Catalyst* called for the resignation of the administrator charged with enforcing drug policy in the dormitories.

The student government at that time, the Colorado College Campus Association (CCCA), was governed by a council composed of students, faculty members, and administrators. The CCCA voted 9–5 to support the College drug policy, but it was faculty and administrator votes that caused the motion of support to pass. The students then proposed a new student government constitution that would eliminate the faculty and ad-

[14]Alan Gottlieb, "Dwigans Revises Escort System," *Catalyst*, 16 January 1976, 1. Anne Reifenberg, "New Escort Service Rolling," *Catalyst*, 13 February 1976, 1.

ministration representatives on the CCCA council, thereby giving total control of the student government to the students. The College faculty rejected the proposed new student government constitution as inconsistent with the educational purposes of the College.[15]

The drug issue continued to divide the campus, but the College had no choice but to enforce national and state laws that made the possession of certain mind-altering drugs a crime.[16] College administrators also had to deal with the effects of the emerging student drug culture. Often students would be unable to meet their academic responsibilities due to addiction to illegal drugs and would have to drop out or be suspended from the College.

GROWTH ISSUES—WORLDWIDE AND ON THE CAMPUS

The early 1970s were a time when there was considerable concern, particularly on the part of the College faculty, about "growth" issues. World population growth had led to increasing sensitivity about environmental problems, so much so that in 1970 the January Symposium was on the subject of ecology, the branch of science devoted to studying the interrelationship of organisms and their environment. "Small is beautiful" became one of the favorite sayings of some faculty and students, and a neo-Malthusian concern gripped many members of the College community as they worried that the steady increase in the number of human beings on planet earth was going to someday exhaust the supply of crucial natural resources, such as coal and petroleum.

There also were worries about the steady rise in enrollment at Colorado College. By 1974 enrollment had reached 1,800 students, an increase of 50 percent over the previous ten years. The College administration had taken advantage of the World War II Baby Boom and the rapid post-War population growth in Colorado, slowly increasing the

---

[15]Reid, *Colorado College: The First Century, 1874–1974*, 284–285.

[16]Ed Goldstein, "C.C.—Police Relationship: Arrest Sparks Questions," *Catalyst*, 1 December 1978, 5. Mark Engman, "Two Arrested In Conspiracy To Sell Cocaine," *Catalyst*, 9 November 1979, 1. "'Window Shopping': C.C. Drug Market," *Catalyst*, 12 October 1984, 1. Brian Armstrong, "Drug Policy: Compassion, Not Hardcore Enforcement," *Catalyst*, 12 October 1984, 11. Lisa Cain, "Student Initiates New Course Focusing On Drugs," *Catalyst*, 31 March 1989, 13.

number of students with each passing year. Older faculty members in particular believed that the increase in the size of the student body was changing the character of the College, doing away with the smaller, friendlier, and more intimate atmosphere they had found so warming and charming when they first came to the College.

Colorado College eventually put a cap on student enrollment. The size of the student body was set at more than 1,900 but less than 2,000 students. This limitation on enrollment growth was a major event in the College's history. It meant that future buildings constructed at the College could be tailored to a student body that was always going to number slightly less than 2,000 persons. Also, as the size of the population of the United States and the state of Colorado continued to grow, Colorado College made itself more "selective" by setting a definite limit on the size of its student body.

GROWTH IN COLORADO SPRINGS

But the most serious growth concerns were directed at the city of Colorado Springs, which had become a military town during World War II and had experienced rapid population expansion as a result. The advent of the Vietnam War had further stimulated growth in the Springs as the local U.S. Army base, Fort Carson, enlarged its training activities. According to a number of sources, by the early 1970s Colorado Springs was one of the fastest growing cities in the nation.

One person who particularly reacted to the problem of rapid population growth in Colorado Springs was Professor of Political Science Fred Sondermann. He had served on the City Planning Commission in the early 1960s, and at that time became concerned that the city was growing so fast that it was being poorly planned and not provided with adequate school facilities and park lands. In 1972 Professor Sondermann founded a political action group, Citizens Lobby For Sensible Growth, to urge the city government to plan well for the future population growth which surely was going to occur.

In the spring of 1973 Fred Sondermann ran for the Colorado Springs City Council on a "Sensible Growth" ticket. Realizing that electing only one person to a nine-member City Council would not really change anything, Sondermann recruited a "ticket" of like-minded individuals to run with him. One of his ticket mates was a younger colleague on the Colorado College faculty—Professor of Economics Mike Bird.

In a city election that many persons described as a "revolution," Sondermann and Bird were elected to the Colorado Springs City Council and the "Sensible Growth" forces gained a narrow majority of the council seats. In addition to pushing for better city planning, Sondermann and Bird supported a successful drive to have housing developers in Colorado Springs contribute land or money to help pay for the acquisition of land for new public schools and new public parks. They also successfully supported using modest amounts of city funds to finance programs at the Colorado Springs Fine Arts Center and provide summer performances by the Colorado Springs Symphony in city parks.

Fred Sondermann voluntarily stepped down from the City Council in 1975 after serving a two-year term in office.[17] Mike Bird, however, served eight years as a City Council member, including two years as Vice Mayor. He put his skills as an economist to work on the city budget, becoming well-known for his ability to find the funds for essential and desirable city programs without having to raise city property taxes.

Sondermann's and Bird's election to City Council did not, of course, significantly alter population growth rates in Colorado Springs. Although there were some periods when growth rates in Colorado College's hometown slowed down a bit, the general pattern throughout the 1970s, 1980s, and 1990s was for the Colorado Springs population to continue to grow at a steady pace.

PACKARD HALL

David Packard, a former member of the Board of Trustees, had been appointed Deputy Secretary of Defense by President Richard Nixon. Packard had made a sizeable fortune in the computer industry, and he put his financial holdings in trust while working for the U.S. Government to avoid a conflict of interest. When Packard left his job at the Defense Department, he gave a portion of the earnings and capital gains from the

[17]Anne Reifenberg, "Sondermann Will Not Run In 1975," *Catalyst*, 14 February 1975, 1.

trust to Colorado College, a sum totaling $7.5 million. The gift was in the form of corporation stock, so the College liquidated the gift over a number of years. The stock appreciated in value, so the final total received by the College eventually reached $12 million.[18]

President Worner went to Washington, D.C., to discuss with David Packard and his wife, Lucille, the best uses for the Packard gift. The three met for dinner and held a long discussion about the money and what to do with it for the College. The Packards were aware that the faculty had voted to make a new fine arts building a top priority, but both David and Lucille Packard questioned whether that really was in the best interests of the College. President Worner recalled Lucille Packard saying: "Now look, . . . we don't need this. We don't want this."

Lew Worner spent the better part of the evening explaining to the Packards that the College art program had outgrown the shared facilities at the Colorado Springs Fine Arts Center. The Music Department was jammed into Armstrong Hall with all the other Humanities departments and woefully lacked sound-proof practice rooms and a small auditorium for musical performances. Furthermore, moving the Art and Music departments into their own new building would free-up badly needed space in Armstrong Hall for the other Humanities, such as English, Philosophy, and Religion.

As the evening went by, President Worner convinced David and Lucille Packard that a new fine arts building was the best use for a substantial part of their gift. Looking back on the evening and its delicate but always friendly negotiations, Worner marveled that David and Lucille Packard focused all their attention on the best use for the money from the College's point of view. Worner concluded: "It's interesting. . . . Bricks and mortar and their name on the building didn't mean a *thing* to them."[19]

Packard Hall was constructed on the southwest corner of Cascade Avenue and Cache La Poudre Street, a location that kept the Art Department close to the Fine Arts Center. The site was formerly occupied

---

[18]Reid, *Colorado College: The First Century, 1874–1974*, 279–281. "CC Receives $7.5 Million," *Catalyst*, 26 January 1972, 1.

[19]Worner oral history, 5 February 1985, 134.

by Hayes House, a private home that had been acquired by the College and used as classroom and faculty office space. Albert Seay, Professor of Music, and James Trissel, Professor of Art, jointly chaired the faculty planning committee for the building. The architect was Edward Larabee Barnes of New York City.[20]

Packard Hall was one of the more adventurous buildings constructed at Colorado College. The red, brown, and dark gray brick that had characterized almost all the new buildings since World War II was not used. Nor did the architect return to the graceful stone construction of the extensive building program under former President Slocum. Most of the walls were of a premanufactured cement material, with one wall of a decorative black and white brick. To add a designer look, the black and white bricks were angled at each other, giving that one wall a saw-tooth appearance. The building's most attractive feature was that the art studios, both small and large, were located in such a way that their plate glass windows provided a magnificent view of Pike's Peak.

The new fine arts building also provided space for a music library, which included many of the historic musical documents collected by Professor Seay. There also was a photography laboratory and a slide-making facility for Art History. A most useful part of the building, for all of the campus, was the small auditorium for musical performances. With its comfortable theater-style seats, upholstered in a relaxing green, the auditorium in Packard Hall quickly became a popular lecture hall as well as a music hall.[21]

One of the most popular uses for the new auditorium in Packard Hall was the weekly "Thursday At Eleven." Once a week, almost always at 11 A.M. on Thursday, there would be some sort of an academic event in Packard auditorium—a lecture by a visiting scholar, a panel discussion on an issue of current political interest, a performance by a visiting musician, etc. Although attendance at "Thursday At Eleven" was voluntary, faculty members were encouraged to end their classes at 10:45 on Thursday

---

[20]Reid, *Colorado College: The First Century, 1874–1974*, 280. "CC Receives $7.5 Million," *Catalyst*, 26 January 1972, 1.

[21]"Packard Hall: Ready For Immediate Occupancy," *Catalyst*, 8 October, 1976, 5.

mornings so that those students who wanted to could troop over to Packard auditorium to attend the program.

OTHER INNOVATIONS

Packard Hall was not the only building project at Colorado College in the early 1970s. The former Van Briggle Art Pottery building at Uintah Street and Glen Avenue was acquired by the College and remodeled to provide offices, shops, and vehicle storage for the Physical Plant Department. Care was taken to preserve the large kiln chimneys, a distinctive feature of the exterior of the Van Briggle building. The College also preserved the ornate brick and tile decorations on the outside of the building.

The ugly but functional building that previously housed the Physical Plant offices was located just to the west of Cutler Hall. Once the Physical Plant moved into the remodeled Van Briggle building, the old Physical Plant building was torn down and removed. The area was leveled and landscaped and renamed Cutler Park. With its grassy expanse and magnificent view of Pike's Peak and the surrounding mountains, Cutler Park became one of the more attractive spots on campus. Some years later, large pink stones were placed there for students to sit and lounge around on while studying, conversing, or just gazing at the Peak.

In 1972 there was significant progress on the computing scene at Colorado College. The age of "time-sharing by long distance telephone" came to an end when the College acquired the first computer of its own. "Smedley," as the new computer was affectionately known, was manufactured by Hewlett-Packard and took up residence in the basement of Armstrong Hall. Direct lines connected Smedley to computer terminals in Armstrong Hall, Olin Hall, Palmer Hall, and Tutt Library.

A combined faculty-administration committee, the Campus Design Board, worked at reducing traffic and parking problems at Colorado College. The Board adopted an overall philosophy of trying to remove automobiles and parking lots to the outside edges of the campus, thereby reserving the center of the campus, as much as possible, for pedestrians. In line with this philosophy, the Board closed the half-circle street in front of Cutler Hall, Cossitt Hall, and Rastall Center to automobile traffic. Once the College had acquired all the property in the 1100 block of

Wood Avenue (the block north of Loomis Hall), the Board closed off that block of Wood Avenue at Uintah Street, turning the block into a quiet cul-de-sac area with only local automobile traffic. This action cut down on traffic through the campus and also reduced traffic accidents at Wood Avenue and Uintah Street.

The Campus Design Board also went to work on the large unpaved parking lot that ran from San Rafael Street to Uintah Street west of Mathias Hall and the fraternity quadrangle. The southern half of the parking lot was leveled, sodded, landscaped, and turned into an intramural soccer field. The northern half remained a parking lot but was paved and decorated with "landscaped islands." Many of the landscaped islands had sunburst locust trees planted in them.

When not worrying about automobiles and parking, the Campus Design Board kept busy urging the College administration to take better care of the many private homes the College had acquired over the years at the fringes of the campus. The Board was suspicious that the College was deferring maintenance on these buildings with a view toward tearing most of them down in the future and replacing them with large dormitory and classroom buildings. The Campus Design Board argued that these former private homes were some of the most attractive buildings on the campus and also were very comfortable places in which to live, have office space, and hold classes and meetings. A policy of preserving the best examples of these former private homes on the campus was called for, the Board concluded.

The chairman of the Campus Design Board during the early 1970s was Professor Robert Loevy, of the Political Science Department, who was teaching an undergraduate seminar in Urban Planning while at the same time serving on the Colorado Springs City Planning Commission.

A Southwest Studies program was created at Colorado College to enhance research and teaching about the unique problems of the peoples of the southwestern United States. The program was particularly, but not exclusively, oriented to studying the history of Spanish-surnamed Americans and American Indians in the region. The first director of the Southwest Studies program was English Professor Joseph Gordon.

An era came to an end in 1971 when Christine Moon, who had been the Dean of Women at Colorado College for 14 years, retired. Her time in office had been characterized by strident demands for change from the student body, and she had presided, at times unwillingly, over a steady reduction in the role of the College in the governance of women students. The *Catalyst* commented that "she was flexible and progressive in that she allowed decisions that she opposed as they reflected the changing attitudes of the times."[22]

There also was innovation and experimentation on the football field at Colorado College in the early 1970s. Under the leadership of Coach Jerry Carle, the football team switched to the single wing offense, a formation which had been discarded from college football some 25 years earlier. Colorado College became one of the few teams which was *not* using the conventional T or I formation. This bold switch in football strategy worked well. Over six years the Colorado College men's football team won 47 games, lost 6, and tied 1.[23]

THE CENTENNIAL CELEBRATION

The study process that resulted in the adoption of the Block Plan had been instituted in anticipation of the celebration of the College's 100th birthday in 1974. The study process moved so swiftly, however, that the Block Plan was adopted by the faculty in 1969 and put into operation in the fall of 1970. By the time the actual date of the College Centennial rolled around in 1974, the Block Plan had been up and operating for three-and-one-half years.

David and Lucille Packard's generous gift to the College was incorporated into the Centennial festivities. The Board of Trustees decided to hold a fund-raising drive, the Centennial Challenge Campaign, to match the $7 million original value of the Packard gift. By the end of the Centennial year—1974—$5 million of the $7 million had been raised.[24]

The Centennial celebration began on January 20, 1974, with a black-tie dinner at the Broadmoor Hotel for a select group of 300 students, fac-

[22]Reid, *Colorado College: The First Century, 1874–1974*, 277.

[23]Reid, *Colorado College: The First Century, 1874–1974*, 275.

[24]Reid, *Colorado College: The First Century, 1874–1974*, 282, 296

ulty members, trustees, and friends of the College. That date was the 100th anniversary of the decision by the Conference of the Congregational Churches of the Territory of Colorado to establish Colorado College in Colorado Springs. President Worner gave the after-dinner speech, which was entitled "A Commitment to be Perpetual," words taken from the Charter of the College.

February 9, 1974, was the 100th anniversary of the day the new College's charter was filed with the Territory of Colorado in Denver. To mark that auspicious event, a dinner for 375 of the College's alumni and friends in the Denver area was held at the Brown Palace Hotel in downtown Denver. Colorado Governor John H. Vanderhoof proclaimed that particular day as "Colorado College Day" throughout the state. Over the remainder of the year, Centennial Dinners were held for alumni and friends of the College across the nation, usually featuring a talk by President Worner and a narrated slide show on the College's history by Juan Reid, the Director of Alumni Relations.

CENTENNIAL MUSIC

The major musical event of the College's Centennial year was a full presentation of Johann Sebastian Bach's *The Passion According To St. Matthew.* This religious masterpiece was conducted by Professor Donald Jenkins of the Music Department and required an enlarged choir of 250 College and community singers accompanied by a 40-piece orchestra. The *Passion* was presented in Shove Chapel in April of 1974 in the traditional manner: three-and-a-half hours of music and singing separated by a two-hour intermission.[25]

THE CENTENNIAL SYMPOSIUM

In September of 1974 there was a Centennial Symposium on the topic, *The Liberal Arts Education: Today and Tomorrow.* The Centennial Symposium was held during the block break at the end of Block One. The Centennial Symposium was organized by Professor Timothy Fuller of the Political

---

[25]Barbara M. Arnest, "The St. Matthew Passion And A Community Of Singers," *Colorado College Bulletin*, May 1975, 31–37.

Science Department. The idea for the Symposium had grown out of a series of Friday lunches held at the home of Professor of Physics Wilbur Wright. It was at these lunches that a group of College faculty decided to have a number of speakers come to the campus and discuss one of the great underlying principles of Colorado College—the furthering of "liberal learning."

The Centennial Symposium included a major address, entitled "A Place Of Learning," by Michael Oakeshott, Emeritus Professor of Political Science at the London School of Economics. Learning "is a self-conscious engagement," Professor Oakeshott said. It is not a reaction to exterior pressure, or environmental conditions, but "a self-imposed task inspired by the intimations of what there is to learn."

Learning is pursued for its own sake, the British scholar argued. It has little to do with "getting on in the world." It is, instead, "an adventure in which an individual consciousness confronts the world."

A college or university, Oakeshott continued, is a "special place of learning. . . . What is special about such a place . . . is its seclusion, its detachment from . . . the here and now of current living." A college and university should be a sheltered place "where excellences may be heard because the din of local partialities is no more than a distant rumble."

Oakeshott criticized strongly the call for "relevance" in education that was sounded so loudly in the late 1960s and early 1970s. The result, he said, was that "history is contracted into what is called contemporary history, languages come to be recognized as contemporary communication, and in literature the book which 'verbalizes what everyone is thinking now' comes to be preferred, on that account, to anything else."

The British scholar also attacked the 20th Century call for an educational process that emphasized "socialization" of the student rather than intellectual achievement. Such a system, Oakeshott said, recognizes the "learner" as "nothing but a role-performer in a so-called 'social system.'"

Liberal learning is not a single set of ideas or beliefs, Oakeshott emphasized. There are many voices speaking, and these voices join in an ongoing "conversation" which is never concluded. The human self-understanding which is the goal of liberal education is a topic that merits ever-continuing discussion.

At the end of his address, the British Political Scientist spoke directly to the students and faculty of Colorado College. Given the pressures and distractions of modern life, Oakeshott concluded: "We must remember who we are: inhabitants of a place of liberal learning."[26]

Another major speaker at the Centennial Symposium was D. S. Carne-Ross, Professor of Classics and Modern Languages at Boston University in Massachusetts, whose topic was "The Grammar Of Humanity." The college or university "needs to withdraw from society and become a separate place," Carne-Ross said. Teachers and students need to choose the "contemplative life" over the "active life." Teachers and students need to escape from the "big blooming buzzing confusion that we call 'real' life."

Carne-Ross saw education tied to particular regions, times, and religions. "The task of education," he explained, "is to teach us the ways of our regions, its cultural, historical, and religious traditions, not because they are part of our past but because they are the determinants of our present and future." But in studying one's own culture and traditions, he pointed out, the student has the responsibility of deciding what to accept and what to reject from that culture and tradition. Some may, if they wish, reject the culture and tradition completely.

Because the Cold War between the United States and the Soviet Union was very much a reality in the early 1970s, Carne-Ross warned that the comfortable college and university campuses of the day could pass away with the civilization that created them. He concluded his talk by urging his scholarly colleagues to set about the work of preserving that which is best and memorable about Western culture and tradition. "We lost too many of these essential works the last time our civilization [classical Greece and Rome] collapsed," Carne-Ross said. "We should aim to do better this time."[27]

---

[26]Michael Oakeshott, *A Place of Learning* (Colorado Springs, CO: Colorado College, 1975), 6–29. Oakeshott's address was delivered 17 September 1974 in Armstrong Hall. For commentary on Professor Oakeshott's speech by a newly-minted graduate of Colorado College, see Paul Reville, "Tale Of Two Symposia: Irritation Vs. Confrontation," *Catalyst*, 18 October 1974, 6.

[27]Professor Carne-Ross's talk was given a new title and published by Colorado College. See D. S. Carne-Ross, "The Nipping Of Our Cultural December," *Colorado College Bulletin*, May 1975, 11–20. Also see Bill Barron, "Centennial Symposium Examines Liberal Arts," *Catalyst*, 4 October 1974, 1. "Centennial Symposium On The Liberal Arts Today And Tomorrow," *Colorado College Bulletin*, May 1975, 9. For student commentary, see David Owen, "Striking Out Against Collegiate Bunk And Hooey," *Catalyst*, 4 October 1974, 5. Also see Lloyd Worner, President of Colorado College, "College Community Should Ponder Goals," *Catalyst*, 4 October 1974, 5.

The theme of the Centennial Symposium—that the college or university is a separate place in society where the thoughts and ideas and writings of the past are treasured—contrasted interestingly with that other aspect of the Centennial, the adoption of the Block Plan. The College stopped to study, recall, and think about its intellectual and cultural roots at the same time that it embarked on a courageous and experimental new academic calendar.

THE CENTENNIAL WEEKEND

In late October of 1974 the College sponsored a Centennial Weekend to correspond with Alumni Homecoming. Former President Louis Benezet returned to the campus and spoke at a special Centennial Convocation. Benezet urged the College to continue to resist the drive for "specialization" and to remain true to the liberal arts ideal. Benezet blamed the desire to compete with the Soviet Union after the launching of the Sputnik satellite in the late 1950s for the pressure that was being put on colleges and universities to offer more specialized courses. Benezet said that an education aimed solely at "fitting the undergraduate into his first job . . . is wrong." The former President also said that Colorado College escaped the major unrest that gripped so many other campuses in the late 1960s and early 1970s because, at Colorado College, "students are involved in the determination of their own liberal educations."[28]

Benezet's speech and the Centennial Weekend festivities marked the end of the College's Centennial Celebration. With 100 very successful years behind them, the students, faculty, and administrators of Colorado College turned from admiring the College's past to living the College's future.

---

[28]"Benezet To Speak At Convocation," *Catalyst*, 11 October 1974, 2. "Benezet: Specialization A Mistake," *Catalyst*, 1 November 1974, 3. For a further explanation of former-President Benezet's ideas on education at Colorado College, see Louis T. Benezet, "Some Passing Thoughts About Change," *Colorado College Bulletin*, February 1975, 17–18.

CHAPTER 8

A Time of Advancement

In the fall of 1974 the 101st academic year got underway at Colorado College. The first year class had 609 students, the largest first year class in the College's history. The class was so large that an overflow of 20 students began the year living at J's Motel on North Nevada Avenue until additional space could be found in the dormitories. The incoming students were said to be more "grade conscious" and conservative than Colorado College students had been in previous years.[1]

Two new assistant deans were hired to provide better counseling and help with recruitment of minority students. At that time there were about 33 Black, 70 Spanish-surnamed, and 6 American Indian students enrolled at the College. William Turner was the new Dean to help Black students, and Rudolph de la Garza was to work with Spanish-surnamed. Dean de la Garza, who also was to teach Political Science courses, took advantage of the Block Plan's flexibility in making out his work schedule. He alternated full-time teaching blocks with full-time blocks working as a Dean.[2]

---

[1]Bob Krimmer, "Biggest Freshman Class in CC History Enrolled In College For Fall Semester," *Catalyst*, 13 September 1974, 1. "Survey Shows Freshmen Conservative," *Catalyst*, 28 February 1975, 2. Randy Kiser, "Changing Student Attitudes Emphasize Academics," *Catalyst*, 9 May 1975, 1. Large first year classes resulting in overcrowded dormitories became a periodic recurring phenomenon at Colorado College. See Laurel Van Driest, "Seventy Students Live At J's Motel; Student Overload Complicates Housing Situation," *Catalyst*, 14 September 1979, 1.

[2]Frank Purdy, "Realignment To 'Unify' Deans' Office," *Catalyst*, 13 September 1974, 1. Frank Purdy, "New Minority Deans, Turner And De La Garza, Express Viewpoints," *Catalyst*, 4 October 1974, 2.

WOMEN PROFESSORS

Important changes were occurring at Colorado College where the hiring of women professors was concerned. In the early 1970s the College quietly dropped an informal and unspoken prohibition against a husband and a wife both working on the faculty. This opened the way for some notable professorial couples—such as Susan Ashley (History) and Robert Lee (Political Science). Another espousal teaching team was Tom K. Barton (History) and Ruth Barton (English).

According to Ruth Barton, who taught part-time in the English Department, sex discrimination against women at Colorado College had mainly taken the form of not considering women for career positions on the faculty. Young women were not considered because they probably would get married and eventually leave the faculty to stay home with their children. Older married women were not considered because it was thought to be wrong to distract them from caring for their families.

Ruth Barton said the situation had improved greatly by the mid–1970s. The hidden prejudices of the past "have come to the conscious level," she said, and "we are more sensitive to the situation." Despite the improvement, however, during the 1975–1976 academic year there were more than 7 men professors at the College for each woman.[3]

By the end of the decade of the 1970s, however, there had been a considerable increase in the number of women professors. Among them were Charlotte Mendoza in Education (hired in 1971), Alexandra Vargo in Biology (1973), Margaret Duncombe in Sociology (1975), Marcia Dobson in Classics (1976), Gale Murray in Art (1976), Marie Daniels in Spanish (1977), Judith Genova in Philosophy (1978), Ruth Kolarik in Art (1978), and Judith Laux in Economics (1979).

THE CANINE CRISIS

During this time Maxwell Taylor, the Associate Dean, was constantly vexed by the problem of dogs on campus. A significant number of students living off-campus acquired canine pets, and the animals often were left to roam

---

[3]Kathy De Shaw, "Female Profs. Air Views On Their Minority Status at C.C.," *Catalyst*, 7 May 1976, 3. Heather Ruth Palmer, "Women Profs. Down But Not Out," *Catalyst*, 13 January 1978, 3.

the campus while their owner was in class or in the library. Some student dog owners would tie their animals to a tree or a railing while in a building, which often resulted in a barking or whining dog disturbing the general peace of the College. Dean Taylor finally posted a long list of rules for dog owners and threatened to have the Humane Society remove any dog found running loose on campus.[4] In a canine case that produced a great deal of student sympathy for the dog, the Dean's Office evicted Alpine, a 14-week-old puppy who was a cross between a doberman and a yellow labrador, from the Phi Gamma Delta fraternity house.[5]

VENTURE GRANTS

To enable students to take full advantage of the extra freedom created by the Block Plan, the College instituted a Venture Grant program to subsidize student travel and living expenses while conducting research away from the campus. A total of $8,000 was budgeted for Venture Grants for 1974–1975, with individual awards totaling as much as $600. Students usually combined a Venture Grant with a one-block independent study course and then traveled to a distant location, often exotic, to do research and writing.

For instance, grants were made for studying coral reefs in the Indian Ocean and for observing bilingual education in Chile. One student used a Venture Grant to intern at a "store-front" neighborhood organization for the poor on Spring Garden Street in Philadelphia, Pennsylvania.[6]

A NEW OLD REGAL

Two faculty members in the Music Department, Albert Seay and Michael Grace, announced they had spent two months painstakingly building a

---

[4]"CC Cracks Down On Pesty Puppies," *Catalyst*, 18 October 1974, 6. Anne Reifenberg, "Canines Stir Fuss," *Catalyst*, 31 October 1975, 1. "Dog Problem Reaches Crisis; Deans Overreact?" *Catalyst*, 21 November 1975, 1.

[5]Le Melcher, "C.C. Evicts Alpine," *Catalyst*, 6 November 1981, 6.

[6]Jay Hartwell, "Venture Grants Funds Going Fast," *Catalyst*, 6 December 1974, 2. The Venture Grant to Spring Garden Street in Philadelphia was undertaken under the author's direction. Also see Michael Santos, "Venture Grants Fund Students' Dreams," *Catalyst*, 11 November 1988, 7. Annette Long, "Student's Grant Leads To New York City," *Catalyst*, 12 May 1995, 14.

regal. "What's a regal?" everyone asked, and Professor Seay happily gave the answer. "It's a small portative organ, modeled after an instrument that was common in the 15th and 16th Centuries." The regal had a 44-note keyboard, was less than half the size of a piano, and, unlike most organs, had no pedals or knobs. Professor Seay, an authority on Medieval and Renaissance music, said the regal would be added to the College's collection of early musical instruments, which included four crumhorns, a harpsichord, a lute, and four recorders.[7]

STUDENT LIFE

For a number of years Colorado College students had been urged to support unionized lettuce workers in their strike against lettuce growers. To this end, the Saga food service had agreed to serve only United Farm Workers (UFW) "approved" lettuce in College dining rooms. In the fall of 1974 a poll revealed that the student body still supported the lettuce workers, but a majority of the students said they disliked the taste and quality of the UFW-approved lettuce being served to them. Despite this unsavory consequence of political action, the *Catalyst* urged the students to continue eating union-approved lettuce.[8]

ENACT, the College organization for environmental action, operated a program for collecting recyclable materials at various points on campus and selling them to appropriate recycling businesses. The bins and containers for newspapers, glass, aluminum, and other recycled materials eventually were housed in little wooden sheds with shingled roofs in order to make the campus look more attractive.[9]

A coffee house, intended to be a campus night spot for students, was constructed in the basement of Rastall Center. Coffee, tea, soft drinks, beer, and snacks were available for purchase, and a dance floor and stereo system were installed. The coffee house was to be a place for intellectual

---

[7]"Professors Get Their Regal Together," *Catalyst*, 18 October 1974, 9.

[8]Jay Hartwell, "A Bite Into The CC Lettuce Situation," *Catalyst*, 20 September 1974, 5. "Lettuce Vote," *Catalyst*, 7 November 1975, 1.

[9]"Recycling Center Reestablished," *Catalyst*, 18 October 1974, 1. Ian Heffron, "ENACT Constructs Recycling Sheds," *Catalyst*, 26 April 1986, 3.

advancement as well as entertainment. A flexible design permitted it to be used for live entertainment, intimate group gatherings, class discussions, student theatrical productions, and showing films. Initiated by the students, the new coffee house received the enthusiastic support of the College administration. It was named Benjamin's Basement in honor of Benjamin Rastall, for whom Rastall Center was named.[10]

MINORITY STUDENTS

For a number of years the Black students on campus had been organized in a group known as the Black Student Union (BSU). Early in 1974 the Black Student Union announced it was going to become more intellectual and political and less of a social organization. In line with this new approach, the organization began preparing a pamphlet to use to recruit more Black students to come to Colorado College. Over the years the Black students brought in lecturers, showed films, and occasionally staged dramatic productions in an effort to heighten student and faculty awareness of Black issues and traditions.[11]

Many of the Spanish-surnamed students belonged to MECHA, which stood for "Movimento Estudiantil Chicano de Aztlan." In English that meant "Chicano Student Movement of Aztlan." The word "Aztlan" represented a region of Mexico that was the birthplace of the Aztecs. It was added to the organization's name to connote cultural pride.

MECHA was founded at Colorado College in 1969 and immediately went to work helping to recruit more Spanish-surnamed students to come to the College. In the six years from 1969 to 1975, the number of Spanish-surnamed students increased from 6 to 70. MECHA also joined in the College's efforts to employ Spanish-surnamed faculty. The hiring of Rudolph de la Garza as both a Political Science professor and a minority dean was a major step forward in MECHA's continuing efforts to enrich campus life for Spanish-surnamed students.

---

[10]Linda Hare, "Coffee House Should Open Soon," *Catalyst*, 18 October 1974, 3. Randy Kiser, "Ben's Basement To Open After Block Break," *Catalyst*, 24 January 1975, 3.

[11]"Black Student Union Announces Events," *Catalyst*, 18 October 1974, 5. Tom Adkinson, "Keith Owens: Building A Black Consciousness," *Catalyst*, 28 October 1977, 5. "Black Awareness Week Set For February, *Catalyst*, 23 January 1981, 9.

MECHA sponsored a number of cultural activities, such as celebrating Chicano Awareness Week each spring. These events were designed to bring awareness of Spanish ideas and Spanish culture to the entire campus, not just the Spanish-surnamed students. MECHA also played a leading role in the political drive to serve only United Farm Worker approved lettuce in the College dining halls.[12]

EXPANSION OF WOMEN'S SPORTS

In the spring of 1975 something new was added to the Colorado College sports program—a women's soccer team. As with many new sports at the College, women's soccer began modestly as a "club" sport rather than as an official athletic activity. About 20 women practiced each evening at Washburn Field, kicking the ball around under the direction of volunteer student coach Steve Paul. The Colorado College women's soccer team won its first game, defeating a club team from the Denver area, the Aurora Riders, by 3 to 0. Some of the star players on this first women's soccer team were Kim Austin, Lynn Harrison, Linda Weil, and goalie Jamie McAllister.[13]

The same process was taking place with the women's volleyball team. Originally a club sport, by the fall of 1975 women's volleyball was being played at the intercollegiate level. A new coach hired by the College, Laura Golden, was working to rid women's volleyball of its previous relaxed, casual, club atmosphere and produce a hard-hitting, hard-practicing varsity team.[14]

Laura Golden had been brought to Colorado College, in something of a crisis atmosphere, with instructions to organize an intercollegiate sports program for women during the 1975–1976 academic year. Her major problem the first year was figuring out which sports the women stu-

---

[12]G. E. Easterbrook, "MECHA: Our Admirable 'Troublemakers,'" *Catalyst*, 14 November 1975, 5. Ken Salazar, "MECHA Represents Chicano Students," *Catalyst*, 14 January 1977, 4.

[13]"Women Tough In Soccer," *Catalyst*, 16 May 1975, 7. Lisa Bryant, "CC Women's Soccer Teams Compete In Tourney," *Catalyst*, 10 October 1975, 10.

[14]Sally King, "Women's V-Ball To Be NCAA," *Catalyst*, 3 October 1975, 5. This *Catalyst* article questioned whether it was really an improvement to introduce the high competitiveness and pressure to win of intercollegiate varsity competition to women's volleyball at Colorado College.

dents wanted to play. By the spring of 1976 it had been decided that Colorado College women would compete in eight intercollegiate varsity sports. There would be field hockey, soccer, and volleyball in the fall, basketball and skiing during the winter, and softball, tennis, and track and field in the spring. In the winter of 1976 there was a major effort to revive the women's swim team, which had disbanded in the early 1970s due to lack of student interest.

Women's sports at Colorado College were to operate under the same rules that applied to men's sports (except for the men's ice hockey team). No scholarships would be offered, the coaches would do no formal recruiting, and the academic orientation at the College would be emphasized whenever perspective students inquired about the intercollegiate athletic program.

Laura Golden, who came to Colorado College from Georgia College in Milledge, Georgia, said there initially would be a disparity between the quality of men's and women's sports at the College because women were not yet receiving good training in competitive sports at the junior high and high school level. But she said Colorado College women would come to appreciate the rewards of intercollegiate competition. Referring to her experience at the College so far, Golden concluded many women students "weren't sure what competition was, but many women want[ed] that intensity."[15]

The Colorado College women were off to a particularly fast start with the sport of basketball. During the 1976–1977 season, the women's basketball team posted a 16–1 record and advanced to the NCAA regional playoffs, quite an achievement for the team's second year of existence. In the final game of the regular season, the Tiger women roundballers defeated Metro State College in Denver by 65–42.

That game had the distinction of being the first women's collegiate basketball game in the history of Colorado to be broadcast over the radio. Jim Vinal and Wess Ster of radio station KVOR-AM in Colorado Springs traveled to Denver to broadcast the game back to a rapidly growing number of College and hometown fans. Standout players on the team

[15]Anne Reifenberg, "CC's 'Second Sex' Receives Jock Status," *Catalyst*, 6 February 1976, 6. Conway Fleming, "Women's Team Resurfaces," *Catalyst*, 10 December 1976, 15.

included Rose Harvey, Lorna Kollmeyer, Ann Pringle, Mary Shifrin, and Ann Shutan.

The 1976–1977 women's basketball team won both games at the regional playoffs in Denver and advanced to the National Division II championship series in Pomona, California. An outstanding season ended there, however, as the Lady Tigers lost to Ashland College and Eastern Connecticut State.

The student newspaper, the *Catalyst*, was quick to give sports-style nicknames to the women basketball stars. Lorna Kollmeyer was referred to in print as "Lanky Lorna," Mary Shifrin was called "Shifty Shifrin," and Rose Harvey was described as "Ramblin' Rose."[16]

By 1979 Colorado College had a women's lacrosse team practicing and playing its home games on Stewart field. The 1979 season got off to a good start when Colorado College won its home opener by defeating Colorado State University by a score of 5 to 4. Leading scorers for the women's lacrosse team that year were Lynn Mestres, Maria Catlett, and Bevo Cathcart.[17]

At the close of the 1980–1981 academic year, the woman who founded the women's sports program at Colorado College moved on. Laura Golden accepted a new position as women's basketball coach at Central Michigan University. In Golden's six years as women's basketball coach, Colorado College had a record of 101 wins and only 39 losses, a significant achievement for a brand new intercollegiate athletic team.

"From the beginning," Laura Golden said, "our philosophy was [that sports are] an extension of the liberal arts education. Anyone can build up one sport. We took the program from scratch and built it, diversified it, so that everyone could participate. Over the years, I've been very satisfied with C.C.'s support for its women's athletic program."[18]

---

[16]Craig Silverman, "Record Moves CC Women To Playoffs," *Catalyst*, 18 February 1977, 11. Craig Silverman, "Double Defeat In California Tourney: But The Weather Was Nice," *Catalyst*, 8 April 1977, 7.

[17]Michelle Giarratano, "Women's Lacrosse Team Sticks-Up C.S.U.," *Catalyst*, 11 May 1979, 6.

[18]Kent Bossart, "Golden Heads North," *Catalyst*, 22 May 1981, 13.

Men's Sports

There were the usual number of occasional triumphs in men's intercollegiate sports during the 1970s. The 1975 football team, under the direction of Coach Gerald Carle, advanced to the NCAA playoffs. The playoff game took place at Washburn Field, so a large Colorado College crowd got to see the football Tigers in post-season action. Unfortunately, Millsaps College won the game 28 to 21. One of the highlights of the 1975 football season was the outstanding place-kicking of junior Ted Swan, who won a number of games with 50-yards-plus field goals and crucial extra points.[19]

The men's soccer team had one of its best seasons ever in the fall of 1975. The team amassed 15 wins against 2 losses and 2 ties. The Colorado College booters went to the NCAA Division 1 tournament but lost a close game by 1 to 0 to California State at Fullerton.[20]

The men's ski team won a league championship in the winter of 1976 by outpointing the favored University of New Mexico Lobos at a ski meet in Red River, New Mexico.[21]

A new era in Colorado College men's sports began when a woman, Meg Nelson, was hired to be one of the three trainers for the football team. She attended football practice and football games, helped administer first aid to injured players, and worked with players on recovering from their sports injuries. Nelson was the first woman ever hired by the College to serve as an athletic trainer in a men's sport.[22]

An era ended when Coach Leon "Red" Eastlack gave up coaching men's basketball for health reasons. Eastlack's career at Colorado College stretched from 1959, when the basketball Tigers were still a power in the old Rocky Mountain Athletic Conference, until the end of the 1976 roundball season. During Eastlack's first two seasons, the men's basketball team

---

[19]Terry Johnson, "Playoff Hopes Shattered: Gridders Bow 28–21," *Catalyst*, 27 November 1975, 1. Gregg E. Easterbrook, "Ted Swan: Feets Don't Fail Him Now," *Catalyst*, 17 October 1975, 5.

[20]George Jackson, "Playoff Hopes Shattered: Soccer Team Loses 1–0," *Catalyst*, 27 November 1975, 1.

[21]"CC Ski Team Schusses To League Victory In New Mexico," *Catalyst*, 20 February 1976, 10.

[22]"Meg Nelson: A Feminine Touch For Football Bruises," *Catalyst*, 24 September 1976, 6.

won the Rocky Mountain championship both years, a real accomplishment for a small liberal arts college playing in a league with large universities.

Perhaps Coach Eastlack's greatest accomplishment was to successfully oversee the de-emphasis of men's basketball at Colorado College. In 1962 the scholarships for men basketball players were ended, but Eastlack was able to field scrappy teams that consistently performed around the .500 mark.[23]

There was a significant addition to the College's athletic plant in the fall of 1980. Stewart Field, located north of Washburn Field, was enlarged so that it became a regulation size soccer field. The area separating Stewart Field from Washburn Field also was increased in size. The project was delayed for one year when, while removing earth for the new field, the Physical Plant accidentally ruptured an unmarked water main and completely flooded the site.[24]

Political Changes

By the fall of 1974 changes in the national political scene had had a quieting effect on the campus. Because of the Watergate scandal, Richard Nixon resigned the U.S. presidency in August of 1974. Vice President Gerald Ford became President of the United States, but Ford lost considerable public support in September of 1974 when he pardoned Nixon for any crimes connected with Watergate.

The international situation changed abruptly in the spring of 1975. The United States had progressively removed its military forces from Vietnam in the early 1970s. With the U.S. military effort so greatly reduced, the North Vietnamese quickly won the war. The United States was forced to use helicopters to hastily remove its diplomats and remaining military personnel from the U.S. embassy in Saigon, the South Vietnamese capital. After the North Vietnamese army had taken complete military control of South Vietnam, U.S. President Gerald Ford officially announced to the American people—and the world—that the Vietnam War was over.

---

[23]Brad Frye, "Coach 'Red' Retires From El Pomar Courts," *Catalyst*, 5 March 1976, 7.

[24]Barbara Terman, "Practice Field Delayed," *Catalyst*, 12 October 1979, 1.

It was the end of a war that had inspired innumerable teach-ins, marches, protests, and panel discussions at Colorado College. The faculty and students responded to the end of hostilities by holding a series of panel discussions on why the war had ended so swiftly and what the implications were for U.S. foreign policy. There was minimal gloating by those who had strongly opposed U.S. military involvement in the war. The mood on campus was mainly one of relief combined with continued concern for the future of international affairs.[25]

Block Plan Refinements

One of the few problems that had developed with the Block Plan was a shortage of good classrooms. The shortage came about because most of the professors wanted to teach their classes in the morning, and there simply were not enough classrooms to go around at that busy hour of the day. Instead of trying to hold classes in lounges and other inappropriate areas, President Worner urged the faculty to teach more classes in the afternoon, thereby "sharing" classrooms with professors teaching in the morning.

Philosophy Professor Glenn Gray stated at faculty meeting that he had been experimenting with teaching after lunch and found that he could hold "satisfactory afternoon classes with better preparation by students." Professors Albert Seay and Donald Jenkins reported that professors in the Music Department had been sharing classrooms for quite some time under the Block Plan. A substantial number of professors began teaching classes after the lunch hour, and afternoon classes became an accepted part of the Block Plan.[26]

As for the overall status of the Block Plan, the faculty voted overwhelmingly in the fall of 1974 to make the Block Plan the accepted calendar of the College "indefinitely." After four full years of teaching under the new plan, the faculty voted 80 to 5 to continue it. There were 5 abstentions. During the debate a recommendation was made that professors

---

[25]Steve Johnson, "Panelists Disagree On Vietnam War Questions," *Catalyst*, 16 May 1975, 2. Also see "Military Aid For Vietnam Said 'Futile,'" *Catalyst*, 18 April 1975, 3.

[26]"Faculty Postpones Plan Debate Till November 11," *Catalyst*, 1 November 1974, 1. "Course Room Situation Called Unsatisfactory," *Catalyst*, 8 November 1974, 1

offer more two-block courses. "There's something dilettantish about new students every three-and-a-half weeks," said Philosophy Professor Glenn Gray. He praised two-block courses as "much sounder pedagogically, not just for myself but for the future of Colorado College."

There was one persistent note of criticism as the faculty reaffirmed its support for the Block Plan. The criticism concerned the heavy workload placed on the faculty by the new teaching system. The faculty adopted a statement that "each full-time faculty member be encouraged each year to schedule one block when his or her sole teaching duty would be the direction of no more than five students in independent study . . . or special projects." The faculty also encouraged its members to "not feel obliged to prepare [for the first time] more than five or six courses a year."[27]

Physics Professor Richard C. Bradley, who succeeded George Drake as Dean of Colorado College, said the College was developing statistical data which put the Block Plan in a most favorable light. According to Dean Bradley, the number of academic suspensions (flunk-outs) had dropped to one quarter of what it had been before the plan was adopted. In addition, Director of Admissions Richard E. Wood reported that the drop-out rate at the College was down. Prior to the Block Plan, only 57 percent of entering first year students stayed until graduated. After the Block Plan went into effect, that figure rose to 68 percent.

The Block Plan had a dramatic impact on class size at the College. In 1969–1970, the year before the plan was implemented, average class size was 21 persons. By 1973–1974, four years into the Block Plan experiment, average class size was only 14 persons.

Associate Dean Maxwell Taylor, in charge of evaluating the Block Plan, commented on the falling flunk-out and drop-out rates. He said the favorable statistics were probably caused by the higher levels of class participation that resulted under the Block Plan. The students "become uniquely involved in the teaching-learning process," Taylor said. "This involvement reflects itself in a consistently high level of preparedness for

[27]Carol Garten, "Block Plan Given 80–5–5 Faculty Vote Of Confidence," *Catalyst*, 15 November 1974, 1. Also see Wade Buchanan, "Block Plan Proves Successful," *Catalyst*, 9 November 1979, 1.

class, accompanied by an attitude frequently described by faculty as one of enthusiasm or a joy of learning."[28]

Away from the campus the Block Plan was receiving a large amount of favorable national publicity. In December of 1974 *Newsweek* magazine ran an article on the Block Plan and the College. The article described how "no bells ring in the halls." It extolled Biology classes which took off from the campus to study whales in Baja, California. It waxed romantically about Astronomy classes that met at midnight "to take full advantage of the starry panorama of the Rocky Mountain skies."

The only criticisms of the plan noted by *Newsweek* were that it could lead to "hurried gorging" with no time "to teach any more than the essentials, the bare machinery."[29] The national news magazine also noted that, under the Block Plan, students were kept busy "cramming" in information, possibly worked too hard, and often did not have enough time for extracurricular activities. The article concluded with a thoughtful comment from President Worner: "As long as it doesn't become the new orthodoxy we'll continue the plan."[30]

In that comment Lew Worner was stating a concern about the Block Plan that also was shared by Glenn Brooks, the plan's designer. Both Worner and Brooks feared that, once it was well-established, the Block Plan would achieve the status of unchangeable holy writ at Colorado College. If that happened, in future years the Block Plan could become as confining and limiting as the old semester system was at the time the Block Plan was adopted.

---

[28]"Fall In Flunk-Outs, Drop-Outs Attributed To Block Plan," *Catalyst*, 7 February 1975, 5. For analysis of and excerpts from Associate Dean Taylor's report on the Block Plan, see "The Plan: Still Loved," *Colorado College Bulletin*, May 1975, 39–42.

[29]These quotes were given to *Newsweek* by George Simmons, Professor of Mathematics, who was one of the 5 faculty members who voted against continuing the Block Plan at Colorado College. Simmons was a senior member of the faculty who had published a number of text books in Mathematics, so his criticisms were taken seriously. For more on Professor Simmon's critique, see Steve Paul, "Math Professors Voice Opposition To Block Plan," *Catalyst*, 31 January 1975, 1.

[30]"Midnight Scholars," *Newsweek*, 30 December 1974. See also Randy Kiser, "CC's 'Midnight Scholars' Featured In National Weekly," *Catalyst*, 31 January 1975, 1. For a more pedagogical evaluation of the Block Plan, see "The Colorado College Plan," *Critique* (a quarterly memorandum from the Center for the Study of Higher Education, The University of Toledo), March 1973

"One of the things I have told people," Brooks said, "is that the Block Plan is simply a vehicle for teaching the liberal arts and sciences. My real commitment is to the liberal arts and sciences. . . . The Block Plan is a way of doing business. If it works, great! If it doesn't work, change it! And if it doesn't *really* work, then abandon it altogether."

But Glenn Brooks acknowledged the Block Plan was becoming a popular academic innovation and was giving Colorado College a new identity. He concluded: "I don't have an emotional stake in the Block Plan, the way some people seem to have. . . . But I think it is part of the institution now. Alumni . . . say, 'Don't mess with the Block Plan!' .. . . They want to keep it because it has been pretty successful."[31]

CLASS PARTIES

One of the unexpected benefits of the Block Plan was the class party. By the mid–1970s it had become almost a tradition that, at least once during a block, the professor and the class would get together in a more informal setting for some social life. After all, one of the goals of the Block Plan had been to build stronger student-faculty relationships, and what better way to work toward that goal than a good class party.

Class parties took many forms. The most popular form was for the students to come to the professor's home in the evening for a meal and a class discussion afterward. This created a "homey" atmosphere for the students, particularly if the professor was married and had small children. It was duly noted by the *Catalyst*, however, that the presence of the professor's spouse and children often had a dampening effect on the celebratory level of the class party.

There were many other ways to do a class party. Sometimes professor and class would go out to a restaurant for lunch or dinner. Some classes would go to a relevant movie film, or a musical performance, or a dramatic production. In those cases where the professor was something of a party-type, the class and the professor would just get together, drink refreshments, and talk. The Drama Department became famous for holding good class parties, but those parties had the advantage of being cast

[31]Brooks oral history, 14 February 1996, 55.

parties as well as class parties. The language departments developed a reputation for taking their classes on picnics.

Soon the class party was institutionalized, at least if there was a home-cooked meal involved. Saga, the food service at Colorado College, agreed to give the class the amount of food and non-alcoholic beverages equivalent to what the boarding students would have eaten and drunk in the dining halls. Professors and culinary-minded students could pick up food supplies and utensils from Saga and prepare the meal in whatever location the class party was going to be held.

As would be expected, particular professors and particular classes became famous for the exuberance and celebratory level of their class parties. But many students said they preferred class parties that dealt with the subject matter of the course as well as providing a more relaxed atmosphere. Such parties gave the discerning student "the chance to look at the class from a different, loosened perspective."[32]

GRADE INFLATION

Colorado College did not escape one of the major college and university trends of the early 1970s—grade inflation. According to the Office of the Dean, there was approximately a 5 percent increase in the number of A grades given at the College in the two-year period from 1972 to 1974. This trend was reflected at prestige universities such as Harvard and Stanford, where there were substantial statistical increases in both grade point averages and the number of students receiving honors at graduation.

There were many theories about why, all across the nation, such readily-observable grade inflation was taking place. One theory was that, with so many Baby Boom students trying to get into graduate and professional schools, professors were unwilling to handicap their undergraduate students by giving them low grades. Another theory held that, with the nation in the midst of an economic recession from 1973 to 1975, college and university students were frightened about their future job prospects and were putting more effort into getting good grades.

---

[32]Colin Crawford, "Blasenheim, Hannigan, and Lewis Social Aces: Class Parties At CC," *Catalyst*, 6 May 1977, 1.

At Colorado College there was an inclination to attribute the grade inflation to the improved quality of the students admitted in recent years. "I think it's a better student body," said Dean Richard C. Bradley. "The quality of students has risen nationally," said J. Douglas Mertz, Professor of Political Science and the College pre-law advisor. According to Admissions Director Dick Wood, the College was selecting 500 to 600 entering students from 2,000 to 3,000 applicants. As a result, Wood concluded, "every year the quality of the applicant pool is a little higher."[33]

Concern with Proper Sex Roles

As the women's liberation movement grew in importance during the early 1970s, the attention of Colorado College students, both men and women, shifted to the proper role each sex should play in modern society. Two guest speakers on campus in the fall of 1974 illustrated the nature of the discussion. Rita Costick and Don Ward, of Michigan State University, lectured in Tutt Library Atrium on "The Role Of Communication In Sexual Behavior."

Costick and Ward argued that, under conventional sexual stereotypes, men and women were unable to escape the roles that society had molded for them. The man was to play the powerful male and the woman was to perform as the female secure in his power. But in these widely-accepted roles, Costick and Ward argued, the man felt burdened and the woman stifled. The two speakers urged the students, men and women alike, to "break out of the role," be their real selves, and "not accept the obvious normal and taught."[34]

Leaves of Absence and Time Off

It was becoming increasingly popular with students at Colorado College to takes leaves of absence during their college career, sometimes for leisure and other times to study at a different institution in a different locale. By the mid–1970s approximately 7 percent of the student body was on a leave of absence at some time during the academic year. Students

[33]Jay Hartwell, "Grade Inflation Hits CC, In Line With U.S. Trend," *Catalyst*, 21 February 1975, 1.

[34]Anne Reifenberg, "Ward And Costick Decry Sexual Stereotypes," *Catalyst*, 8 November 1974, 3.

often took a leave of absence to get away from the collegiate world and try to get in touch with what was called "the real world."

Dave Drake, a pre-medical student, took a leave of absence and returned to his hometown to work in a pizza place and a record store. He then got a job transporting wheelchair patients for an ambulance company. He ended up working as an ambulance driver, an experience which reaffirmed his commitment to going to medical school and becoming a physician. At the end of his leave of absence, Drake took a bicycle tour of Japan and visited Hong Kong and Taiwan. He said he came back to Colorado College with an improved sense of himself and his life as a college student.

A different kind of leave was taken by Carol Gregory, who took a semester away from Colorado College to work and study at an environmental education center in Smoky Mountain National Park in Tennessee. She earned 9 semester hours of credit (subsequently accepted by Colorado College) and said the unique courses and the different environment contributed much to her Environmental Studies major.[35]

It also was becoming popular among the students to "take a year off" after graduating from Colorado College before going on to graduate school or professional school. There was great variety in what students might do when taking such time away from academic pursuits. One popular option was to get a job as a bartender, a waiter or waitress, or a member of the ski patrol at a Colorado ski resort, such as Vail or Aspen. Students could earn some money and get some real skiing and socializing done at the same time. Other students returned home and worked hard during their year off, saving badly-needed money and building up "psychic energy" for graduate or professional school.

PSYCHIATRIC CARE

By the mid–1970s the College had instituted a Counseling Center as an integral part of the health care services of the Boettcher Health Center. Psychiatrists and psychologists on the staff of the Counseling Center were available to offer free and confidential advice to students experiencing

[35]Taffy Bond, "Leave Of Absence Accessible And Self-Enriching," *Catalyst*, 31 January 1975, 2.

emotional difficulties. The kind of counseling that previously might have been given by faculty and administrators to students on an amateur basis now was available from full-time paid professionals.

Part of the need for psychiatric and psychological counseling of students arose from the increasing quality of the student body. According to Barbara MacDougald, one of the counseling psychologists, many students at Colorado College were at the top, or close to the top, of their high school classes academically. This gave them a sense of identity and distinction. At Colorado College, however, these top performers from high school found themselves only one among many top performers that had come to the campus. The competition to stand out at the College was much greater. Students had to learn, MacDougald said, how to cope with no longer being the outstanding student, or the most successful campus leader, or the most famous athlete in the institution.

MacDougald gave Colorado College high praise for building academic and intellectual type skills, but she noted it was the job of the Counseling Center to help students acquire emotional management and assertiveness skills. Students needed to learn how to handle anger, frustration, and anxiety, MacDougald said, and how to act independently from their parents.[36]

PALMER HALL RENOVATIONS

In the fall of 1975 the College began an extensive renovation of the classrooms in Palmer Hall. The project was directed by Alvin Boderman, Professor of Sociology, and was undertaken with a view to making the classrooms more compatible with the smaller class sizes and emphasis on seminars brought about by the Block Plan.

The walls were scraped and painted, old radiators were removed and replaced with baseboard heating, and the fluorescent lights were located further down from the high ceilings to make the rooms feel smaller and more intimate. In an effort to preserve the historic character of one of the

---

[36]Janet Odlaug, "Depression And The CC Student: Help Is Available," *Catalyst*, 20 May 1977, 5. JL Spradley, "Counselors Promote Mental Health," *Catalyst*, 17 April 1981, 11. Tragically, psychological counselor Barbara MacDougald died of injuries suffered while skiing. Donna Sanders, "MacDougald Memorial," *Catalyst*, 22 April 1983, 3.

College's finest old buildings, the paint was stripped from the woodwork around the windows, doors, and blackboards. The natural oak wood was stained and varnished.

The renovation of 23 classrooms in Palmer Hall represented another step in the transition of that gigantic stone structure from a Natural Science building to a Social Science building. Palmer Hall was originally constructed to house the classrooms and laboratories of the Natural Science departments, but all of the Natural Sciences except Anthropology, Geology, Mathematics, and Psychology had moved into the new Olin Hall of Science when it was completed in the early 1960s. That had greatly expanded the space available in Palmer Hall for the Social Sciences. One of the goals in renovating the Palmer Hall classrooms in the mid–1970s was to reduce their somewhat sterile, laboratory-like appearance and replace it with a softer, more human, and comfortable atmosphere.[37]

WAITING LIST EVALUATIONS

One of the byproducts of the 25-student class limit, implemented with the Block Plan, was the class waiting list. When more than 25 students wanted to take a particular course, the first 25 were put in the class and the names of the additional students went on the waiting list. When a course developed a long waiting list, that was a pretty good sign that the course was a popular one with a skilled and interesting professor. In the fall of 1975 the student newspaper, the *Catalyst*, printed the names of the courses at the College with the longest waiting lists.

In first place was *Introductory Geology*, taught by John Lewis, with 67 students waiting to get in. The *Catalyst* attributed the course's drawing power to the fact it was taught in the fall (students could admire the yellow aspen trees while chopping rocks in the mountains) and the popularity of the professor. In second place was *Children's Literature*, taught by Ruth Barton, an adjunct professor and also the wife of History Professor Tom K. Barton. The *Catalyst* theorized that 50 additional students wanted this course so they could "revert to some childhood security for a block."

---

[37]Kathie DeShaw, "Palmer Renovation Hammers Away," *Catalyst*, 19 September 1975, 1.

In third place was *International Politics: Versailles To The Cold War*, taught by Political Science Professor Fred Sondermann and History Professor Susan Ashley, with 39 students on the waiting list. The *Catalyst* attributed this course's popularity to the teaching skills of Sondermann and Ashley. It opined: "These two professors could teach Foam Rubber Maintenance and still draw a crowd."[38]

ALCOHOL ABUSE

Early in 1976 the College confronted the problem of student misuse of alcoholic beverages. At a party for new recruits to one of the fraternities, an overly enthusiastic new recruit drank so much alcohol he went into a coma and nearly died. The young man survived only because his prospective fraternity brothers rushed him to the hospital and secured prompt medical attention for him.

Encouraging and allowing a student to drink so much alcohol was deemed to be a violation of the College's liquor policy. Associate Dean Maxwell Taylor promptly put the fraternity on probation. That meant the fraternity could hold no social functions for the remainder of the academic year. If there were further violations of College social rules, the fraternity could be kicked off campus.

The student leaders at the fraternity defended their behavior and objected to being placed on probation. "People at this school misunderstand [us]," one of the fraternity's officers told the *Catalyst*. "They think we're a bunch of typical rich preppies who just spend their money on liquor and getting wasted. Actually, what we do is add diversity to the frat system at this school. The probation was due to the fact that the administration doesn't understand that we're conscientious. We got the guy to the hospital; we took the responsibility. . . . We realize he almost died. After that, even without probation, we would have toned the whole thing down."

---

[38]"Top Waiting Lists," *Catalyst*, 19 September 1975, 8. This issue of the *Catalyst* contained editorial evaluations of a variety of things at Colorado College, from the College administration to the academic departments to the fraternity/sorority system to the availability of drugs on campus. The evaluations should be read with caution. The student newspaper was striving for humor first and accurate judgement second.

The young man who almost died returned to good health and continued to be a fraternity member.[39] But over the next few years the College community struggled with the problem of alcohol abuse, and periodically there would be student-led drives to reduce alcohol consumption at student social events. There also were repeated attempts to convince students to select non-alcoholic beverages rather than just mindlessly guzzling beer, wine, and liquor.[40]

OFF-CAMPUS STUDY PROGRAMS

One popular feature at Colorado College during the 1970s was the off-campus study programs, some lasting an entire semester and some only for one or two blocks. Colorado College faculty and students could set off together for an interesting location and pursue both learning and research. It was a way for students to get to interesting places while at the same time earning academic credit and advancing their college careers.

One such program was the French Department's spring semester program in Menton, France. In this charming village on the French Riviera, Colorado College students did "home-stays" with local French families and thereby were able to rapidly perfect their conversational French. Using Menton as a base, the Colorado College students were able to travel to other places of scenic and historic importance in the general area. Over and above its language benefits, the Menton semester contributed to the "international understanding" of the students who participated in it.

In the spring of 1976 the faculty Committee on Instruction surprised everyone by voting to discontinue the Menton semester. Leading the attack on Menton and similar types of off-campus programs was College Registrar Al Johnson, who also was a Professor of Economics. Johnson pointed out that off-campus study required the student to come up with substantial extra funds for airline tickets and overseas living expenses. Since

---

[39]Alan Gottlieb, ". . . Placed On Probation," *Catalyst*, 6 February 1976, 1.

[40]James Lewis, "Want A C.C. On The Rocks?" *Catalyst*, 5 March 1982, 6. James Lewis, "C.C. Looks At New Programs," *Catalyst*, 19 March 1982, 4. James Lewis and Jennifer Lewis, "One More For The Road," *Catalyst*, 23 April 1982, 4. David Klein, "Alcohol Awareness; Alcohol Related Emergency," *Catalyst*, 15 November 1985, 11. Kevin Haley, "Student Combats Alcohol, Drug Abuse On Campus," *Catalyst*, 4 October 1996, 3.

College scholarships or subsidies for these extra expenses were virtually nonexistent, Johnson argued that only well-to-do Colorado College students from upper middle class backgrounds were able to participate in most off-campus programs. Johnson thus concluded that programs such as the Menton semester were furthering economic discrimination at the College.[41]

Registrar Johnson had put the spotlight on a problem that was to vex the Colorado College faculty for many years. One of the real advantages of a small liberal arts college, and particularly one with the scheduling freedom of the Block Plan, was that faculty could organize courses that traveled to locales relevant to the material being studied. On the one hand, should wealthier students at Colorado College be denied the benefits of off-campus study because *all* the students at the College could not afford to go on such programs? On the other hand, was it really fair for the College to pour considerable resources (the Menton program had a budget of $13,000) into off-campus programs that many students lacked the extra money to participate in?

The question was never really answered. The faculty reversed the decision of the Committee on Instruction and renewed the Menton semester. The College faculty continued to organize exciting, and usually expensive, off-campus programs for students to go on. A notable one was a Spanish language and Mexican culture semester in Cuernavaca, Mexico. No one ever was able to find an adequate way to completely eliminate the economic discrimination implicit in these programs.[42]

EDITOR FIRED

Controversy gripped the campus in the spring of 1976 when the *Catalyst* published a photograph of two young women in revealing bikini bathing suits frolicking in the ocean. The photograph, taken from a recent issue of

---

[41]"Off-Campus Programs: A Controversy Is Born," *Catalyst*, 20 February 1976, 1. For a description of the Menton Semester, see Paul Butler, "Menton Semester Offers Academics, Culture," *Catalyst*, 2 December 1977, 1.

[42]"Off-Campus Programs: Faculty Renews Menton Semester," *Catalyst*, 5 March 1976, 1. For information on additional off-campus study programs, see "Cuernavaca Offers Variety," *Catalyst*, 22 January 1982, 7. Kaaren Bock, "Cuernavaca Program," *Catalyst*, 10 February 1984, 8. Patrick Shea, "German Culture At Hochschule Luneburg," *Catalyst*, 17 February 1984, 8.

Sports Illustrated magazine, was used to highlight the *Catalyst* report that the faculty had decided to continue the off-campus semester in Menton, France. The implication of the photograph was that a student could attend the Menton program and have a really good time playing in the nearby waters of the Mediterranean Sea.

Many women and women's groups on campus took immediate exception to the photograph, labeling it "sexist" and "exploitive." One group of women students was seen marking out approximately 500 of the photographs in copies of the *Catalyst* that had been put in Rastall Center for pick-up by students. The editor of the *Catalyst* who had decided to publish the photograph was publicly accused of "irresponsibility."

Cutler Board, the student organization in charge of the College's student publications, felt the need to hold a public hearing. The problem of sexism raised by the photograph was discussed at length, but there were also concerns that the *Catalyst* editor had failed to get permission from *Sports Illustrated* before publishing the photograph. The editor was dismissed, and new editors of the student newspaper were appointed.

The *Catalyst* reported all of these events in its next issue. The story was illustrated with a different photograph of the same two young bikini-clad women leaping around in the water. A line of print at the bottom of this new photograph noted that permission to publish it had been granted by *Sports Illustrated*.[43]

This second photograph aroused as much feminist ire and as many charges of sexism as the first photograph had. Between 1,500 and 2,000 copies of this issue of the *Catalyst* were illegally confiscated by unknown persons and found their way into various recycling centers around the community. Similar to any student newspaper, the *Catalyst* had wanted to stir up controversy on campus, but it had not expected to become, itself, the center of a controversy.[44]

The flap over the *Sports Illustrated* photographs was an important event in the history of Colorado College. It symbolized the emerging voices and

---

[43]"Editor Dismissed For Copyright Violation," *Catalyst*, 12 March 1976, 1.

[44]Ed Goldstein, "Photo Prompts Irate Feminists To Paper Theft," *Catalyst*, 19 March 1976, 1. A humor supplement to a future issue of the *Catalyst* presented a photo layout of two Colorado College men in bathing suits frolicking in Monument Creek. *Catalyst*, 14 May 1976, "Enzyme" supplement.

the growing political activism of women on the campus. For the first time, many members of the male community at the College came to realize that the women were serious about redefining their status and reshaping their role in the College community.

College-Funded Abortions?

As part of its student government, Colorado College had a fund known as the Student Emergency Aid Association (SEAA). The purpose of the fund was to grant money to students to help them get through certain emergency situations. In the spring of 1976 money from the fund was being granted to women students to pay for terminating unwanted pregnancies.

This fund and its use came to general campus attention when the student government (CCCA) decided only to *loan* money for abortions rather than to fund them outright. Shortly after that announcement was made, the student government suspended the activities of the Student Emergency Aid Association and announced that the entire matter was going to be restudied by both the student government and the College administration.

It subsequently became known that President Worner seriously questioned the advisability of student activity funds being used for so controversial a purpose as student abortions. "If something went wrong there, even with the best of care and the parent is told," Worner said, "we made the money available . . . well, I suspect there would be a great many problems that would arise there. . . ."[45]

The Presidency Mini-Symposium

One of the casualties of the adoption of the Block Plan was the January Symposium, that week-long feast of speakers, movies, and panel discussions that had been held prior to the start of second semester classes. The January Symposium had been a big part of College intellectual life during the 1960s. It was discontinued in 1971 because the Block Plan calendar,

[45]Jay Hartwell, "C.C.C.A. Reverses Abortion Decision," *Catalyst*, 23 April 1976, 1. Gregg E. Easterbrook, "Guest Commentary: Where Is The Real C.C.C.A.?" *Catalyst*, 30 April 1976, 4. Alan Prendergast, "S.E.A.A.: Paying For Other People's Mistakes," *Catalyst*, 7 May 1976, 4. Also see Molly Parrish, "C.C. To 'Restudy' Student Policy For Abortion Loans," *Colorado Springs Gazette Telegraph*, 15 April 1976.

with nine blocks per academic year, was so tightly packed. There simply was not enough time to take an entire week in January for a Symposium.

In April of 1976 Fred Sondermann, Professor of Political Science, decided to organize a shortened version of the Symposium. He scheduled the various events in the late afternoon and the evening so they would not conflict with most Block Plan classes.

This mini-Symposium was on the subject of the upcoming 1976 presidential election. The major speaker was Theodore Sorensen, the speech writer for former President John F. Kennedy prior to Kennedy's assassination in 1963. Although it had been 13 years since President Kennedy's death, there was standing-room-only in Armstrong auditorium when Sorensen took the podium.

Referring to the recent Watergate scandal under former President Nixon, Sorensen said he opposed reducing the powers of the presidency but did think the American people had to work harder at making their presidents more accountable. Sorensen somewhat shocked his audience by predicting that Jimmy Carter, the little-known former governor of Georgia, would win both the Democratic nomination and the presidential election in November. Sorensen later revealed that he was supporting Carter for President but believed his predictions to be accurate ones nonetheless.

Another guest speaker at the 1976 mini-Symposium was Thomas E. Cronin, Professor of Political Science at Brandeis University in Massachusetts. Speaking in Tutt Library, Cronin argued that the American people expect too much of their presidents, wanting them to be attractive personally as well as have great skill at solving all of the nation's social and economic problems. No person could live up to such demands, Cronin concluded, which is why the American people so often become disillusioned with the person who is elected President.[46]

Tom Cronin made a strong impression on both the students and the faculty at Colorado College. He was asked back to teach a number of courses under the Block Plan, and those courses worked out so successfully he eventually became a permanent member of the Political Science

---

[46]Recollection of the author. Also see Mark Anderson, "Diary Of A Presidency Symposium," *Catalyst*, 16 April 1976, 4.

Department. He specialized in teaching courses on the United States presidency and political leadership.

WATSON FELLOWSHIPS

One of the exciting intellectual developments of the 1970s was the large number of Colorado College seniors who were winning Watson Fellowships for post-graduate travel and study. The Watson Fellowship was created by Thomas J. Watson, the founder of International Business Machines (IBM), for the purpose of allowing students to take a full year to travel to a place that interested them and further their knowledge on a particular topic. This scholarly endeavor was to be undertaken for its own benefit and *not* to earn the student an advanced degree at a graduate institution.

Colorado College was one of 50 colleges and universities selected to nominate graduating seniors to win a Watson. Every year one and often two Colorado College applicants were named Watson Fellows.

The class of 1976 at Colorado College won a total of three Watson Fellowships. Michael Nava proposed to travel to Mexico City, Mexico, and Buenos Aires, Argentina, to research the life of South American poet Ruben Dario. A poet himself, Nava hoped to translate Dario's major poems from Spanish to English.

A second Watson winner in 1976 was Anne Berkeley, who had been active in drama production at Colorado College and a past president of Theater Workshop. She planned to travel to Paris, France, to work in an experimental repertory theater and study recent developments in drama on the European continent.

The third winner was Peter Offenbecher, a Political Economy major, who worked part time as an investigator for the juvenile courts in Colorado Springs while attending Colorado College. He proposed to go to Scotland to learn about the juvenile justice system there, which concentrated on changing the juvenile offender's behavior rather than emphasizing his legal rights in court.[47]

The faculty member who most strongly managed and supported the Watson Fellowship program at Colorado College was Professor John Riker

---

[47]Harlan Feder, "Three Seniors Win Watson," *Catalyst*, 30 April 1976, 1.

of the Philosophy Department. Riker's efforts were typical of many of the College's faculty. He gave long hours of his time to the Watson program, advertising it among the student body and counseling students on the best ways to frame a Watson proposal so it would have a chance of being selected. Whether it was some other graduate program, such as the Rhodes Scholarship, or an off-campus program, such as the Chicago Urban Semester, faculty members such as Professor Riker were putting forth a great deal of effort—without extra financial remuneration—to make these programs a successful and meaningful part of a Colorado College education.

Theme Houses

Jackson House, a large former private home used by the College for additional dormitory space, inspired the development of the "theme house" concept at Colorado College. Originally the College had doled out rooms in Jackson House, located on North Nevada Avenue across from the main campus, on the basis of a room lottery. In the spring of 1976, however, a group of students came forward and asked that Jackson House's accommodations for 29 students be assigned exclusively to them. The students wanted to use the house for cooperative living.

Instead of giving Jackson House to the cooperative living group, it was decided to invite a wide variety of student organizations to apply to occupy the house and organize intellectual and social life in the house around a central theme. A group calling itself "Creative Awareness Through The Visual And Performing Arts" eventually was chosen, mainly because it was felt the group's artistic endeavors would favorably effect the broader campus community as well as the students living in the theme house.[48]

The students living in Jackson House delivered on their promise to provide an artistic uplift to the student body. During the 1976–1977 academic year they held an outdoor music festival, sponsored workshops on madrigal singing and life drawing, scheduled a regular series of musical performances known as the Firelight Series, and started a jazz improvisation workshop.[49]

---

[48]Christie Balka, "Art Group Gets Jackson," *Catalyst*, 14 May 1976, 1.

[49]"Jackson House Presents . . . ," *Catalyst*, 11 February 1977, 2.

Theme houses became increasingly popular at Colorado College over the ensuing years. Houses were organized around such themes as environmental action, experimenting with solar energy, and volunteering personal time and energy to help solve social and economic problems in the Colorado Springs community. Best of all, theme houses provided activist groups of students the opportunity to further in their daily living some of the concepts and ideas they were learning about in the classroom.[50]

PROFESSOR DISMISSED

During the mid–1970s the College found it necessary to dismiss a tenured professor who had falsified his academic credentials. The faculty member, first hired in the mid–1960s, claimed to have received a Ph.D. from a well-known university. When the College, acting on a tip, checked the professor's credentials, it turned out he had never even attended that particular university, let alone received a Ph.D. It was College policy that falsification of credentials was sufficient grounds for immediate dismissal.

The most interesting aspect of the case was that the professor apparently was doing a creditable job of teaching courses at Colorado College. He joined the faculty as a part-time instructor and did well enough that he was hired full-time and eventually granted tenure. Many members of the College community were genuinely shocked to learn the man did not possess the credentials he claimed to have.

ELECTRONIC MUSIC

The post-World War II trend toward electronic music reached Colorado College in the fall of 1976 when the Music Department purchased a "Synthi 100" music synthesizer and installed it in the electronic music studio in Packard Hall. Professor of Music Stephen Scott used the machine both for teaching students and writing and playing his own compositions. The new machine generated musical sounds by changing the voltage sent through an electronic oscillator.

---

[50]Laurel Van Driest and Lara Roberts, "Group Tackles 20th Century Survival," *Catalyst*, 18 May 1979, 2.

Chess in Packard Courtyard

A large outdoor chess board, measuring 40 feet by 40 feet, had been set up in the courtyard of Packard Hall. Sixteen students volunteered to dress in appropriate costumes and serve as chess "pieces" so that History Professor Tom K. Barton could play an al fresco chess match with student Jim Hamilton, a member of the senior class. Barton and Hamilton surveyed the chess board and shouted their moves down from the second level balcony of the studio wing of Packard Hall. The contest lasted one hour and was won by Professor Barton.[51]

Career Counseling

One area in which Colorado College was somewhat behind other colleges and universities was career counseling. There was no one person in charge of helping graduating seniors to get jobs or get into graduate and professional school. Perhaps most important, there were no trained professionals on campus who could help the students explore their own career desires and develop a coherent plan for getting a good job. Colorado College also lacked a full-time employee who made it a point to make contacts in the business world and turn those contacts into job interviews for the students.

This situation changed in the fall of 1976 when Carol Leavenworth was hired as the College's new career counselor. A 1974 graduate of the University of Wisconsin with a Masters degree in Guidance and Counseling, Leavenworth worked at setting up a full-service Career Center on campus. She conducted group counseling sessions to help students become aware of the wide variety of career opportunities open to prospective graduates of liberal arts colleges. She also encouraged students to prepare their resumes, practice interviewing for jobs, and take advantage of the increasing number of job recruiters she was bringing to the campus. An extensive collection of university catalogs was assembled for those students interested in going on to graduate and professional school.

---

[51]"Time Warp; A Look Back In C.C. History," *Catalyst*, 4 October 1996, 2.

The Career Center quickly became a permanent part of the administrative structure at Colorado College with its own offices and interviewing rooms for use by job recruiters.[52]

THE PLAZA HOTEL CRISIS

President Worner and the Board of Trustees faced a very difficult situation in the late fall of 1976 when Colorado Technical College, a small private college offering mechanical and commercial courses, tried to lease the old Plaza Hotel. The building, located at the corner of Cache La Poudre and Tejon streets across from Armstrong Hall, had been offered for sale to Colorado College some years earlier, but the Board of Trustees passed up that opportunity, allegedly because the asking price was too high.

Colorado Technical College planned to move all 250 of its students, almost all of them local residents of Colorado Springs, into the old hotel building, which for many years had been operated as an office building. President Worner regarded this as a major threat to Colorado College because of traffic congestion and security problems.

J. Douglas Mertz, a former Professor of Political Science who was Colorado College's full-time legal consultant, explained that Colorado College had spent over $1 million to solve parking problems on the campus, an investment that would have been lost if 250 additional students—with 250 additional automobiles—were allowed into the area. Mertz also noted that Colorado College had no worries about the caliber and character of Colorado Technical College students, but anytime the number of people in a given locale is increased, the number of robberies, rapes, and other crimes is going to go up. Mertz noted that his position "had nothing to do with snobbery."

Colorado College had other concerns, largely unexpressed, about accepting Colorado Technical College as such a close neighbor. The names of the two institutions were highly similar, which meant that Colorado Technical College, a brand-new institution, would be able to

---

[52]Cathy McCall, "Career Counselor Chosen," *Catalyst*, 8 October 1976, 1. The author served on the Career Placement Committee, which monitored the early development of the Career Center. Also see Patrick Shea, "Nish Revamps Career Center," *Catalyst*, 10 February 1984, 6.

trade somewhat on the strong reputation which Colorado College had been building for more than a century. It also was inevitable that Colorado Technical College students, if located next door, would avail themselves of such open-to-the-public Colorado College facilities as the Hub snack bar in Rastall Center, Tutt Library, and the lawns and walking paths of the general campus.

After conferring with Robert Loevy, the Political Science Department's resident authority on state and local government issues, President Worner decided to oppose Colorado Technical College with every publicity weapon at his disposal. In order to legally move into the Plaza Hotel building, Colorado Technical College needed a zoning variance from the Colorado Springs City Council. President Worner recruited a phalanx of powerful friends of Colorado College to go down to the City Council chambers and strenuously oppose the zoning variance for Colorado Technical College.

Leading the charge was Russell Tutt, the Chairman of Colorado College's Board of Trustees and the President of the Broadmoor Hotel and El Pomar Foundation. He was joined by William Wells, President of the Board of Trustees of the Colorado Springs Fine Arts Center, and William Mueller, the former president of Colorado Interstate Gas. Along with President Worner, these men testified at length before City Council as to why Colorado College should not have a somewhat similar educational institution located just across the street.

The attorney for Colorado Technical College listened to all the Colorado College testimony and then quickly withdrew from the battle. "We have been made to appear as Attilla the Hun storming the gates of the city," he lamented.[53] Robert Turkisher, the President of Colorado Technical College, acknowledged that his institution had been hit with "a preponderance of heavyweights." The City Council voted 6 to 1 to deny Colorado Technical College the zoning variance required to move into the old Plaza Hotel.[54]

---

[53]Related to the author by Mike Bird, Professor of Economics at Colorado College, who at that time was a member of the Colorado Springs City Council.

[54]Niles Lathem, "Polytec Move Vetoed By CC And Council," *Catalyst*, 14 January 1977, 12 (page misdated 14 January 1976).

The near loss of the Plaza Hotel building to Colorado Technical College was a learning experience for Colorado College. When the opportunity presented itself in the summer of 1991, the College bought the old Plaza Hotel and began the process of converting it into a College office building. It was renamed Spencer Center for longtime College benefactor William Spencer, who was chairman of the Board of Trustees in the 1980s.[55]

In fact the College began making a concerted effort to buy as much property as possible on the south side of Cache La Poudre Street where it adjoined the campus. In the spring of 1977 the College purchased the Meadow Gold building, a large one-story brick commercial building that at one time housed a major dairy operation. In the years prior to World War II students and townspeople had been able to buy ice cream cones and other dairy products in the building, and it became something of a campus meeting place. The College's short range plan for the building was to tear down part of it for a badly needed parking lot.[56]

Palmer Hall Museum Removed

In 1977, as part of the continuing renovation of Palmer Hall, the College began to dismantle and remove the natural history museum located on the third floor. The whale skeleton and the stuffed animals were transferred to a variety of locations in Colorado, such as the Museum of Natural History in Denver. A small bit of Colorado College history and tradition died when the Palmer museum was sent elsewhere. No longer could irate students, as they had done in the past, demonstrate their displeasure with the College administration by secretly moving the Palmer museum's stuffed animals to various inappropriate locations around the campus.

The large space occupied by the Palmer museum was redecorated with wall-to-wall carpeting and comfortable chairs and sofas. During the day it was designed to function as a faculty common room, a place where the faculty could go to read, converse, and hold small meetings. The

---

[55]Randy Grow, "College Expands Across Cache La Poudre," *Catalyst*, 18 October 1991, 4.

[56]"CC Buys Meadow Gold Building," *Catalyst*, 22 April 1977, 1.

College arranged for Saga food service to serve a delicatessen-style buffet lunch in the new common room, thus creating an opportunity for faculty and administrators to get together and socialize during the noonday meal. Almost immediately, a small group of faculty became lunchtime "regulars" in the common room and very much enjoyed this new opportunity for faculty intellectual exchange combined with conviviality.[57]

In the late afternoon and evening the faculty common room was available for lectures, receptions, and catered meals that were open to all members of the College community. The new common room immediately became the location for faculty meetings (one per Block Plan block) as well as a popular spot for retirement parties and, for persons connected with the College, wedding receptions. The new facility was named Gates Common Room in honor of the charitable foundation that donated most of the money for the project.[58]

YET ANOTHER ANTI-MILITARY PROTEST

For a brief moment in the spring of 1977, Colorado College returned to the political protests of the late 1960s and early 1970s. Prior to a scheduled campus visit by a U.S. Army recruiting officer, more than 100 persons gathered in Rastall Center to protest military officer recruiting at Colorado College. The protest was organized by a student, Frank Lane, who told the crowd not to "forget Vietnam so quickly." He added: "We must stop people who offer bribes and other enticements in order to recruit professional killers."

Also speaking at the protest was Michael Parenti, a Visiting Professor in the Political Science Department. Parenti added a bit of a Marxist twist to the proceedings when he charged that the United States was "a military machine committed to the goal of global counterrevolution." Parenti then asked the assemblage a question: "Are we really making the world

---

[57]Members of this initial group of lunchtime regulars in the common room included the author and professors Carl Roberts (Psychology), Bill Champion (Chemistry), Dirk Baay (German), and Fredrick Keller (Psychology and Computer Services).

[58]Colin Crawford, "Whale To Be Removed: Palmer Renovation Begins," *Catalyst*, 4 February 1977, 1. Mary Brown, "New Breath Of Life For Palmer Hall," *Catalyst*, 21 October 1977, 4.

safe for democracy with our military installations in 109 countries, or are we making it safe for General Motors and ITT (International Telephone and Telegraph)?"

But the protesters made no effort to stop the Army recruiters from setting up their table and talking to interested students. As the demonstration broke up, one of the Army recruiters privately affirmed the group's constitutional right to assemble and speak out.[59]

JESSIE ERWIN BROWN

One of the memorable elements of college and university life is the members of the service staff who become well known to and good friends of large numbers of students. Such a staff member was Jessie Erwin Brown, the custodian in Tutt Library during the late 1970s. Brown was drafted into the Army during the Korean War and, following his military retirement in 1974, came to work for the College. He became famous for having a ready smile and a friendly greeting for anyone who came into the library. He typified the large numbers of staff persons who worked at the College over the years and, in a very different way from the faculty and administrators, had an important impact on the lives and values of the students.

"I didn't get out of the Army to make money but to be happy," Brown said during a *Catalyst* interview. "At [Colorado College] I work with people, and working with people means a lot." Brown said students tended to talk to him, not about academic problems, but about adjusting to life at Colorado College.[60]

THE WRITING PROGRAM

By the late 1970s there was increasing concern at Colorado College over the writing abilities of many of the students. There also was much discussion over whether the College was doing as much as it should to improve the quality of student writing. The problem stemmed from the fact that, during the 1967–1968 academic year, the faculty had voted to eliminate the requirement that all first year students take a combined writing-

---

[59]Andrew Wolfson, "ROTC Demonstration Hits Rastall," *Catalyst*, 15 April 1977, 1. Also see Frank E. Lane, "More For Your Money: ROTC: A Multi-Issue Issue," *Catalyst*, 6 May 1977, 3.

[60]Cindy Butler, "Library Personality: Jessie Is Exceptional," *Catalyst*, 15 April 1977, 8.

literature course in the English Department. At that time the English Department argued that the responsibility for teaching writing rested with every academic department and every course, not just the English Department and one required freshman year literature course.

The difficult national economy in the late 1970s made the student body particularly sensitive to the issue of future employment after graduation. It was the era of "stagflation," when increasing unemployment rates were combined with a high rate of inflation. There was much student discussion centering on the idea that students who had not been trained to write well would not succeed very well in such a challenging economic environment. The final result was a grass roots movement among the student body to have some sort of a writing program at Colorado College. A faculty leader in this effort was History Professor Tom K. Barton.

After much discussion, the faculty adopted a plan to create a number of courses, in a variety of academic departments, to be taught "with Emphasis on Writing." These "writing courses" would all involve a definite subject matter, such as *Foundations of Classical Culture* or *Politics, Ethics, and Journalism*, but the professors teaching the courses would give heavy writing assignments and meet personally with the students to help them improve their writing skills. In order to compensate the faculty for the extra time required to grade all the additional student papers in a "writing course," the maximum class size for such courses was cut from 25 students to just 12.

In addition to the "with Emphasis on Writing" courses, the College set up a Writing Center where students in any course could go and get tutored on their writing problems. Students were encouraged to bring in the rough drafts of their course papers and go over them line-by-line with a writing tutor. Undergraduate students with strong writing skills were trained to help with the tutoring. A full-time administrator was hired to organize the Writing Program, train the student tutors, and get the word out to the undergraduates to take advantage of this helpful service.[61]

---

[61]Kristin Lau, "Students Have Writing Problems," *Catalyst*, 6 May 1977, 1. Sue Royce, "Writing Institute Offers Improvement To Students," *Catalyst*, 24 February 1978, 3. Ed Goldstein, "Writing Given Priority By C.C. Faculty," *Catalyst*, 22 September 1978, 1. Eric Trekell, "Help On The Way For Poor Writers," *Catalyst*, 19 January 1979, 2. Donna Sanders, "Writing Assistance Begins Anew," *Catalyst*, 17 September 1982, 2.

At many other colleges and universities, only those students with demonstrated writing deficiencies were entitled to get writing help. This was not the case at Colorado College. Students at all levels of writing ability were encouraged to use the Writing Center, and many of the better student writers willingly and enthusiastically did so.

The Writing Center subsequently acquired a Texas Instruments (TI) computer with a word processor with a spelling correction program. The *Catalyst* subsequently noted: "There's no other place in town that has a room full of English buffs dying to sit down with a cup of coffee and help improve a student's writing skills. Set up an appointment."[62]

SAGGING APPLICATIONS

Anxiety levels began rising among faculty and administrators at Colorado College in the late 1970s when the number of applicants for admission began to drop. From the peak years of 1971 and 1972, when some 3,500 high school seniors applied each year, the number of applicants dropped to only 2,100 in 1977. Many observers worried that, in such a situation, the academic caliber of students entering Colorado College had to be declining.

One reason for the drop in applications was the slowly advancing end of the World War II Baby Boom. High school seniors applying for admission in the late 1970s were born in the late 1950s, when the unusually high post-World War II birth rate was starting to decline. The future looked challenging. The size of the applicant pool—the number of high school seniors available to apply to all colleges and universities—was expected to decline steadily until the year 1992.

Dick Wood, the Admissions Director at the College since 1961, sought to relieve some of the worry. It was pointed out that average Scholastic Aptitude Test (SAT) scores were down among Colorado College first year students, but average SAT scores were dropping for entering freshmen at colleges and universities all over the nation. Also the Admissions Office did not see SAT scores as the best measure of whether a student could do the work required at Colorado College.

---

[62]Paul Fenn, "Writing Buffs Polish Skills; Center Adds Word Processor," *Catalyst*, 14 September 1984, 7.

Dick Wood also saw the number of applications falling because Colorado College had been required to send out so many rejection letters in previous years. The word had gotten around that Colorado College was difficult to get into, and mediocre students declined to apply—or were advised not to apply—as a result. "Self-selection is stronger now," Wood observed. The College's growing reputation for competitive admissions had resulted in higher quality levels among those high school seniors who did actually apply for admission.

The College was making real progress in the late 1970s in recruiting minority students. In an effort to attract more Spanish-surnamed students, the Admissions Office intensified its minority recruitment efforts in the southwestern United States. The number of Spanish-surnamed students, referred to in everyday conversation as Chicanos, was expected to reach as high as 100 students during the 1977–1978 academic year, up from 70 students the previous year.

The College was continuing to make a major investment in minority student recruitment. In 1976–1977 some 6–7 percent of the student body qualified as minorities, but these students were receiving 27 percent of the College's financial aid. That level of monetary support for minority students—primarily Blacks and Chicanos—was expected to be sustained into the foreseeable future.[63]

---

[63]Ross Barker, "52% Of Applicants Accepted: Freshman Class Of Questionable Academic Caliber," *Catalyst*, 20 May 1977, 3. Also see Gabriele Harstrick, "Admissions: C.C. Remains Competitive," *Catalyst*, 11 May 1979, 1.

CHAPTER 9

THE CLOSE OF THE WORNER YEARS

The 1977–1978 academic year began with Colorado College having the highest enrollment in its history. There were 1,927 full time students, an increase of over 100 students from the previous year. Because of the increased willingness of the College administration to give students permission to live off-campus, the record-setting size of the student body did not produce a great deal of overcrowding in the dormitories. Only about 12 students were sleeping in study lounges or other makeshift quarters. There was no need, as had been done in past years, to rent out extra rooms at J's Motel.

A number of faculty grumbled that the College was using off-campus housing to slowly increase the size of the student body and thereby take in more tuition income. Many professors wondered if Colorado College was not admitting too many students, thereby causing too many classes to fill up to the Block Plan's 25-student limit. Professor of Philosophy Harvey Rabbin complained in the *Catalyst* that the growing size of the College was inevitably having adverse effects on the student-faculty ratio.

For its part the College administration said it was aiming each year for a student body of 1,880 students. There also was the consideration that the annual budget at the College was based on getting a specific number of paid tuitions. Given the uncertainties of the admissions process, and the difficulty knowing exactly how many students would return each semester after a leave of absence, the administration argued it was better to err on the side of too many students rather than too few. Dean Richard Bradley did say, however, the College's goal was to bring enrollment "back down to 1,800 over the next few years."

One effect of allowing so many students to live off-campus was an apartment shortage in the residential neighborhoods immediately adjacent to the campus. With 600 Colorado College students living off-campus (compared to about 1,200 on campus), and with most of those students trying to live within 5 blocks or so of the campus, adequate but inexpensive apartments in the College's neighborhood had become very difficult to find.[1]

In line with the College's goal of having equal numbers of men and women students, the incoming first year class in the fall of 1977 was perfectly balanced. Including the Summer Start members of the class, there were 296 women and 296 men. As had been true for a number of years, one-third of the first year class was from Colorado.[2]

A NEW DEAN OF WOMEN

A wave of protest swept through the student government at Colorado College when President Worner appointed a new Dean of Women without involving any students in the selection process. The former Dean of Women, Elizabeth Sutherland, had resigned and taken a new job at Mercy College in Detroit, Michigan. After conferring with top administrators and key faculty members but no students, President Lloyd Worner filled the vacant post with Laurel McLeod, the Assistant Dean of the Summer Session. The students did not object to the new Dean of Women personally but to the manner in which she was chosen for her job.

President Worner said it was not "normal procedure" to consult students when filling a job with "in house" personnel. If the College had done a national search to fill the position, the President said, then student opinions would have been officially solicited. In this case, Worner concluded, it was "a normal promotion with the College that did not require that widespread input."[3]

---

[1]Alan Gottlieb, "Increase In Enrollment Effects Every Phase," *Catalyst*, 16 September 1977, 3. Tracy Curts, "Students And Housing Office Confront Dilemma," *Catalyst*, 16 September 1977, 3. Chris Nordlinger, "C.C.C.A. Attacks Dean Selection, Enrollment," *Catalyst*, 23 September 1977, 1.

[2]Ted Stavish, "Freshpersons: Easy Adjustment To The CC Scene," *Catalyst*, 7 October 1977, 3.

[3]Chris Nordlinger, "Students Ignored In Dean Selection Process," *Catalyst*, 16 September 1977, 1.

The students based their case on an official publication of the College that stated that "students at Colorado College work closely with faculty and administrators in policies that affect student life." The position of Dean of Women was viewed as one directly related to student affairs, given the large number of students who came to that particular Dean for counsel and advice.[4]

For her part, Laurel McLeod said she hoped to break out of the traditional role of the Dean of Women being the "old-fashioned moral leader." She explained: "At this historical period, this job conjures up an entirely new image—with new activities and new possibilities." Although part of her job entailed working with women's issues, such as the proposed Equal Rights Amendment, McLeod said most of her work would be concerned with both men and women students.[5]

When reminded that the Dean of Women used to be a combination mother and policewoman who set dress codes and dormitory curfews for "coeds," Dean McLeod laughed and said: "I am told . . . that part of my budget is . . . for me to go out and buy a bunch of old women's dresses and put my hair up in a bun."[6]

MELLON BLOCKS

A continuing concern at the College had been the heavy workload imposed on the faculty by the Block Plan. Most professors had signed up to teach a course in each of the 9 blocks in the academic year, but that had proved to be a very time-consuming and tiring process. Once the excitement of teaching under the new calendar had dimmed somewhat, professors found it a long haul from September to June with no relief from the strain of preparing and teaching classes.

---

[4]Chris Nordlinger, "C.C.C.A. Attacks Dean Selection, Enrollment," *Catalyst*, 23 September 1977, 1. Chris Nordlinger, "C.C.C.A. Reasserts Selection Discontent: Council Drafts Study Committee," *Catalyst*, 7 October 1977, 1.

[5]The Equal Rights Amendment was an amendment to the United States Constitution providing for equal treatment on the basis of sex. Although approved by the United States Congress, the Equal Rights Amendment failed to be adopted when it was not approved by 3/4 of the state legislatures.

[6]Thom Shanker, "College Deans Shift Positions," *Catalyst*, 16 September 1977, 1. Tom Adkison, "Laurel McLeod: Quiet Strength In The Dean's Office," *Catalyst*, 16 September 1977, 4. Ed Langlois, "Close-Up On Deans," *Catalyst*, 21 September 1984, 6.

There was the additional problem that, as professors put so much of their time into teaching classes and advising students, there was no time left, other than summer vacation, for scholarly reading and contemplation. This meant that many professors were unable to keep up with new developments and ideas in their particular academic disciplines. Professors also lacked the time under the Block Plan to conduct research and write books and articles. This limited their ability to represent the College by reading papers at scholarly meetings and publishing in their field.

To relieve some of the teaching pressure on the faculty under the Block Plan, the College applied for and received a $192,000 grant from the Mellon Foundation to be used to give faculty "blocks off" for writing and research. Faculty were to apply to a committee of their peers for a "Mellon block" by stating how they would use the free time from teaching to advance their academic development. The money from the Mellon grant would be used to hire one-block replacements for Mellon block recipients.

Glenn Brooks, the designer of the Block Plan, was one of the authors of the Mellon grant proposal. He noted that the grant would permit faculty members to have block-long sabbaticals in which they would work on projects, travel away from the campus to do research, or study "the horizons of their field to better keep up with important developments." Brooks added: "It must be understood that this is not a salvage operation. The grant should be viewed as a continuing opportunity to help an already solid faculty maintain its professional competence."

Brooks explained that all liberal arts colleges, not just Colorado College, faced the problem of keeping the faculty intellectually honed. The Mellon grant funds were to enable the professors at Colorado College, who were particularly burdened with teaching duties under the Block Plan, to find "the crucial balance between immediate obligations to students and course work, and long range obligations as professional scholars."[7]

The Mellon Block program became an important and enduring part of faculty life at Colorado College. Even after the money from the original grant was used up, the College allocated sufficient funds to enable fac-

---

[7]Thom Shanker, "College Receives $200,000 Grant," *Catalyst*, 23 September 1977, 1.

ulty to take blocks off for research and writing. Although these blocks off were officially renamed "development blocks," for several years many members of the faculty continued to refer to them as Mellon blocks.[8]

Four Professors

Sad times came to Colorado College in the late 1970s when, within the space of two years, four professors died in the midst of their active teaching careers. The four professors were of different ages, and the four of them had pursued very different academic careers at the College. Taken together, their lives illustrated what the faculty was like and what the faculty was doing in the decade of the 1970s.

Arthur Pettit

The Colorado College community was saddened during the summer of 1977 to learn of the death of Professor of History Arthur Pettit. He was only 39-years-old at the time he passed away. He died of cancer after only nine years at the College. He represented a new wave of professors who were taking teaching jobs at liberal arts colleges in the 1970s—younger professors who were good teachers but also were accomplished scholars with significant publications to their credit. Pettit also was a member of that new generation of professors who were devoting much of their teaching time and research interest to minority issues in the United States.

In 1974 Arthur Pettit published his major work, *Mark Twain And The South,* a study of Twain's attitudes toward Blacks and the peculiar institution of American slavery. The book was nominated for the Bancroft prize, a prestigious award in the field of American History. Pettit also studied the racial problems of the American southwest, and his research on United States attitudes toward Spanish and Mexican peoples led him to develop close relationships with the Chicano students on campus.[9]

---

[8]The author applied for and received a number of development blocks to allow released time for the preparation of this book.

[9]"CC Loses Revered Prof.," *Catalyst,* 16 September 1977, 1.

J. Glenn Gray

In the fall of 1977 the College lost a man said by the *Catalyst* to be the most distinguished member of the faculty of his time. J. Glenn Gray, Professor of Philosophy, died of a heart attack at the age of 64. He had completed 29 years of teaching at Colorado College and was slated to retire the following June.

Glenn Gray's academic career was typical of many of the professors at Colorado College. He was born in an East Coast state, Pennsylvania, near Mifflintown. He attended a small liberal arts college, Juniata College, and then did his advanced work at the University of Pittsburgh and Columbia University in New York City. He served as a combat soldier and intelligence officer in the European theater during World War II, which led him to write his best known work, *The Warriors: Reflections On Men In Battle*. The book was a study of the unique thoughts and experiences of men in an intense wartime environment.

Gray was said to be an outstanding teacher, with students "clinging to every word spoken." He intellectualized about his experiences teaching undergraduates at Colorado College in another book, *The Promise Of Wisdom: A Philosophical Theory Of Education*. He concluded that the general goal of the teacher was to further human individuality but with an appreciation for the needs and values of the larger community. Professor Gray also edited translations of the works of existential philosopher Martin Heidegger.

Although Gray could give brilliant lectures, he spent much of his time in class discussing the views and ideas of his students. Polly Strong, a 1975 graduate of the College and a Philosophy major, described Gray's classroom technique this way: "We knew that if he would only speak openly and fully he would give us things so valuable. . . . We were impatient that he was a teacher intent on drawing out students' ideas, and not a lecturer." A senior Philosophy major, Kelly Shaw, said that Gray's teaching style was based on Heidegger's idea that "the hardest task for any teacher is to let learn, and he was a master at doing exactly that."[10]

---

[10]Thom Shanker, "College Mourns Death Of Professor J. Glenn Gray," *Catalyst*, 4 November 1977, 1. For a sample of Professor Gray's writing and his educational philosophy, see "J. Glenn Gray: An Articulate Legacy of Insight And A Challenge To Freedom," *Catalyst*, 4 November 1977, 6.

Prior to Glenn Gray's untimely death, his colleagues had been writing a series of essays to commemorate his distinguished career as both a teacher and a scholar. The essays, edited by Professor Timothy Fuller of the Political Science Department, were published as a memorial to J. Glenn Gray under the title *Something Of Great Constancy*. Colorado College faculty who contributed essays to this book included Professor of Philosophy Jane Cauvel, Professor of Religion Douglas A. Fox, Professor of History William R. Hochman, and Professor of Music Albert Seay.[11]

Robert Armstrong

Professor of English Robert Armstrong died of a self-inflicted gunshot wound in February of 1978. A committed teacher with an interest in all aspects of literature, including 20th Century poetry and modern novels, he was only 42 years of age. He had just returned from a 7-month sabbatical devoted to a combined travel and reading program.

Bob Armstrong was typical of the Colorado College professor who devoted his career completely to his teaching and his students. He did not publish extensively, preferring to put all his energies into his own study of English literature and the sharing of the fruits of that study in the classroom. His classes became famous for his exuberance and his passion for the material he was presenting. The *Catalyst* commented:

"His students will recall the times when he became so excited and engulfed by a piece of literature that in his analysis he seemed to temporarily transcend the realm of the classroom and become surrounded by a poem or a passage, letting it sweep him away from consciousness."

Armstrong graduated from Carleton College in Northfield, Minnesota, in 1957. Named a Fulbright Scholar, he spent a year studying at the University of Bordeaux in France. He did graduate work at Johns Hopkins University in Baltimore, Maryland, and received an M.A. in English Literature from the University of Arizona in Tucson. He was one of a limited number of professors at Colorado College who were so talented in their teaching they were allowed to become tenured members of the faculty without earning a Ph.D degree.

---

[11]Timothy Fuller, ed., *Something Of Great Constancy: Essays In Honor Of The Memory Of J. Glenn Gray, 1913–1977* (Colorado Springs, CO: Colorado College, 1979).

By not taking a doctorate, Bob Armstrong eschewed becoming a specialist in a narrow area of English literature. But it was his commitment to all phases of literature, and his dedication to knowledge in a wide variety of areas, that made him particularly moving and inspiring as an undergraduate teacher.[12]

Fred Sondermann

A man said to be one of the best teachers who ever taught at Colorado College died of lung cancer in the fall of 1978. Fred Sondermann, Professor of Political Science, had been at the College for 25 years. Characteristically, despite suffering through a long and debilitating illness, he was still actively teaching a class in International Relations the same week that he died. He was 54 years old.

Fred Sondermann was born in Germany in 1924. A big part of his charm was the slight German accent he retained from his youth. Because he and his family were Jews, they emigrated to the United States in the late 1930s, barely escaping Nazi persecution.

Sondermann joined the U.S. Army during World War II and served in the South Pacific. It was during this period that he first demonstrated his phenomenal ability to type on a typewriter at a very high rate of speed. This skill served him well as a faculty member, because he became famous for his ability to effortlessly and quickly type out long memos on a wide variety of subjects pertaining to Colorado College.

Sondermann attended Butler University, where he graduated *magna cum laude* in 1949. He received an M.A. from Indiana University and then took a Ph.D. in International Relations from Yale University. He joined the Colorado College faculty in 1953 and quickly established himself as both an excellent teacher and a ready source of new ideas for exciting programs at the College. He served for a time as Associate Dean of the College and, from 1962 to 1965, headed the College's Summer Session.

Fred Sondermann perhaps was best known for planning and organizing the week long January Symposium that was held for a number of years at the beginning of second semester. He demonstrated his intellectual ver-

---

[12]Sue Royce, "CC Loses Prof.; Bob Armstrong Dies," *Catalyst*, 17 February 1978, 1. Dan Merewether, "Bob Armstrong, 'Joy With A Shy Reservation,'" *Catalyst*, 17 March 1978, 9.

satility by managing symposiums on such diverse topics as the *American Presidency*, the *New Science*, *Urban America*, and *World War II*.

His approach to International Relations was to serve as a voice of reason. He saw foreign affairs as exceptionally complex, and he strove to avoid overly simple solutions to international problems, such as an over-reliance on military power. Sondermann took a questioning attitude toward the United States military role in the Vietnam War, but he saw the nation's political leaders struggling to come up with a workable policy and thus made no radical pronouncements opposing the war. Despite his qualms about U.S. policy in Vietnam, Sondermann strongly supported the nation's defense program.

Fred Sondermann was an active scholar as well as teacher. He helped to organize the International Studies Association and for a time edited the organization's influential journal—*International Studies Quarterly*. He was the coauthor of a major text book, *Theory And Practice Of International Relations*, and he taught at the graduate level at the Denver University Graduate School of International Studies. He was that most desirable commodity at a small liberal arts college—a faculty member who succeeded at being both a great teacher and a respected and published scholar.

The onset of Professor Sondermann's cancer and the 25th anniversary of his coming to Colorado College both occurred in the same year. The College held a formal tribute in Sondermann's honor, with more than 200 persons from the College and the community of Colorado Springs gathered in Gates Common Room to recall his many contributions and give him a standing ovation. Despite the pain of his illness, Fred Sondermann struggled to the podium and said: "Nothing at this College has ever equaled this moment. You have touched me deeply."[13]

In gratitude for Sondermann's service on the City Council and his many efforts to improve community life in Colorado Springs, a new city park, located west of Interstate 25 and north of Uintah Street, was named

---

[13]Ed Goldstein, "Fred Sondermann: All That A Man Was Meant To Be," *Catalyst*, 3 November 1978, 1. Greg Easterbrook, "A Tribute To Professor Fred Sondermann," *Catalyst*, 3 November 1978, 9. The author organized the formal tribute to Professor Sondermann with the help of the Political Science faculty.

Sondermann Park. The 77 acre facility was left mainly in its natural state to encourage such activities as horseback riding, trail walking, and studying the natural environment.[14]

In retrospect it could be said that Fred Sondermann's greatest contribution to Colorado College was chairing the faculty committee that suggested that the 100th anniversary of the College in 1974 be more than just a celebration and also include a review of the College's academic program. It was this recommendation, carried by Fred Sondermann to President Lloyd Worner, that resulted eventually in the development and adoption of the Block Plan. Fred Sondermann started and initiated many new things at Colorado College. One of the most important was the review process that produced the College's most distinguishing modern feature—the Block Plan.[15]

NO MORE MAID SERVICE

A bit of the gentility and pampering that once characterized dormitory life at Colorado College was removed in the fall of 1977 when the College ended all maid service in student bedrooms in the dormitories. From that point on, it was up to the individual students to keep their room floors swept, their desks and chests-of-drawers dusted, and their rugs (if there were any) vacuumed. The College continued to provide maid service to bathrooms, lounges, and hallways in the dormitories.[16]

ALTERNATE ROOM COED HOUSING

In a move that surprised many students, the Board of Trustees approved an experiment in alternate room coed housing for 16 rooms in Mathias Hall. Instead of the sexes being separated into different floors and wings of coed dormitories, men and women could live in adjacent rooms. However, separate toilet and bathing facilities for women and men would be available.

---

[14]Dave McKinnie, "To Cover 77 Acres: Sondermann Park Dedicated," *Catalyst*, 2 November 1979, 1.

[15]For a retrospective on Professor Sondermann's years at Colorado College, see Fred Sondermann oral history, 7 February 1978.

[16]Tom Adkison, "Maids Swept Away," *Catalyst*, 21 October 1977, 3.

President Worner initially announced his opposition to alternate room coed housing, but he changed his opinion upon learning that men and women were already living in adjacent rooms in the French, German, and Spanish language houses. It also was revealed that, back during the 1971–1972 academic year, the College had conducted an alternate room coed housing experiment for 55 students in Mathias Hall, apparently without incident.[17]

The decision to allow alternate room coed housing greatly improved the standing of the College administration in the eyes of the student body. The student newspaper, the *Catalyst,* had been hammering President Worner hard for all the new regulations being enforced on the students. There was general discontent with all the rules concerning dogs, not to mention the strict enforcement of College liquor policies undertaken since that first year student almost drank himself to death at a fraternity house. The students also were upset that student representatives were not participating in the hiring of new deans and the selection of commencement speakers. The approval of adjacent room coed housing by the Board of Trustees quieted this campus furor down a bit.[18]

Coed housing was not the only victory scored by the student body in the fall of 1977 in the drive for a larger student role in College policy making. President Worner accepted a series of guidelines proposed by the student government that allowed for more student input on hiring administrators. That put to rest the controversy over the "in-house" hiring of Dean of Women Laurel McLeod. Also the junior class, set to graduate in 1979, was given a role to play in the process of selecting the 1979 graduation speaker.[19]

---

[17]Nancy Joseph, "Coed Housing Plan To Face Final Hurdle," *Catalyst,* 11 November 1977, 1. Nancy Joseph, "Coed Housing Passes In A Surprise," *Catalyst,* 18, November 1977, 1. Ross Rabin, "Coed Housing: How Changes Are Really Made At CC," *Catalyst,* 10 February 1978, 1.

[18]For a detailed account of the student unrest that was brewing in the fall of 1977, see Jay Hartwell, Anne Reifenberg, and Thom Shanker, "Is CC Running Scared, Or Just Running Away?" *Catalyst,* 11 November 1977, 1. Also see "Presidential Praise," *Catalyst,* 18 November 1977, 6.

[19]Robert S. Lackner, "Worner Accepts C.C.C.A. Hiring Guidelines," *Catalyst,* 16 December 1977, 3. "Grad Speaker Cops Plea: 'Wait And See' Says Jordan," *Catalyst,* 15 September 1978, 1.

PROGRESSIVE DEMOCRATIZATION

One could see by the late 1970s that, in the history of Colorado College, there had been three major periods in terms of the governance of the College. From the College's founding in 1874 to the involuntary retirement of President William Frederick Slocum in 1917, the College had essentially been run by the President and the Board of Trustees. There next ensued a period of rising faculty power, and this drive for faculty power had contributed to Slocum's departure. From 1917 to the late 1960s the faculty was in the ascendancy on the campus, gaining almost complete control over the curriculum and other internal academic matters.

The late 1960s and the entire decade of the 1970s, however, were a period of strident student demands for power, particularly when it came to the social lives of the students. The College administration, with the tacit approval of the faculty, accommodated many of those demands, so much so that the student role in the governance of Colorado College had been greatly enhanced by the late 1970s.

It thus could be said that the history of Colorado College was one of progressive democratization. In the late 19th and early 20th Centuries the College was run very much like an autocracy, with the President and the Board of Trustees setting almost all policies. This gave way to a somewhat aristocratic form, with the faculty (the aristocracy) wresting a great deal of power from the President and the Board (King and Council). In the late 1960s and 1970s a more democratic system of campus governance came about with the student body (the general populace) and its representatives playing an important role in what previously had been exclusively administration and faculty decisions.

When President Worner agreed to have student representatives participate in the hiring process for College administrators, student body leader Neil Morganstern said: "This shows that we are successfully able to cooperate. The strength of the campus community is that when there are problems, parties with differences, including students and the President, [they] can sit down and solve them." The *Catalyst* commented: "The whole affair indicates that the CC community is strong enough to surpass any controversy, and can work together to find solutions to the problems that exist."[20]

[20]Robert S. Lackner, "Worner Accepts C.C.C.A. Hiring Guidelines," *Catalyst*, 16 December 1977, 3.

The Aspen Bike Trip

By the late 1970s one of the great by-products of the Colorado College Block Plan was the annual Aspen Bike Trip, always scheduled for the first block break of the academic year in late September. Between 50 and 100 students would ride their bicycles westward from Colorado Springs over Wilkerson Pass and Independence Pass to Aspen. They were able to enjoy both the mild early fall weather (usually) and the golden colors of the turning aspen leaves.

The student cyclists departed on Wednesday afternoon of block break and spent two nights camping out on the road, arriving in Aspen late Friday afternoon. Trucks and small buses loaded with sleeping bags and food would follow the pedaling entourage. Stragglers who could not make it over that last hill could hitch a ride in a vehicle known as the "sag wagon." On Friday, after reviving themselves the night before at the Twin Lakes Bar and Grill, the cyclists would attack the high spot of the trip, 12,095 foot high Independence Pass, and then enjoy the long downhill coast into the town of Aspen.

The students spent Friday and Saturday nights in Aspen, resting up from their recreational labors in a jacuzzi or a sauna, often at the St. Moritz Hotel. True two-wheel aficionados could spend their one full day in Aspen, Saturday, on an optional pedal trip to the Maroon Bells scenic area a few miles to the south of Aspen. On Sunday both bicycles and bicyclists were loaded into trucks and buses and transported back to the campus.

The Aspen Bike Trip grew famous over the years as a great way for students to get some exercise, see some scenery, and enjoy some social life in an informal setting. Without that unique feature of the Block Plan—the four-and-a-half-day block break—the Aspen Bike Trip might never have come into existence.[21]

ROTC Leaves the Campus

One of the longest student-administration conflicts came to an end at Colorado College when the Board of Trustees voted to terminate the

---

[21]The Aspen Bike Trip was written up in the *Catalyst* almost every year of its existence. For typical coverage, see Beverly Cathcart, "Aspen Biking Is Traditional," *Catalyst*, 3 October 1980, 5. Dan Friedlander, "Exhilarating Challenge: Mile After Beautiful Mile," *Catalyst*, 9 October 1981, 4.

Reserve Officers Training Corps (ROTC) use of office space in Cossitt Hall. The College had hosted the ROTC program for itself, the University of Colorado at Colorado Springs, the local community college, and Colorado Technical College, but only about 5 percent of the students in the program were Colorado College students. The practical effect of the decision was that the ROTC program would have to find office space at one of the other local institutions.

In announcing this decision by the Board of Trustees, President Worner made it clear that Colorado College students would still be able to take ROTC. Military oriented students would simply have to attend classes and participate in training drills at one of the other participating colleges and universities. Worner repeated his well-known belief that the U.S. military would be better off with more officers trained at liberal arts colleges rather than military academies. He explained: "I still believe more officers should come from civilian colleges, and [I therefore] support Colorado College participation in ROTC."[22]

PATTERNS IN NATURE

The variety of courses that can be offered under the Block Plan was ably illustrated when a number of Natural Science professors got together and organized the new course *Patterns In Nature.* The three-block class was designed for non-science majors, allowing them to study under a number of different Natural Science professors in a wide variety of scientific fields. The word "patterns" in the title of the course referred to the idea that many of the same methods of studying and categorizing data are used in all the major sciences.

Perhaps the most interesting feature of the new course was its schedule. After meeting together for two blocks, the students in *Patterns In Nature* separated and all took different courses for a block. This was designed to prevent the students from getting overexposed to the material and to keep them from getting on each other's nerves. Then the class came back together for the third and final block, which was designed to help the stu-

[22]Chris Nordlinger, "ROTC Terminated," *Catalyst,* 18 November 1977.

dents integrate the scientific knowledge gained in the first two blocks with what they were learning in their non-science courses.

The first semester *Patterns In Nature* was scheduled for Blocks 1, 2, and 4. Second semester it was to meet Blocks 5, 6, and 8. Geologists, biologists, chemists, physicists, and mathematicians were signed up to teach various sections of the course, and guest lectures by Social Science and Humanities faculty were included to help show the influence of scientific discoveries on non-scientific disciplines.

The new course was developed by Chemistry Professor Keith Kester and Biology Professor Jim Enderson with the aid of a $55,000 grant from the National Science Foundation. Because the United States was experiencing energy shortages in the late 1970s, *Patterns In Nature* included a major unit on the nation's use and abuse of energy supplies.[23]

A SECOND BLOCK PLAN COLLEGE

In the fall of 1978 the Block Plan concept expanded beyond the campus of Colorado College for the first time. Cornell College, a small liberal arts college in Mount Vernon, Iowa, became the second college to adopt the Block Plan calendar. The faculty at Cornell College voted in the Coloradc College version of a modular schedule after extensive administrator, fac ulty, and student visits to the Colorado College campus.

At that time Cornell College had an enrollment of 850 students, thus it was about half the size that Colorado College was when it developed the Block Plan in the fall of 1968. Colorado College and Cornell College knew each other well, however. Both were members of the Associated Colleges of the Midwest (ACM), the consortium of midwestern liberal arts colleges that had banded together to offer joint off-campus study programs. Another ACM college, Coe College in Cedar Rapids, Iowa, studied the Colorado College Block Plan at the same time Cornell College did, but Coe College made no move to adopt it.

The many visits by Cornell College persons to Colorado College revealed that the biggest drawback of the Block Plan was the heavy faculty workload. Cornell College made a number of adjustments in its version

[23]Tracy Curts, "Enderson, Kester Start Science Semester," *Catalyst*, 17 February 1978, 3.

of the Block Plan to try to answer this loud complaint and gain a favorable vote from the Cornell College faculty. Instead of having to teach nine blocks per year, as Colorado College faculty had to do, Cornell College faculty would only teach seven blocks per year. The two "blocks off" per academic year would be treated as a sabbatical, with individual faculty making the choice as to whether to do research and writing, do committee work and other non-teaching tasks, or simply take the time off.

One of the strong advocates of adopting the Block Plan at Cornell College was Dean Robert Lewis. He commented: "It's a better way of teaching because of the increased interaction between faculty and students, and because it would prevent interference from other classes. It would insure the liberal arts education." Lewis also made it clear the Cornell College was benefitting from the fact that Colorado College had operated the Block Plan successfully for eight years (1970–1978) and had gotten the bugs out of the system. "Visiting CC put an end to the argument that it can't work," Lewis concluded. "It certainly can work."[24]

Because the term Block Plan was so closely associated with Colorado College, Cornell College searched for its own name for this inventive new modular college calendar. Cornell College came up with the descriptive phrase, "One Course At A Time." Some observers at Colorado College thought that "One Course At A Time" gave a better description of the plan than the term Block Plan, the use of which always required a lengthy discussion about just what a block was and exactly how the plan operated.

The adoption of the Block Plan at Cornell College had a definite impact on the faculty at Colorado College.[25] Some 800 miles to the east, another faculty was teaching under the Block Plan but was only having to teach *seven* blocks per academic year. The Colorado College faculty also was aware that the administration at Cornell College had heard the many Colorado College faculty complaints about the heavy Block Plan work-

---

[24]Tracy Curts, "Cornell College Adopts Block Plan," *Catalyst*, 21 April 1978, 3.

[25]Recollection of the author. Cornell College experienced increases in the number of applicants and the number of students enrolled after it adopted "One Course At A Time." The number of students from the state of Colorado applying to and attending Cornell College went up substantially. It was probably the case that Colorado College had made the Block Plan well-known in the state of Colorado, and this made Cornell College's version of the Block Plan more familiar and desirable to Colorado high school seniors looking to apply to a liberal arts college.

load and had believed those complaints—and had adjusted the Cornell College version of the Block Plan accordingly. The final message was that the Block Plan was working the Colorado College faculty too hard, and that something needed to be done about it.

The Unit-Session Plan

In addition to Cornell College, there were two preparatory schools in the United States that had adopted innovative new curricular calendars based on the Colorado College Block Plan. The first was the Cambridge School at Weston, Massachusetts, which divided its academic year into seven "mini-terms," each four and one-half weeks long. The major difference with the Colorado College Block Plan was that Cambridge School students could take one, two, or three courses simultaneously, rather than just one course, in each mini-term.

The new program at the Cambridge School was called the Unit-Session Plan. The underlying idea was that the student and the academic adviser would create a schedule for each mini-term that best served the needs and abilities of the individual student. The Cambridge School adopted its Block Plan variation in 1972, just two years after the Block Plan had been instituted at Colorado College.

The Cambridge School's version of the Block Plan, copied from Colorado College, then was adopted by Colorado College's close neighbor, the Colorado Springs School. The idea had moved from a college in Colorado Springs to a prep school in Weston, Massachusetts, and then back to a prep school in Colorado Springs. The Unit-Session Plan worked well at the Colorado Springs School, but it produced a number of complaints about the high demands on faculty time, leading to faculty "burn-out."[26]

South African Investments

In April of 1978 in a front page story with a banner headline, the *Catalyst* charged that Colorado College owned almost 100,000 shares of stock,

---

[26]Mike La Mair, "Students Challenge Ideas, Authority At Colorado Spgs. School," *Catalyst*, 13 April 1979, 4.

valued at more than $3.5 million, in 50 companies that did business in South Africa. Because the South African government pursued an official policy of rigid segregation of the races, known as apartheid, the student newspaper implied that Colorado College was tacitly supporting racial discrimination by continuing to hold stock in companies that operated in, loaned money to, or sold military weapons to South Africa.

The *Catalyst* article noted that Colorado College had collected almost $170,000 in dividends the previous year on its apartheid-tainted investments. A particular point was made that Citibank, the second largest bank in the United States, had loaned more than $700 million to the South African government in the past three years. The President of Citicorp, the holding company that owned Citibank, was William I. Spencer, an alumnus and a member of the Board of Trustees at Colorado College. In addition to that close connection, the student newspaper revealed that the College owned 10,000 shares of Citicorp stock.

The student newspaper then printed the names of leading colleges and universities, such as Harvard University, the University of Massachusetts, Tufts University, and the University of Wisconsin, that had already divested their portfolios of the stocks of companies doing business in South Africa. These colleges and universities decided that, rather than support corporations that might be operating segregated factories or selling their products in segregated stores, they would invest their money only in socially-responsible companies that operated exclusively in non-racially segregated nations.

The College administration was caught somewhat off-guard by this revealing article in the *Catalyst*. Robert Broughton, the College Vice President for Business, said that Colorado College had never paid attention to how its money was invested where social considerations were concerned. In fact the bulk of the College's investments, some $20 million, were managed by a professional investment firm, John W. Bristol & Company of New York. The only instruction the College had given for the investment of its funds was "slow but steady growth, without large risks."

In an interview printed in the same issue of the *Catalyst*, President Worner said the College administration would be willing to review its investment policies with a view to their possible effect on racial segregation in

South Africa. It "should be looked at," Worner said, "and I think we'll be glad to do so." Worner acknowledged that the College had a responsibility to review the possible social and political impacts of any of its investments. He concluded: "I think it's the school's responsibility to be informed."[27]

Thus began a long and hotly debated issue on the Colorado College campus. Various members of the student body and the faculty lobbied long and hard to get the Board of Trustees to divest the College of all its South African investments. The College administration and the Board resisted, arguing that it might be better in the long run to keep United States business corporations, with their more progressive employment policies, involved in the South African economy. The argument also was made that pulling U.S. corporations out of South Africa would not change the government's apartheid policy and mainly would cause individual Blacks in South Africa to lose good jobs with U.S. companies.

The battle had been joined at Colorado College over the College's investments in South Africa. It was a battle that would continue—off and on, cold and hot—for more than a decade.[28]

An Addition to Tutt Library

On October 21, 1978, the newspapers in Colorado Springs announced that a two-story addition was going to be built on to Tutt Library. The money for this project—$1.5 million—had been contributed by El Pomar Foundation. The architect, Carlisle B. Guy and Associates, already had been hired and the plans already drawn. A model of the new addition, which was to be built on to the south side of Tutt Library, already was available for viewing. A photograph of the model appeared in the newspapers along with the story announcing El Pomar Foundation's generous gift.[29]

---

[27]John Weiss, "CC-South African Connection Found," *Catalyst*, 21 April 1978, 1. Tracy Curts, "Worner: Investments 'Should Be Looked At,'" *Catalyst*, 21 April 1978, 1.

[28]"C.C.C.A. Tackles Housing, S. Africa," *Catalyst*, 28 April 1978, 1. "Trustees Act On S. Africa," *Catalyst*, 15 September 1978, 1. Mark Greidinger, "South African Investments Questioned," *Catalyst*, 11 May 1984, 1. Bruce Allen, "Investment Or Divestment; Our Money In South Africa," *Catalyst*, 25 February 1985, 4. For an essay by Professor of Economics Chris Griffiths opposing divestment in South Africa, see "Divestment Not The Answer," *Catalyst*, 11 October 1985, 7. Also see Liz Gratton, "Awesome Apartheid Panel," *Catalyst*, 6 December 1985, 4.

[29]"Knowledge Marches Southward," *Catalyst*, 3 November 1978, 13.

The library needs of Colorado College had increased substantially in the 20 years since El Pomar Foundation gave the money to build the original Tutt Library building. The size of the student body had almost doubled, and there had been a substantial proliferation in the number and variety of printed materials available for scholarly research. The library also needed space for its own archival materials on the history of the College and for a computer room for student use. There also were to be additional rooms so that professors could bring their classes to the new building to watch the library's growing collection of educational videotapes.

The library addition was to be slightly smaller than the original Tutt Library building, rising only two stories high instead of three. It was to be built out of the same type of cast concrete slabs. It was to be a separate building but connected to the original library by a two-story enclosed hallway.

Since the new addition would block the busy main sidewalk running from Olin and Palmer halls to Loomis Hall, a set of downward ramps connected by an open air tunnel was to be constructed under the hallway between the two buildings. This would permit pedestrian traffic to conveniently pass through the building but without having to enter the building.

As with any new college or university building project, the Tutt Library addition had its critics. A number of faculty and administrators complained privately that it was wrong to allow a new building to penetrate so deeply into the large grassy area that comprised the main quadrangle of the College. The library addition would break up the open feeling generated by the existing large landscaped area between the old Tutt Library building and Armstrong Hall. But these critics could suggest no alternative location for the library addition that they liked better, and few persons wanted to see the existing Tutt Library expanded by becoming a five-story high-rise building.[30]

President Worner thanked El Pomar Foundation for its continuing support of the College, describing the gift as "a simply wonderful lift for

---

[30]Ken Abbott, "Fagan Has Plans For Quad," *Catalyst*, 23 February 1979, 2. For a satirical comment on the Tutt Library addition and the growth problems that necessitated it, see "Worner Hall Devours Quad, Trees, Relieves Congestion," *Catalyst*, 13 April 1979, insert.

us." Worner concluded: "El Pomar Foundation's action in providing the funds for Charles Leaming Tutt Library two decades ago was in a very real sense the beginning of the redevelopment of the Colorado College campus into the splendid facilities that we have today. This new act of generosity on the part of the Foundation is not only a means toward a still finer physical plant for us, but a very real encouragement to us to continue to offer liberal arts education of the first rank."[31]

The Tutt Library addition also was a reminder that the College was continuing to be the beneficiary of the Cripple Creek and Victor gold strikes, even though it was almost three-quarters of a century since the large-scale gold mining had come to an end. It was the lure of Cripple Creek gold that first brought the Tutt family to Colorado, and it was a successful Cripple Creek gold mine that laid the foundation of the Tutt family fortune. The Tutt Library addition was simply the latest item in the Cripple Creek-Victor legacy to Colorado College.

A Politically Active Faculty

The late 1970s saw continuing political activity on the part of the Colorado College faculty. Professor Richard L. Taber of the Chemistry Department was elected to and served six years on the School Board in District 2, the school district located south and east of Colorado Springs that included Harrison High School. Professor Robert Loevy of the Political Science Department designed a successful election campaign to win voter approval to build a performing arts hall in Colorado Springs. The result was the Pike's Peak Center, constructed near the corner of Cascade Avenue and Colorado Avenue, a large auditorium which became the new home of the Colorado Springs Symphony and a popular venue for traveling Broadway musical shows.

Professor Loevy also served as the President of the North End Home Owners Association, an organization which sought to preserve the interesting group of mostly Victorian-era homes located to the north of the

[31]"Knowledge Marches Southward," *Catalyst*, 3 November 1978, 13. Also see Velva Price, "New Building Relieves Tutt Growing Pains," *Catalyst*, 19 September 1980, 1.

Colorado College campus. Professor Loevy organized and led a successful drive to have the North End neighborhood designated a National Historic District.

ELLSBERG SPEAKS

There is a constant parade of speakers coming to a liberal arts college campus, and periodically one of those speakers draws an unusually large crowd and seems to have a lasting impact on campus thought and opinion. Such was the case when Daniel Ellsberg spoke at Colorado College in the fall of 1978.

Ellsberg first gained fame as the man who "leaked" the Pentagon Papers to the news media. Those papers detailed how the United States slowly but inevitably became involved militarily in the war in Vietnam. Although the United States Government had prepared the Pentagon Papers, the Government did everything in its power to see that they were not released to the public. Ellsberg's "leak" prevented the papers from being kept "Top Secret" and out of the public view.

Daniel Ellsberg spoke at Shove Chapel to an audience estimated at close to 1,000 persons. He arrived at the talk having just been convicted of trespassing at the Rocky Flats nuclear plant near Denver, where he led a protest against the continued United States manufacture of nuclear weapons. The Rocky Flats facility made plutonium triggers for nuclear bombs and was a favorite protest target for those opposed to the continued production of weapons of mass destruction.

Ellsberg urged his audience to embrace organized activism as the best way to effect nuclear disarmament. He noted that "the kind of changes we are talking about can't be done without some risks." He referred to the Rocky Flats nuclear plant as "the scene of the crime," but he was not referring to his own arrest. It was "the scene of the crime" because of the radioactive materials that would "contaminate the land for the next 500,000 years." If he could be arrested for trespass, but the Government was not punishable for contaminating the land for half a million years, then Ellsberg concluded there was a "fatal flaw" in current property laws.

If more people did not became politically active and go on the road demonstrating against nuclear weapons, Ellsberg said, then "the nightmare of nuclear possibilities of the present will become realities."[32]

Daniel Ellsberg was typical of many of the speakers who came to the Colorado College campus during the 1970s and the 1980s. He urged the students, who often were accused of being overly concerned with their own personal problems, to move beyond self-interest and become involved in the major political issues of the day. Ellsberg's particular issue, the Rocky Flats nuclear plant, continued to be the scene of protest demonstrations, and over the years a significant number of Colorado College students participated in those demonstrations.[33]

War, Violence, and Human Values

This continuing concern over the problem of nuclear war was highlighted when the Henry Luce Foundation awarded Colorado College a grant of $65,000 to offer academic courses and hold a lecture series on the issues of "War, Violence, and Human Values." This new program was designed to emphasize the humanistic and philosophical aspects of war and violence. It augmented the existing studies of war and violence that tended to stress international diplomacy, competitive economics, power politics, and maintaining an international balance of military forces.

The Luce Foundation Grant was to be administered by a committee chaired by William Hochman, Professor of History, who was the principal author of the grant proposal. A U.S. Navy officer during World War II whose ship was torpedoed and sunk during the Normandy invasion, Professor Hochman had long been concerned that the issues of war and

---

[32]Laurel Van Driest, "Ellsberg Speaks On Anti-Nuclear Bomb Protest," *Catalyst*, 1 December 1978, 1. Ed Goldstein, "The Ellsberg Message," *Catalyst*, 7 December 1978, 5 (some pages misdated).

[33]Shirin Day, "Protesters Rally At RFP," *Catalyst*, 27 April 1979, 1. Jim Reed, "Commoner Addresses CC Crowd: 'Nuclear Power Is An Economic Bust,'" *Catalyst*, 27 April 1979, 1. Wade Buchanan, "Rally Calls For Rocky Flats Conversion: 18,000 Protest," *Catalyst*, 25 April 1980, 1. Mary McClatchey, "Rocky Flats: Thousands Demand Plant Conversion," *Catalyst*, 8 May 1981, 2. Anne Kerwin, "20,000 Protest," *Catalyst*, 21 October 1983, 2. Patrick Shea, "C.C. Offers Nuclear Peril Minor," *Catalyst*, 13 April 1984, 7. Marc Phillips, "C.C. Students Arrested In Nuclear Weapons Protest," *Catalyst*, 25 January 1991, 2.

violence be approached in terms of their personal human impacts rather than just their political and economic impacts.[34]

One of the first speakers to be brought to campus under the Luce Foundation Grant was Harvard University Professor Michael Walzer. Author of the book *Just And Unjust Wars*, Walzer argued that the state, and not the individual soldier, fights a war, thus it is the leaders of the state, and not the rank and file military, who should be held responsible.

Walzer argued that unjust acts can be committed during wartime if the final outcome, victory of the correct participant, is just. It thus was acceptable for Great Britain to violate Norwegian neutrality during World War II, an unjust act, because that kept Adolph Hitler from getting iron ore for German factories. Defeating Hitler was a just outcome from an unjust act.[35]

Another Luce Grant speaker was U.S. disarmament expert Paul Warnke. He argued that, for United States foreign policy, "our ultimate moral value is to prevent nuclear war." He said the best way to do this was through MAD, the Mutually Assured Destruction that would come to both sides if a nuclear war ever started. Warnke concluded it was a positive step for the United States to negotiate nuclear arms limitation with the Soviet Union provided neither side ever got the mistaken impression it could win a nuclear war.[36]

AN OLD PRESS AND A NEW COMPUTER

One of the more interesting faculty projects during the late 1970s was the construction of an old printing press by Professor James Trissel of the Art Department. The press was an early 20th Century version of the type developed by Gutenberg in the 15th Century, with all letters and designs set entirely by hand. The purpose of the press was to demonstrate that a

---

[34]Bill Anschuetz, "Luce Money Broadens College Program," *Catalyst*, 19 January 1979, 1.

[35]David McKinnie, "Luce Program Sponsors War Discussion," *Catalyst*, 7 March 1980, 1.

[36]Michael LaMair, "Warnke Sees No Alternative To Salt: Keeps Things From Going MAD," *Catalyst*, 11 April 1980, 1. For more information on the Luce Grant, see Carol Wright, "Luce Foundation Offers Insight To The Intense Experience Of War," *Catalyst*, 2 October 1981, 8. James Atkinson, "Hacker Examines Terrorists," *Catalyst*, 16 October 1981, 1.

printer could be an artist who, instead of merely rendering copies like a copy machine, could produce beautiful works of art.

In line with this idea, all prints rendered on the press were numbered in a small limited edition, with each piece of paper specially selected and left to cure after being printed. Professor Trissel began using his hand-built press by printing a collection of poems by Joan Stone, an English Professor at the College. Trissel and Stone worked together choosing the poems, the paper, the type, and the engravings to go with the poems.

Professor Trissel also printed a book of poems by Alistair Reed, a poet from New York who occasionally taught a block of poetry at the College. Trissel named his antique printing device The Press at Colorado College.[37]

At the other end of the technological spectrum, the College replaced its old (nine years) Hewlett-Packard computer with a more powerful machine named the Burroughs B–6803. The new computer cost almost $500,000 but had 40 times the computing capacity of the machine it replaced. It was located in the basement of Armstrong Hall, and a small computer classroom with 15 computer terminals was installed next door.[38]

The new Burroughs was a fine machine, and it did its work well, but it never gained the affection that had been showered on the old Hewlett-Packard machine. The nickname of the old computer, "Smedley," was widely used on campus. An attempt was made to nickname the new machine "Mnemosyne," for the goddess of memory, but the nickname did not stick and the new machine was known mainly as "the Burroughs."[39]

---

[37]Carol Chidsey, "Antique Press Immortalizes Art," *Catalyst,* 26 January 1979, 6. Also see Sharon Yanagi, "Announcing 'The Press,'" *Catalyst,* 11 September 1981, 4. James Kent, "Press Most Un-Type-Ical," *Catalyst,* 22 January 1982, 7. Courtney Murphy, "Art Professor Teaches Antiquated Print Method In Eighth Block Class," *Catalyst,* 5 May 1989, 14. Evan Michael, "Pressing Matters," *Catalyst,* 13 December 1996, 11. For information on Joan Stone, see Matthew Holman, "Writer Finds Home At CC," *Catalyst,* 9 February 1979, 4.

[38]Jim Collins, "Old Reliable Smedley To Be Burroughed Under," *Catalyst,* 7 December 1978, 1.

[39]When asked during an oral history interview for the nickname of the Burroughs computer, President Gresham Riley replied: "I don't remember that it had a name." Gresham Riley oral history, 27 May 1992, 24.

Lincoln and Douglas Return

The College community received a treat early in 1979 when two History professors, William Hochman and Tom K. Barton, staged one of their periodic reenactments of the Lincoln-Douglas debates. Professor Hochman, a tall man who projected an imposing presence, played Abraham Lincoln. Professor Barton, who possessed a suitably rotund figure, portrayed Stephen Douglas. The two men recreated the highlights from Lincoln's and Douglas's seven debates during the 1858 U.S. Senate election campaign in Illinois.

Because Hochman and Barton both were popular professors, there were many students in the audience who had had one or both men teach them a class. That just added to the excitement. Although a number of persons came to the debate to be amused by Hochman's and Barton's accentuated speaking styles, they quickly found themselves caught up in the compelling issues that divided pre-Civil War America. A number of the quotes spoken by Hochman and Barton revealed that both Lincoln and Douglas opposed complete social and political equality for the nation's minorities, thereby illustrating how significantly different one time in history could be from another.

Those in the audience could sense the great affection which many students felt for these two History professors. The Hochman-Barton recreation of the Lincoln-Douglas debates was one of those unique intellectual events that distinguish a liberal arts college.[40]

Draft Registration Revived

In January of 1980 the Soviet Union invaded the Asian nation of Afghanistan. The Soviets sent 85,000 troops to try and suppress a revolution against the pro-Soviet government there. U.S. President Jimmy Carter, a Democrat, saw this Soviet military expansion as a threat to the security interests of the United States. He recommended to Congress the reinstitution of the Selective Service System to provide an up-to-date list

---

[40]"Hochman, Barton Revive 1858 Rhetoric," *Catalyst*, 23 February 1979, 2. Also see Laurie Pfeiff, "Lincoln-Douglas Reenactment," *Catalyst*, 7 February 1986, 1. J. Scott Robertson, "Professors Reenact Lincoln-Douglas Debates," *Catalyst*, 17 February 1989, 1.

of young Americans who could be drafted into military service if needed at a future date.

With the end of the Vietnam War just five years in the past, a number of students at Colorado College criticized the revival of compulsory registration for the draft. The *Catalyst* ran an article reminding students that they could legally avoid registering for the draft by either going to another nation, such as Canada, or by joining a religious or social organization that was morally opposed to warfare.[41] But this controversy never went beyond the rational discussion level at the College. Registration for the military draft was reinstituted, and the young men of Colorado College quietly accepted it.

A NEW DOCTOR

There was a major change at Boettcher Health Center when a Colorado College graduate, Judith Reynolds, became the new College doctor. She replaced Dr. Hugh Rodman, who retired. The new campus physician received her M.D. from the University of South Florida, interned at Yale University hospital in Bridgeport, Connecticut, and served her residency in family practice at Thomas Jefferson University Hospital in Philadelphia, Pennsylvania.

Dr. Reynolds said her major goal was to change the image of Boettcher from a place for the sick to a place where students go to learn how to be healthy and stay well. She said she would set aside 10 hours each month for gynecological examinations and conferences, and she would provide birth control counseling. She also said she would instruct students on proper methods of weight-loss.[42]

MINORITY HIRING

Student concern over the lack of racial and ethnic diversity in the Colorado College faculty resulted in a student demonstration in front of Packard Hall early in 1981. About 20 students met to protest the fact that

---

[41]Laura Hershey, "Draft Age Showdown," *Catalyst*, 8 Feburary 1980, 1. Laura Hershey, "Cost Of Oil, Vital Interests, And The Price of Life," *Catalyst*, 14 March 1980, 1.

[42]J. Spradley, "Doctor To Change Boettcher's Image," *Catalyst*, 12 September 1980, 1. James Schmid, "Boettcher Offers Complete Care," *Catalyst*, 24 April 1981, 3.

the Minority Education Committee was not being consulted in the recruitment of a new Art History professor. The protest was led by the Black Student Union and MECHA, the organization representing Spanish-surnamed students. The new professor was to teach Baroque and Renaissance Art.

The group then marched over to the Dean's Office in Armstrong Hall and staged a friendly sit-in. The students debated minority employment issues with all four deans. The problem seemed to be that the Minority Education Committee had not been told an applicant was going to be interviewed for the Art History job until just 24 hours before the interview took place. The demonstrators also said that Colorado College needed an Affirmative Action Program with a full-time director to ensure equal employment opportunity at the faculty level. "It shouldn't be the Dean's responsibility," said Velva Price, one of the demonstrators. "It should be done by an objective third party."[43]

President Worner subsequently suspended the effort to hire an Art History professor and said the College would resume the job search with a fresh start in the fall of 1981. That way all hiring procedures could be carefully followed and all relevant persons and committees given ample notice of interviews and meetings.[44] The entire affair illustrated the increasing sensitivity at the College, among both the minority students and the administration, over the issue of hiring more Blacks and Hispanics on to the faculty.

Debate Thrives

Although the men's and women's oratorical societies that had characterized the College at the turn of the 20th Century were long gone, the idea of students honing their verbal and presentation skills was still very much alive in the late 1970s and early 1980s. The Colorado College Debate Team was one of the most active and successful extra-curricular activities on campus. The team competed with some of the best collegiate debate

[43]Vince Bzdek, "Students Hold Demonstration And Sit-In To Protest Faculty Hiring Methods," *Catalyst*, 23 January 1981, 1.

[44]Carolyn Case, "President Scraps Art Post Interviews," *Catalyst*, 6 February 1981, 1.

squads in the country—Harvard, Northwestern, and Stanford, for example—and repeatedly sent its star members to the National Tournament for college and university debaters.

The Debate Team was coached by Al Johnson, the Registrar at the College and a Professor of Economics. In 1979–1980 the Colorado College Debate Team was ranked in the top ten in the United States for colleges and universities under 2,500 enrollment. "Debate vastly improves students' ability to express themselves orally," debate coach Johnson pointed out. "More than that, it forces them to think through a problem carefully and to consider both pro and con. Debate quickly shows a student what opinions [he or she] can and cannot support. The faculty can spot a debater every time because of [his or her] logic and reason."

Al Johnson noted that the real reward for organizing and leading the debate team was the faculty-student contact. He explained: "It's a closeness not otherwise possible; you can get closer to students than you can as a teacher because of all the hours spent together traveling to tournaments."

In 1980–1981 Al Johnson marked his 25th year as the debate coach at Colorado College. In addition to working with students on topic debating, Johnson also helped to develop a new form of collegiate debate where students argued "values" rather than "just the facts."[45]

A NEW DEAN

In the fall of 1979 Glenn Brooks, the designer of the Block Plan, became the new Dean of the College. He replaced Richard Bradley, who resigned in order to return to his teaching position in the Physics Department. Bradley's six years in the "deanery" had been marked by quiet but steady progress. Dean Bradley had successfully presided over the College's 100th anniversary celebration in 1974, and he had worked hard to help resolve some major conflicts on the campus, such as those over dogs and adjacent room coed housing.

Dean Bradley was particularly pleased with the moves away from academic over-specialization that occurred during his deanship. He believed

[45]Anne Doty, "Debaters Aim For Nationals Under Johnson's Guidance," *Catalyst*, 13 February 1981, 2. Mike Smith, "Johnson Leads And Coaches From The Heart," *Catalyst*, 16 December 1994, 9.

the development of interdisciplinary, multi-professor courses, such as *Patterns In Nature*, had helped turn the College back toward the true meaning of a liberal education. An avid musician as well as a Physics professor, Bradley hoped that, once away from the constant hubbub and turmoil of the Dean's office, he would have more time to compose classical music.[46] He was able to achieve that goal. During the 1990s a Richard Bradley composition, "Sierra Song," was performed by the College Choir at a number of College events.

Upon being named the new Dean, Glenn Brooks acknowledged that, in the past, he had preferred to continue teaching rather than accept administrative posts at the College. But, he said, "I'm [now] at a stage of my own career that I should meet some larger obligation to the College." Glenn Brooks had long had a sign in his faculty office that read: "Administration Rots The Mind." He promised that the sign would travel with him to the Dean's office and be displayed there as well.[47]

Glenn Brooks also told close confidants on the faculty that he had taken the deanship in order to provide for continuity between the end of Lloyd Worner's presidency and the start of the presidency of whoever was Worner's successor. Worner had told Brooks that he expected to retire in two years, and he wanted Brooks in the Dean's office to smooth the path to a new presidential administration. Although Worner's retirement plans were generally known on campus, they had not yet been officially announced.[48]

"NO NET ADDITIONS BROOKS"

At the time Glenn Brooks became Dean, student enrollment at the College had stabilized at just under 2,000 students per year. In view of that fact, Brooks pursued a policy throughout his deanship of not adding

---

[46]Paul Butler, "Bradley Leaves 'Unpredictable' Job With Enriched Understanding," *Catalyst*, 25 May 1979, 6. For a review of Richard Bradley's teaching career at Colorado College and his service as Dean, see Richard Bradley oral history, 12 December 1988.

[47]Tim Zarlengo and Ed Goldstein, "Glenn Brooks Appointed New Dean Of Faculty, College," *Catalyst*, 16 November 1978, 1. Ed Langlois, "Administration Doesn't 'Rot The Mind,'" *Catalyst*, 5 October 1984, 6.

[48]Recollection of the author.

to the number of faculty. Professors were replaced as they retired or did not have their employment contracts renewed, and by and large no academic department was permitted to increase in size.

"I was known as 'No Net Additions Brooks,'" the new Dean later recalled. "I was arguing for a trade-off there; that we would keep the size of the faculty constant and increase salaries. . . ."

Glenn Brooks did succeed in limiting growth in the size of the faculty while he was Dean, but during his tenure the number of non-academic staff at the College began to increase rapidly. The reason for this, Brooks explained, was that the faculty had become more professionalized and no longer took responsibility, for the most part, for creating leisure-time activities for the students. A significant number of new administrators had to be hired to help students with foreign study arrangements, citizen service in the community, etc. Faculty members used to carry out such functions "as just a side pocket operation of their own job," Brooks concluded, but "now professional staff people run that stuff."[49]

TOWARD A CORE CURRICULUM

As the Block Plan became increasingly accepted and praised at Colorado College, there was a growing concern that there needed to be a common core of courses taken by every student at the College. Under the "laissez-faire" system in use at the time, students were free to choose their schedule of classes from a wide variety of courses, with no two students likely to have taken any, or very many, courses in common. This "right to choose" system was called "hop-scotching" by its critics.

In 1982, following a major study by Professor of English James Yaffe, the faculty was presented with a set of four proposals:

(1) Each student at Colorado College would be required to take a two-block course that emphasized the values of the Western intellectual tradition. The course could be a Political Science course, or a History course, or a Religion course, but its subject matter would be based on Western European and American ideas and values. For convenience, these Western courses would be called "A" courses.

[49]Brooks oral history, 14 February 1996, 52.

(2) In addition, each student would have to take two courses with non-Western subject matter, such as courses in Asian politics, African anthropology, Middle Eastern international relations, etc. For convenience, these non-Western courses would be labeled "B" courses.

(3) Minor fields would be created at Colorado College which students could take on a voluntary basis. These "thematic minors" would not be similar to the conventional major fields, such as Economics or Physics or Philosophy, but would be in specialized interdisciplinary areas, such as Urban Affairs, Journalism, American-Ethnic Studies, etc.[50]

(4) The three-unit Natural Science requirement would remain unchanged.

These proposals for a modified core curriculum at Colorado College were adopted by the faculty.[51] The proposals provided a degree of commonality to each student's course of study, but not enough, it was believed, to be viewed as overly restrictive. This curricular change introduced three main questions into conversations with students about their course schedules. What is your two-block "A" course? What are your two "B" courses? Are you taking a thematic minor and, if so, what is it?

This curricular change was a durable one. Creating a dual-core curriculum, with one core Western and the other non-Western, proved to be a viable way of organizing a student's academic program at the College. Although this curricular change was a major one, it was not unique to Colorado College the way the Block Plan was. A number of other colleges and universities reorganized along a Western and non-Western studies line, very much the way Colorado College had.[52]

---

[50]Initially students were going to be required to take a thematic minor in order to graduate, but the faculty later decided this was too rigid a requirement and made the thematic minor optional. Ed Langlois, "51 Faculty Want A Change," *Catalyst*, 10 May 1985, 3. Katie Kerwin, "Minor Headaches," *Catalyst*, 17 May 1985, 10. Rob Lynch and Kristen Dillon, "Thematic Minors Optional; Faculty Shuffles Requirements," *Catalyst*, 13 September 1985, 1.

[51]"C.C. Should Go All The Way With Curriculum Changes," *Catalyst*, 5 March 1982, 8. Peter Anderson, "A.P.C. Proposes Changes," *Catalyst*, 23 April 1982, 1. Timothy Peek, "Look: Course Requirements To Change," *Catalyst*, 15 October 1982, 4. George F. Simmons, Professor of Mathematics, Colorado College, "The West Is Best," *Catalyst*, 22 October 1982, 8. Anne Grignon, "Faculty Vote 'Yes . . . '" *Catalyst*, 5 November 1982, 1. Timothy Peek, "But Not Without Opposition," *Catalyst*, 5 November 1982, 1. Ed Langlois and Anne Kerwin, "General Education Proposal Launched," *Catalyst*, 14 January 1983, 1. Paul Burge, "General Ed. Requirements Enter Second Year," *Catalyst*, 12 October 1984, 3. Matt Berger, "Fair Launches New Minors Program," *Catalyst*, 25 February 1985, 1.

[52]This particular curriculum reform originated during the Worner presidency but was completed under his successor, President Gresham Riley. See Gresham Riley oral history, 27 May 1992, 11, 28.

THE EIGHT-BLOCK TEACHING LOAD

In the spring of 1980 the College administration decided to act on the increasing number of complaints about the faculty workload under the Block Plan. Dean Brooks announced that the normal teaching load for faculty would be cut from nine blocks to eight blocks per year, with each faculty member left free to determine the best use for this new "Block Without Teaching."

Instead of hiring new faculty to teach the various courses that would be eliminated by this reform, Dean Brooks proposed instead to increase the enrollment in a limited number of courses from 25 to 50 students. This would be done in classes such as English Professor Joe Gordon's *American Life in Literature* and Political Science Professor Robert Loevy's *American Government and Politics*—courses which were suited to a lecture form of presentation and thus would not be substantially harmed by having additional students. Dean Brooks made it clear that at least 90 percent of the courses at Colorado College would continue to be subject to the Block Plan's 25-student limit.[53]

The eight-block teaching load was implemented without incident, but there were loud and long student complaints about the limited number of courses that were allowed to increase enrollment to as much as 50 students.[54] Gradually over the following years the College quietly eliminated these oversize courses, adjusting the course schedule incrementally so that, eventually, individual faculty members were only teaching eight blocks per year and the 25-student limit applied to almost every course the College offered.

Adoption of the eight-block teaching load was a giant step in reducing faculty complaints about the workload under the Block Plan. But it did not succeed in eliminating those complaints altogether. Even when only required to teach eight blocks per year, a number of faculty continued to argue strenuously that the Block Plan left insufficient faculty time for the reading, research, and writing required for proper scholarly development.

---

[53]George Garfield, "Teaching Load Shrinks; Some Classes Will Expand," *Catalyst*, 8 February 1980, 1.

[54]David McKinnie, "Class Size Crucial," *Catalyst*, 8 February 1980, 2.

PRESIDENT WORNER RETIRES

On October 22, 1979, Colorado College President Lloyd E. Worner announced his retirement, to take effect one-and-a-half years later in June of 1981. Worner said he revealed his retirement plans early so that the College would have ample time to recruit his successor. Worner was 61 years old at the time he decided to step down, and he noted that, by June of 1981, he would have completed 18 years in the presidential office.

Worner said: "I think it's time for a change for me and time for a change for the College—a change that inevitably comes in the life of an institution." He added: "These have not been easy years for traditional learning, and a number of liberal arts colleges have found it necessary or expedient to turn in other directions in order to ensure their survival. I'm proud that Colorado College has gone forward with unfaltering commitment to the kind of learning that has been proved through hundreds of years."[55]

THE SEARCH FOR A NEW PRESIDENT

Worner's early announcement of his departure enabled the College to proceed swiftly with a nationwide search for his successor. By the late spring of 1980 a search committee had narrowed the hunt to two candidates, both of whom were from "outside" the Colorado College community. In an effort to have an "inside" candidate, Dean Glenn Brooks became a third candidate for the College's presidency.

Brooks was simultaneously a committed but reluctant candidate. The outgoing President, Lloyd E. Worner, was the ultimate Colorado College "insider," having been a student, a professor, and a dean as well as a president of the College. Glenn Brooks agreed with the widespread opinion that the College now needed an "outsider" President, someone to bring in new ideas and new experiences to the job. Furthermore, Brooks had been named the College Dean for the explicit purpose of providing for an orderly transition in the Dean's office from Worner's presidency to that of

---

[55]Samuel B. Montgomery, "President Worner To Retire After 18 Years At CC," *Catalyst*, 2 November 1979, 1.

his successor. Brooks thought he should be completing that assignment rather than competing for the presidency.

As it turned out, the Board of Trustees hired one of the "outsider" candidates for the new President. He was Gresham Riley, at that time the Dean of the Faculty of Arts and Sciences at the University of Richmond in Virginia. Gresham Riley and Glenn Brooks had spoken frankly together about Brooks's ambivalent quest for the presidential office. The end result was that Brooks served comfortably as Gresham Riley's Dean of Faculty for the first six years of the Riley administration, ably fulfilling his assignment as a "transitional Dean."[56]

THE WORNER PRESIDENCY

Lloyd Edson Worner's 18 years as President of Colorado College had been record-breaking ones. Student enrollment increased by more than 50 percent to over 1,900 students, but throughout the period the student-faculty ratio held steady at 14 to 1. The value of the College's endowment increased from nearly $9 million to almost $40 million. Under Worner's guidance, Colorado College was able to make these outstanding gains at a time when many other small liberal arts colleges were experiencing dwindling enrollments and financial crises. And Worner brought the College safely through a period of national student turbulence and protest without experiencing any major disruptions or student riots.[57]

One anecdote nicely summed up Worner's presidential character during the discordant 1960s. In the midst of a protest demonstration a student shouted at Worner: "I'm not satisfied with my education here." Worner instantly replied: "Neither am I."[58]

Most remarkable were the additions to the College's physical plant during Worner's presidency. Six major buildings were constructed:

---

[56]Both Gresham Riley and Glenn Brooks commented on this delicate situation. Gresham Riley oral history, 27 May 1992, 5. Brooks oral history, 14 February 1996, 35–38.

[57]For a detailed evaluation of Worner's first ten years as President, see Reid, *Colorado College: The First Century, 1874–1974*, 287–289. Also see Wade Buchanan, "Worner Cultivates Change," *Catalyst*, 15 May 1981, 7.

[58]"Lloyd Worner Honored," *Catalyst*, 8 May 1981, 3.

Boettcher Health Center, Armstrong Hall, Mathias Hall, El Pomar Sports Center, Packard Hall, and the Tutt Library addition. Also, the Van Briggle Art Pottery building, at Uintah Street and Glen Avenue, was acquired to house the College's Physical Plant offices and shops.

But the most outstanding achievements of the Worner years were in the College's academic program. Lloyd Edson Worner presided over and gave his whole-hearted support to the adoption of Colorado College's Block Plan. By the time President Worner left the presidential office on June 30, 1981, the Block Plan had become the distinguishing feature of the College.

Lloyd Worner lived the remainder of his life in Colorado Springs, close to the College to which he had devoted his entire professional career. He was occasionally seen about the campus attending an academic lecture or enjoying a dramatic or musical presentation. He returned to academic life briefly to co-teach a Religion course in 1984. In April of 1985 he was awarded $10,000 by the Bonfils-Stanton Foundation for his "significant and unique contribution" in the field of higher education.[59] He died in Colorado Springs in the fall of 1996.[60]

Ever true to the liberal arts college tradition, Lloyd Worner never weakened in his devotion to the idea that what was being done at Colorado College was very important and would prove to be enduring. Immediately after he left the presidency, he said: "I *am* confident, and I'll admit this is an act of faith, but . . . I'm convinced . . . that a hundred years from now, that this kind of education, this kind of college, and this particular College will be about its business. I believe that."[61]

---

[59]Scott Meskin, "Worner Is Honored," 12 April 1985, 1.

[60]"Former C.C. President Dies At 78," *Catalyst*, 6 December 1996, 1.

[61]Worner oral history, 5 February 1985, 160.

CHAPTER 10

THE RILEY ERA BEGINS

On July 1, 1981, Gresham Riley became the ninth President of Colorado College.[1] He took office at a time of great well-being in the history of the institution. There was the now-customary enrollment of just under 2,000 students. The endowment stood at an all-time high. The Block Plan had operated successfully for eleven years and was regarded as the established—not the experimental—academic program at the College.

Gresham Riley was born in Jackson, Mississippi, on June 27, 1938. He attended public schools, graduating from Provine High School in Jackson. He grew up in a racially segregated society where state and local governments firmly supported rigid social separation of the Black and the White races. This early experience with government-sanctioned racial discrimination sensitized the young Gresham Riley to social injustice. It also convinced him that freedom and equality for minority groups would come only from the United States Government in Washington, D.C. Riley came to distrust state and local government and the doctrine of state's rights that was used to justify racial segregation.

But there was another Mississippi that influenced Gresham Riley while he was in high school. It was the Mississippi of such great writers as William Faulkner, Eudora Welty, and Richard Wright, all of whom Riley read as a teen-ager. "Mississippi was segregated but had a great literary

[1]For Gresham Riley's first speech to the College community, see Stephen Hinchman, "Riley Issues Challenge," *Catalyst*, 11 September 1981, 1. For Gresham Riley's inauguration, see Le Melcher, "CC Inaugurates Riley," *Catalyst*, 9 October 1981, 1.

tradition," Riley commented. "I was reading these writings as a youth, which may have led me to my career in academe."[2]

In 1956 Gresham Riley left Mississippi to attend Baylor University in Waco, Texas. He never returned to Mississippi to live. He graduated magna cum laude from Baylor in 1960 as a Philosophy major. He spent a year in Germany on a Fulbright Scholarship. He then went to graduate school in Philosophy at Yale University, in New Haven, Connecticut, where he earned his M.A. in 1963 and his Ph.D. in 1965. Riley focused his graduate studies on the philosophical writings of C. S. Peirce.

One of the most important things Riley observed during his years at Yale University was that an academic person can successfully pursue a career as both a teacher and a scholar. "While at Yale," Riley said, "I saw clearly there was no serious conflict between teaching and a scholarly life. A balance can be achieved between a faculty member's relationship to students and to his or her scholarly endeavors."

Gresham Riley went from graduate study at Yale to the faculty at New College in Sarasota, Florida. It was at New College that Riley was first exposed to adventurous innovation in undergraduate education in the United States. New College had been founded for the specific purpose of finding new and exciting ways to provide a challenging and fruitful college education. At New College students studied for only three years rather than the more customary four years. The academic program was completely unstructured, with students making contracts with faculty members to read certain books, write research papers and essays, etc. The student and the faculty member also worked together to evaluate what the student had accomplished once the contract was completed.

Because of his youthful experience at New College, Gresham Riley had no problem understanding or adjusting to or supporting the Block Plan at Colorado College.

In 1973 Riley made his first foray into the ranks of academic administration. He became acting Provost at New College in 1973 and subsequently was named Provost. At New College the Provost is the chief aca-

---

[2]This and subsequent quotes from Gresham Riley are from the author's notes, interview with Gresham Riley, former President of Colorado College, Philadelphia, Pennsylvania, 11 June 1997. Also see Gresham Riley oral history, 27 May 1992, 1–7.

demic officer, the equivalent of the academic Dean at Colorado College. To his surprise, Riley found that he enjoyed administrative work, and that many of the skills he had developed as a professional philosopher were readily transferable to academic administration.

In 1975 Gresham Riley became the Dean of the Faculty of Arts and Sciences at the University of Richmond in Virginia. He joined the administration at Richmond just as the University was about half-way through a major ten-year fund-raising campaign. Riley thus had the opportunity to get hands-on experience in institutional fund-raising, and he saw clearly that colleges and universities could not achieve their major future goals if they did not have an effective apparatus for raising the required money.

Gresham Riley thus came to Colorado College as both a highly trained college teacher and a well-experienced college and university administrator. He had been brought in from outside the Colorado College community in an effort to infuse the College with new ideas and new programs. Riley, only 43-years-old at the time he became President, set about his work with the proverbial youthful vim and vigor.

"The 1980s were a transitional period in American higher education," Gresham Riley noted. "College and universities moved from an era of general approval to one of considerable criticism. A rash of books charged that college professors were retreating from teaching and spending all their time doing obscure research that had little value and writing scholarly tomes that hardly anyone ever read. Colleges and universities were accused of making indefensible and unconscionable increases in tuition. In the name of political correctness—not wanting to offend anyone—it was said that freedom of inquiry and freedom of speech no longer really existed on most campuses. The political left, critics charged, was progressively destroying the cherished value of academic freedom."

Gresham Riley saw the task of defending academic freedom as one of his most important responsibilities as the new President of Colorado College. "I worked to guarantee the widest possible application of First Amendment rights to those who teach and study at the nation's colleges and universities," Riley said. "I was critical of those who pretended to have all the answers and could not analyze reality from a variety of points of view. I strongly opposed the overbearing advocates of certainty and consistently advocated the truth-producing qualities of doubt."

But at the same time he staunchly defended academic freedom, Gresham Riley worked to further the cause of minority groups and women's groups at Colorado College. A hallmark of his presidency was a strong emphasis on the goal of increasing racial, ethnic, and gender diversity in the student body, on the faculty, and within the College administration. Riley saw the United States Government, specifically the Department of Health and Human Services, as the driving force behind the slow but steady increase in the number of minority persons participating in the life of the College. By threatening to cut-off U.S. Government funds for various College programs, the U.S. Government guaranteed that race, ethnicity, and gender considerations became a part of the admissions process as well as the faculty and administration hiring process. Riley explained: "The Department of Health and Human Services was the conscience of the colleges and universities on race and gender issues."

Gresham Riley also saw the enhancement and perfection of the Block Plan as an important part of his mission at Colorado College. "I was attracted to the College by the Block Plan," Riley said. "I saw the Block Plan as indicative of a faculty and a student body that was open to change." Riley saw an important next step to be a continued emphasis on interdisciplinary courses—courses which brought together professors from different disciplines, such as Biology and Philosophy, to teach on a related subject of general interest. "I believed that a college or university had to take an interdisciplinary approach to produce real learning and get at the real truth," Riley concluded. "The large number of interdisciplinary courses was one of the things I liked best at Colorado College."

Riley also placed an emphasis on students playing a more active role in their own education. His experience with the "contract" system at New College was an important influence here. Riley supported the creation of more independent study courses at Colorado College. He endorsed having more students write a senior thesis, and he wanted more students working directly with their professors on research and writing projects. "I believed students of the caliber we had at Colorado College would learn

Gresham Riley

President Riley strived during the 1980s to make Colorado College a nationally "preeminent" liberal arts college. Worner Campus Center and Barnes Science Center were constructed during the Riley administration.

best when actively involved in their own education," Riley said. "I knew our students had the ability to work on their own if we would just let them do it more often."

Gresham Riley had only one concern with the Block Plan as he found it at Colorado College in the early 1980s. Some of the faculty, many of the students, and most of the young alumni of the College had become, in Riley's view, too protective of the Block Plan and overly resistant to various proposals for changing and improving it. Riley lamented: "The irony was that a brilliant innovation had, for too many persons associated with the College, become an unchangeable position."

The President's House

Lloyd Worner's wife Mary had been seriously ill for most of the years that Worner was President. As a result the President's House on Wood Avenue just north of Uintah Street had not functioned, as many persons had wished, as the social center of the campus. This situation changed dramatically when Gresham Riley took over as President. Gresham's wife, Pamela Riley, happily took on the job of making the President's House a "hospitable and warm place for students and faculty and trustees and community members."[3] Faculty members and administrators who had never been in the President's House, some of them after working more than a decade at the College, suddenly were being invited, along with their spouses, to Gresham and Pamela's home for receptions, cocktail parties, and dinners.[4]

Professionalization of the Decision Making Process

The men who preceded Gresham Riley in the presidential office at Colorado College had tended to take an ad hoc and eclectic approach to the construction of new campus buildings. They usually decided on their own what new buildings were needed and then went quietly looking for

---

[3]Gresham Riley oral history, 27 May 1992, 44–45. Also see Ernie Luning, "First Lady: Pam Riley," *Catalyst*, 30 November 1984, 6.

[4]Recollection of the author.

wealthy donors to provide the money needed to build the building. They often picked the site for the building according to their own tastes and desires for the future appearance of the campus. In no instance had a professional campus planner been brought in to systematically assess the physical needs of the College and provide a coherent future plan for meeting those needs.

Gresham Riley changed all that. If there was one thing President Riley contributed to administrative procedure at Colorado College, it was the professionalization of the decision making process. Decisions that had previously been made by presidents and deans, often on the basis of personal experience and little more, soon were being made with the help of professional consultants with specialized knowledge of the area under consideration. The final decisions were still being made at Colorado College, but suddenly much of the information and expertise on which those decisions were based was coming from paid professionals outside the College community.

Even as early as when he was being interviewed for the job of President of Colorado College, Gresham Riley saw clearly that there were "bricks-and-mortar" needs at the institution. The Natural Science professors made it clear that their space needs had outgrown the Olin Hall of Science, despite the fact that Olin was one of the newer buildings on the campus. There was the additional problem that the laboratories in Olin had become antiquated, particularly in view of the rapid technological changes that were occurring in all the physical sciences.

And Olin was not the only "new" building with problems. The Humanities professors in Armstrong Hall complained that the classrooms were poorly ventilated, the windows were too small, and that certain spots in the building were too hot and others were too cold. Some of the loudest complaints came from the Drama Department, which contended that Armstrong Theater was too large and formal for the more intimate and informal theatrical productions that characterized contemporary dramatic instruction. Meanwhile, over at Rastall Center, it had become obvious that more space was badly needed to meet the social and activity needs of a student body that now numbered almost 2,000.

Which of the various building projects suggested by these complaints should have the highest priority? Were these the only complaints that existed, or were they just the loudest complaints? And were there future needs of the College which would soon need to be met but which were not yet clearly visible and generating discussion? To answer these questions, President Riley called in a group of high-powered college and university consultants. Riley's program had three major parts: (1) the development and presentation of a campus physical plan, (2) a needs assessment study to establish and prioritize all the needs of the College, both physical and academic, and (3) a campaign feasibility assessment to ascertain how much money the College could reasonably expect to raise to pay for the beautiful new buildings and exciting new programs that would be generated by (1) and (2).

The 1983 Campus Plan

The first consultant called in by President Riley was campus planning expert Richard P. Dober of Belmont, Massachusetts. Dober and his planning firm, Dober & Associates, had made a specialty of planning college and university campuses, and Dober had written a book on the principles of campus design.[5] For more than a year during 1982 and 1983, Dober studied the Colorado College campus in depth and then published a book-length summary of his findings and recommendations.[6]

Dick Dober's planning style called for extensive faculty and student involvement in the planning process. A steering committee, chaired by Political Science Professor Robert Loevy, was set up to carefully channel faculty and student needs and opinions to Dober and his planning cohorts. Academic departments met together to determine their needs and priorities, and the resulting reports were sent to Dober's headquarters in Massachusetts by air express. Student committees met and debated at length what improvements were needed in the student center and the dormitories, and soon even more reports and data sheets were on their way

[5]Ed Langlois, "Dober Rebuilds," *Catalyst*, 3 December 1982, 1.

[6]"The Colorado College Planning Study 1983," Dober & Associates, Inc., Planning Consultants.

to Massachusetts. Dober did an excellent job of personally involving every significant leadership group at the College—faculty, student, and administration—in his planning process.[7]

Dober found some interesting things about the Colorado College campus that might otherwise have gone unremarked, and perhaps undiscovered. Compared to most other premier liberal arts colleges, Colorado College had a campus that was relatively small and compact. About the longest walk anyone had to take on the campus was from Mathias dormitory at the northeast corner to El Pomar Sports Center at the southwest corner. Dober therefore recommended that the College accelerate its efforts to acquire more land for future expansion, mainly to the east and the south of the existing campus. He particularly recommended looking east, so much so that the eclectic group of houses and vacant lots to the east of Nevada Avenue was soon nicknamed "the Dober zone."[8]

Dick Dober conducted a survey of where students lived when they moved to off-campus apartments and houses. He found that off-campus living was not taking place very far off-campus. The vast majority of students not living on campus domiciled themselves within a three-block distance of the College campus. Dober concluded from this that off-campus students were not really all that anxious to remove themselves from the life of the College. He concluded that, if the College would provide housing with the privacy and the freedom from immediate supervision that characterized off-campus housing, most off-campus students would be more than happy to move back to the campus.

CLOSING CASCADE AVENUE

One of the major characteristics of Colorado College that concerned Dick Dober was the way Cascade Avenue, with its heavy automobile traffic, cut right through the center of the campus. As Colorado Springs grew in population and the traffic on Cascade Avenue inevitably increased,

---

[7]For a description of Richard Dober's interactive planning style, see Art Vander Veen, "A Speculative Bonanza," *Catalyst*, 17 December 1982, 3. Tim Peek, "Dober Lives," *Catalyst*, 18 February 1983, 3.

[8]Author's notes, interview with Gresham Riley, 11 June 1997.

Dober believed the problem would become a major one. In his opinion, it was not a question of *whether* Cascade should be closed but a question of *when*. He recommended that the College make a maximum effort to close Cascade Avenue and turn the central part of the campus into an exclusively pedestrian environment.[9]

Knowing that the wide boulevards, such as Cascade and Nevada avenues, were an important part of the design and history of Colorado Springs, President Riley was skeptical that the city government ever would give permission for Cascade Avenue to be closed. The Board of Trustees bought Dober's suggestion, however, and asked Riley to make a maximum effort to, once and for all, eliminate the Cascade Avenue problem at Colorado College.

Riley, with the all-out help of his Planning Committee Chairman, Robert Loevy, made the effort. Community leaders were lobbied hard, and many responded positively to the College's overtures, but the city government remained strongly opposed to closing Cascade Avenue across the campus. To President Riley's amazement, however, the city conducted no traffic studies, opposing the closing of Cascade Avenue on principle rather than with up-to-date traffic statistics.

So President Riley did a typical Riley thing. He hired his own traffic consultant to evaluate the effect of closing Cascade Avenue on overall traffic patterns in Colorado Springs. The results of the study were ambiguous: Cascade Avenue could effectively be closed, but it would divert a great deal of traffic onto nearby streets. In the end President Riley was able to convince the Board of Trustees that there was too much political opposition to closing Cascade and that the College would have to find some other way to solve its major traffic problem.[10]

DOBER'S RECOMMENDATIONS

The Dober planning study was issued in 1983 in the form of a 157-page book with a take-out map in a folder at the back. The map detailed visu-

---

[9]Meg Dennison, "Cascade: Can CC Close It?" *Catalyst*, 7 October 1983, 3.

[10]Gresham Riley oral history, 27 May 1992, 14–16. Also see "Trustees Will Not Close Cascade," *Catalyst*, 9 March 1984, 2.

ally all of Dick Dober's future plans for the College. The campus plan contained five major recommendations. (1) Construct a new science building as an addition to Olin Hall of Science. (2) Construct a new student center building, possibly in the air space over Cascade Avenue (between Tutt Library and Boettcher Health Center) if Cascade Avenue could not be closed. (3) Convert the existing Rastall Center into a Drama and Dance facility. (4) Acquire more land to the east of Nevada Avenue and construct intramural athletic fields on it. (5) Extensively renovate Armstrong Hall and the major student dormitories.[11]

As expected and desired, the 1983 Campus Plan produced a great deal of discussion in the College community. There was much skepticism as to the wisdom of constructing a major building in the air space above Cascade Avenue, although there were many who liked the idea of making rolling automobiles and trucks on Cascade less visible and noisy by covering them with a building. There also were many grumbles, mainly from the Humanities faculty, that Dober and his planners had failed to see the immediate necessity for tearing down Armstrong Hall as quickly as possible.

But, as it moved into the mid–1980s, Colorado College had a professionally prepared campus plan. The Dober Plan, as it came to be known, provided the Riley administration with a number of rational options for the future development of the College's physical plant. President Riley was very pleased with this brand new campus plan. "Dick Dober did serve us extremely well," Riley commented, "and out of his study came some quite practical results."[12]

NEEDS ASSESSMENT

A college or university is more than just a grassy campus filled with buildings. There are many programs other than the physical plant that require planning and money to make them a reality. For one thing, President Riley wanted to be certain he had the money to seek out and hire the best

[11]"The Colorado College Planning Study 1983," Dober & Associates, Inc., Planning Consultants. Also see Sharon Brady and Darrend Brown, "CC: A Quantum Leap . . . ," *Catalyst*, 20 May 1983, 3. Taylor Stockdale, "Planning The Perfect Campus," *Catalyst*, 23 September 1983, 3.

[12]Gresham Riley oral history, 27 May 1992, 14.

possible new faculty members. Starting salaries for new professors would have to be raised if the College was going to compete seriously for the best teacher-scholars coming out of the graduate schools.

There also needed to be money for curricular changes, such as bringing in visiting professors to teach new courses in non-Western studies and minority studies. And more money was desired to strengthen the athletic programs at the College and subsidize student activities, such as the *Catalyst*, the student newspaper. The point was often made at faculty meetings that the College should be "spending its money on people, not buildings."[13]

To tabulate and prioritize the various needs of the College, Gresham Riley appointed a Needs Assessment Committee. Although made up primarily of faculty, the committee also had students, administrators, trustees, and alumni on it. The committee reported back that it had identified $80 million worth of needs, both physical and human, at the College.

THE CAMPAIGN FEASIBILITY STUDY

Once again President Riley turned to a national consulting firm to help with the decision-making process. This time it was Barnes and Roach, a consulting firm in Philadelphia, Pennsylvania, that specialized in analyzing college and university fund-raising campaigns. Bob Roach, the President of Barnes and Roach, conducted a national study of the fund-raising prospects for Colorado College. He talked with alumni, influential friends of the College, key figures in the foundation world, and looked at how well colleges the size of Colorado College had done in recent fund-raising campaigns. Bob Roach reported to Gresham Riley that Colorado College could not raise $80 million—but that it could successfully raise between $40 and $50 million.[14]

---

[13]Recollection of the author, who was asked by a *Catalyst* reporter to make the case for "buildings, not people." The author said he regarded the choice between "buildings" and "people" as an artificial one. He told the *Catalyst*: "The College spends money on both aspects all the time. The Dober Plan allows the money for physical development to be spent rationally." Sharon Brady and Darrend Brown, "CC: A Quantum Leap . . . ," *Catalyst*, 20 May 1983, 3.

[14]Gresham Riley oral history, 27 May 1992, 19. News of the fund-raising campaign made its way into the student newspaper, the *Catalyst*, at a very early date. See Art Vander Veen, "CC Plans Major Fund Drive," *Catalyst*, 24 September 1982, 1. Tim Peek, "Campaign Escalates," *Catalyst*, 11 March 1983, 2.

With this information firmly in mind, President Riley and the Board of Trustees set a goal of raising $43.5 million in a major, five-year fund-raising drive. The job of cutting $80 million in perceived needs back to just $43.5 million fell to the Needs Assessment Committee. After much anguished deliberation, it was decided to build a new science building. It also was decided to build a new student center, but the new building would be constructed on the present site of Rastall Center, incorporating some of the steel structure and exterior walls of the old building into the new building. The dormitories would be rehabilitated as quickly as possible.

Deleted and therefore delayed were the proposed Drama and Dance building and the new intramural athletic fields east of Nevada Avenue. Those were important improvements, but the case for them was not as compelling as the arguments for a new science building, a new student center, and rehabilitation of the dorms. It was decided that Drama and Dance could get along a little longer with the existing facilities—the large theater in Armstrong Hall and the former basketball court in Cossitt Hall, recently converted into a large dance studio. Intramural sports would remain concentrated on the small fields on the main quadrangle in front of Armstrong Hall.

President Riley commented that both he and the Board of Trustees had to stay in the realm of the practical. "We did not want to adopt a goal, such as $60 million or $80 million, that we could not meet. We did not want to promise a component, such as a new Drama and Dance building, that would not be built." President Riley himself wanted to set the goal a little higher than $43.5 million because he thought the College would do better with large foundations than Bob Roach had predicted. But the Board wanted the lower figure because, so the argument went, the fund-raising campaign "could not afford to fail."[15]

TRUSTEE INVOLVEMENT

Robert Brossman, who had been the College's chief fund-raiser during the Worner years, was slated to retire in 1982.[16] President Riley con-

[15]Author's notes, Gresham Riley interview, 11 June 1997.

[16]Carrie Printz, "Committee Seeks Brossman Replacement," *Catalyst*, 22 January 1982, 3.

ducted a nationwide search and hired Richard Chamberlain as the new Director of Development. Dick Chamberlain previously had worked on major fund-raising campaigns at Brown University in Rhode Island and the University of California-Los Angeles. As one of their first priorities, Riley and Chamberlain set about involving the Board of Trustees as completely as possible in the upcoming fund-raising campaign at Colorado College. Riley explained:

"One of the first things Dick [Chamberlain] and I had to do was to sort of educate the Board of Trustees to the fact that, if we were going to be successful, they had to claim ownership of the campaign. I remember very vividly during the first couple of years, key members of the Board would often refer to the forthcoming campaign as 'Gresham and Dick's campaign.' A major turning point . . . was a retreat that Dick and I organized at Keystone [a Colorado ski resort]. We took the Board of Trustees up to Keystone for a long weekend, . . . and that was when the Board gained ownership of the campaign. . . . After that time, the Board really threw themselves into this effort in a way that essentially guaranteed success."[17]

THE COLORADO COLLEGE CAMPAIGN

Now officially named the Colorado College Campaign, the five-year fund-raising drive kicked off on September 13, 1985, with a giant banquet, paid for by the College, at the Broadmoor International Center at the Broadmoor Hotel. Faculty members, administrators, trustees, alumni, students, and prospective donors sat down to a sumptuous meal and a rousing round of speeches touting the College and its ambitious fund-raising plans. Each person who attended was presented with a nice souvenir—a small square china plate used to protect a dining table from hot dishes of food. The china plates were covered with white enamel with the image of Cutler Hall outlined in blue.[18]

---

[17]Gresham Riley oral history, 27 May 1992, 18–19. Jerry Lanosga, "Board Of Trustees Rally In Keystone; Board Evaluates Need For Funds," *Catalyst*, 21 September 1984, 3. Pat Chisholm, "Board Of Trustees Enthusiastic," *Catalyst*, 5 October 1984, 4.

[18]Recollection of the author. Also see Jeff Shaw, "Boffo Affair Tonight!" *Catalyst*, 13 September 1985, 1. Blair Sanford, "16.3 Million Raised," *Catalyst*, 20 September 1985, 1.

As so often happened in the history of Colorado College, El Pomar Foundation of Colorado Springs got the campaign off to a roaring start by making an initial commitment of $6 million—$5 million for the new student center and $1 million for student scholarships. Another key contribution came from David and Lucille Packard, who had previously donated the money for Packard Hall. They gave $2 million for the new science building. Before the five-year campaign was over, the Board of Trustees, from their own resources, committed more than $6.5 million.[19]

The Colorado College Campaign became the centerpiece of the middle years of the Riley presidency. Gresham Riley estimated that, from 1984 to 1989, he devoted 40 to 50 percent of his time and energy to the campaign. Small and medium-sized contributions were sought as assiduously as large ones. From September to June during the five-years of the campaign, President Riley was "on the road continuously" speaking to alumni groups. As a result, 85 percent of the living alumni of the College contributed to the campaign.[20]

When the Colorado College Campaign ended in 1989, a total of $49.9 million had been pledged. That was $6.4 million more than the campaign goal of $43.5 million. The $49.9 million final figure was just within the feasibility consultant's estimate that the College could raise between $40 to $50 million.[21]

THE NEW STUDENT CENTER

The first major project to result from the Colorado College Campaign was the new student center. President Riley gave that effort top priority because of the inadequacy and unattractiveness of the old student center. "My most vivid memory with regard to that project," Riley said, "was relief as they began to demolish the old Rastall Center. From the very outset, I considered that building to be an eyesore, and it was on such a

---

[19]Gresham Riley oral history, 27 May 1992, 20. Ernie Luning, "Capital Campaign [Rarin'] To Go," *Catalyst*, 25 February 1985, 1.

[20]Gresham Riley oral history, 27 May 1992, 21. Markus Hartman and Blair Sanford, "Gresham Riley: An Interview," *Catalyst*, 17 January 1986, 18.

[21]"C.C. Raises $49.2 Million," *Catalyst*, 15 September 1989, 1.

strategic corner of the campus that we really needed to upgrade. . . . And so it was a great deal of satisfaction to see the . . . outside shell of that old building being demolished."[22]

A committee of faculty, administrators, and students, chaired by Residence Hall Director Dana Wilson, worked with campus planner Dick Dober to determine the general functions to be served by the new student center.[23] The emphasis was on student thoughts and opinions, and this consulting with students also was carried on by the architects who designed the new building. President Riley described the process:

"In the early design phases, . . . the architects actually set up tables in the old Rastall Center at noontime and would capture students as they were going into lunch and would force them to sit down and talk to them about what they wanted in a campus center. What sort of spaces did they want? And what kind of use did they want to make of such a center? And so the students were enormously helpful in aiding us in conceptualizing that space."[24]

What the students said they wanted were more meeting rooms and more office space for student organizations. They also saw a need for a larger and more attractive snack bar. But, most of all, they wanted the new student center to serve as a unifying point on the campus, a place designed to bring the student body together for activities and social events as well as for eating meals and buying coffee and snacks.

In order to facilitate this stated goal of campus unification, President Riley decided to locate all the student mailboxes in the new student center. Previously students had received their mail in their individual residence halls, and many students said they liked the intimacy and conve-

---

[22]Gresham Riley oral history, 27 May 1992, 21.

[23]As chairman of the Steering Committee for the 1983 Campus Plan, the author participated in the meetings on the design of the new student center. Because the snack bar at the author's alma mater, Williams College, had been designed in the form of a semi-circle coming out into the campus, the author suggested the same semi-circular design for the new student center at Colorado College. That design concept was subsequently adopted for the new snack bar.

[24]Gresham Riley oral history, 27 May 1992, 22. Katie Kerwin, "Rastall Architect Discusses Renovation," *Catalyst*, 11 October 1985, 1. "Making Tentative Rastall Plans," *Catalyst*, 15 November 1985, 3.

nience of having their mail delivered directly to their campus home. President Riley saw it differently, however. He explained:

"We had received a lot of advice to the effect that a powerful magnet in a campus center would be to have student mail delivered there. . . . And even though we had a good bit of student opposition, we decided to put mailboxes in the campus center, and I think that has proven to be a very wise choice on our part."[25]

When finally constructed, the new student center was considerably bigger than its predecessor. The student dining areas were greatly expanded, and an outdoor porch area was provided where students could eat their meals alfresco on warm days and evenings. The new building included two meeting areas. The larger one, Gaylord Hall, was used for either lectures or for lunch and dinner gatherings. The smaller one, the Women's Educational Society (WES) Room, was equipped with film and slide projectors and other visual aides.

The lounges, offices, and the snack bar entrance in the new building were gathered around an atrium that stretched from the basement, where the book store and mailboxes were located, to the second floor. The building was constructed of red, brown, and dark gray brick with white cement block trim. It thus matched the appearance of other post-World War II campus buildings such as Armstrong Hall and Olin Hall. There were many large glass windows, which gave the structure an interior atmosphere that was light and airy.

The new student center was named for Lloyd Edson Worner, the recently retired longtime President of the College. It proved to be a very popular building and became, as hoped, the focal point for much faculty, administration, and student activity.[26]

---

[25]Gresham Riley oral history, 27 May 1992, 22. Future events bore out the wisdom of President Riley's assessment. The campus mail box area in the new student center became a lively place, with students constantly coming and going and much student interaction taking place.

[26]Judith Reid Finley, who conducted the Colorado College Archives Oral History Project, described the new Worner Center as "a wonderfully vibrant building with lots of use." Gresham Riley oral history, 27 May 1992, 22.

Worner Campus Center

Dedication ceremonies were held on the lawn in front of this larger and more spacious campus center, which replaced the former Rastall Center. Worner Campus Center included a major dining area and a semi-circular snack bar.

THE NEW SCIENCE BUILDING

As part of the 1983 Campus Plan, planner Dick Dober compared the space available for Science study at Colorado College to that at similar-sized colleges throughout the United States. This study revealed that Colorado College was seriously deficient in space for Science study compared to its competitors. The need for more Science space was made even more compelling by the desire of the Natural Science faculty to move away from the traditional lecture-demonstration style of teaching to a more hands-on, student-project-oriented, laboratory-centered approach. "Dober's comparison space studies showed that we were badly short on Science space," President Riley said. "Those studies made a new science building a top priority in my mind."[27]

Input from the Natural Science faculty was the major influence on the design of the new Science building. Professor Harold Jones of the Chemistry Department chaired a committee of Science professors that met frequently and struggled hard to create a building in which students would be encouraged to "do Science" rather than "see Science." The result was a four-story building which also had an astronomical observatory and biology greenhouses on the roof.

The new Science building was attached at a right angle to the existing Olin Hall of Science. The new structure had the same brick exterior as the old Olin Hall, but considerably more windows. It included space for the Anthropology Department, which moved over from the basement of Palmer Hall, and new offices and laboratories for the rapidly-expanding academic computing services at the College.

The new Science building was named the Barnes Science Center in honor of Otis and Margaret Barnes. Otis Barnes was a Professor of Chemistry at Colorado College who married Margaret Tyson Barnes of the class of 1927. Professor and Mrs. Barnes bequeathed more than $9 million to the Chemistry Department and to the Natural Science program of the College.[28]

---

[27]Author's notes, Gresham Riley interview, 11 June 1997. Also see L. C. Rivera, "Tinkering With Olin," *Catalyst*, 27 January 1984, 4. Steve Geraghty, "Students Discuss Olin Renovation," *Catalyst*, 1 November 1985, 3.

[28]David Klein, "Barnes Boosts Budget," *Catalyst*, 5 December 1986, 1.

Barnes Science Center
This major Science facility was attached at a right angle to the north end of Olin Hall of Science. It included an astronomical observatory and Biology greenhouses on the roof.

The new structure, because of its right-angle connection to Olin Hall of Science, created an attractive new quadrangle of buildings on the campus. This new quadrangle, landscaped with trees and grass, had the Olin Hall of Science to the east, the glass-enclosed Olin Hall lounge to the south, the east end of Palmer Hall to the west, and the new Barnes Science Center to the north.

Similar to the new Worner Campus Center, the new Barnes Science Center drew many compliments, both from those who taught and studied inside it and those who observed it while walking about the campus.[29]

OTHER BRICKS-AND-MORTAR PROJECTS

Colorado College was growing in size, but so was the Colorado Springs Fine Arts Center adjacent to the campus. The art museum needed to take back some space that it had rented to the College for its sculpture program, so the College hastily constructed a temporary building for a sculpture studio on the south side of Cache La Poudre Street across from Slocum Hall. The new building also included badly needed space where the Drama Department could build sets for its theatrical productions. After the sets were completed, they were transferred across the street and set up in Armstrong Theater.[30]

Although it was the least visible of the bricks-and-mortar projects undertaken during the Riley years, the residence halls were extensively renovated at a cost of some $2.5 million.[31] In addition to fresh paint and spruced up bathrooms and showers, the dormitory rehabilitation included the creation of more of the "suite" type of rooms that had been requested by the students.

TUTT ALUMNI HOUSE

During the 1985–1986 academic year the College took a beautiful home located just north of the campus and renovated it as an alumni house.

---

[29]Linda Baynham, "The New Olin – A Scientific Wonderland," *Catalyst*, 16 September 1988, 9.

[30]Gresham Riley oral history, 27 May 1992, 23. The author's description of the sculpture and set production building as temporary was something of a prayer. The building was constructed at the sidewalk line without any landscaping and in no way appeared to relate to or be a permanent part of the Colorado College campus.

[31]Gresham Riley oral history, 27 June 1992, 23.

The home had belonged to the Tutt family and was given to the College in 1959. The home had been used for faculty housing prior to being turned into offices, reception rooms, and a dining area for alumni activities. The completely repainted and spruced up facility was named Tutt Alumni House.

The new alumni center was located on the northeast corner of Cascade Avenue and Uintah Street. A unique feature was a bedroom and bath that were made available to alumni who returned to the campus on official College business and needed a place to stay overnight. Tutt Alumni House symbolized the strong emphasis on good alumni relations that was an important part of Gresham Riley's presidency. Diane Benninghoff, a graduate of Colorado College, took over as Director of Alumni Relations when the new facility opened.

The Baca

In the mid–1980s the College acquired a large tract of land down in the San Luis Valley of southern Colorado. The land totaled approximately 300 acres, was 175 miles from Colorado Springs (a three-hour drive one way), and included a small conference center. The nearest town was Crestone, with a population of some 50 permanent residents. Rising dramatically to the east of this facility were the snow-capped Sangre de Cristo mountains.[32] Towering above all was Crestone Needle, a mountain peak 14,197 feet high, a full 87 feet higher than Pike's Peak.

This new facility was particularly attractive as a place where classes could go to get away from the distractions and stresses of the main campus. Professors took their students down to this new facility by bus for anything from a four-day stay to an entire block. The College enhanced the existing conference center by constructing a $550,000 southwestern style lodge and library, three town houses, and a mini-computer laboratory.[33]

---

[32]When Spanish explorers first saw the red color of a morning sunrise reflecting off the snow on the tops of these mountains, they named the mountains Sangre de Cristo, or "Blood of Christ."

[33]Gresham Riley oral history, 27 May 1992, 23. *Colorado College Catalog 1997–98*, 13. Ted Craig and David A. Fitzgerald, "C.C. Contemplates Baca Extension," *Catalyst*, 12 September 1986, 1. Owen Perkins, "Baca Grande: C.C.'s New Horizon," *Catalyst*, 20 February 1987, 1. "C.C. Purchases Baca Townhouse, Conference Center; Trial Lease Deemed Successful," *Catalyst*, 16 February 1990, 3.

This San Luis Valley facility was named the Baca Campus, but it soon was called "the Baca" in everyday parlance. In addition to being an excellent place to get away from city life and hike in the Sangre de Cristo mountains, the Baca was a comfortable base from which to study the archeology, anthropology, and cultural history of southern Colorado.[34]

FRATERNITY ENTERPRISE

One of Lloyd Worner's toughest decisions before leaving the presidential office was to suspend College approval of one of the fraternities and evict the fraternity members from their College-owned fraternity house. This had been very difficult for President Worner because he had been a fraternity member as an undergraduate at Colorado College. But the problems at this particular fraternity house had been of major concern. The brothers were accused of breaking College rules as well as state laws by selling alcohol and illegal drugs at their fraternity parties.

It fell to Gresham Riley, as the new President, to decide if and when this fraternity would get renewed College approval and its house back. The second week Riley was in office, all of the officers of the fraternity came in to see him. "You'd never seen such a clean, well-scrubbed group of young men in your life," Riley said. "They came trooping into my office with three-piece, pin-striped suits, all very serious, and proceeded to explain the circumstances of the punitive action that had been taken against them. . . . Their position was that they had been more sinned-against than they had sinned. . . . [They said] they were simply enterprising entrepreneurs, raising money for fraternity parties."

Gresham Riley saw immediately that the fraternity men were hoping that, as the brand-new College President, he would be naive and anxious to please and might possibly buy such an argument. Riley told them: "Gentlemen, you are *not* enterprising entrepreneurs; you *really* are felons! And it's a wonder that you're not in the slammer in the state of Colorado, rather than being in this office trying to hoodwink me with regard to how enterprising you are!"[35]

---

[34]Matthew Lewis, "The Baca: Far And Away From The Everyday," *Catalyst*, 11 December 1992, 5.

[35]Gresham Riley oral history, 27 May 1992, 7–8..

President Riley then held a realistic and firm discussion with the officers of the fraternity to the effect that College rules and Colorado and United States laws had to be obeyed at Colorado College. Riley restored College approval of the fraternity, but he made the errant fraternity men wait another year before they could reoccupy their fraternity house. The new President also clearly established himself as someone who could not be flim-flammed by the students, no matter how adept and inventive their arguments.

A Ph.D. Is Required

Another major crisis during Gresham Riley's first year as President concerned terminal contracts given to two popular young members of the College faculty. Both had failed to complete their doctoral dissertations in the four-year period allowed by College rules. The situation was complicated by the fact that, after vociferous debates and close votes, the appropriate faculty committees had recommended that both teachers be retained and promoted rather than terminated.

The issue landed on Gresham Riley's desk accompanied by a strong recommendation from Dean Glenn Brooks that terminal contracts be issued. Brooks argued, and Riley strongly agreed, that promoting faculty members without Ph.D.s would lower the academic reputation of the College. Riley explained:

"[This] was not establishing the kind of precedent for the faculty that we thought was important. . . . The integrity of the faculty and the kind of standards that we wanted to establish and maintain really were at issue. . . . It was important to me, early on in my presidency, to make clear what my own academic values were as it pertained to the faculty."

This decision made the College's new President very unpopular with certain members of the faculty and the student body. There were no sit-ins in the presidential office, but Riley received many office visits from upset professors and students. The student newspaper, the *Catalyst*, gave the story front-page coverage, and more than 750 students, one-third of the student body, signed a petition asking President Riley to reconsider the matter. An all-campus outdoor rally was held in behalf of keeping the two young teachers on the faculty. The students took their arguments to the

Board of Trustees, but the Board confirmed the decision made by President Riley on the recommendation of Dean Brooks.

These two faculty dismissals were symptomatic of an important change that was taking place at Colorado College in the early 1980s. The College had long ago established itself as a premier *teaching* institution, and that idea had been solidly confirmed by the adoption of the teaching-oriented Block Plan. But now the time had come to start building the *scholarly* reputation of the College, and that called for an all-Ph.D. faculty and an increase in publishing by the professors, both new and old. Dean Glenn Brooks was considered to be the major advocate of increasing the scholarly output at Colorado College, but there was no question that he was strongly supported by President Riley in this effort. Particularly when it came to hiring new faculty at the College, an extra emphasis was being placed on seeking young persons with good scholarship potential as well as good teaching potential.[36]

AN ACADEMIC ATHLETIC DIRECTOR

In 1982 the new emphasis on improving the academic stature of the College was extended to the Athletic Department when President Gresham Riley appointed a tenured professor as the new Athletic Director. Richard Taber, Professor of Chemistry and a member of the College faculty since 1963, moved into the top spot at El Pomar Sports Center following the resignation of Jerry Carle, who had served as Athletic Director for 25 years. Carle continued to serve as football coach but stepped down as Athletic Director so that the post could become a full-time position at the College.[37]

Noting that 70 percent of the student body participated in organized athletic activity while at Colorado College, Taber said he switched from the Chemistry Department to the Athletic Department because he wanted "to help students establish life-time athletic habits." As for intercollegiate athletics, Taber said he saw them as athletics at a higher level that required

---

[36]Recollection of the author.

[37]Ernie Luning, "Carle Resigns: Full-Time Athletic Director Considered," *Catalyst*, 22 January 1982, 1. Hockey coach Jeff Sauer briefly served as acting Athletic Director after Carle, but Sauer then left Colorado College for the head coaching job at the University of Wisconsin.

greater skills. "A lot of the justification for an intercollegiate athletic program is strictly historical," he commented. "It's been going on for years."

Dick Taber explained that he took this new and different job partly because big universities were fielding "semi-professional teams" and recruiting athletes "solely for their athletic prowess, not their academic prowess." At Colorado College there was the opportunity "to guide a program important to the liberal arts setting." As for men's ice hockey, Colorado College's one big-time (NCAA Division I) sport, Taber said the Athletic Department would continue to "recruit the best hockey players we can find, but we will also recruit students who will benefit from a Colorado College education."[38]

Division I Women's Soccer

One of the first tasks facing Professor Taber in his new position as Athletic Director was achieving more equality between men's and women's sports at Colorado College. Because the College had an NCAA Division I men's ice hockey team, it was deemed essential to elevate one of the women's sports to NCAA Division I status. Much of the pressure for this change came from a U.S. Government law (Title IX, as it was known) mandating that colleges and universities that receive U.S. Government funds treat men and women equally.[39]

The proposal to elevate a woman's sport to Division I status kicked off a flurry of faculty suggestions that demoting men's ice hockey from Division I status was a better idea. President Riley rejected that option, citing the fact that the College had been one of the institutions that first developed Division I men's ice hockey back in the late 1930s. After a lively faculty debate, in which there was much support to elevate the women's basketball team to Division I status, it was decided to upgrade the women's soccer team instead. Because of the larger number of players on

---

[38]David Davis, "Academics Meet Athletics In Taber," *Catalyst*, 17 September 1982, 1. Richard Taber served as Athletic Director from 1982 to 1990. See Tim Lambert, "Taber To Step Down As Athletic Director; Wants To Return To Teaching Chemistry Full-Time," *Catalyst*, 2 February 1990, 1.

[39]The specific law was Title IX of the 1972 Amendments to the Civil Rights Act of 1964. For discussion of the issues involved with Title IX, see Dan Rohlf, "Colorado College's Athletic Catch 22: Title IX," *Catalyst*, 25 February 1983, 10–11.

a team, and because more young women were playing soccer than were playing basketball, it was argued that Colorado College could field a competitive women's soccer team at the Division I level. "As we studied the matter," explained President Riley, "it seemed to a lot of us that we would be able to recruit the kind of students who could do well in soccer."[40]

The major point was that the College was giving ample athletic scholarships to women soccer players as well as men ice hockey players. Very quickly that money appeared to have been well-spent, especially where results on the athletic field were concerned. For a number of years in the mid–1980s, the Colorado College women's soccer team made the "Final Four" in the NCAA Division I women's national soccer championships. In 1986 Colorado College had the second best women's collegiate soccer team in the United States, losing the NCAA Division I championship game to the University of North Carolina by a score of 2–0.[41]

But there were other benefits from the Division I women's soccer program rather than just chalking up numbers in the win column. Young women from throughout the nation—and in some cases the world—received athletic scholarship aid that enabled them to come to Colorado College, something they otherwise might not have been able to do. These top-level women athletes became role models for other women students at the College, demonstrating that women can excel and succeed in athletic as well as other forms of endeavor. The women's soccer program also created a new set of Division I athletic heroes on the campus, and for the first time in the history of Colorado College those Division I athletic heroes were women. From 1980 to 1990, 14 Colorado College women's soccer players were named All-Americans.[42]

With the transition to Division I women's soccer, there was an important coaching change. Steve Paul, who began as an undergraduate coach-

---

[40]Gresham Riley oral history, 27 May 1992, 30–31. Also see Stacie Oulton, "Title IX Options Considered," *Catalyst*, 16 March 1984, 13.

[41]Kathy Mahoney, "Awesome," *Catalyst*, 6 December 1985, 17. Anna Shortt and Karen Willoughby, "America's Number 2 Team," *Catalyst*, 5 December 1986, 1.

[42]*1997 Colorado College Women's Soccer Media Guide*, produced by the Colorado College Sports Information Office, 34.

ing the women's soccer team at Colorado College back in 1975, gave up his part time job as women's soccer coach and moved on to other opportunities. Paul had been a founder and solid supporter of women's soccer at Colorado College. He was replaced by Dang Pibulvech, who promptly announced his intention to lead the College's Division I women's soccer team to a national championship, a goal he almost but never quite attained.[43]

TOWARD A NATIONAL PROFILE

As he gained a firmer grip on the presidential reins at Colorado College, one of Gresham Riley's major goals was to gain more national recognition for the College. "It became clear to me in my many conversations that there was an aspiration on the part of the College community which many people felt had not been fulfilled," Riley said. "And that was the movement of the College into a posture of national recognition—recognition for being the kind of institution that, in fact, it was."

Riley saw Colorado College in the early 1980s as comparable to other liberal arts colleges with national profiles but still having something of a regional profile. He felt the time was right for the College to take positive steps to be "acknowledged as a national institution of distinction." One part of this effort was to mobilize the alumni of the College by restructuring the National Alumni Council so that there were strong alumni chapters, where possible, in the major metropolitan centers of the country. "The result," Riley explained, "was that we were able to put in place a national network of graduates of the institution who began talking about Colorado College in their own cities. And so Colorado College began to be talked about in Boston, and New York City, and San Francisco, and Chicago, by people who knew the College well. And . . . that . . . served us very well."

Another effort to build the reputation of the College involved hiring national news media consultants to steer reporters and writers toward the Colorado College faculty as expert sources to be quoted in newspaper and

[43]Camille Bzdek, "Paul Leaving C.C.," *Catalyst*, 11 February 1983, 17. Maxwell Cohen, "Fundamentals, Optimism, Pibulvich, *Catalyst*, 23 September 1983, 17. For a general review of the status of women's sports at Colorado College in the early 1980s, see Camille Bzdek, "Women's Sports Assessment," *Catalyst*, 25 March 1983, 16.

magazine articles. Reporters and writers could telephone the consultants, state the subject matter on which they were writing, and get the names and telephone numbers of those Colorado College professors who had expertise in that subject area. The result was a number of stories quoting Colorado College professors that ran in national publications such as the *New York Times*, the *Christian Science Monitor*, *Time*, and *Business Week*.

President Riley also sought to build the national profile of the College by recruiting new members of the Board of Trustees from across the country. "Just as our alumni were scattered from coast to coast," Riley noted, "so we had a national profile in our Board of Trustees, and they were very vigorous in promoting the College."[44]

TECHNOLOGICAL ADVANCES

Although liberal arts colleges have traditionally emphasized the importance of the intellectual heritage of the past, there is also a need to keep up with the latest technological developments in a rapidly-changing society. In the early 1980s three major technological shifts impacted on the College. One was the change from movie film to video. A second was the shift from large mainframe electronic computers to smaller personal computers. A third was the change from rotary-style dial telephones to push-button touch-tone telephones.

Video

Gus Mundt, the Director of Technical Services, led Colorado College into the video age. Two shoulder-carried video cameras and a portable videotape recorder were acquired. Mundt made the equipment available to all interested students and encouraged them to begin inaugurating their own video projects, such as taping visiting speakers and student dramatic productions.[45]

Meanwhile, Tutt Library was busy acquiring a collection of significant videos to be used as instructional aides. The videos ranged from old movies, such as "All The King's Men" for Political Science classes, to pub-

---

[44]Gresham Riley oral history, 27 May 1992, 12–13.

[45]Angela Padilla, "Video Workshop Set," *Catalyst*, 18 September 1981, 1.

lic television productions such as "Civilization," which was shown in a variety of history and literature classes. Faculty members were encouraged to order appropriate videos for course use. The videos were cataloged in the same manner as books, and all members of the College community could check out a video for home viewing.

Tutt Library also installed two large video rooms so that professors and their students could come and watch the videos in a comfortable setting. The video playing machines used were the large-screen type, which made seeing a video in Tutt Library somewhat like going to the movie theater.

Personal Computers

The Burroughs computer was aging rapidly by the early 1980s. It had become so obsolete that the College could not get repair parts for it. One of the first decisions President Riley had to make in the fall of 1982, when he first took office, was what would be the next step in computing at Colorado College. It was determined that the College would replace the Burroughs with two small mainframe computers, a "VAX" and a "Prime 750," for administrative uses, such as course registration and keeping business records.[46] For faculty and students, however, the College would decentralize the computing process and equip each individual, as much as possible, with his or her own personal computer. The College began by buying 58 Texas Instruments (TI) personal computers and locating them where they could readily be used by administrators, faculty, and students.[47]

To encourage more members of the faculty to get into personal computing, the College subsidized the purchase of a TI personal computer for home use for each faculty member who wanted one. The subsidy took the form of both a price reduction and a no-interest loan to be paid back through monthly salary deductions. Almost all of the faculty took advantage of this low-cost opportunity to get into personal computing on the home front. The new faculty computers were used mainly for word pro-

---

[46]Sharon Brady, "VAX Overtakes The B6800," *Catalyst*, 13 April 1984, 7. "New Computers," *Catalyst*, 7 September 1984, 2.

[47]Gresham Riley oral history, 27 May 1992, 24. Melissa Hyde, "More Computers For C.C.," *Catalyst*, 18 February 1983, 4. Scott Riney, "Into The Information Age," *Catalyst*, 16 September 1983, 5. Holly Ornstein, "Computers In Dorms," *Catalyst*, 14 December 1984, 2.

cessing, and the College standardized on using Word Perfect 3.0 as the common word processing system.[48]

Personal computers were made available to the students by installing large numbers of the machines in "computer labs" scattered at strategic places around the campus. One large set of machines was placed in the basement of Tutt Library, and another group was located in two adjoining subterranean and windowless rooms in the depths of Palmer Hall. Students used these personal computers for word processing, mathematical calculations, or learning how to program computers. Games were available on the student personal computers and often were played quite avidly by procrastinating undergraduates.

Touch-Tone Telephones

Advancing technology also caught up with the Colorado College telephone system in the early 1980s. Unable to secure replacement parts for its old rotary-style dial telephones and switching equipment, the College installed a new American Telephone & Telegraph (AT&T) "Dimension 2000" telephone system in the fall of 1981. A fleet of white telephone company trucks and vans descended on the campus to carry out the necessary rewiring and equipment installation.

The new telephone system brought touch-tone phones to the Colorado College campus for the first time. It provided call-waiting signals, and it allowed outgoing calls to be touch-toned directly without going through the campus operator. It also permitted students to use credit cards when making long-distance calls.[49]

GOODBYE TO HANYA HOLM

The hallowed and treasured relationship between Hanya Holm and the Summer Session at Colorado College came to an end in the early 1980s. Hanya Holm first taught Dance at Colorado College in the 1941 Summer

---

[48]A significant portion of this manuscript was rough drafted on the author's old Texas Instruments computer in Word Perfect 3.0. The T.I. had been purchased with a College subsidy in 1983 and was still very much operative in the author's office at home in the late 1990s.

[49]James Atkinson, "CC Plugs Into Ma Bell," *Catalyst*, 6 November 1981, 1.

Session. For 43 uninterrupted years her summer dance classes were an integral and inspiring part of summertime at Colorado College.

Hanya Holm's dance classes were legendary for their high quality, and the former Broadway dancer and choreographer brought a touch of star quality to the campus during the summer months. The dance performances put on by Hanya Holm's students during the Summer Session were enthusiastically attended by dance connoisseurs at the College and throughout the Colorado Springs community.

There was great sadness at Colorado College over Hanya Holm's departure. Many had hoped she could go on teaching dance at the Summer Session—and producing such wonderful dance performances—forever. Her more than four-decades-long tenure at the Summer Session was a major artistic highlight of the College's history.

The Golden Anniversary of Shove Chapel

In 1981 the College marked the 50th anniversary of the construction of Shove Chapel, which was built in 1931. In honor of this event, Political Science Professor Timothy Fuller wrote a book, *This Glorious And Trancendant Place*, which described in detail the architectural significance of the building, its various sculptural features, and its beautiful stained glass windows. The book was illustrated with a large number of photographs by Benschneider, an independent photographer who did much work for the College at the time. Enlargements of Benschneider's photographs for the book on Shove Chapel were displayed in Tutt Library.[50]

Student Musicals

Periodically throughout the late 1970s and early 1980s there would be student productions of classic Broadway musicals. These performances were exciting, because they brought together a variety of talents from both the faculty and the student body. The dramatic, vocal, dance, and instrumental music abilities of the College community would come together

---

[50]Scott Patton, "Happy Semi-Centennial," *Catalyst*, 2 October 1981, 1. Timothy Fuller, ed., *This Glorious And Transcendant Place* (Colorado Springs, CO: Colorado College, 1981).

briefly in a major entertainment effort. Particularly notable were productions of *Carousel*, *Finian's Rainbow*, *Cabaret*, *Hair*, and *Kiss Me Kate*.[51]

In the fall of 1981 *West Side Story* was presented. This musical version of Shakespeare's *Romeo And Juliet* highlighted the conflict on the streets of New York City between rival teen-age gangs, one of them Anglo and the other Puerto Rican. The show was regarded as particularly significant because of the increasing attention to ethnic diversity issues at the College at that time.

Professor of Drama James Malcolm directed *West Side Story*, and Professor of Dance Peggy Berg did the choreography and trained the student dancers. Berg was particularly complimented for the hilarious and vivacious dance number "America," where a group of Puerto Rican young women humorously compared life in New York with life in Puerto Rico. Students David MacDonald and Sarah Van Scoy played and sang the roles of Tony and Maria, the ill-fated young lovers, and students David Ammons and Jon Khoury were highly praised for their high-pitched performances as leaders of the two rival gangs.[52]

A Conservative in the White House

In 1980 a conservative Republican, Ronald Reagan of California, was elected President of the United States. There was no question that Ronald Reagan's presidency had an effect on the political atmosphere of the Colorado College campus. Many students, and particularly student political leaders, opposed Reagan's conservative economic philosophy and his confrontational attitude toward the Soviet Union. There were periodic reminders of the turmoil and tumult of the late 1960s and early 1970s as students in the 1980s staged demonstrations opposing Reagan's efforts to suppress the spread of Communism in Latin American nations such as El Salvador and Nicaragua.[53] But as Reagan's presidency became

---

[51]Valerie Feder, "Hair: Rehearsals Underway; Get Your Beads Out," *Catalyst*, 5 October 1984, 12. Shaun Avery, "Hair '84," *Catalyst*, 19 October 1984, 10. Jeannie Anselmi, "Successful Start For C.C. Drama; 'Kiss Me Kate' Opens On A High Note," *Catalyst*, 16 October 1987, 17.

[52]Peter Russell, " 'West Side Story' High Energy," *Catalyst*, 16 October 1981, 7.

[53]Photograph by Steve Wilson, "Marchers . . . ," *Catalyst*, 5 February 1982, 1. Tim Fitzgerald, "U.S. Funding Adds To El Salvador Turmoil," *Catalyst*, 5 February 1982, 3. Tim Peek, "El Salvador Policy: Blind Ideology," *Catalyst*, 5 February 1982, 5.

more popular with the American people, campus opposition to him and his policies quieted down. By the mid–1980s, in fact, there were substantial numbers of students who were willing to identify themselves publicly as conservatives and strong supporters of President Reagan.[54]

JOJOBA RESEARCH

One of the more interesting research projects on campus in the early 1980s was Biology Professor Richard Storey's work with the jojoba plant. Storey earned his bachelor's degree from the University of New Mexico and his Ph.D. from the University of Oklahoma. He became interested in the jojoba plant because it grows in desert areas and a high-speed lubricant can be extracted from its seeds. After the lubricant is removed, an edible meal for animals is left behind as a byproduct.

Using jojoba oil as a high-speed lubricant would reduce the need for sperm whale oil, also a high-speed lubricant, and would thereby reduce the pressure to hunt and kill sperm whales. But what really interested Professor Storey was the animal meal left behind after the oil was removed. Since the jojoba plant is drought, heat, and salt resistant, it could be grown in largely unproductive desert areas, provide jobs manufacturing the lubricant, and then also become an indirect food source for the local population.

"The world is becoming a desert," Storey said, "so there is an incredible amount of interest in the world in the physiology of arid plants." If the jojoba could be developed as a cash crop, "it could help alleviate some of the economic and social problems of the under-developed countries, which are often located in arid regions."

Professor Storey's research involved studying the metabolism of the seed proteins in the jojoba plant. His work also was significant because, typical of much scientific study at Colorado College under the Block Plan, Storey involved 13 of his students in the jojoba research project. "I believe that if you're going to do research at a place like CC," Storey concluded, "you ought to involve students."[55]

---

[54]For national data on the conservative tendencies of college and university students in the 1980s, see "Freshmen Become Greedier," *Catalyst*, 5 March 1982, 2.

[55]"Storey Receives Grant, Jojoba Research To Continue," *Catalyst*, 9 April 1982, 2. Anne Grignon, "Jojoba: CC Researches Applications For A Renewable Resource," *Catalyst*, 24 September 1982, 5

CHANGING STUDENT SOCIAL PATTERNS

Question: What is the difference between Colorado College women and the trash? Answer: The trash still gets taken out!

A variation of this joke was printed in the student newspaper, the *Catalyst*, in the early 1980s. It summed up the way in which men-women relationships among the students at the College were changing. Formal dating, where one person asked another person out at a specific time for a specific event, had come almost to an end. Students were more likely to do social things in groups, with no one man being with any particular one woman. Most of all, casual and uncommitted dating had been greatly reduced. If two students went out together more than once, they were immediately viewed by their friends as a "steady" couple.

One woman student, Velva Price, told the *Catalyst* that she was no longer depressed by the lack of formal dating at Colorado College. She wrote: "I've adjusted to it quite well. I've already picked out my convent in California. . . . But, if anybody would like to change my mind, just give me a call.[56]

The students at the College had no ready explanation for how this "no more formal dating" situation had come about. Some blamed the Block Plan, arguing that three-and-a-half-weeks was not long enough to get to know someone in a class and then want to ask them out. The situation was complicated by the intensity of the last week-and-a-half of the block. Students became so busy with classes, homework, extracurricular activities, and athletics that there was no time to follow up on a relationship that might have blossomed during the first two weeks of the block.[57]

The *Catalyst* told about a woman student who characterized her best recent date as going with a man student to a lumber yard and a hardware store to buy the materials to build a chalk board. The two of them then sat around and drew pictures on the chalk board. It was about as far from a formal date as a couple could get. "If [Colorado] College dating exists," this women student concluded, "it doesn't follow any pattern or make any

---

[56]Velva Price, "Dating Game," *Catalyst*, 12 February 1982, 7.

[57]Katherine Eastman, "Students Have Sex On The Block Plan; Campus Sexual Activity Conforms To Class Rigors And Natural Cycles Of The Block Plan," *Catalyst*, 4 May 1990, 10.

sense. Confusion has surfaced and isn't likely to subside. We can only try to 'be excellent to each other.'"[58]

In the late 1990s the *Catalyst* officially declared that "the dating scene here is almost non-existent." One student, Ben Fowle, described going on a formal date as a "myth." He explained: "You just hook up at parties and then say 'Hi' in [Worner Center] the next day." But there were some positive social aspects to going to a school with the Block Plan. A number of students said they started going out with each other after they went on a Block Break service project together. B. J. Stone started seeing Chelsea Newby regularly after they both went on a 1997 spring break Community Service Trip to New Orleans, Louisiana.[59]

The "no formal dating" situation was something of an anomaly. Over the previous three decades, the College had eliminated dormitory curfews for women, had permitted opposite sex visitation in dormitory rooms, and had provided both wing and alternate-room coeducational housing. The College, in response to student demands, had very much placed the men and women students in each other's physical presence. But apparently the age-old problem of how do men find compatible women—and how do women find compatible men—had not been completely solved.

But despite the lack of formal dating, Colorado College men and women still found a way to meet, fall in love, and get married. Every spring and early summer throughout the 1980s and 1990s, Shove Chapel continued to host a significant number of student weddings.[60]

STUDENT FADS

In the early 1980s a new fad swept the campus, particularly among the men students. It was hackey-sack, where a player worked hard at keeping a small leather pouch in the air by bouncing it off his or her knees and

[58]Sara Phillips, "Dating Practices Change With The Times; Student Wonders If College Dating Really Exists At Colorado College," *Catalyst*, 16 February 1990, 7.

[59]Andrea Godsman, "The Campus Dating Scene: What It Is, What It Isn't, And What Some Think It Should Be," *Catalyst*, 31 October 1997, 6.

[60]Christine Andresen, "C.C. Students Head To The Altar; Spouses-To-Be Discover Promise And Frustration In Matrimonial Futures," *Catalyst*, 4 May 1990, 7. Anne Lucke, "'Till Death Do Us Part . . . C.C. Students Take The Plunge," *Catalyst*, 10 February 1994, 9.

ankles. The point of the game appeared to be to keep the hackey-sack up in the air as long as possible.[61]

Throwing the frisbee around continued to be popular, but that old pastime had developed some interesting new variations. One was frisbee golf. Competing players sailed the circular plastic discs toward specific points on the campus and then counted the number of "strokes" required to get to the specific point. The player with the lowest number of strokes won that particular "hole." Occasionally bystanders or passing pedestrians, some of them faculty members or administrators, would get hit by an errant frisbee golf shot, which was a one-stroke penalty. Students often sipped beverages as they played around the "official" eleven-hole frisbee golf course on campus. There were periodic informal frisbee golf "tournaments" for the truly dedicated.

The highest form of frisbee was "ultimate" frisbee, where teams of students would play a variation of touch football using a frisbee instead of a football. Ultimate frisbee was sometimes played as a coeducational sport. By the early 1980s there were both upper class and first year leagues with avid competition for the ultimate frisbee championships.[62]

FACULTY POLITICIANS

The Colorado College faculty continued to participate actively in the political life of the Colorado Springs community. To give proper credit, the accomplishment sheets which each faculty member filled out each year had a place for listing "community service."

One of the most exciting political ventures by a Colorado College faculty member was undertaken by Professor of Political Science Thomas Cronin. Although Colorado Springs was considered Republican Party territory, Cronin courageously ran as a Democrat for the local seat in the United States House of Representatives in Washington, D.C. Cronin's political effort sparked a great deal of interest at the College, and a large number of students "spent a block" working in his campaign by taking the internship course *Political Campaigning*. Although Professor Cronin polled

---

[61]Photograph by Greg Anderson, *Catalyst*, 22 January 1982, 6.

[62]Mark Tindall, "Frisbee Gains Popularity As Legitimate Sport," *Catalyst*, 23 April 1982, 13. David King, " 'Shrubbery Belligerence!' Frisbee Golfers Invade Campus," *Catalyst*, 3 April 1992, 7.

more votes than any Democrat had ever received in that particular congressional district, it was not enough for victory and Cronin's conservative Republican opponent was elected.[63]

In 1982 Economics Professor Mike Bird, following eight years of service on the Colorado Springs City Council, ran for a seat in the lower house of the Colorado state legislature in Denver. After winning a hard-fought Republican primary against an arch-conservative incumbent legislator, Bird was unopposed in the general election.[64] Four years later Mike Bird was elected to the Colorado state Senate, where he served an additional eight years. As Chairman of the state legislature's powerful Joint Budget Committee, the Colorado College economist became famous for his skill at maintaining state services and programs while at the same time keeping state finances on a solid footing.

Student Scholars

For the first time in 17 years, a Colorado College student won a Rhodes Scholarship to study at Oxford University in England. In the spring of 1983 Wade Buchanan, a senior History major with an approximate 3.8 grade point average (on a 4.0 scale), became the College's first Rhodes Scholar-elect since the late 1960s. Buchanan said he planned to take a course of study at Oxford entitled *Philosophy, Politics, and Economics*.[65]

The class of 1983 also turned in an outstanding performance when it came to winning Watson Fellowships to travel and think overseas. Four Colorado College seniors won a Watson, a very unusual event for a single college or university. Donna Sanders planned to use her Watson funds to study family violence in Asia, Dyan Gershman was going to intern with a historic preservation program in France, Laura Hershey intended to travel to the United Kingdom to work with political groups involved in handicapped rights, and Shawn Sigstedt was heading for the People's Republic of China to study that nation's usage of medicinal plants.[66]

---

[63]Dave Davis and Tim Peek, "Analysis: Congressional Race Unique At Best," *Catalyst*, 22 October 1982, 4. Anne Kerwin, "Cronin Defeated," *Catalyst*, 5 November 1982, 1.

[64]Mary Mashburn, "Bird Got Grass-Roots Vote," *Catalyst*, 15 October 1982, 3.

[65]Linda Knufinke, "Buchanan Wins," *Catalyst*, 14 January 1983, 1.

[66]Linda Knufinke, "Watson Pocket Money," *Catalyst*, 18 March 1983, 2. Also see Thomas Walsh and Brian Armstrong, "The Watson," *Catalyst*, 7 September 1984, 10. "Laura Hershey – C.C. Fellow '83," *Catalyst*, 7 September 1984, 11.

ALL-AMERICAN SWIMMERS

Coach Jerry Lear's swimming teams continued to perform at a consistently high level. The 1982–1983 season ended with two Colorado College women swimmers named All-Americans at the NCAA Division III Nationals in Canton, Ohio. Sue Wolfe qualified by placing 12th nationally in the backstroke, and Laura Luckett was honored for finishing 9th in 3 meter diving. The women's and men's swim teams combined to give Colorado College the best scores it had ever received at a Division III National swim meet. At the close of the season Coach Lear was voted Intermountain Swim League Coach Of The Year.[67]

A COACHING LEGEND

Although he officially retired from the College faculty a decade earlier, Professor of Biology Robert Stabler was still going strong in the early 1980s helping to coach the men's lacrosse team. Known as "Doc" Stabler to the students, he drove down to Stewart Field in his famous maroon pick-up truck and performed a variety of handyman chores for the lacrosse players, everything from planning the schedule to fixing broken helmets. More than anyone else at the College, it was Stabler's lacrosse team. He founded men's lacrosse at Colorado College in the early 1960s and served as the first coach (in addition to his Biology teaching duties).

"Doc" Stabler was born in 1904 in Washington, D.C. He played lacrosse at Swarthmore College near Philadelphia, Pennsylvania, and developed a great love for the game. After graduating from Swarthmore in 1927, Stabler received a degree in medical Zoology from the Johns Hopkins University in Baltimore, Maryland, and began his teaching career at the University of Pennsylvania in Philadelphia. He joined the Biology Department at Colorado College in 1947, a time when "lumberjack" shirts were the latest craze in student clothing and attendance at weekly chapel services was compulsory.

On his 80-acre ranch near what became Interstate 25 and Garden of the Gods Road, Professor Stabler kept a variety of animals that were part of his study of parasitology and other diseases of animals. He published more than 170 articles in academic journals on parasitology.

---

[67]Kate Fuller, "2 Big Cat All-Americans, Lear Coach-Of-The-Year," *Catalyst*, 25 March 1983, 15.

But "Doc" Stabler was best known for his after-hours interest in student athletics. He served as coach of the swimming team back before Colorado College had its own swimming pool and the team had to practice at the YMCA or the Broadmoor Hotel pool. In his years as lacrosse coach, he serviced all the lacrosse equipment in his cellar at home, a big job in view of the fact each player wore more than $100 worth of equipment. He said he stayed at Colorado College and in Colorado Springs for so long because of the "good kinda people" he found at both places.[68]

Broadway Bound

In the early 1980s a play by Colorado College English Professor James Yaffe was presented at a Broadway theater in New York City. The play, entitled *Immorality Play*, was a "thriller" designed to attract large audiences rather than make a deep intellectual statement. Professor Yaffe joked that the play was so "very commercial" it might wreck his reputation as a teacher and scholar.

The play enjoyed a very popular three-week run at the Alliance Theater, a major regional playhouse in Atlanta, Georgia. It was then picked up by a Broadway producer and performed on the Great White Way. For a few weeks, the work of a Colorado College professor was showcased on the New York stage.

James Yaffe typified the college professor who comes to teaching at the mid-point rather than the beginning of his professional career. Yaffe was a television writer, and one of his most successful scripts was *Charly*, a teleplay about a mentally challenged man who became normal for a brief period of time. That script subsequently became a theater movie starring actor Cliff Robertson in the title role. Yaffe also wrote *The Deadly Game*, a television play that was adapted for the New York stage in 1960 and was performed by summer stock groups throughout the nation.[69]

In the late 1960s James Yaffe began teaching creative writing at Colorado College. His courses were very popular, and he found teaching very enjoyable. He subsequently pursued both careers simultaneously,

---

[68]George Brown, "Colorado College's Lacrosse Doctor," *Catalyst*, 29 April 1983, 16. Also see Chris Carson, "The Little Pond," *Catalyst*, 9 May 1980, 6.

[69]Peter Andersen, "Yaffe On Broadway?" *Catalyst*, 20 May 1983, 12.

helping to develop a strong creative writing program at the College while at the same time continuing to write novels, historical accounts, and theater plays. In the late 1980s and early 1990s Yaffe published the "Mom" series of mystery novels, in which a mother helped her detective son solve a variety of crimes.[70]

A Week on Skid Row

One of the more interesting courses offered at the College in the early 1980s was Sociology Professor Robert Dunne's one-block class *Powerlessness In The Inner City*. This course required students to live for one week "on the streets" in the run-down skid row section of Denver, Colorado. Professor Dunne explained the rationale for this particular form of experiential education:

"In this course, one confronts reality, unmediated by the interpretations of a writer. One learns in the real world, not in the library. This immediacy appeals to me. I look forward to the course every year, when I, like my students, can become bummy, walk the streets, eat in the soup kitchen, and observe Denver's inner-city area."[71]

Students taking the class were encouraged to meet and talk with the street people of Denver, many of them homeless, and compare such life experiences with their own. Although the course tended to deglamorize the life of freight-train-hopping bums, it enabled Colorado College students to see and react to a significant portion of the human family. It was the kind of experiential, do-it-differently course that was made possible by the Colorado College Block Plan.

Minority Recruitment

By the early 1980s Colorado College was beginning to make progress at hiring minority faculty members. In 1977 the College had only two minority faculty—Jim Coleman and Rudolph de la Garza—and both doubled as minority deans. By the spring of 1983, however, there were eight full-time and five visiting minority faculty members.

---

[70]Amy Jenkins, "Yaffe: Professional Writer At C.C.," *Catalyst*, 19 October 1984, 9. Bill Porter, "C.C. 'Best Of Both Worlds,'" *Catalyst*, 12 September 1986, 7. Megan McKee, "An Author In Our Midst: Jim Yaffe's Mystery Novels," *Catalyst*, 16 September 1994, 15.

[71]Amy Rubin, "Denver's Skid Row," *Catalyst*, 27 May 1983, 6.

There were a number of reasons for this increase. Deans Coleman and de la Garza devoted a great deal of time in the late 1970s to recruiting minority faculty as well as minority students. Academic departments at the College began defining vacant faculty positions more broadly, stating they were looking for professors with expertise in minority studies or a third world emphasis. When minority candidates for faculty positions came to the campus, the minority students made an extra effort to convince them that there was an important goal to be achieved by increasing racial and ethnic diversity on the Colorado College faculty.

By the early 1980s it was believed that Colorado College was well ahead of comparable liberal arts colleges in terms of hiring minority faculty. There also was general agreement that much more remained to be done.[72]

As for recruiting minority students, the College in the fall of 1983 hired an assistant admissions director, Lloyd Peterson, Jr., for the specific task of encouraging more Black and Spanish-surnamed students to come to Colorado College. Peterson worked particularly hard at recruiting minority students from high schools that had a good ethnic mix, seeking individuals who already were comfortable studying and socializing in a majority White and European-origin environment.[73] By early 1984 the minority student population at the College stood at 8.6 percent.[74]

DEBUTANTES RETURN

In a satirical look back at the past, a group of Colorado College students in the early 1980s staged a mock debutante party on the front steps of Palmer Hall. Young women dressed in long white evening gowns ceremoniously walked down the Palmer steps escorted by young men in formal attire. This simple but solemn act was said to represent the symbolic acceptance of the young women into "CC society."

At a time when shorts and levis were the all-too-common dress of the average woman college or university student, it was a pleasant break in the routine to see young men and women so impeccably dressed and properly behaved. But there was historic irony in this event. Seventy to

[72]Eleanor Milroy, "Minority Faculty," *Catalyst*, 27 May 1983, 8.

[73]Michelle Kearns, "CC Wants Minority Students," *Catalyst*, 11 November 1983, 3.

[74]Thomas Rudolph Caplan, "Minor Diversion," *Catalyst*, 20 January 1984, 4.

eighty years earlier, when the Victorian values of Dean of Women Ruth Loomis held sway at the College, such social graces and formal niceties were an intrinsic part of a Colorado College education.[75]

WRITING IN LONDON

Continuing to exercise the inventiveness and spirit of adventure that came with the adoption of the Block Plan, the faculty in the early 1980s came up with some interesting courses for the students. One of the more unusual and rewarding was a Summer Session course taught in London, England, which combined attending dramatic productions with learning to write well. For eight weeks students lived in a Chelsea College dormitory, went to a large number of theatrical productions, and then wrote about their experiences, both in London itself and at the theater.

Students received three blocks of credit for attending the *Summer Writing Institute In London.* In the summer of 1984 the program was directed by Mark Stavig, Professor of English, a Shakespeare scholar who also was interested in contemporary theater in London. During one previous visit to the British capital, Stavig attended 24 plays in only 21 days. Professor Stavig knew London and England well, having previously studied at Oxford University as a Fulbright Scholar.[76]

The summer writing program in London both symbolized and accomplished two of the major goals of the College in the early 1980s. One was the goal of internationalizing the curriculum and giving Colorado College students many opportunities for foreign travel and study. The second goal was to improve, through close faculty critique, the writing abilities of the students.

MEN'S SOCCER POWER

The fall of 1983 was a banner time for men's soccer at Colorado College. The team made it to the NCAA Division III Midwest regional playoffs, winning the first game but losing in the finals. The real triumph was breaking the "first round of the playoffs" jinx. Previously the men's

[75]M. Francis Patrick, "Elegance And Sophistication: The CC Debs," *Catalyst*, 20 May 1983, 13–14.

[76]Ed Langlois, "Around The Corner," *Catalyst*, 18 November 1983, 7.

soccer team always had lost its first playoff game when participating in post-season play.

The mainstay of men's soccer was Horst Richardson, a Professor of German who spent his fall afternoons out on Stewart Field serving as head coach of the team. Richardson came to Colorado College in 1965 and quickly went to work furthering both the teaching of the German language and men's soccer. Over the years Richardson often produced and directed an annual German play, in which the students in German courses would present a dramatic production in the German language.

In addition to coaching men's soccer, Horst Richardson conducted summer soccer camps for the youth—both male and female—in the Colorado Springs area. He was joined in this activity by his wife, Helen, who also spent many hours of time operating the video camera that videotaped Colorado College men's soccer games.

Horst Richardson was the son of a German soldier who was killed in World War Two. Richardson gathered together, edited, and published a book based on the letters that his father wrote to his family while serving on the Russian front. Richardson also served on the Colorado Springs District 11 School Board and was elected President of the Board.

In the fall of 1983 Richardson was elected Division III Midwest Coach of the Year for men's soccer. It was the second year in a row he received that honor.[77]

ALBERT SEAY RETIRES

The year 1982 marked the retirement of one of the brightest lights of the Colorado College professorate—Music Professor Albert Seay. Known to the students as "Dr. Seay," he came to the College in 1953 and taught for 29 years. His major interest was the musical works of the Renaissance, and a special library was created in the basement of Packard Hall, the

[77]Patrick Shea, "CC Soccer = Consistency," *Catalyst*, 9 December 1983, 16. Mike Rabinovitch, "Men's Soccer Nets Two Accolades; Coach Of The Year Horst Richardson Joins All-American Rob Lipp," *Catalyst*, 12 February 1993, 17. Also see Beth Skelton, "Between Racism And Heritage," *Catalyst*, 26 April 1986, 18. Todd Walker, "An Author In Our Midst: Richardson Compiles Letter; 'Sieg Heil' Recounts The Harrowing Experiences Of A Young Soldier," *Catalyst*, 23 September 1994, 14.

new art and music building, to house the many copies of Renaissance music that he collected in a lifetime of scholarly work.

A native of Louisville, Kentucky, Albert Seay earned his master's degree in Music from Louisiana State University and took his doctorate at Yale University in New Haven, Connecticut. At various points in his academic career he was a Fulbright Fellow, a Guggenheim Fellow, and a Senior Fellow of the National Endowment for the Humanities. When asked why he liked Colorado College, he said it was because it was a place where, if you wanted to do something, people would "beat their brains out to help you do it."

Professor Seay was particularly admired for his work in the classroom. He had a talent for describing musical ideas in a particularly colorful way. He would show students how to "take an old cliche and drive it into the ground." He would comment that certain musical tones could behave like "treacherous beasts . . . wanting to go down, shoving other places." This piece was composed to "make a buck," and that piece was "killingly dull," and a third piece was "sharp as a pistol," and a fourth would scare "the pants off you." Albert Seay often said that he wanted his students to note the "little ghosties" going "dee, dee, dee all over the place," and to listen to the tone color "going like crazy."

In 1956 Albert Seay founded the Colorado College Music Press. The purpose of the Music Press was to publish and make accessible good music that had not been published—or played and listened to—for centuries. In its early days the Music Press was supported by the income from a soft-drink machine, but it soon received foundation support and became highly acclaimed for publishing translations, critical texts, and transcriptions. Professor Seay worked to keep Music Press publications simple and inexpensive so that a wide-variety of music lovers could afford to buy and use them.

Albert Seay taught courses about all of the arts as well as Music. He emphasized that students needed to read great writers but also should read *True Confessions* magazine. "How can students appreciate the best," he concluded, "if they haven't [experienced] the worst."[78]

---

[78]Albert Seay died on January 7, 1984, at the age of 67. See Anne Kerwin, "Albert Seay, 67, Dies," *Catalyst*, 20 January 1984, 1.

CHAPTER 11

ON A WAVE OF SUCCESS

In the spring of 1984 Russell T. Tutt stepped down as Chairman of the Board of Trustees of Colorado College. His departure from the chairmanship represented the end of an era—an 18-year era which began in 1966 and saw the College complete four major buildings: Armstrong Hall, El Pomar Sports Center, Packard Hall, and the Tutt Library addition. Russell Tutt also provided a smooth transition at the Board level from Lloyd Worner's presidency to Gresham Riley's presidency, and he ably presided over the early stages of the campus planning and major fund-raising campaign that became the hallmarks of Gresham Riley's years in the presidential office.

But Russell Tutt was most famous for the way he had worked in tandem with President Worner. For the 15 years during which their terms as President and Board Chairman overlapped, the two men seemed to work in perfect harmony and synchronization. Much of the credit for the major achievements of the Worner years—guiding the College through the turbulent late 1960s and early 1970s, greatly increasing the endowment, smoothing the way for the adoption of the Block Plan—was shared equally between the two men.

Russell Tutt was the son of Charles Leaming Tutt, Jr., a Colorado College trustee from 1934 to 1950 and a major benefactor of the College through his family's El Pomar Foundation. Tutt Library was named in the older Tutt's honor.

Russell Tutt graduated from Princeton University in 1935 with a degree in engineering. He served in the U.S. Army during World War II, seeing duty in the European theater and rising to the rank of Major. At the same time he was Chairman of the Board of Trustees at Colorado College, Russell Tutt also was Chairman and Chief Executive Officer of both El Pomar Foundation and the Broadmoor Hotel. He served on the boards of numerous other business and charitable organizations. He was married to Louise Honnen, whose family name is on the ice rink at Colorado College.

When Russell Tutt gave up the chairmanship and became just another member of the Board of Trustees, he received high praise from former-President Lloyd Worner. "Mere words cannot express the difference his strong and sensitive leadership has made," Worner said. "His devotion to and concern for CC have never wavered."

William I. Spencer of New York was elected to succeed Russell Tutt as Chairman of the Board of Trustees. A native of Grand Junction, Colorado, Spencer was a 1939 graduate of the College who majored in Economics. Following his graduation, he traveled to New York City to visit the 1939 World's Fair, and while there he took a job at Chemical Bank. At the conclusion of his banking career he retired as President of both Citicorp and Citibank in New York.

To William Spencer would fall the task of maintaining Board of Trustees participation and support for the ambitious program of improvements that President Gresham Riley was undertaking at the College.[1]

THREE FACULTY RETIREMENTS

During the 1983–1984 academic year three prominent members of the Colorado College faculty retired. It was a sign of things to come. In the 1940s and 1950s the College had greatly increased its enrollment and hired additional faculty to carry the load. By the 1980s this post-World War II crop of professors was coming up for retirement.

"Some of the superstars of the faculty . . . retired during this period of time," noted President Gresham Riley. "Many, many of the outstanding faculty of the past . . . reached retirement age. And so we had a major task of replacing those individuals. . . . Among the major accomplishments that I look back upon with great pride is the fact that we have re-

[1]"Board Of Trustees Elects Spencer As Chairman," *Catalyst*, 9 March 1984, 1.

cruited a new generation of teacher-scholars who, I think, will secure the future of this institution.[2]

But as the College welcomed this talented new faculty, it had to pause periodically throughout the 1980s to honor those who were leaving active teaching.

Lester Michel

Dr. Lester A. Michel hired on at Colorado College in 1947 while still working on his Chemistry doctorate at the University of Colorado in Boulder. The Block Plan was more than 23 years in the future, and one of the first classes Les Michel taught at the College was a beginning Chemistry class with more than 140 students. He had logged 36-and-a-half years of service to the College when he stepped down in December of 1983.

Les Michel's career spanned a period of accelerating change at Colorado College. He worked for five presidents—Davies, Gill, Benezet, Worner, and Riley—and saw the Chemistry Department grow from two faculty members to eight. He played a major role in the movement of the Chemistry Department from Palmer Hall to the newly-constructed Olin Hall in 1962.

Professor Michel was a strong supporter of the Block Plan when it was adopted in the fall of 1969. He said he voted for the Block Plan "with fear and trembling," but he found its effects so positive that he later argued that students benefit greatly from participating in "grand educational experiments." He concluded that a college or university should change its program every ten years so that both faculty and students could experience the challenge and the excitement.[3]

Van Shaw

Van Shaw grew up in a small rural town where everyone shared the one party-line telephone. He described his youth as "really provincial." It was

---

[2]Gresham Riley oral history, 27 May 1992, 25–26.

[3]Valerie Feder, "Admired Prof. Retires," *Catalyst*, 20 January 1984, 5. Professor Michel compiled a history of the Chemistry Department at Colorado College. See Lester A. Michel, *111 Years Of Chemistry At Colorado College*, 1988. Copy available at Colorado College Archives.

quite a shock to him when he went to a small state college in western Kansas and discovered that people in small cities behaved differently from people in small rural places. This observation convinced him that Sociology was the academic field where he wanted to spend his time and increase his knowledge.

From 1938 to 1946 Shaw slowly worked on getting a master's degree at the University of Minnesota in Minneapolis. Teaching high school to make a living and serving 38 months in the U.S. Army during World War II slowed down his graduate education. He went on to the University of Missouri at Columbia to get a doctorate, and did his field research by going and living, with his wife and daughter and dog, in Nicodemus, Kansas, an all-Black community. Shaw wanted to find out if discrimination against Blacks was less in all-Black communities than it was in racially-mixed communities. His conclusion: no community was large or remote enough that, in the American society of the 1940s and 1950s, Black Americans could escape racial discrimination.

Van Shaw's teaching career spanned the 1950s, the 1960s, and the 1970s. He observed college students change from being conformist "status-strugglers" in the 1950s to being rebellious, "questioning," disbelievers in the 1960s. He saw the students of the 1970s returning to many of the "forget about the ills of society" values of the 1950s.

During his final semester at Colorado College, Sociology Professor Van Shaw received the student government's award for being an outstanding member of the College faculty.[4]

Norman Cornick

When Norman Cornick returned from World War II, he entered the McCone School of Music and Art in Salt Lake City, Utah. He was bound for a career as a musician, and only took dance classes to meet requirements for graduation. After getting a Bachelor of Science degree in Music from the University of Utah, Cornick found himself playing as an accompanist at a dance recital in Salt Lake City. It was at this point that he turned his interest—and his future teaching career—to Dance.

---

[4]Liz Lewis, ". . . And Goodbye To Shaw . . ." *Catalyst*, 25 May 1984, 6.

Cornick came to Colorado College in the summer of 1953 to take a Dance course taught by Hanya Holm. He did so well under Holm's direction that he subsequently was asked to head the Dance Department at the College. He built the Department and at the same time actively danced in many local Colorado Springs productions. Along with his wife, he helped to start a children's and laymen's dance program in the community. He was best known for directing 14 different productions of "The Nutcracker Suite," all of them staged prior to the Winter Break. Professor Norman Cornick's "Nutcracker" became an integral part of the holiday season in Colorado Springs.

When asked why he never took his dancing talents to New York City, the center of professional dance, Cornick always responded that he was happier in Colorado Springs "than I would have been somewhere else. I don't have the mind or the personality to be a New Yorker."

"I've met some wonderful students here," Cornick said during his final semester of teaching. "Watched them grow and learn. I love to work with young people. That's what I'll miss."[5]

A SEXUAL HARASSMENT POLICY

In January of 1984, in response to a recommendation from a United States Government agency, Colorado College adopted a sexual harassment policy. The policy provided for informal consultation on sexual harassment matters, noting that the Dean of the College (Glenn Brooks), the Boettcher Health Center Director (Dr. Judith Reynolds), and other members of the College administration were available for consultation in confidence. If informal discussion failed to resolve the matter, a formal grievance procedure was established that could serve as the basis for future court action.

Dean of Students Laurel McLeod noted that the policy arose from theoretical need and was not the result of a particular incident. "People tend to think that sexual harassment doesn't exist," McLeod said. "It's a real problem in this culture."

---

[5]Sharon Brady, "Goodbye To Norman Cornick," *Catalyst*, 25 May 1984, 6.

The College struggled to come up with a policy that would protect victims of sexual harassment but which would not, at the same time, interfere with the friendly and cooperative atmosphere so essential to a small liberal arts college. Dean McLeod pointed out that the first goal of the new policy was to "preserve the educational environment." She explained: "We don't want to cause a backlash—to cause professors to be afraid to have students in their houses. We don't want to inhibit healthy interaction. It is a well-publicized possibility to have a negative spin-off."

The promulgation of a sexual harassment policy was a typical example of the increasing legalism that was being applied to professional and personal relationships at Colorado College in the decade of the 1980s. With so many more disagreements ending in court suits, the College really had no choice but to formalize and put in writing its various policies and procedures. The result was a need for more paperwork and more administrators to do the paperwork. Originally the sexual harassment policy was going to be a short statement by President Riley. After Dean McLeod, College legal consultant Mary Greenwood, the Women's Concerns Committee, and President Riley's cabinet of College officers finished working on it, the short statement had turned into a three-page formal legal policy.[6]

A New Librarian

Upon the retirement of Head Librarian George Fagan, the College embarked on a nationwide search for his successor. The process reflected the way recruitment of faculty and top administrators at the College had changed in recent years. The job was advertised nationally in academic publications, and more than 83 persons responded by sending a letter of interest, a vita, letters of recommendation, or some combination of the three. From those 83 persons five finalists were selected to come to the campus and be interviewed.

This sort of large response to a job offer by the College was not that unusual. In some instances in the 1980s, more than 150 persons would apply for a faculty or administrative vacancy. Although it was rewarding

[6]Michelle Kearns, "Harassment Policy," *Catalyst*, 17 February 1984, 6.

to have such a rich pool of talent from which to choose, sifting through all the applications to pick finalists to be interviewed became a major consumer of faculty and administration time.

But, as would be expected with so many enthusiastic applicants, the qualifications of the people hired by the College as new faculty and administrators were quite exceptional. John Sheridan, the applicant finally hired as Head Librarian, received his B.A. degree in Classics in 1970 from City College of New York (CCNY). He held two M.A. degrees, one from the University of Indiana in Classics (1972) and one from the University of Wisconsin at Milwaukee in Library Science (1973). He did library work at Kearney State College in Nebraska and Knox College in Illinois. Prior to coming to Colorado College, he was Head Librarian at the University of Transylvania in Lexington, Kentucky, for seven years.[7]

The retiring Head Librarian, George Fagan, had begun the process of computerizing much of the work and the records of the Colorado College Library. Fagan arranged for the Library to be connected to a number of off-campus computerized data bases.[8] When John Sheridan took over as Head Librarian, he took charge of a project to computerize the Library's own card files.

As it turned out, Sheridan and the Tutt Library staff pioneered the development of computer software for liberal arts college libraries. President Riley particularly noted Colorado College's leading role in this area. "We found ourselves sort of out front in terms of, at least, liberal arts and sciences colleges. We tried to learn from other institutions, and we discovered that no other comparable colleges were really thinking about automating their library systems."[9]

THE TRIBES PROGRAM

In the continuing effort to reach out to minority groups in the United States, the College created a Summer Session program for Native

---

[7]Stephen Rockwell, "Committee Selects New Head Librarian," *Catalyst*, 24 February 1984, 1.

[8]David Pye, "Tutt Enters Computer Age," *Catalyst*, 12 November 1982, 1.

[9]Gresham Riley oral history, 27 May 1992, 24. Aklilu Dunlap, "'The Cat Is Here,'" *Catalyst*, 20 March 1987, 3.

American high school graduates who were thinking about going to college. During an intense eight-week study period, 40 young Native American students simultaneously furthered their education and got a sense of what going to college was all about. The program was called *TRIBES*, for *Tribal Resource Institute in Business, Engineering, and Science.*

The *TRIBES* program was directed by Val Veirs, Professor of Physics at Colorado College. Veirs studied air pollution problems in the southwestern United States and thus was familiar with many of the Native American reservations and their surrounding territory. Part of the *TRIBES* program was to simulate an imaginary Native American reservation in southwestern Colorado and have students formulate solutions to the reservation's political, economic, and social problems.

Victor Mojado, a Native American from Las Vegas, Nevada, enrolled in the *TRIBES* program in the summer of 1983 and then attended Colorado College as a first year student. Mojado said the program was challenging, particularly with its emphasis on engineering and science, but he and his fellow *TRIBES* students had been warned to expect that. "I was totally impressed with Veirs," Mojado concluded. "He really worked our butts off, but it was definitely worth it."[10]

The *TRIBES* program eventually moved on to other colleges and universities in Colorado. While it was at Colorado College, however, the College gained influence in the Native American community and was able to recruit a number of *TRIBES* participants to come to the College as full-time students. As a result, at one time there were more than 30 Native Americans studying at Colorado College.[11]

THE DEAN'S CUP

During the 1980s there was increasing interest among faculty and students in running and jogging as a way to maintain physical health. To honor this trend, Dean Glenn Brooks created the Dean's Cup 10k Race, an opportunity for all those who enjoyed running and jogging to get out

---

[10]L. C. Rivera, "Program For Native Americans," *Catalyst*, 13 April 1984, 8.

[11]Author's notes, interview with David Finley, former Dean of Colorado College, 4 December 1997.

and do it in an organized but light-hearted fashion. "There were a lot of us [in the Dean's office] that liked to run," Brooks explained, "and we decided to challenge the rest of the College at the 10k run. . . . The spirit of the thing is to have fun and get a bunch of people out—whether they are serious runners or joggers or walkers."

Brooks and his office cohort, Associate Dean Maxwell Taylor, anchored a fleet-footed group of five administrators known as "The Dean Machine." There were other team entries, one of the most notable being the English Department's "Lord Byron's Foot Club." The Economics Department ran under the name of "Long Run Dead," taken from economist John Maynard Keynes's famous statement: "In the long run we are all dead."

Occasionally contestants showed up for the race dressed in elaborate costumes. "One of the more memorable moments was when I was passed by a giant caterpillar," Dean Brooks lamented. He said the shock of losing to a caterpillar inspired him to "do a little better the next year."[12]

Staying on Track

The mid–1980s were a time of confusion and struggle for many liberal arts colleges in the United States. There were no more World War Two Baby Boom students, with the result that the "applicant pool" of available young people to go to college continued to shrink rapidly. In this trying and highly competitive situation, a number of liberal arts colleges around the country began straying away from the liberal arts curriculum in an effort to attract more students. Some began offering highly specialized courses designed to prepare students for specific careers. Others began offering night school and weekend programs aimed at so-called non-traditional students, such as parents, mainly women, whose children were now in school and who wanted to prepare themselves to return to the work force.

---

[12]Dan Rohlf, "Sportlight: Dean Brooks Enjoys Running," *Catalyst*, 18 May 1984, 13. Alec Rekow, Allison O'Neall, and Scott Allen, "Dean's Cup: The Challenge Continues," *Catalyst*, 15 May 1987, 1. Photographs of "The Dean Machine," *Catalyst*, 15 May 1987, 8. Professor of Economics Mike Bird provided the recollection that the Economics and Business Department ran under the name of "Long Run Dead."

Speaking at the Opening Convocation of Colorado College in the fall of 1984, Dean Glenn Brooks firmly committed Colorado College to continued and unshakable devotion to the pure liberal arts education. Brooks explained:

"One affliction of contemporary higher education has been that a great many institutions have lost their nerve about the validity of their enterprise. Faced with declining enrollments and increasing costs, they have branched out helter-skelter in search of new customers. In too many cases, the result is a sad confusion of activity, a dissipation of institutional energies, and, ultimately, financial disaster, as a college finds itself with too many programs and faculty members who are not adequately prepared to handle new demands."

This sorry state should never be allowed to come about at Colorado College, Dean Brooks said. "Early College catalogs as well as our current pronouncements state the same consistent theme," he concluded. "We are a small undergraduate institution devoted to teaching the liberal arts and sciences."[13]

Falling enrollments were *not* the problem at Colorado College in the fall of 1984. More that 50 students had to be housed in "temporary space," lounge areas in Bemis, Loomis, Mathias, and Slocum halls that were hastily turned into triple and quadruple occupancy dormitory rooms. Things were so crowded the first week of school that a number of first year women students were housed in the sick bay in Boettcher Infirmary. Other students found themselves living in some Spanish-style apartments that the College owned on Glen Avenue, over on the other side of Monument Creek just north of the Monument Valley Park duck pond and just east of the railroad tracks.

Dana Wilson, the Director of Housing at the College, said the crowding was mainly the result of the continuing desire of junior and senior students to live on-campus rather than off-campus. Wilson noted: "On-campus living seems to be the new trend. More kids wish to stay on campus; more parents want their kids to stay on campus."[14]

---

[13]Paul Burge, "111th Academic Year Officially Underway, *Catalyst*, 7 September 1984, 1.

[14]Jamie Barnett, "Freshmen Living 'Temporarily,'" *Catalyst*, 7 September 1984, 3. Claire Patterson, "Dorm Life In Demand," 14 September 1984, 7.

KRCC MOVES AND IMPROVES

Major changes were taking place in the mid–1980s at the Colorado College radio station—KRCC-FM. Long a fixture on the second floor of Rastall Center, the student-operated broadcast facility moved to a home of its own on Cache La Poudre Street across from Slocum Hall. The College had acquired the building that contained Peggy's Beauty Salon, and this narrow but lengthy commercial structure proved ideal for housing both broadcast studios and transmitting equipment.

The strength of KRCC's signal was increased when the station installed a radio tower atop Cheyenne Mountain. This replaced the old radio tower located adjacent to Rastall Center. The station beamed its signal from its new Cache La Poudre Street headquarters up to Cheyenne Mountain by microwave. This new, more powerful signal could be heard all the way from the top of Monument Hill to the north down to the city of Pueblo to the south.

KRCC acquired a satellite disk which permitted it to pick up National Public Radio (NPR) and provide this popular educational radio feature to its listeners. Styling itself the "Alternative Radio Station," KRCC presented music and information shows that were not generally available on commercial radio stations in Colorado Springs and Pueblo. Much of the music was Jazz, but there were also selections of Soul, Reggae, Celtic, New Wave, as well as traditional Classical music. In the fall of 1984 the leading musical groups being presented on KRCC included the Psychedelic Furs, the Violent Femmes, the Big Sky Mudflaps, the Twinkle Brothers, and the Wiser Dead.

As the equipment improved and the radio signal grew stronger, KRCC began to evolve from a student activity into a major community educational and entertainment facility. Colorado College students continued to work on a volunteer basis at the radio station, but a paid professional staff took charge of managing the facility. Community members joined the students working as disk jockeys, engineers, and production staff. Managing the enterprise and supervising all the new changes was longtime Station Manager Mario Valdes.[15]

---

[15]Matthew Kite, "KRCC Moving Forward," *Catalyst*, 7 September 1984, 14. Libby Swanson, "Radio Magazines Air," *Catalyst*, 19 April 1985, 1.

HONNEN ICE RINK ENCLOSED

The Honnen Ice Rink was constructed in the early 1960s to be a covered but open-air facility. Walls were installed that permitted cold outside air to flow easily into the facility so that skating at Honnen would have the feel and ambiance of an outdoor activity, particularly in the wintertime.

By the mid–1980s this simulated outdoor atmosphere at Honnen Ice Rink had become a financial liability. The rink was in use throughout much of the year, and refrigeration costs for maintaining the ice were substantially higher, particularly in the spring and fall, because of the open-air character of the building. At the suggestion of Ed Honnen, who contributed the money to build the ice rink, the walls of Honnen were enclosed, the lighting improved, and a natural gas heating system installed to provide a constant temperature for skaters in the wintertime. The anticipated savings in utility costs from these improvements was 25 percent.

Similar to the campus radio station, Honnen Ice Rink had become as much a community facility as a College facility. A variety of local groups, from juvenile ice hockey teams to competitive ice skaters to speed skaters, rented and used the rink when it was not needed for College functions.[16]

A MISPLACED AWNING

The campus got a surprise when the awning of a maternity shop on North Tejon Street was placed in front of the Phi Gamma Delta fraternity house on the fraternity quadrangle. The ten-foot-long semi-circular awning had the name of the maternity shop, Mothers-To-Be, emblazoned on it. The misplaced awning was first seen by students walking to class on a Tuesday morning in the fall of 1984.

There was no vandalism involved. Workers had removed the awning to repair the store building and left it unguarded on the sidewalk. At 3 o'clock the following afternoon a group of the Phi Gams cheerfully returned the awning, none the worse for wear, to Mothers-To-Be. No person or group admitted responsibility for the prank. The *Catalyst* reported that, while the awning was in front of the Phi Gam house, "no customers came to their building in search of nine month smocks."[17]

---

[16]"Honnen Enclosed," *Catalyst*, 14 September 1984, 3.

[17]"Fiji's Open Shop," *Catalyst*, 14 September 1984, 3.

SOLOMON NKIWANE

Symbolic of the new emphasis on non-Western studies at Colorado College was Solomon Nkiwane, a visiting professor from the University of Zimbabwe in Africa. A native of Africa and a graduate of Colorado College, Nkiwane returned to his alma mater a number of times during the 1970s, 1980s, and 1990s to teach courses on Africa. After graduating from Colorado College, Nkiwane earned a masters degree from the University of East Africa in Uganda and a Ph.D. from McGill University in Montreal, Canada.

Nkiwane was a stern critic of the rigid racial segregation practiced by South Africa prior to the 1990s, and his classes helped to generate and focus student opposition to the White-dominated South African government.[18] Because he was as comfortable in the most primitive parts of Africa as he was in the most developed sections of the United States, Nkiwane described himself as "someone who has lived in the Stone Age, but is quite able to live in the 21st Century." He viewed the United States as trying to force the rest of the world to fit into its way of thinking, and he saw Zimbabwe as distorted by Western influences. Solomon Nkiwane's overall view: "The Western world is overrated at the expense of the [non-Western] world."[19]

POOR RICHARD'S

By the mid–1980s one of the most popular "campus hangouts" was Poor Richard's Feed and Read, a sandwich shop located a few blocks south of the College on North Tejon Street. This distinctive restaurant featured natural foods and was combined with a bookstore. Customers were encouraged to come in, get a meal or snack, and read a book while dining. When the Flick Theater closed, and there was no longer a place in Colorado Springs to see classic and foreign films, a film series was launched at Poor Richard's.

---

[18]Tim Fitzgerald, "Solomon Nkiwane: Interview," *Catalyst*, 21 September 1984, 10. "Zimbabwe: Solomon Nkiwane," *Catalyst*, 19 October 1984, 8.

[19]Stephen Schmid and Elizabeth Skelton, "Solomon Nkiwane: Out Of Africa," *Catalyst*, 7 February 1986, 18. Brian Smith, "Nkiwane Speaks On Zimbabwe And South Africa," *Catalyst*, 14 February 1986, 3.

This restaurant-bookstore-movie theater was the brainchild of owner-operator Richard Skormann, a 1975 graduate of Colorado College with an Art major. For seven years Skormann ran the restaurant himself, but then he turned more responsibility over to his staff and began spending much of his time developing the movie theater and finding quality films to show. Skormann subsequently became active in local politics in Colorado Springs, strongly supporting minority rights and environmental causes.

Skormann found the Colorado College students who ate his sandwiches and read his books and attended his movies to be a "good bunch." But with a conservative Republican, Ronald Reagan, serving as President of the United States, Skormann said he found the students of the 1980s to be more on the political right than when he was at the College. "The student body seems more conservative than in the '70s," Skormann explained. "We used to be more progressive." He added: "But, there seem to be some innovative new faculty members."[20]

FACULTY EARLY RETIREMENT

Early in November of 1984 the Board of Trustees approved a modified early retirement plan for the Colorado College faculty. Known as Special Senior Status (SSS), the plan permitted faculty members 60-years-old and older to stop teaching completely but still collect 45 percent of their base salary and all College benefits. Faculty who accepted this early retirement option were required to enter full regular retirement at age 65.

The motivating force behind this early retirement plan was a law passed by the United States Congress that declared mandatory retirement at age 65 to be illegal. Congress thus enabled Colorado College faculty to teach into their 70s and beyond if they wanted to and enjoyed the good health to do so. The purpose of SSS, as it came to be called, was to en-

[20]Paul Burge, "Whatever Happened To Richard Skormann?" *Catalyst*, 5 October 1984, 6. Amy Hightower, "Poor Richard's Provides Campus Cultural Outlet," *Catalyst*, 28 April 1989, 6. Richard Skorman received an honorary degree from Colorado College at the opening Convocation on 1 September 1997. "Two Return For Honorary Degree, *Access*, October 1997, 1.

courage longtime faculty members to retire at age 65 in return for getting up to five years at almost half salary for no work.[21]

The plan was designed so that faculty members could ease out of teaching. Those faculty who wished to do so, and whose academic departments needed their services, could teach up to four blocks per year under SSS and receive an additional 6.1 percent of their salary per block taught. Many faculty who entered SSS took advantage of this provision, cutting back substantially on their teaching but not eliminating it altogether in their first years of early retirement.

The financial logic behind SSS was that the College could take the 55 percent of salary it did not pay the early retiring professor and use it to hire a younger replacement. New faculty members finishing graduate school or with a brand new Ph.D. could be hired for just about one-half the full salary of a senior professor. College President Gresham Riley noted that the hiring of more young professors, made possible by the early retirements stimulated by SSS, would enable the College to "maintain our commitment to affirmative action—with respect to women and minorities."[22]

Special Senior Status (SSS) quickly became an intrinsic part of the faculty culture at Colorado College. Most senior professors "went on SSS" for at least a few years before reaching age 65, but there were a number of stalwarts who decided they loved to teach and kept on teaching into their late 60s and early 70s. Overall, the program functioned the way it was designed. It encouraged the older professors to leave the classroom early. It provided the necessary funds to hire a younger and more diverse faculty at an earlier point in time.

BYPASS SURGERY FOR PRESIDENT RILEY

The College community received a minor shock in April of 1985 when President Gresham Riley was hospitalized for quadruple coronary by-

---

[21]To comply with U.S. laws, Special Senior Status at Colorado College was subsequently modified so that it was not tied to specific ages such as age 60 and age 65. A faculty member became eligible for SSS when his or her salary reached an annually-adjusted figure. This figure was set so that most faculty members were about 60 years old when their salary equaled the figure and SSS could begin.

[22]Gerry Lanosga, "Trustees Approve, Revise At November Meeting," *Catalyst*, 16 November 1984, 1.

pass surgery. Riley experienced chest pains on a trip to Washington, D.C., and entered Penrose Hospital for cardiac laboratory tests upon his return to Colorado Springs. When an angiogram revealed two partially obstructed coronary arteries, surgeons bypassed the occluded arteries with four bypasses. The bypasses, which carried blood around the obstructed arteries to the heart, were made with blood veins from elsewhere in President Riley's body.

Gresham Riley recovered rapidly from his surgery and, within a few days, was walking and riding an exercise bicycle. During the operation and recovery period, daily management of College affairs was taken over by Dean Glenn Brooks, who noted that the College had a pre-arranged agreement to handle such situations.[23]

TONY FRASCA RETIRES

A Colorado College sports and administrative legend came to an end when Tony Frasca, the longtime Director of the intramural athletic program, retired in the spring of 1985. A native of Massachusetts, Frasca played ice hockey for Colorado College and starred on the team that won the National Collegiate Athletic Association (NCAA) championship in 1950. Playing at center, Frasca was named to the all-tournament team.

But that was only the beginning of Tony Frasca's association with Colorado College. In 1958 he was named men's ice hockey coach, a position which he relinquished in 1963 when he became Manager of Honnen Ice Rink and Director of Intramural Athletics. Frasca also assumed the duties of varsity men's baseball coach, a position which he held for 22 years until his retirement.

In the course of his career, Tony Frasca knew, played with, was coached by, and coached many of the biggest names in Colorado College sports history. He played football at Pueblo Junior College with longtime Colorado College track coach Frank Flood. While an undergraduate at Colorado College, Frasca was coached in men's baseball by legendary football coach Jerry Carle. While he was ice hockey coach, Frasca coached such outstanding men's ice hockey players as goalie Eddie Mio,

[23]Stephen Renwick, "Riley Is Recovering," *Catalyst*, 10 May 1985, 1.

who subsequently played professional ice hockey in the National Hockey League. But most of all, Tony Frasca directed an intramural athletic program that grew in size and offered an ever-wider variety of intramural sports to Colorado College undergraduates.

When Tony Frasca retired, Athletic Director Dick Taber told the *Catalyst*: "He has a heart as big as you can find. He always held the best interests of the kids (non-varsity) first. His continuing interest is behind the success of the intramural program. We're going to miss him."[24]

Tony Frasca impacted the taste buds of Colorado College as well as the intramural athletic program. He started an Italian pizza restaurant, Panino's, down on North Tejon Street close to the College, which became a popular eating place and hangout.

SPORTS STANDOUTS

Although intercollegiate sports (except mens ice hockey and women's soccer) were de-emphasized at Colorado College, a number of College athletes in the mid–1980s excelled as individuals and earned national recognition for themselves and the College. Paul LaStayo, the captain of the 1984 men's lacrosse team, became the first Colorado College player in history to be selected for the national North-South Lacrosse All Star game. The following year the 1985 men's lacrosse captain, Tom Sulger, followed in LaStayo's footsteps and became the second Colorado College stickman to be a North-South All Star player.[25]

Another individual standout was Julie Dunn, who ran women's cross country. Sidelined during her junior year, Julie came back in her senior year and qualified for the 1985 national women's cross country meet at Ohio Wesleyan. She placed 23rd and was named an All American.[26]

---

[24]Roger T. Mullarkey, "Tony: A History," *Catalyst*, 17 May 1985, 9. Reid, *Colorado College: The First Century, 1874–1974*, 181, 221, 237.

[25]Kathy Mahoney, "National Recognition," *Catalyst*, 24 May 1985, 5.

[26]"Senior Sports Stars: Julie Dunn," *Catalyst*, 24 May 1985, 6.

THE LOOMIS LAST LECTURE SERIES

In an effort to increase faculty-student interaction outside of the classroom, the students living in Loomis Hall organized a series of faculty "last lectures." There were just two rules. The faculty member had only one hour to speak, and he or she was to give the lecture as if it would be the last one he or she would ever deliver.

The first faculty member to give a Loomis Last Lecture was Owen Cramer, Professor of Classics. Cramer decided to speak on "The History of the World" and "The Meaning of Life." He carefully noted what he considered to be the high points in the history of humanity, from the discovery of language (40,000 years earlier) to the development of agriculture (12,000 years earlier) to the invention of cities (5,000 years earlier). Cramer concluded that, at each change in its history, humanity had gained something (more food, more convenient life in cities) but had lost something (a less-populated planet and a less complicated social and economic life). Cramer concluded by questioning whether the great "step-ups" of human history had really improved human life.[27]

Owen Cramer was a logical choice to give the first Loomis Last Lecture. He was in many ways the typical small college professor. His father had been a Humanities professor at the University of Chicago, so Owen Cramer had grown up in a lively academic atmosphere. He attended the University of Chicago Lab School, which was a private school operated by the University for faculty children. Owen Cramer graduated from high school in Athens, Greece, where his father was teaching on a Fulbright Fellowship.

Cramer did his undergraduate work at Oberlin College. He almost majored in Chemistry but soon decided on Classics. He elected to earn his Ph.D. at the University of Texas because of its "iconoclastic" Classics Department. He committed himself to a career of teaching Classics because he believed that one could not know the modern without carefully studying the ancient. Even as an undergraduate at Oberlin, Cramer knew that he would spend his life as a college professor.

---

[27]Jon-Mark Patterson, "L.L.L.S. And The Meaning Of Life," *Catalyst*, 18 October 1985, 2.

Owen Cramer's advice to his students: "Have courage—courage in the sense of not being afraid to risk your identity on strange material, . . . or not being afraid of doing more than you can do. Really dive into things. Let your full weight down. Be yourself as completely as possible."[28]

The second speaker in the Loomis Last Lecture Series was Professor of Physics and former Dean of the College Richard Bradley. Since Professor Cramer had already discussed "The Meaning of Life," Bradley chose to speak about "some things that give life meaning." He told of a memorable event of his youth, a challenging but spectacularly beautiful cross-country ski trip he went on with his father and his brothers through the back country of Yosemite National Park in California.[29]

STRATEGIC DEFENSE INITIATIVE

One of the major political issues discussed on campus in the mid–1980s was the Strategic Defense Initiative (SDI), President Ronald Reagan's proposal to use high technology to develop a system for shooting down nuclear-tipped Soviet missiles fired at the United States. Because the SDI would use a mix of high speed computers, air defense missiles, and perhaps even laser beams, it was often referred to as "Star Wars," the name of a very popular science-fiction movie about military battles in outer space.

A number of students and faculty members at the College strongly opposed the Strategic Defense Initiative, arguing that it was technologically impossible to achieve and, even if successfully built and tested, would exacerbate relationships between the United States and the Soviet Union rather than improve those relations. Opponents of Reagan's "Star Wars" plan called for more arms reduction agreements with the Soviet Union rather than building an expensive, perhaps unreliable, missile defense system. Leading faculty critics of the SDI included Professor of Physics Richard Bradley, Professor of History William Hochman, Professor of Sociology Jeff Livesay, and Professor of Economics William Weida.[30]

---

[28]Brian Smith, "Owen Cramer At A Glance," *Catalyst*, 8 November 1985, 12.

[29]Caroline Bryan, "The Adventures Of Dr. Richard Bradley," *Catalyst*, 8 November 1985, 11.

[30]Rob Lynch, "Shooting Down Star Wars," *Catalyst*, 15 November 1985, 10. Mary Beth Barron, "Weida On SDI: Asking The Right Questions," *Catalyst*, 21 February 1986, 1.

A group of Colorado College students, calling themselves the "Nuclear Age Players," staged a protest against the Strategic Defense Initiative during a conference on space issues at the Broadmoor Hotel in Colorado Springs. The students turned the sidewalk in front of the hotel convention center into a "street theater" and periodically performed a skit entitled "The Emperor's New Defense System." The satirical play implied that President Reagan thought he was protecting the nation with the SDI but actually was not protecting it at all.

There was a considerable public reaction to the students' "street theater" production. One local newspaper, the *Colorado Springs Sun*, labeled the anti-SDI skit "boorish and naive" and accused the students of "all but advocating unilateral disarmament." An accompanying political cartoon, by local cartoonist Chuck Asay, contrasted a caricature of the protesting students, portrayed as silly and juvenile, with a heroic drawing of U.S. military personnel, presented as serious and committed.

But while the students were protesting on the outside of the convention hall, three Colorado College faculty members—Professor of Political Science Curtis Cook, Professor of Political Science David Finley, and Professor of History William Hochman—were inside the convention hall participating in a series of presentations and panel discussions on space related issues.

And, after the convention adjourned, Richard MacLeod, the executive director of the U.S. Space Foundation, which sponsored the convention, came out to Colorado College to speak with interested students about space issues. MacLeod told the students he had no problem with their "street theater" commentary. He lamented the fact that two local television stations interviewed him but failed to broadcast his official comment that he "didn't disapprove" of the students' actions, that the skit "didn't disrupt anything," and that the students "conducted [them]selves well."[31]

The advisability of the Strategic Defense Initiative was an issue which led to much discussion and protest at Colorado College during Ronald Reagan's second term as President of the United States.[32] The issue was

---

[31]Chris Weaver, "Broadmoor SDI Conf. Sparks Debate At CC," *Catalyst*, 6 December 1985, 1.

[32]For a variety of Colorado College student views on the Strategic Defense Initiative, see the *Disparaging Eye*, 7 March 1986, 3–5, inserted in the *Catalyst*, 7 March 1986.

never resolved completely. The U.S. Congress funded the SDI, but mainly at the research and development level rather than the implementation level.

COMMUNISM IN LATIN AMERICA

Another political issue that divided the campus during the mid–1980s was United States military and financial aid to the Contras, a group of armed revolutionaries trying to militarily overthrow the allegedly pro-communist government of Nicaragua. Many Colorado College faculty and students, the most active being Professor of Spanish Salvatore Bizzarro, accused the United States of encouraging death and destruction in a small nation that constituted no strategic threat to the United States.[33]

A contrasting point of view was provided by U.S. Representative Richard Cheney, a Republican from Wyoming, whose wife and daughters attended Colorado College. Congressmember Cheney gave the Lopat lecture on Public Life and Politics, named in honor of Marianne Lopat, a Colorado College graduate who had worked in politics in Washington, D.C., prior to her untimely death.

Representative Cheney argued that the United States constituted the best source of hope for people living in underdeveloped nations who were being oppressed by communist regimes. He called for aiding the rebel forces in Nicaragua with military weapons, financial support, and advice. He accused the Nicaraguan government of threatening "democratic values" and described Nicaraguan military forces as "not a friendly lot."

United States foreign policy, Cheney said, should be motivated by a mixture of moral and strategic objectives. Actions which further democracy (moral objective) simultaneously guarantee the safety of the United States (strategic objective). "There is little or no possibility [pro-communist] governments can be changed by peaceful means," Cheney concluded. "The forceful interventions of the U.S. and the forceful interventions of the Soviet Union are not the same. . . . To suggest that force is force is force denies the difference between the force that liberates [U.S.] and that which subjugates [Soviet Union]."[34]

---

[33]For a full discussion of campus viewpoints on the situation in Nicaragua, see *The Disparaging Eye*, 13 December 1985, 1–4, inserted into the *Catalyst*, 13 December 1985. Also see Salvatore Bizzarro, "Contra Aid As 'Deceitful Scheme,'" *Catalyst*, 14 March 1986, 9.

[34]Ed Langlois, "Congressman Cheney Gives Lopat Lecture," *Catalyst*, 17 January 1986, 1.

United States resistance to pro-communist governments in Latin America continued to stir much controversy at Colorado College. The issue was finally resolved when, following free elections, a non-communist government came to power in Nicaragua.

"THE PROCESSORS"

Unrestrained free enterprise enjoyed one of its best moments at Colorado College when Wayne Rudner, a senior, noticed that the College had a large number of computer terminals but very few students who knew how to use them to type research papers. Rudner got a group of students with good typing skills together and made them available to type student papers on a College computer for a fee. Apparently there was pent-up student demand for an on-campus typing service, because in the first semester of the 1985–1986 academic year more than 100 students availed themselves of Rudner's neat, efficient, convenient, and fast paper-typing service.

Because his "employees" were using computer word processing to type papers, Rudner named his rapidly expanding business "The Processors." Furthermore, because the papers were "computerized," students could easily make corrections and print additional copies. According to the *Catalyst*, Wayne Rudner and his business associates produced "well-printed papers, easy to read with few errors, on quality paper, all for a reasonable price." One student commented: "I couldn't survive without the Wayner!"

But then Wayne Rudner's thriving business enterprise ran afoul of the College administration. When Dean of Students Laurel McLeod learned what was going on, she pointed out to Rudner that U.S. Government laws forbade operating a "for-profit" enterprise within a "non-profit" organization such as Colorado College. There also was the problem that Rudner and his small army of student typists were making money while using expensive College computers free-of-charge. If Rudner wanted to continue in the paper-typing business, he would have to go off-campus and provide his own office space and his own computers.

The *Catalyst* argued in its news columns that Rudner had illuminated the need for a good paper-typing service on the Colorado College campus.[35] The College administration appeared to prefer that students type

---

[35]Anne Huffman, "Rudner's Processors Shut Down," *Catalyst*, 17 January 1986, 1.

their own papers and thereby gain the typing and word processing skills that were rapidly becoming necessary for success in a computerized world. "The Processors" went out of business, and most of the students went back to learning how to write on the new computers themselves.

Goodbye to the Business Economics Major

In February of 1986 Dean Glenn Brooks issued an official memorandum declaring "a moratorium on further declarations of Business Economics majors by freshmen, sophomores, and prospective students." Colorado College's most vocationally-oriented academic major, the Business Economics major, had begun the process of coming to an end.[36]

It was a tough decision given that Business Economics was one of the most popular majors at the College. The action was brought about by the difficulty and expense of hiring competent faculty to teach the Business curriculum. Persons with Ph.Ds in Business generally were not willing to work at the Colorado College faculty salary scale. Most were being hired by state universities and business graduate schools that could pay considerably higher salaries than Colorado College was either willing or able to afford.

As the *Catalyst* noted, the problem with the Business Economics major was essentially one of that old economic law of supply and demand: "Too much demand from students and too few faculty members to fill that demand."

Dean Brooks and Walter Hecox, the Chairman of the Economics Department, made it clear that the College and the Department would see to it that all current Business Economics majors would be able to successfully complete the major. But once those students had finished, there would be no more Business Economics major—only a "straight" Economics major—at Colorado College.

Professor Hecox counseled first year and second year students thinking about a Business Economics major to consider an Economics major instead. Except for three courses, the two majors were almost the same. Furthermore, students could major in Economics with a "Business emphasis" by selecting additional elective courses in Business.

---

[36]In earlier years the Business Economics major was named Business Administration.

Professor Hecox made an important final point. The best Business graduate schools, he noted, wanted students with a *liberal arts education*, not a Business major.[37]

A PROFESSOR DEPARTS

In the spring of 1986 Professor Barry Huebert of the Chemistry Department announced he was leaving his teaching job at Colorado College for an executive research position at SRI International (formerly the Stanford Research Institute). Huebert had taught at Colorado College for 15 years, specializing in Atmospheric Chemistry and sensitizing the College community to the twin problems of air and water pollution. He became known and respected among students and faculty alike for his scientific approach to environmental problems and his commitment to urging government at all levels to act in a technologically correct manner to end urban air pollution.

Huebert was famous for his class field trips, mainly because they went to such seemingly mundane places as the Colorado Springs city sewage plant and the Martin Drake electrical power plant. The city sewage plant was a working example of efforts to curb water pollution. The Martin Drake electric plant, located just to the southwest of downtown Colorado Springs, was a coal-fired steam generation plant and one of the major sources of air pollution in the Pike's Peak region.

Barry Huebert symbolized the many talented individuals who, over the years, make a major contribution to the intellectual and scholarly life of Colorado College but do not spend their entire professional careers at the College. A considerable number of teachers and administrators come to the College, do an excellent job and make a major impression while they are on campus, and then move on to other pursuits. In some cases these "shorter-time" members of the faculty and administration become as beloved and respected by the students as those who stay at the College for their entire career.[38]

---

[37]Jeff Blair, "Business Economics Major Axed," *Catalyst*, 14 February 1986, 1. Brian Smith, "Business/Econ. Follow Up," *Catalyst*, 21 February 1986, 2.

[38]Charlie Brown Hershey, in his history of Colorado College, paid particular homage to those who stay a short time and then go on to other jobs. Hershey wrote: "The faculty of Colorado College

Huebert's departure also symbolized the continuing tension at Colorado College between research and teaching. A growing number of faculty, many of them newly-tenured, were arguing that Colorado College should become a "research college," somewhat similar to a "research university." Teaching undergraduates would still remain the fundamental purpose of the College, but those faculty inclined to do research would be given more time-off from teaching and more financial support for equipment, research travel, and attendance at scholarly meetings.

Those supporting the "research college" concept argued that, in order to become one of the truly distinguished liberal arts colleges in the United States, Colorado College would have to recruit a more research-oriented faculty and give that faculty the time and money it needed to study, experiment, and publish.

Barry Huebert said the intense teaching load at Colorado College was one of the major reasons he was leaving for a "pure" research position. The pressure to teach, he said, was very great at the College. He explained: "I began to feel that some of my colleagues didn't believe that I was giving the Department all I should. . . . You're not doing your job if you're not teaching eight courses (every year).. . . Once professors here recognize their mobility [to move to jobs involving] less work and higher pay, . . . the College isn't going to have a prayer of keeping good faculty."[39]

The twin issues of faculty workload and the teaching/research balance would play prominently at Colorado College in the late 1980s and early 1990s. President Gresham Riley had repeatedly said a major goal of the College was to achieve "national recognition." A number of faculty believed this could not be done because, in their view, the College faculty was both overworked and insufficiently provided with research time. Professor Barry Huebert's departure highlighted these two issues dramatically.

---

does not differ from the faculties of other institutions in that, while many of its members have given most of their active years to its classrooms and laboratories, others have gone from the College, as from a springboard, into other institutions to achieve distinctions and honors that have reflected a kind of glory on the place in which their first experiences and promises of success gave them confidence." Hershey, *Colorado College: 1874–1949*, 166.

[39]Jeff Blair, "Huebert Resigns," *Catalyst*, 23 May 1986, 4.

THE EIGHT BLOCK YEAR

In the fall of 1986 an independent group of Colorado College faculty members proposed shortening the academic year from nine blocks to eight blocks. The main reason for doing this was to cut the normal faculty teaching load from eight blocks to seven blocks. Eliminating the ninth block would add two weeks in January to the winter holidays vacation and two weeks in May to the start of summer vacation.

The faculty members who made this proposal called themselves the Committee for the Eight Block Year. The group was co-chaired by Professor of Philosophy Judith Genova and Professor of Art Gale Murray. After studying the academic calendars and faculty workloads at a select group of midwestern and Ivy League colleges and universities, the faculty committee concluded that Colorado College had a heavier teaching load and a longer academic year than any other prestige institution of its type. "Many high quality colleges have dramatically changed their calendars and requirements since we inaugurated the Block Plan," the faculty committee reported, "and it is time for us to make our own adjustments."

The Committee for the Eight Block Year described the teaching load at Colorado College as "uncommonly heavy." Their report emphasized: "Faculty need time for research and reading, not only for their own independent projects but to keep up-to-date in their fields and to revitalize their classes." The underlying assumption of the Eight Block Year proposal, the committee said, was that "the quality of the classroom experience is determined to a great extent by what faculty and students do with their time and minds outside the classroom."[40]

The Eight Block Year proposal stirred up considerable controversy on the Colorado College campus. A random sampling of student opinions conducted by the *Catalyst* found 62 percent opposed to the Eight Block Year, 35 percent for it, and 3 percent undecided. In an open discussion at a faculty meeting, Professor James Yaffe of the English Department proposed that the College keep the Nine Block Year but cut the faculty teaching load to only seven blocks. Professor of Art Gale Murray, co-chair of the Committee

[40]Aklilu Dunlap, "Chopping The Ninth Block," *Catalyst*, 12 September 1986, 1. Kate Wilkinson, "CCCA Discusses Eight Block Plan," *Catalyst*, 19 September 1986, 2.

for the Eight Block Year, rejected that option by noting that combining a Nine Block Year with a seven block teaching load would put excessive upward pressure on class sizes at the College, an unacceptable side effect.[41]

Progressively the Eight Block Year turned into a battle between the faculty, most of whom supported the proposal, and the students, most of whom opposed it. At the time the proposal came up for a vote by the College faculty, the student newspaper, the *Catalyst*, put out a special edition airing all sides of the hotly-debated issue.[42]

At a special faculty meeting on Monday, October 28, 1986, the Colorado College faculty adopted the Eight Block Year by a vote of 82 to 30 with 2 abstentions. John Riker, Professor of Philosophy, strongly supported the proposal and noted that eight quality blocks should be a sufficient year's work for any college student. Owen Cramer, Professor of Classics, also in support of the proposal, said the Eight Block Year would cut the number of courses offered by 11 percent. That would not harm the students, Cramer concluded, because "we offer too many courses at Colorado College."

In line with the democratic spirit of the College, students were allowed to address the faculty and express their opposition to the Eight Block Year. Mike Fine, a senior, argued that the Eight Block Year would not create more faculty research time and would not stimulate more student research. Many critics of the proposal hinted that the real result would simply be an additional four weeks of vacation for faculty and students alike.

Judy Genova, Professor of Philosophy and co-chair of the Committee for the Eight Block Year, reminded the faculty that the real purpose of the plan was to attract more qualified teachers and researchers to come to work at the College. After the vote, Professor Genova said she hoped that the overwhelming 82–30 faculty vote in favor of the Eight Block Year would encourage the Board of Trustees to adopt the proposal as official College policy.[43]

---

[41]David Klein, "An Eight Block Update: Faculty Decides To Hold On Vote," *Catalyst*, 3 October 1986, 1. Carey L. Ewing, "Eight Block Debate," *Catalyst*, 17 October 1986, 1.

[42]Blair Sanford, "Eight Block Plan Revised: Overview And Commentary," and Devon Peña, "In Defense . . . ," *Catalyst*, Special Edition, 17 October 1986, I-IV.

[43]David A. Fitzgerald, "Faculty Passes Eight Block Proposal," *Catalyst*, 31 October 1986, 1.

Once the faculty had voted for the Eight Block Year, President Gresham Riley put his power and prestige behind the proposal. "This is the kind of plan I feel I can and should support," Riley said in an informal discussion with students held in Bemis Hall. Riley said he had confidence in the faculty's ability to make the plan work. He concluded that, by giving the faculty more time for research and publication, the Eight Block Year would further Riley's stated goal of making Colorado College a premier liberal arts institution.[44]

On March 14, 1987, the Board of Trustees adopted the Eight Block Year as the official calendar of Colorado College, to take effect in the fall of 1988.[45] Although there were loud protests from many of the students, this innovative proposal to lighten the workload of the College faculty went forward.[46]

A WIRED CAMPUS

During the 1986–1987 academic year the College began installing the wiring that would permit all of the personal computers on campus to be connected into a single network. The American Telephone & Telegraph (AT&T) Information Systems Network gave students, faculty, and administrators immediate computer access to the College's five main computer systems. Once the network was wired up, students and faculty were able to peruse the Tutt Library catalog from their computers rather than having to go over to the Library. Faculty members could pull up the transcripts of their student advisees on their computers rather than having to visit the Registrar's office. An elaborate checking system was installed so that unauthorized persons could not gain access to secure computer files.

The network gave rise to an increasingly popular form of communication at the College called E-Mail, or Electronic Mail. Instead of having to type memorandums or write notes to each other, students and faculty could type messages into their computers and then transmit them electronically to any other computer user on campus. Eventually the

---

[44]Jerrel Armstrong, "Riley Stumps For Eight Block Year," *Catalyst*, 5 December 1986, 2.

[45]"Board Decisions Announced: Eight Block Plan Passes," *Catalyst*, 20 March 1987, 4.

[46]Kevin Drennan, "Forum On Eight Block Faults," *Catalyst*, 17 November 1989, 1.

Colorado College network was linked to those at other colleges and universities. Faculty members and administrators were able to communicate with colleagues at other educational institutions by E-Mail. Students were able to send messages to their friends on distant campuses.

The Colorado College computer network also was connected to the World Wide Web, an internationally interconnected computer system where various scholars and other organizations placed computerized information for use by others. Students and faculty at Colorado College could find information by using computers to locate various information sources on the World Wide Web. Accessing information in this manner often was referred to as "driving the Information Highway." When useful information was found on the World Wide Web, it could be printed out with a computer printer. By the late 1990s sizable numbers of students were using their computers to access the World Wide Web and find information that could be used for writing papers.

Presiding over the early phases of the development of the computer network at Colorado College was Frederick Keller, the Director of Academic Computing. Although he was trained as a psychologist, Keller applied his scientific knowledge of the operations and capabilities of computers to improving and encouraging computer usage on the Colorado College campus. Faculty and students alike came to rely on Keller to guide them into the rapidly advancing world of computer information technology. One close observer of the process concluded that "Frederick Keller *dragged* the College into the 21st Century where computers were concerned."[47]

Keller pointed out that the new Information Systems Network cost Colorado College $200,000, but he said the expenditure was worthwhile for exposing students and faculty to the rapidly changing nature of storing, transmitting, and accessing information. Keller also noted that the College was establishing itself as something of a pioneer in this area. He concluded: "Colorado College will become the first college of this size to install a system of this complexity."[48]

---

[47]Author's notes, interview with David Finley, former Dean of Colorado College, 4 December 1997.

[48]David A. Fitzgerald, "Information Systems Network To Link Campus Terminals," *Catalyst*, 10 October 1986, 1.

The growing importance of computers on college and university campuses presented a number of challenges to the College administration. The technology was changing and improving so quickly that the College had to struggle to keep its computers and computer network up-to-date. There was the corresponding problem that expensive equipment became obsolete very quickly and had to be replaced after only a few years of use.

A subtle and largely unspoken tension was created. On one hand there were the high-end users, mainly scientific researchers who needed the very latest, the most powerful, and the most expensive computers. On the other side there were the low-end users, who argued for buying large numbers of less-expensive machines and thereby making computing available to as many members of the College community as possible. These two groups competed for the limited funds available for new computer technology. The College continued to be a leader in the field of liberal arts college academic computing in the late 1980s and early 1990s, but it required a constant and unrelenting effort on the part of the College administration and computer services personnel.[49]

SHANTY TOWN

The issue of Colorado College's investment in corporations that did business in South Africa boiled to the surface again during the 1986–1987 academic year. A student-faculty group called the Colorado College Community Against Apartheid decided to protest the College's remaining investments in that racially segregated nation. The group began by constructing a shanty town of wooden shack buildings on the campus quadrangle in front of the administrative offices in Armstrong Hall. The shacks were said to resemble the shabby housing in which racially oppressed South African Blacks were forced to live.

The shanty town was readily visible to the large number of automobiles passing by the campus on Cascade Avenue. The reaction of some elements of the Colorado Springs community to this hastily-assembled group of structures was highly negative, at least when measured by news media editorials and letters-to-the-editor of local newspapers. In an editorial, one

---

[49]Author's notes, interview with David D. Finley, former Dean of Colorado College, 4 December 1997.

Colorado Springs television station accused the protesting students of being enrolled in "Hypocrisy 101" and called on them to drop out of Colorado College if they did not like the College's investment policies.

The shanty town was constructed in an effort to influence the College's Board of Trustees. As a result, two members of the Sociology Department, professors Margaret Duncombe and Jeff Livesay, were allowed to address the Board of Trustees and make the case for withdrawing all Colorado College investments in South Africa. Duncombe and Livesay were joined in their presentation by two students, Tim Fitz and Teddy Matera. After the presentation, President Riley agreed to give the Colorado College Community Against Apartheid two hours of time at a subsequent meeting of the Board of Trustees to hold a major discussion with the Board on the South Africa divestment issue.

The protesters left their shanty town standing, but it was attacked by unknown vandals late at night the following weekend. One shack was demolished and several others were overturned. At the same time, opponents of the protest pointed out that the shacks were illegal dwelling units under Colorado Springs zoning laws and could possibly subject the College to a $300 fine. However, the shanty town remained standing throughout the rest of the 1986–1987 academic year and, periodically, was the target of additional vandal attacks.

For its part, the College administration saw the shanty town as "a form of symbolic speech, protected by the [United States] Constitution and school guidelines." Such political protest activities were legitimate as long as there was no disruption of educational activities at the College. This fit with President Riley's frequently stated position that "Freedom of Speech," no matter what the views being presented, would be the hallmark of political discussion and political activity at Colorado College.[50]

One faculty member who was willing to publicly oppose College divestment of South African holdings was David Hendrickson of the Political Science Department. In an article in the *Catalyst*, Hendrickson argued that those supporting divestment were hoping to foment a political revolution in South Africa—a revolution that could lead to years of polit-

---

[50]Aklilu Dunlap, "Shanty Town Sparks Constructive Dialogue," *Catalyst*, 5 December 1986, 1. Peter W. Loach, "C.C.C.A.A. Overcomes Violence, Looks To Future," *Catalyst*, 12 December 1986, 3.

ical and economic instability and "a scene of starvation, disease, and death on a scale we really cannot fathom." Hendrickson concluded that the United States would have more influence over events in South Africa if it retained its economic investments and political ties to the nation and continued to press for a peaceful end to the rigid racial segregation there.[51]

On March 14, 1987, William Spencer, the Chairman of the Colorado College Board of Trustees, emerged from a Trustees meeting to announce the Board's vote on the issue of South African divestment. Spencer, a longtime executive of Citicorp, stood in bright sunshine at the west entrance to Armstrong Hall. Standing next to him was Colorado College President Gresham Riley. Spencer said the Trustees appreciated the student and faculty concern about the issue of South Africa and apartheid, but the Board had decided it was in the best interests of the College "to reaffirm its long-standing policy of investing in American companies who conduct business in South Africa." He made it clear the College would continue to support bringing about change in South Africa by peaceful means.

As Spencer spoke, a group of disgruntled students, who appeared to have anticipated the Board's negative vote on divestment, flipped hundreds of pennies in the air that landed at William Spencer's and Gresham Riley's feet. The pennies were said to symbolize the College's greater interest in making money from its investments rather than helping the people of South Africa. The *Catalyst* reported there was a "continual clanking of pennies on the ground." Student protesters in the crowd began chanting: "We won't rest 'till you divest!"[52]

The following Monday a number of students staged a vigil outside of President Riley's office in Armstrong Hall. They taped their mouths shut in an effort to symbolize their contention that the Board of Trustees had refused to listen to the desires of the students on the South Africa issue. At 5 P.M., when it was time to secure the building, the protesting students refused to leave. President Riley then arranged for campus security guards

---

[51]David Hendrickson, "South Africa And Divestment," *Catalyst*, 6 March 1987, 13.

[52]Katie Kerwin, "Trustees: No Divestment," *Catalyst*, 20 March 1987, 1.

to remain through the night with the protesters to protect the important College records kept in Armstrong Hall. On subsequent days, the protesters decided to confine their vigil outside President Riley's office to normal business hours when extra security guards would not be required.[53]

The rift between the College Board of Trustees and the students and faculty supporting South African divestment defied resolution. Individual members of the Board of Trustees held a series of panel discussions on the issue on campus, debating student and faculty advocates of divestment face-to-face. But the two groups remained at odds, and positions began to harden rather than move toward compromise.[54]

SOUTHWESTERN STUDIES

In the spring of 1987 the College received a grant of $500,000 from the National Endowment for the Humanities (NEH) to establish the Hulbert Center for Southwestern Studies. The "challenge" grant was to be matched three-to-one, with the College raising another $1.5 million and thereby producing a total $2 million endowment for Southwestern Studies.

The NEH grant permitted a major expansion of the existing Southwestern Studies Program at the College, which was organized in 1984 and directed by Professor of English Joseph Gordon. The expanded program was named in honor of Professor of History Archer Hulbert, who taught at Colorado College in the 1920s and wrote extensively about western United States history, particularly the various trails in the West.

The Hulbert Center for Southwestern Studies represented a major effort by the College to take advantage of its location in a southwestern state, Colorado, and the geographical closeness of the Native American pueblos and Hispanic cultures of northern New Mexico. The Center helped to organize courses in Southwestern Studies. Under the Block Plan, the Center granted "blocks off" to Colorado College faculty doing

---

[53]Katie Kerwin, "'Voiceless' Students Protest Outside President's Office," *Catalyst*, 20 March 1987, 1. Katie Kerwin, "Events Support Divestment: Teach-In, Rallies And The Leeches," *Catalyst*, 20 March 1987, 3. Also see photograph entitled "Voiceless," *Catalyst*, 10 April 1987, 6.

[54]Ian Campbell, "87–88: The Year Of Southern Africa," *Catalyst*, 10 April 1987, 5. Mike Fraterelli, "Panel Discussion On South Africa," *Catalyst*, 8 May 1987, 1.

research and writing on the subject of the American Southwest. The NEH challenge grant was specifically designated to establish an endowed professorship that would be used to bring in a visiting scholar on southwestern subjects each year. The visiting professor could pursue his or her own research but would so some teaching at the same time.

The Hulbert Center for Southwestern Studies was housed in Dern House, a large stucco home located at the northeast corner of Cascade Avenue and San Rafael Street. Built in the 1920s and given to the College in the 1940s, Dern House previously had been used as a small dormitory. With its dark wood trim, French doors, and large fireplace, Dern House proved to be a comfortable and productive home for Southwestern Studies at the College.[55]

TELEPHONING THE ALUMNI

By the mid–1980s a well-established practice at Colorado College, and many other colleges and universities, was having members of the student body telephone the alumni in an effort to raise more funds. The program was called *DIALogue* and had been established some ten years earlier by Barbara Yalich of the College Development Office. Groups of students, working at a bank of telephones, spent two-hour and thirty-minute shifts calling alumni who had contributed to the College in past years and asking them to renew their gift or give more money in the current year.

Students working in *DIALogue* were encouraged to call alumni who had participated in the same activities the students were participating in. Thus current members of the men's lacrosse team would call former men's lacrosse players, and students currently on the debating team would call former debaters. Students were rewarded for their efforts with hamburgers and fries donated by a local McDonald's restaurant and hot pizza given by a nearby Pizza Hut. When the two-week *DIALogue* program was completed, the students who had put in the most hours of telephoning received door prizes donated by local merchants. The more a student worked, the better the prize he or she was likely to receive.

[55]Nan Ellsworth and Joe Barber, "CC Scores Cool Half-Million," *Catalyst*, 23 January 1987, 1.

DIALogue was a financial success as well as being a mixture of work and fun for the students. Throughout the 1980s the program raised approximately $100,000 in alumni contributions each year it operated.[56]

A NEW MAJOR IN COMPARATIVE LITERATURE

The curriculum of a college or university is in a perpetual state of evolution. Periodically existing courses that appear to have lost relevance are removed from the curriculum, while at the same time new courses are developed and added to the curriculum. Adoption of proposed new courses is one of the major duties of the Colorado College faculty when it gathers for its monthly (one per block) faculty meetings.

In the spring of 1987 the College faculty created a new major in Comparative Literature. It was designed to be a "joint major" composed of courses from existing departments and taught by faculty members from existing departments. There was *not* going to be a Comparative Literature Department with its own Comparative Literature faculty.

Comparative Literature was not a traditional major in United States higher education but had been adopted at a number of prestige colleges and universities before being instituted at Colorado College. The new program was similar to the Literature/Comparative Literature major being offered at the time at Yale University in New Haven, Connecticut. Two senior class students, Becky Bark and Amy Schroth, were the first at Colorado College to select a Comparative Literature major.

The concept of Comparative Literature first emerged in the 19th Century and referred to the influence of one nation's literature on that of another nation. Thus early practitioners of Comparative Literature studied the influence of French authors on English authors, or English authors on United States authors, etc. In the 20th Century, however, the field of Comparative Literature was expanded to include the study of the relationships and influences among the various *types* of literature, i.e., anthropological, historical, philosophical, psychological, etc.

The Comparative Literature major was supported by the creation of the Maytag Chair, an endowment gift of $1 million which permitted

[56]Margo Levi, "Dialing For Dollars," *Catalyst*, 6 February 1987, 1.

a Comparative Literature specialist to be brought to the campus each year to teach relevant courses in this exciting academic field. The first Maytag Professor was George Konrad, a Hungarian novelist who at one time was arrested by Communist authorities in Budapest for his anti-socialist writings.[57]

ALUMNUS WRITES *NEWSWEEK* COVER STORY

Every so often an alumnus or alumna of Colorado College distinguishes himself or herself in a way that breaks into the national consciousness and reflects favorably on the College. Such an event occurred in the spring of 1987 when Gregg Easterbrook, Colorado College Class of 1976, authored a byline cover story for *Newsweek* magazine.

Easterbrook wrote an expansive article entitled "The Revolution in Medicine." The article ran 26 pages long, setting a precedent at *Newsweek* for such in-depth coverage. In the article Easterbrook summarized the way advancing technology was altering the way people received medical care and the way they related to their physicians.

Gregg Easterbrook symbolized a growing number of Colorado College graduates who were seeking careers in journalism. When interviewed by the *Catalyst*, however, Easterbrook encouraged Colorado College undergraduates to pursue a general liberal arts education rather than transfer to a journalism school. "The rules and basic procedures of journalism you can learn pretty fast if you're a smart person," Easterbrook said. He concluded that having a "general knowledge of society" was the best preparation for a writing career.[58]

In the first semester of 1992 Gregg Easterbrook returned to Colorado College to receive an honorary degree and give the address at the opening Convocation. His subject was the tendency of environmental reform-

---

[57]Mary Butcher, "Comparative Literature Initiated At CC," *Catalyst*, 6 February 1987, 9. George Butte, Professor of English, "Hungarian Writer To Teach At C.C.; George Konrad Will Be First Maytag Professor," *Catalyst*, 15 January 1988, 3.

[58]Katie Kerwin, "CC Grad Published," *Catalyst*, 7 March 1987, 1. Katie Kerwin, the student author of the *Catalyst* story about Gregg Easterbrook, subsequently became a well-known political reporter for the *Rocky Mountain News* in Denver.

ers to overstate environmental threats to humanity. The talk was entitled "The Annual End of the World."[59]

GLENN BROOKS STEPS DOWN AS DEAN

Effective at the end of the 1986–1987 academic year, Glenn Brooks submitted his resignation as Dean of the College. He had served as Dean for eight years, which he said was twice as long as he had intended. "Being a Dean at Colorado College is never dull," Brooks said when his departure from the post was announced. "You are constantly fired at from all directions. But there are great satisfactions that go along with it."

Brooks said he had striven as Dean to always work "through collaboration, and never in isolation." The most rewarding part of the job, he explained, was in watching the College's graduates go on to lead "interesting and significant lives." Brooks said his one regret as Dean was that he missed the daily interaction with students that comes with teaching, and he said he intended to return to the classrooms of Colorado College following a sabbatical.

The major curricular change at Colorado College during Glenn Brooks's deanship was the adoption of the Western and non-Western course requirements for all students and the institution of voluntary thematic minors. Dean Brooks also cut the faculty teaching load from nine blocks per year to eight blocks, and he strongly supported the Eight Block Year proposal, which further cut the faculty teaching load from eight blocks per year to seven blocks. Brooks said that final adoption of the Eight Block Year by the Board of Trustees enabled him to end his time as Dean with "an extremely constructive step towards academic excellence."[60]

---

[59]Sean McLaughlin, "Easterbrook Advises Students," *Catalyst*, 11 September 1992, 4.

[60]Caroline Bryan, "Brooks Resigns," *Catalyst*, 5 December 1986, 1.

CHAPTER 12

A Time of Tumult

President Gresham Riley wasted no time in naming a new Dean. He selected David Finley, Professor of Political Science and the College's resident expert on the Soviet Union and Communist China. There was a well-established tradition at Colorado College of recruiting deans from within the existing faculty, and President Riley carefully followed that tradition.

David D. Finley was born in Indianapolis, Indiana, on November 4, 1933. He was the son of an Army officer, and the Finley family followed the father as he moved from military post to military post during World War II. One of those posts was Fort Carson, and the family settled in Colorado Springs when David Finley's father retired from the Army in 1947.

David Finley thus spent his high school years in Colorado Springs, graduating from Cheyenne Mountain High School in 1951. He went on to the United States Military Academy (West Point), where he chose to study the Russian language and thereby first kindled his lifelong interest in Soviet affairs. Finley graduated from West Point in 1955 and then served in a missile battalion with the U.S. Army in Europe. After completing his military service, he did graduate work in Political Science at Stanford University in Palo Alto, California. He joined the faculty at Colorado College in 1963 while still writing his doctoral dissertation. He received his Ph.D. from Stanford in 1966.

David Finley traveled extensively in Eastern Europe, the Soviet Union, and Communist China in order to personally observe the peoples and governmental institutions about which he was teaching. He was married to Judith Reid Finley, Colorado College class of 1958, the daughter of longtime Colorado College Dean of Men J. Juan Reid. At the height of student unrest on campus during the late 1960s, David Finley chaired the Committee on Student Rights and Responsibilities, which set out to determine the areas of campus life that would be governed by the students rather than the faculty or administration. The committee succeeded at its work at a very difficult and volatile time.

When the College held a week-long January Symposium on *World War II,* David Finley was recruited to present the Soviet view of that mighty conflict. From 1981 to 1985 he served as Chairman of the Political Science Department.

There were some slightly raised eyebrows when it became known that one Dean from the Political Science Department, Glenn Brooks, was going to be succeeded by a second Dean from Political Science, David Finley. Some faculty members were of the opinion that the deanship, when vacancies occur, should be rotated around the various academic departments. But appointment of the Dean is clearly the prerogative of the President, not the faculty, and therefore no one publicly questioned Gresham Riley's choice of a second Political Science Dean.[1]

Given the increased sensitivity in the 1980s to the various constituencies in the College community, Gresham Riley made it a point to consult with a variety of campus groups about Finley's appointment as Dean. These groups included the Minority Concerns Committee, the Women's Concerns Committee, and the faculty Committee on Committees (the major policy recommending committee for the faculty).

President Riley told the *Catalyst* that he had specifically searched for a "non-special interest candidate," someone who would be in a position to mediate the conflicting demands of the wide variety of groups found at Colorado College. Riley said he also looked for someone who strongly supported his efforts to enhance the national reputation of the College and who would be a strong spokesperson for the faculty's interests.

As for David Finley himself, he said at the time of his selection: "The central purpose of Colorado College is to provide the best teaching for undergraduates in the traditional liberal arts, and I will do my best to keep that commitment central."[2]

---

[1]Recollection of the author.

[2]Katie Kerwin with Joe Barber, "Finley Named New Dean," 6 February 1987, 1.

Colorado College was an optimistic place when David Finley assumed the deanship in September of 1987. The Block Plan had been operating for 17 years and could now be regarded as a mature and proven academic program. The two major buildings to arise out of the 1983 Campus Plan, Worner Center and the Barnes Science Center, were in the final stages of construction and soon would be placed in operation. The College's major fund-raising effort, the Colorado College Campaign, was well underway and clearly was going to reach its high monetary goals. The time had come to move the College to "the next plateau," and President Gresham Riley and Dean David Finley were in complete agreement that the next plateau "was seeking greater eminence among liberal arts colleges."[3]

IMPLEMENTING THE EIGHT BLOCK YEAR

The biggest challenge facing Dean Finley was to make the Eight Block Year work. The new calendar was to take effect in the fall of 1988, just one year after Finley assumed the deanship in the fall of 1987. A mock scheduling was held during the 1987–1988 academic year as faculty and students both worked to accomplish in eight blocks what had previously taken nine. Thanks to the yeoman efforts of Registrar Al Johnson, the bugs were quickly worked out of the registration process and the Eight Block Year got off to a smooth start.[4]

But the student body and many of the alumni continued to direct harsh criticism at the Eight Block Year. The faculty of the College frequently was accused of being lazy and of emulating research university professors by staging a "flight from the classroom." David Finley spent many hours during his early years as Dean "fending off the brickbats over the Eight Block Year." Finley strongly supported the new program, however, arguing that the long and demanding Nine Block Year had been "burning the intellectual capital of the faculty."[5]

---

[3]Author's notes, interview with David Finley, former Dean of Colorado College, 4 December 1997.

[4]Katie Kerwin, "Students Register For No Apparent Reason: Mock Registration Slated For Next Week," *Catalyst*, 30 October 1987, 3.

[5]Author's notes, interview with David Finley, former Dean of Colorado College, 4 December 1997.

It soon developed that there were some operating problems with the Eight Block Year. Normally, students are expected to spend four years at Colorado College. If the academic year is eight blocks long, students can earn a total of 32 one-block units for graduation over those four years. But, under the Eight Block Year, the College required each student to have completed 32 units in order to graduate. That meant that, if a student became ill and missed a block, or failed or withdrew from a course in a block, the requisite 32 units for graduation could not be acquired in four years. The new calendar needed some flexibility so that students could miss a block or two during their careers at Colorado College but still graduate in just four years.

A faculty committee chaired by Professor Timothy Fuller of the Political Science Department came up with a successful solution. *Half-Block* courses were offered in the first two weeks following Winter Break (Christmas vacation). Students attended class for two weeks and received 1/2 unit of credit. If a student took a Half-Block course in each of the four years he or she was at Colorado College, that would add two full units of credit for graduation.

The College administration set to work recruiting a limited number of faculty to teach these newly created Half-Block courses. The faculty responded with imagination, offering two-week courses with exciting titles such as *Freud*, *Winter Field Biology*, *The Films Of Federico Felini*, and *The Civil Rights Movement.* About 30 Half-Block courses were offered each January, which meant that roughly 400 to 500 students, or approximately one-quarter of the student body, took advantage of this novel addition to the College calendar.[6] Technically students and faculty should have begun referring to the Eight-And-One-Half Block Year, but the Eight Block Year remained the preferred nomenclature.

Another reform designed to relieve the strains of the Eight Block Year was the Summer Session *Wild Card.* Colorado College students pay extra tuition to take Summer Session courses at the College, but the Wild Card program allowed each student to take one Summer Session course for free. Any summer during his or her Colorado College career, a student

---

[6]Stephanie Van Auken, "New Half-Block Draws Nearly 500," *Catalyst*, 31 January 1992, 2.

could take a Summer Session course at no extra charge. The wild card program strengthened the Summer Session, because a number of students used their Wild Card to take one course and then, since they were on campus anyway, paid tuition to take a second or third summer course.

A third idea for making the Eight Block Year more palatable to the students was to allow them to take *Extended Format Courses*. These were special courses in the late afternoon or evening that were spread over an entire semester. Such courses were taken at the same time as the regular one or two-block courses but, because they were scheduled over an entire semester, did not unduly load students down with extra work. Extended Format Courses earned students one-half unit of credit per semester. These courses often had a practical, hands-on character to them. Students could take Extended Format Courses in such subjects as book production, choral conducting, journalistic writing, coaching methodology, and emergency medical training.[7]

These three reforms—the Half-Block, the Summer Session Wild Card, and the Extended Format Course—successfully eliminated almost all of the scheduling problems created by the Eight Block Year. The reforms also helped to silence the frequently-heard criticism that, by cutting from nine blocks to eight, the College was giving the students less education but charging the same amount of tuition. There had been some rough spots, but, within two-to-three years of the adoption of the Eight Block Year, the new program was operating smoothly to the general satisfaction of the faculty and student body.[8]

DIVERSITY PROGRAMS

The on-going effort to diversify the student body and faculty of Colorado College accelerated in the late 1980s. There was a substantial increase in the number of women faculty members. In 1980 women constituted only 18 percent of the College faculty, but by the end of the decade the faculty was 28 percent female. The gains were substantial enough that College

---

[7]Michele Santos, "Faculty, Trustees To Consider Plan; Recommendation Is In: 'Eight-Plus Year,'" *Catalyst*, 16 November 1990, 1. Jay Marx, "Eight-Plus Block Year Approved," *Catalyst*, 25 January 1991, 1.

[8]Seth Fisher, "Half-Block Critiqued By Students," *Catalyst*, 16 October 1992, 4.

administrators were predicting that the lack of women on the faculty would soon be a "non-issue" at Colorado College.[9]

The College was enjoying moderate success at recruiting Hispanic faculty members. For example, Douglas Monroy was added to the History Department in 1978. He subsequently became Director of the Southwest Studies program. Devon Peña joined the Sociology Department in 1984 and made the San Luis Valley in southern Colorado his area of special study. Clara Lomas began teaching Romance Languages at the College in 1987, and Mario Montaño was added to the Anthropology faculty in 1992.

A major addition to the Hispanic faculty and staff at Colorado College was Victor Nelson-Cisneros. He was hired in 1981 as a minority dean and to teach some History courses. In 1994 he was appointed Associate Dean of the College.

It was a continuing struggle, however, to find, hire, and retain African-American faculty members and administrators. College and universities across the nation were competing for the services of Black academics. The College made a notable gain in this area of endeavor when it succeeded in hiring Mike Edmonds, an African-American from Mississippi, as the Dean of Students. African-American faculty members in the late 1980s and early 1990s included professors Adrienne Lanier Seward and Claire Garcia, both in the English Department.

In an effort to connect with minority teachers and scholars at the beginning of their academic careers, the College participated in a Minority Scholar in Residence program. It was aimed at African-American and Hispanic graduate students who had finished their course work for the Ph.D. degree but had not yet completed their doctoral dissertations. These young and promising scholars were invited to come to Colorado College for a full academic year, teach only one or two blocks, and spend the remaining time completing their doctoral dissertations.

The Minority Scholar in Residence program was designed to expose minority graduate students to the unique atmosphere and teaching styles

---

[9]Author's notes, interview with David Finley, former Dean of Colorado College, 4 December 1997.

of a liberal arts college, an atmosphere and teaching style that contrasted with the university environments in which these students previously had been working and studying. As the College administration had hoped and intended, a number of the minority scholars liked what they found at Colorado College and subsequently accepted tenure track appointments to the faculty.

One such minority scholar was Vera Leigh Fennell, an African-American and a Political Science graduate of Princeton University in New Jersey. Fennell was working on her Ph.D. at the University of Chicago in Illinois. Her major area of interest was Asian studies, with particular emphasis on the condition of working women in mainland China. Another minority scholar was W. Ryan Rommel-Ruiz, a Hispanic and a Ph.D. candidate at the University of Michigan. Rommel-Ruiz taught courses in the History Department.

The College joined with other colleges in the Associated Colleges of the Midwest (ACM) in instituting the Minority Scholars in Academic Careers program of summer studies. This program encouraged minority students at Colorado College to spend their summers studying and doing research with a minority member of the faculty. The goal was to give minority students a strong dose of academic life and thereby encourage them to consider going to graduate school and pursuing a career in college or university teaching.

There was a particular emphasis in the late 1980s on making Colorado College "a hospitable world for minorities." The College administration worked very hard at eliminating and mitigating the inadvertent slights and thoughtless remarks that can create an unpleasant atmosphere for minority students and faculty.[10] At the same time, however, a strong emphasis was placed on preserving freedom of speech and creating a welcome atmosphere for open discussion at the College. At times resolving conflicts between minority sensitivities and freedom of speech standards proved challenging for administrators, faculty, and students.

---

[10]Author's notes, interview with David Finley, former Dean of Colorado College, 4 December 1997.

The 1988 Recertification

Every ten years Colorado College was required to get "recertified" by the North Central Association of Colleges and Schools. For an institution of the stature and longevity of Colorado College, a successful recertification was a foregone conclusion. The once-a-decade recertification process, however, gave the College community the opportunity to look back over the previous ten years, highlighting major successes and setting bold goals for the future.

The major item supporting the 1988 recertification at Colorado College was a 72-page printed document entitled "Years of Change; Plans for More." This elaborate self-study of the College outlined in great detail how the Block Plan had been perfected with the Western/non-Western studies curriculum and voluntary thematic minors. It noted how Development Blocks were being used to encourage research and writing on the part of the faculty, and how the Writing Center was increasing the writing skills of the students. The Eight Block Year, this optimistic report concluded, would successfully eliminate the major criticism of the Block Plan—a much too heavy faculty workload. The cover of the 1988 recertification report featured a sunshiny photograph of the new Worner student center, which had been completed and dedicated on October 10, 1987.[11]

When representatives of the North Central Association made their recertification visit to Colorado College, however, a somewhat different picture of the College emerged. Minority faculty and minority students complained long and loud to these important visitors that the College was not making a sufficient effort where recruiting more minority faculty and students was concerned. Lack of racial and ethnic diversity was cited as the major shortcoming of a College where virtually all other aspects were favorable. It was acknowledged that many colleges and universities were failing to meet high standards where diversity was concerned, but that did not excuse Colorado College from making a more sincere and, hopefully, more successful effort.[12]

---

[11]The author was the anonymous author of "Years of Change; Plans for More; Self-Study of The Colorado College, 1987–1988." President Gresham Riley and deans Glenn Brooks and David Finley critiqued and polished the final version of the document.

[12]Recollection of the author.

THE CHALLENGES OF DIVERSITY

What the College was experiencing was a phenomenon that became known as the *challenges of diversity*.[13] As students and faculty from varied backgrounds were recruited to come to the College, there was an increasing level of animated discussion and argument between and within these groups. Ironically, as the College community came to include a variety of racial and ethnic groups, these groups pressed hard for their particular societal goals and thereby introduced an element of intellectual discord that had not been seen previously at the College. On second thought, however, many people in the College community concluded that it was healthy for strong minority spokespersons to be adding vociferously expressed minority points of view to campus discussion and thought.

There was a degree of pressure put on the College's administrators in the late 1980s to lower hiring standards in an effort to get more diversity on the Colorado College faculty. Dean David Finley noted that he strongly "resisted bending standards for new hires who were women and minorities."[14]

INTERNATIONALIZING THE CURRICULUM

The late 1980s found the College making a major effort to increase international awareness on the part of both students and faculty. Colorado College students were encouraged to spend at least part of their college career studying abroad, and students from foreign nations were heavily recruited to come to Colorado College. Particular emphasis was placed on recruiting international students from outside of western Europe. To this end, the College had ten scholarships that it offered to prospective foreign students. These international scholarships were ample ones in that they paid tuition and room and board for all four years at Colorado College.

The College established an Office of International Programs in Worner Center with a paid administrator, Tiggy Shields, to publicize and

---

[13]Author's notes, interview with former Dean of Colorado College David Finley, 4 December 1997.

[14]Author's notes, interview with David Finley, former Dean of Colorado College, 4 December 1997.

counsel students on the various opportunities for study abroad.[15] An off-campus study fair was held in the lounge in Worner Center each year at which students could pick up printed information on the various overseas programs offered by the College. Students who had previously attended foreign study programs came to the fair and reported personally on the nature and rewards of their overseas study experiences.

Under the leadership of Professor of Religion Joseph Pickle, the College organized an Associated Colleges of the Midwest (ACM) study program in the African nation of Zimbabwe.[16] Another new international program encouraged Colorado College students to live and study for a while in the city of Olomouc in the Czech Republic.

By the early 1990s almost 25 percent of Colorado College students were spending part of their college career studying abroad. The College participated in overseas programs in nine countries in Africa, Asia, and Europe. In addition, the College operated semester-long language programs in three countries—France, Germany, and Mexico.[17]

At the same time, minority student organizations on the Colorado College campus had instituted the practice of "adopting" international students with similar ethnic or racial backgrounds. This made life at Colorado College more friendly and welcoming for international students, particularly those from non-European nations. In another effort on behalf of international students, a former private residence on Cascade Avenue, Tenney House, was designated the International House. It functioned as a central place for international students to congregate and hold intellectual and social events. A number of international students lived in Tenney House.[18]

With the full moral and economic encouragement of Edith Gaylord Harper, a member of the Colorado College class of 1946, the College hired new faculty and offered a variety of new courses in the field of

---

[15]"Int'l Office Created," *Catalyst*, 22 September 1989, 1.

[16]Jonathan McMurray, "CC-Zimbabwe Connection Opened, Program To Begin This Summer At University Of Zimbabwe," *Catalyst*, 27 January 1989, 9.

[17]"Int'l Office Created," *Catalyst*, 22 September 1989, 1.

[18]Akua Akotto, "Illegal Alien Refuge Prospers," *Catalyst*, 16 October 1987, 9.

Asian studies. Harper, who was a member of the Board of Trustees, contributed over $1 million to help the College focus on the problems and prospects of the Asian continent. Dean David Finley noted: "Harper was way ahead of the College administration and faculty in terms of seeing the future economic and political importance of Asia."[19]

The effort to emphasize internationalism at Colorado College was very successful in encouraging students to study overseas. It was effective but somewhat less successful at getting international students to come to the College.[20] The program could not have been better timed, however. In 1989 the Soviet Union relaxed its iron grip on Eastern Europe. The famous Berlin Wall, which symbolically separated the democratic nations from the various communist states, was torn down. Two years later the Soviet Union itself voluntarily broke apart into a number of separate nations, the foremost of which was Russia. The United States emerged as the leading world power with primary responsibility, many observers argued, for furthering and institutionalizing world peace. These events strengthened the importance of the new emphasis on internationalism at Colorado College.

HARMONIZING TEACHING AND SCHOLARSHIP

The enduring question of "teaching" versus "scholarship" continued to be raised at Colorado College during the late 1980s. Because of the large supply of Ph.D. candidates being turned out by the graduate universities, Colorado College was hiring new professors from prestige schools where research and writing were held in very high regard. A "generation gap" thus began to develop on the College faculty between the older professors, who believed great teaching was the most important goal, and the younger professors, who continued to press the College for more time and more money for research and publication. Dean David Finley quickly learned that "harmonizing" scholarship with teaching was a major part of his job.

[19]Author's notes, interview with David Finley, former Dean of Colorado College, 4 December 1997.

[20]Author's notes, interview with David Finley, former Dean of Colorado College, 4 December 1997.

"I fought hard against there ever being a 'publish or perish' ethic for the Colorado College faculty," Dean Finley explained. "I kept research and writing in a supporting role and clearly defined teaching as the 'primary mission' of the College. The goal was to encourage scholarship on the part of our faculty, but only as a way of building our reputation as a 'teaching' institution."

President Riley and Dean Finley customarily worked together when interviewing prospective faculty for the College. The two administrators formed the habit of President Riley asking most of the questions about a candidate's scholarly accomplishments and Dean Finley making most of the inquiries about the candidate's teaching experience and abilities. Soon President Riley had a reputation for being research oriented, and Dean Finley became known as the great supporter of good teaching. Ironically, both Riley and Finley saw eye-to-eye on the issue. Teaching would always be the most important concern at Colorado College.[21]

Professor Beidleman Retires

In the spring of 1988 one of the College's best-known faculty members, Professor of Biology Richard Beidleman, retired. Thus ended a 40-year teaching career, 31 of those years at Colorado College.

Dick Beidleman was well-known for teaching about the environment. He began arguing for environmental awareness and reform years before those subjects became popular with college students and the general public. But Beidleman did more than teach about the world of nature. Along with his wife, Reba, he took a leadership role in supporting more parks, open space preservation, and urban beautification in Colorado Springs. He worked particularly hard to expand the size and preserve the scenic backdrop of the Garden of the Gods, the spectacular natural rock formations located in west Colorado Springs.

Because of Dick and Reba Beidleman's concern and work for the environment, the Colorado Springs Parks Department named a new park education facility in their honor. The Richard and Reba Beidleman

---

[21]Author's notes, interview with David Finley, former Dean of Colorado College, 4 December 1997.

Environmental Center was located in Sondermann Park, just a mile or two northwest of the College. Housed in a former residence located at the edge of the park, the Beidleman Center was used for public lectures, museum-type displays, and as a departure point for nature walks and biological projects in the park.

Professor Beidleman's field courses in Biology were popular with the students. He encouraged them to notice the way birds, from the natural world, quickly learned to build their nests under highway bridges, products of the human world. Riding the bus from one natural study site to another, Beidleman would amuse his students by pointing out that NORAD, the major U.S. Government facility for defending against attacking bombers or missiles, was located on an earthquake fault line. When his field courses included overnight camping trips, he encouraged his students to crawl out of their sleeping bags early and join him for some pre-breakfast bird watching. An ice cream addict, Beidleman seemed to know, and lead his students to, all the best places to get an ice cream cone in the American Southwest.

Dick Beidleman received his B.A., M.A., and Ph.D. degrees from the University of Colorado at Boulder, completing his Ph.D. in 1954. While at Colorado College, he spent many of his summer vacations working as a naturalist and lecturer for the National Park Service at such scenic locations as Rocky Mountain National Park in Colorado, Dinosaur National Monument in Utah and Colorado, Grand Canyon National Park in Arizona, and Yosemite National Park in California. One of his academic interests was the study of scientists working in frontier environments. He traveled to both Australia and England to research Charles Darwin's visit to the Australia frontier in 1836.

During his final year of teaching, Beidleman noted that Colorado College had a reputation as a party school when he first joined the faculty in 1957. He saw the College evolve into an institution where much work was demanded of the students, a movement that was helped along by the adoption of the Block Plan. Beidleman explained: "The Block Plan is ideal for field work. We have more elasticity in developing a good field program." Working with his departmental colleagues, Professor Beidleman helped turned the Biology Department at Colorado College into what one survey claimed was one of the top ten undergraduate biology departments in the nation.

When he retired, Professor Beidleman left Colorado Springs as well as Colorado College. He and his wife moved to Pacific Grove, California. Reba Beidleman gave two reasons why. "There is no possibility of anyone allowing Dick to retire here," she explained, noting that he would receive countless requests to give talks and work on local environmental projects. Also, she noted, "we've given our years to this community, probably two decades of intensive work. And it's still going to the dogs [because of rapid population growth and bad city planning]. I guess we just don't want to be around to see that happen."

Dick Beidleman said he was not enthusiastic about retiring and leaving the educational mainstream. "You lose a lot of stimulation when you leave academia," he explained. "I'll miss the challenge of not keeping up to date on developments in the sciences. I enjoy passing this knowledge on and seeing people develop."[22]

Sadly, shortly after Professor Beidleman's retirement, his wife, Reba, was killed in an automobile-pedestrian accident in California.[23] Dick Beidleman returned periodically to Colorado College, however, taking advantage of the Block Plan by teaching one or two blocks of Biology every once in a while.

CHAPLAIN BURTON RETIRES

More than a quarter century of religious history at Colorado College came to an end in the fall of 1987 when Kenneth Burton stepped down as Dean of Shove Chapel. He had served as campus chaplain and a member of the Religion Department for 26 years. Shove Chapel, built in 1931, was 56 years old when Kenneth Burton ended his tenure there, so Burton had been chaplain at Shove for almost half of the building's existence.

---

[22]Katie Kerwin, "The Man Behind The Lab Coat," *Catalyst*, 11 September 1987, 9.

[23]See Richard G. Beidleman's letter to the Colorado College community written following his wife's death. "Former Faculty Member Feels C.C. Presence At Time Of Need," *Catalyst*, 30 November 1990, 1.

Kenneth Burton was best known to the Colorado College community as the campus pastor. "He has baptized our children; he has married us; he has buried us; he has comforted us in our moments of sadness," noted a College administrator. Burton performed hundreds of weddings in Shove Chapel for the students, alumni, faculty, and staff of the College, and he was often the first College official on the scene when someone had a bad mishap or suffered a personal loss.

But Kenneth Burton made a significant scholarly as well as pastoral contribution to Colorado College. He convinced the College administration that it needed full-time professors teaching about the various religions of the world. During his time as department chairman, the Religion Department added three new faculty members: Douglas Fox in 1963, Joseph Pickle in 1964, and Sam Williams in 1974. Professor Pickle explained: "In a very real sense, Ken built the Religion Department as it is now."

And Kenneth Burton also was a prodigious presence in the classroom. In his early days at the College he taught all the basic Bible courses as well as the history of Christianity. In his later years he ran discussion courses on liberation theology, a religious philosophy that called for personal intervention in the political and social world in addition to seeking spiritual values. Reverend Burton took an interdisciplinary approach, helping to teach general studies courses such as *Contemporary Britain* and *Renaissance Culture.* He twice directed and taught the London portion of the Associated Colleges of the Midwest (ACM) program in London and Florence.

Perhaps Father Burton's most significant contribution was making Shove Chapel a part of the daily life, not just the spiritual life, of the campus. He opened the building to various choral and dramatic productions, and in 1984–1985 he sponsored a series of lunchtime chamber concerts in the Chapel. In 1975 Burton created Shove Council, a student group which met weekly to plan panel discussions on current issues from a spiritual perspective. In all his efforts, Ken Burton worked to keep the Chapel and all its programs fully open to students of all faiths or no faith.

And there was another Kenneth Burton who was a big part of campus life at Colorado College. This was Kenneth Burton the actor. Because

Burton was from England, he had a delightful English accent that equipped him to play any theatrical role calling for a middle-aged Englishman. He often took parts that spoofed the various eccentricities of the English people.

The end of Kenneth Burton's career at Colorado College did not mean the end of his career as a pastoral minister. At the same time he went on Special Senior Status (SSS) at the College, he became assistant priest at the Chapel of Our Saviour, an Episcopal Church located in the Broadmoor area of Colorado Springs.[24]

Kenneth Burton's successor as Chaplain of Colorado College was Bruce Coriell, who earned his B.A. degree at Wheaton College of Illinois and his Master of Divinity at Princeton Theological Seminary. Bruce Coriell said he intended to build upon Reverend Burton's established Chapel programs at the College with an extra emphasis on interdenominational and nondenominational activities. He said he wanted to serve as a bridge between the various religious groups functioning on the campus.[25]

ALTERNATIVE SPRING BREAK

One of the first programs the new Chaplain, Bruce Coriell, introduced to Colorado College was Alternative Spring Break. Instead of going skiing or hitting the beach in some tropical paradise, students were encouraged to spend their spring vacation working to help the poor and homeless. For spring break 1990, Chaplain Coriell organized student work trips to Alamosa, Colorado, and Tiajuana, Mexico. "We're not going in with 'savior' notions [or bringing in] outside ideas," Chaplain Coriell explained. "We will work with the community on what they are already doing."

In Alamosa the students helped with roofing, fencing, and painting the Alamosa Community Greenhouse. They also helped to cook and serve lunch in a homeless shelter. In Tiajuana the students joined Habitat for Humanity, an established international charity, in its efforts to build

---

[24]Dixie Goodenagh, "Burton Bids Shove Chapel Farewell," *Catalyst*, 2 October 1987, 2.

[25]Aaron Moore, "New Chaplain Seeks Unity And Spirituality," *Catalyst*, 3 February 1989, 2. Also see Evan Michael, "Chaplain Excited About Position At C.C.," *Catalyst*, 18 October 1996, 1.

homes for the homeless. The students fashioned a family home out of styrofoam and stucco, and the family that was to live in the home fixed lunch for the students every day.

Chaplain Coriell noted that Alternative Spring Break was designed to benefit the students as well as the communities in which they worked. It is a chance to "get out of your own personal ghetto," Coriell concluded, and observe firsthand the devastating impact of low incomes and homelessness on people.[26]

THE CHILDREN'S CENTER

In September of 1987 Colorado College took a pioneering step by opening a full-time child care center for the children of faculty, administrators, support staff, and students. The College was the first major employer in Colorado Springs to open such a "work place" child care center, and in the ensuing years the facility was frequently visited and studied by private business firms planning their own "at work" child care centers.

The Colorado College Children's Center, as it was officially called, was located in a former private residence at 931 North Nevada Avenue, right across the street from the back of Shove Chapel. It was very convenient for a College employee to drop his or her children at the center and then proceed across campus to the building where he or she worked. The center was designed to take infants, toddlers, and preschoolers. The College provided the building and the equipment for the child care center, but parents paid fees to meet the day-to-day operating expenses.

The founding director of the Children's Center was Kim Fitzgerald. She was a graduate of Tufts University and earned a Master of Science in Elementary Education at the Bank Street College of Education in New York City. She stressed that the College child care facility would emphasize "personalized care" and seek to build "a partnership between the parent and the caretaker." Colorado College parents were encouraged to come over to the center at lunch time or break time to visit with and play with their children.

---

[26]Robert A. Neer, "Spring Break '90; Volunteerism Takes A Vacation," *Catalyst*, 26 January 1990, 7. Robert A. Neer, "Spring Break Offers Rewards; Volunteer Efforts Bring Real Sense Of Satisfaction To Student Participants," *Catalyst*, 23 March 1990, 8.

Colorado College invested $28,000 in the new child care center in order to bring the building up to Colorado state child care requirements. Professor of History Carol Neel chaired the planning board of College employees that pressed for and helped to design the new center. "Even if you don't use the center yourself," Professor Neel said, "it really makes you feel good. It's a worthy project. . . . I've gotten such a good feeling from working on it."[27]

Although men employees made use of the center just as women employees did, the major effect of the Children's Center was to free women to pursue careers and not have to worry about adequate daily care for their small children. The "students" at the child care center soon became a visible and active part of College life. They made good use of the general campus area, often playing outdoor games in the main quadrangle on nice days.

NON-DISCRIMINATION AGAINST GAYS AND LESBIANS

In the fall of 1987 the Board of Trustees added "sexual orientation" to the College's non-discrimination policy. The new policy was adopted unanimously with one abstention. As amended, the policy read: "The Colorado College does not discriminate on the basis of race, color, age, religion, sex, national origin, *sexual orientation*, or physical handicap in its educational programs, activities or employment practices."

President Gresham Riley first proposed an official College policy of non-discrimination toward gays and lesbians in the spring of 1985. "In practice, Colorado College has not discriminated because of sexual orientation," Riley said. "I wanted to see the College's policy fall in line with its practice. The fact is that something like 10 percent of the population (of the United States) is gay or lesbian. I don't know what the population at CC is, but I would imagine that the profile would be about the same. I felt like this minority deserves the same consideration as other minorities concerning discrimination."

Three members of the faculty helped to organize campus support for an official policy of non-discrimination against gays and lesbians. They

[27]Katie Kerwin, "Campus Children's Center Opens," *Catalyst*, 18 September 1987, 1.

were Professor of Anthropology Paul Kutsche, Professor of Sociology Margi Duncombe, and Professor of Geology Bruce Loeffler. During the 1985–1986 academic year between 700 and 1,000 student signatures were collected on a petition supporting the new policy. The day the Board of Trustees adopted the policy, about 75 students and faculty held a rally outside of Armstrong Hall while the Trustees were meeting inside. During the rally a student and gay rights activist, Stefanie Bryson, led a chant that went: "Two, four, six, eight—what makes you think we're all straight."

The Board of Trustees twice rejected the new anti-discrimination policy before finally voting it in. The first rejection was in the spring of 1985, when the Trustees said it was sufficient that the College did not discriminate against gays and lesbians. The second rejection was in the spring of 1986, when the Trustees noted that the policy was not required in order for the College to receive U.S. Government funds.

Once the policy was officially adopted by the Board of Trustees, those who argued for it made it very clear there had been no major discriminatory incidents at Colorado College concerning sexual orientation. "In the 20 years that I've been here," Professor Kutsche noted, "the College has not fired or declined to hire anyone on the basis of sexual orientation."[28]

RHODES SCHOLARS

Todd Breyfogle, a senior majoring in Classics-History-Politics, became the ninth student in Colorado College history to win a prestigious Rhodes Scholarship. A member of the Class of 1988, Breyfogle planned to study Ancient and Modern History at Balliol College at Oxford University in England. His eventual career goal was either college teaching or to go into the ministry.[29]

One year later Paul Markovich, also a member of the Class of 1988, won a Rhodes. He was from Grand Forks, North Dakota, and

---

[28]Don Silver, "Board Adopts Non-Discrimination Clause: Gay Rights Codified," *Catalyst*, 4 December 1987, 1. Also see "Students Rally For Gay Rights And Divestment," *Catalyst*, 4 December 1987, 2.

[29]Brenda Spoelstra, "Breyfogle's On The Rhode," *Catalyst*, 11 December 1987, 1.

graduated *magna cum laude* from Colorado College with a major in Political Economy.

Eight years after that, another Rhodes Scholarship was won by a Colorado College student. Ryan Egeland, Class of 1997, won the prestigious graduate study award to Oxford University in England. A native of Plymouth, Minnesota, Egeland had a 3.9 grade point average and did independent research on the effects of de-icing salts on fresh water lakes. He planned to devote his graduate program to either Bio-Chemistry or Economics.[30]

Then, in 1998, Gregory Criste of Denver, Colorado, won a Rhodes. Criste was a *magna cum laude* graduate of Colorado College with distinction in Classics-History-Politics.

During the two decades of the 1980s and 1990s, Colorado College had five winners of Rhodes Scholarships, an average of one winner every four years. The faculty adviser to Rhodes Scholarship applicants throughout this period was George Butte, Professor of English. A Rhodes Scholar himself in 1968–1970, Professor Butte expanded the Rhodes application process at the College to include confrontational on-campus interviews. During these interviews Colorado College students were prepared for the probing questions and intellectual cross-examination they would receive later at Rhodes Scholarship final interviews.[31]

Colorado College students won prestigious graduate fellowships other than Rhodes Scholarships. For example, in the spring of 1989, Colorado College senior Christina Chamberlain received a Fulbright Fellowship to study post-World War II German literature at the University of Augsburg in Bavaria.[32] One year after that, in the spring of 1990, Colorado College sophomore Mark Glaze won a Truman Fellowship, a cash award to be

---

[30]Megan McKee, "C.C. Boasts Rhodes Scholar," *Catalyst*, 13 December 1996, 3.

[31]Author's notes, interview with George Butte, Colorado College Professor of English, 27 May 1988. Also see George Butte, "The Rhodes Scholarships: Coveted, Misunderstood," *Colorado College Bulletin*, June 1983, 8. Rhodes Scholars from Colorado College were Albert Ellingwood—1910, Walter Barnes—1912, Everett Jackson—1914, Andrew McHendrie—1927, Edward Pelz—1938, Max Power—1963, Philip LeCuyer—1966, Wade Buchanan—1983, Todd Breyfogle—1988, Paul Markovich—1988 (selected in 1989), Ryan Egeland—1997, Gregory Criste—1998.

[32]Julie Ingwersen, "C.C. Senior Receives Fulbright Award," *Catalyst*, 21 April 1989, 13.

used to complete undergraduate school and do two years of graduate study preparing for a career in public service.[33]

OFF ROAD BICYCLE RACING

Bicycles had long been a continuing part of the Colorado College scene, but something new had been added by the late 1980s. A new style of bicycle—called an "off road" or "mountain" bike—was increasingly popular with the students, both for pedaling around campus and in competition. These new bicycles were manufactured with strong frames and large tires so they could be ridden "cross-country" over unpaved dirt paths and similar types of rough terrain.

In the fall of 1987 the Colorado College Cycling Club hosted a collegiate Off Road Challenge. Cyclists from Colorado College, Colorado University at Boulder, and Western State in Gunnison competed for glory and inexpensive prizes on an off road course set up on Stewart Field. Artificial obstacles, such as sharp curves, barriers, and even a log jump, were designed to make the races more exciting and led to such exciting visual events as *slide outs*, *barrier collisions*, and *jump crashes*.

The contest began with a women's competition that attracted eleven contestants. Colorado College's Cathy Porter crossed the finish line first in this race. There was a men's novice contest, with 28 leg-straining participants, which was won by Nate Porter of Colorado College. The final highlight was the Collegiate Expert race, wherein 14 experienced riders pumped, jumped, dodged, and slid around the course for a full 30 minutes. Colorado College junior Nelson Repenning experienced two flat tires but still succeeded in finishing first.[34]

In addition to the three off road bicycle races, there was a special contest called "stylish bike-handling maneuver." This was won by Colorado

[33]"Glaze Awarded Truman Scholarship In National Competition; C.C.C.A. President Recognized For Scholarship, Character, And Leadership," *Catalyst*, 27 April 1990, 4.

[34]Nelson Repenning graduated in 1989 and earned a Ph.D. at Massachusetts Institute of Technology. He joined the faculty at M.I.T. as a Professor of Management. Colorado College Alumni Development Records.

College's Ted Hubbard. His prize? A velvet Elvis Presley rug nicknamed the "Shroud of Memphis."[35]

The bicycling craze at Colorado College, both on road and off road, peaked in the spring of 1989 when the College hosted the Collegiate Cycling National Championships, with both men's and women's teams competing. Over thirty colleges and universities sent bicycle teams to this three day event. The team from the University of Colorado at Boulder won the national title, but the Colorado College pedalers finished fourth, a significant achievement in view of the fact that the top ten teams, except for Colorado College, were all from major universities.[36]

In the fall of 1991 a Colorado College student, Curtis Gunn, won the gold medal in the one kilometer time trial at the National Collegiate Track Cycling Championships in Northbrook, Illinois.[37]

DRINKING AGE RAISED

In order to conform with a new law passed by the United States Congress in Washington, D.C., the Colorado state legislature raised the drinking age in Colorado from 18 years to 21 years. At about the same time, all alcoholic beverages were banned from being served to rushees during the spring 1988 fraternity rush at Colorado College.

The new rules concerning alcohol consumption changed the nature of fraternity rushing at the College. Friday night of rush weekend had traditionally been beer night, with the five fraternities on campus throwing beer parties for their future prospects that generated a "let's show them a good time" atmosphere. Under the old rules beer also was available on Saturday night, but drinking was de-emphasized as fraternity men and

---

[35]Nelson Repenning, "Biker Madness," *Catalyst*, 11 December 1987, 14. Elvis Presley was a popular recording artist from the 1950s who lived in Memphis, Tennessee, and had died unexpectedly in his middle years. Also see Neil Kopitsky, "Cyclers Dominate Early Season Competition," *Catalyst*, 22 April 1988, S–1. Christopher Merriam, "Tiger Cyclers Finish Second In Conference," *Catalyst*, 13 May 1988, S–1.

[36]Alison Dunlap, "C.C. To Host National Cycling Championship; Repenning Becomes C.C.'s First Conference Champion," *Catalyst*, 5 May 1989, 15. Alison Dunlap, "Cycling Team 4th In Nationals," *Catalyst*, 22 September 1989, 19.

[37]Brian Davis, "C.C. Cyclist Finds Gold At National Championship," *Catalyst*, 18 October 1991, 17.

rushees began somewhat more serious conversations about which rushees were going to join which fraternities. Sunday parties were completely dry as the picking and choosing advanced toward final decisions.

Since virtually all fraternity rushees were well under 21 years in age, the new drinking age law required that fraternity rush weekend become completely dry for all three days for all rushees. The fraternity men came up with some imaginative ideas, however, for impressing the rushees as they passed through and made judgements about the various fraternity houses. Kappa Sigma changed its previous International Beer Day to International Food Day. The Kappa Sigmas also decided to keep their Casino Night but with the bar closed. Beta Theta Pi added a non-alcoholic Casino Night to its rush schedule. Sigma Chi continued its German Januaryfest, but minus the traditional German beer.[38]

Another change appeared to be in store for fraternity rushing at Colorado College. Traditionally a number of women students were invited by the fraternities to act as hostesses at rush parties and serve refreshments. In the spring of 1988 this activity was criticized by the Feminist Collective, a campus organization which presented and supported feminist points of view. In a long letter to the student newspaper, the *Catalyst*, the Feminist Collective argued that it was more honest and straightforward for fraternities to rush with their own men members than to bring in women to help with the job. There was also the consideration that the women were allowed to be present only in secondary roles of greeting at the door and serving food and drink. Finally, the Feminist Collective pointed our that the sororities at Colorado College did *not* invite men students to help with their rush parties.[39]

By the early 1990s there was a movement at Colorado College to deemphasize and deglamorize social drinking. In the fall of 1991 the fraternities agreed to stop supplying kegs of free beer at their house parties. Students over the age of 21 who wanted to drink beer at a fraternity party would have to bring their own. Hard liquor was banned completely. The

---

[38]Steve Geraghty, "No Booze For Fraternity Rushees; Frat Houses Gearing Up For First Night Of Dry Rush," *Catalyst*, 15 January 1968, 1.

[39]"The Feminist Collective Speaks; Women: Boycott Frat Rush," *Catalyst*, 15 January 1988, 12.

aisleways for President Riley and his administrative aides to go about their duties.[45]

Dean David Finley was particularly concerned about the confrontational direction the argument over South African divestment was taking at Colorado College. "At one point I became concerned about the physical safety of one of the Trustees," Finley explained. "She was an elderly woman who had done a great deal for the College, and she had to make her way through a group of pushing and shouting students to get to the Armstrong Hall elevator." At another divestment demonstration, one of the active protesters was Dean Finley's daughter, Laura Finley, then an undergraduate student at Colorado College. Finley noted later that a number of College faculty members told him they admired Laura Finley's "courage" in protesting against a College administration that included her own father as Dean.

There was a grim irony to the situation at Colorado College concerning the South African divestment issue. The College had avoided the breakdown between students and administration that had occurred on so many other campuses during the war in Vietnam in the late 1960s and early 1970s. Now, 15 years later, the Colorado College community was experiencing just such a sharp division, with bitter arguments and hurt feelings, over the South Africa issue. "By the late 1980s," Dean David Finley explained, "relationships between the protesting students and the Board of Trustees over South African divestment were rubbed raw."[46]

GENDER-BASED CONTROVERSY

In the late 1980s the hiring and retention of women on the faculty at Colorado College became a hotly debated issue. Margi Duncombe, the chairperson of the Sociology Department, released a study of the outcomes of tenure and third-year review decisions at the College from 1981 to 1988. Of the eleven faculty members who were terminated during that

---

[45]Paul Holchak, "Student Protesters Force Board Of Trustees To Deal With Divestment," *Catalyst*, 18 March 1988, 1. Matt Case, "Rally For Divestment," *Catalyst*, 18 March 1988, 10. Priscilla Pettit, "Board Calls Moratorium On Divestment," 18 March 1988, 11. See also Michelle Chalmers, "Board Decides Not To Divest," *Catalyst*, 16 September 1988, 2.

[46]Author's notes, interview with David Finley, former Dean of Colorado College, 4 December 1997.

period, Professor Duncombe reported, nine were women or members of minority groups. Professor Duncombe said she believed there was no racism or sexism *per se* at Colorado College but that there were structural problems. She explained:

"You have a disparity between the older faculty department heads (who tend to be white males) and the newer faculty, many of whom are women or minorities. What is happening is a greater regard for the established department members than the newer faculty, who represent a less traditional canon and tend to be more involved with non-departmental programs (i.e., Women's Studies, Southwest Studies, Comparative Literature)."

President Gresham Riley was quick to defend the employment policies of the College and the institution's commitment to hiring and retaining a more diversified faculty. He noted that, in the 1981 to 1988 period covered by Professor Duncombe's study, 11 of the 29 professors granted tenure were women. In fact, Riley continued, 50 percent of the women on the Colorado College faculty with tenure received their tenure during the period Riley had been President. In addition, Riley concluded, the terminations cited in Professor Duncombe's study were all carefully reviewed under the College's established procedure for terminations and there was strong documentary support for negative decisions.[47]

The College administration thus reaffirmed its established procedures for reviewing new faculty members. However, the task of defining and achieving racial, ethnic, and gender diversity continued to be a challenging one for Colorado College.[48]

FOOD SERVICE CHANGES

In the late 1980s the Saga food service at Colorado College was taken over by Marriott and renamed Marriott. That was not all that had changed, however, about the College's food service.

---

[47]Professor Duncombe's charges and President Gresham Riley's responses were reported in David Lazerwitz, "Riley Administration Accused Of Bias; Something's Amiss In Renewals Of Women And Minority Faculty Contracts?" *Catalyst*, 20 May 1988, 4. Also see Justin Blum, "Disparity In Faculty Dismissals," *Catalyst*, 1 February 1991, 1. Also see Letter to the Editor from David D. Finley, Dean of the College, entitled "Female And Minority Profs," *Catalyst*, 15 February 1991, 16.

[48]For further information on gender related activities at the time, see Michele Santos, "Committee Strives To Recruit Female Faculty, Set Up Women's Center," *Catalyst*, 16 December 1988, 7.

The days of all the students eating the same meal were long gone. A variety of optional meals were made available to the students at any particular mealtime. In addition to the conventional "meat-and-potatoes" meals, students could choose from a Mexican food bar or a delicatessen-type service. Meats were available at breakfast every day of the week, and students could get "Omelettes to Order" every morning. For fast-food addicts, hamburgers and hot dogs were offered every day for lunch.

Increasing numbers of students expressed concern about eating healthier meals. Marriott responded by offering more vegetarian items, fish, turkey, and whole fruits. Under another new food program, students were no longer required to eat *all* their meals at one of the College dining halls. Flex Plans enabled students to pay for only 11 meals or 15 meals out of the 21 served each week. According to Marriott officials, 80 percent of Colorado College students elected either the 11 meal Flex Plan or the 15 meal Flex Plan.

One thing had not changed about the food service at the College. It remained a major source of student employment. In the fall of 1988 about 250 students, more than 12 percent of the student body, earned money by working for Marriott.[49]

MICHAEL HARRINGTON SPEAKS

A leading social theorist, Michael Harrington, spoke at Colorado College in the fall of 1988 to a standing-room-only crowd in Packard Hall. A professor of Political Science at Queens College, Harrington was the author of a famous book, *The Other America*, which was credited with inspiring the "War on Poverty" social programs of the 1960s.

Harrington's views typified those held by a vocal group of Colorado College students and faculty at that time. He argued that the United States had passed from a "virtuous circle," where the national economy continuously created more demanding and higher-paying jobs, to a "vicious circle," where the only new jobs were low-paying service jobs, such as working in a fast-food restaurant. Harrington argued the most disadvantaged group in U.S. society was the "working poor," persons who had jobs but were not making enough money to lead a decent life.

---

[49]Peter Padilla, "Marriott Isn't Saga Anymore," *Catalyst*, 7 October 1988, 3.

The solution, according to Harrington, was to take away special tax benefits from wealthy Americans. In addition to ending tax welfare for the rich, he called for giving workers a larger voice in running the companies for which they worked. He called for democratization of the economy to go along with the existing democratic political system.

Harrington said the United States was "having the wrong debate." He argued it was a mistake to debate whether or not the U.S. Government should intervene in economic affairs. "That question was answered 50 years ago. The issue is who the [U.S.] Government *is*, and who the government will intervene on behalf of."

In the international sphere, Michael Harrington saw the United States economy internationalizing "to an unprecedented degree." He characterized large multi-national corporations as "the enemy." He lamented there were no worldwide people's institutions or worldwide trade unions to check the power of the multi-national giants.

At the end of his talk, Professor Harrington called on the students in the audience to do as he had done and live their lives dedicated to an ideal. He described such an action as living a "life of joy." He concluded that only visionaries who "marry their visions" could bring real reform to an existing society which strongly resists change.[50]

The One-Week Symposium Returns

One of the casualties of the Block Plan had been the week-long January Symposium held at the beginning of second semester. This five-day academic festival of speakers, panel discussions, films, and artistic performances had not fit into the crowded calendar created by the Nine Block Year. When the College went on the Eight Block Year in the fall of 1988, however, that freed up enough time in the schedule to bring back the week-long Symposium in January of 1989.

The topic chosen for the revived January Symposium was *Intimacy*. Professor Alvin Boderman, who had organized the *Violence* and *Ecology* symposiums in 1969 and 1970, once again assumed the task of lining up the speakers, organizing the panels, ordering the films, and attending to

[50]Rachel Berrington and Mark Glaze, "Democratic Socialist Speaks Beyond Election," *Catalyst*, 4 November 1988, 4.

the myriad other duties required to produce five full days filled with learned lectures, challenging thoughts, and lively discussions.

The subject of *Intimacy* enabled students, faculty, alumni, and members of the Colorado Springs community to explore the various ways in which human beings relate to one another and to their natural environment. Most of the speakers focused on love relationships between men and women. Two of the most popular lectures were entitled "Intimacy, Passion, Commitment: The Triangle of Love" and "Men, Women, Sex, and Intimacy: Different Strokes, Common Misunderstandings." The program also included Romanovsky and Phillips, a homosexual singer-songwriter duo who performed a concert of their own works.

But a number of the speakers attempted to find a broader definition of intimacy than sexual attraction. Germain Grisez concluded that the most intimate relationships are created when the people in them are working toward a common goal, such as volunteering in the community, doing a research and writing project, creating an artistic or dramatic production, or raising and educating children.

The revived January Symposium was a success, with many of the lectures drawing overflow crowds. As with past symposiums at Colorado College, the opportunity to meet with the various speakers and performers at coffee-and-conversation meetings was rated one of the best aspects of the *Intimacy* Symposium.[51]

In following years the College held January symposiums on such topics as *Wealth*, *The Future*, and *Spirituality And Religion*.[52]

In-Room Telephones

In the fall of 1989 Colorado College students acquired an important convenience and luxury—the ability to have one's own telephone in one's own dormitory room. The College installed the requisite campus-wide wiring so

[51]Dianna Litvak, Nicole Condit, Susan Anderson, Courtney Jackson, and Julie Ingwerson, "Intimacy: Was It More Than Just Sex?" *Catalyst*, 27 January 1989, 12–13. Also see Ian Blake Newman, "Gay Duo Returns For Second C.C. Concert," *Catalyst*, 7 April 1989, 18.

[52]Alexander Durst, "Symposium On Wealth," *Catalyst*, 1 December 1989, 1. Jennifer Jose, "Crowds Came Back For The Future," *Catalyst*, 25 January 1991, 3. Lakis Polycarpou, "Symposium Features Christian Writer," *Catalyst*, 4 February 1994, 7. Lakis Polycarpou, "C.C. Symposium Lacks Real Diversity, *Catalyst*, 4 February 1994, 9.

that there was a telephone jack in every room in all the residence halls. Students could buy a telephone or bring one from home, plug it in, and start making and receiving telephone calls. A Personal Security Code (PSC) was given to each student so that long distance calls could be properly charged.

Previously there were one or two telephones located in the hallway of each wing of a dormitory. Students whose rooms were close to these telephones felt pressure to answer them all the time, and it was bothersome to have to take messages for students who were not in their rooms when they received a call. Jenn Kuehner, a member of the junior class, said she liked the new system. "When we get phone calls, we get them," she explained. "On our wing last year, people wouldn't come to get us. It's also nicer because you can sit in your room and talk and there's not people walking by and listening. Privacy is a big factor."[53]

LENNOX HOUSE BECOMES A DORMITORY

The fall of 1989 also saw the conversion of the large former residence at 1001 North Nevada Avenue from a fraternity house to a coed dormitory. The previous occupants of the building, a well-known national fraternity, lost their charter following a series of disciplinary incidents. The College spent about $30,000 to recarpet and repaint the house as well as strip, sand, and revarnish the woodwork. As soon as it was known these new dormitory rooms were going to be available, they were quickly taken in the College's annual residence hall "lottery" for room assignments.

This large and commodious Moorish style house had long been a colorful part of the history of Colorado Springs and Colorado College. It was built in 1900 for William Lennox, a Cripple Creek millionaire who served as a Trustee of the College from 1901 to 1936. In 1937 the structure was given to the College, named Lennox House, and for 22 years served as the student social center. In 1959 the student center was moved to the newly built Rastall Center, and Lennox House became the home of a fraternity for the next 30 years. The name Lennox House was revived when the building became a dormitory in 1989.

---

[53]Christina Ganong, "New Phone System 'Brrings' Varied Reactions," *Catalyst*, 15 September 1989, 2. Also see Jennie Randall, "College Tries New Phone System," *Catalyst*, 16 September 1994, 1. Ondine Boulter, "Phone Changes Add Options," *Catalyst*, 16 September 1994, 9.

ENTER WOOGLIN'S

A new campus hangout came into existence when two Colorado College students, Dan Cross of the class of 1989 and Linda LaFollette of the class of 1990, founded Wooglin's Deli. This new restaurant, which served hot and cold sandwiches in a wide variety of combinations, was located in the little group of College-oriented stores at the southeast corner of Cache La Poudre and Tejon streets. Wooglin's had the atmosphere of a New York or Chicago delicatessen, with wooden booths as well as dining tables available for its customers to sit, eat, and chat. Dan Cross was a recent Philosophy major at the College, and Linda LaFollette was an Art Studio major.

Almost instantly Wooglin's became a big part of campus life at Colorado College. The food was more substantial and considerably more interesting than the fare provided at Benjamin's, the snack bar in the Worner Center. In addition, Wooglin's was willing to deliver its sandwiches to the dormitories and meeting rooms at the College. It became popular with both administrators and faculty to set up luncheon meetings in the Spencer Center office building or Armstrong Hall and order in a batch of sandwiches and beverages from Wooglin's.

The student newspaper, the *Catalyst*, commented at length on the need for a casual and relaxed rendezvous close to the campus. The raising of the drinking age to 21 years, and a recent series of College and police crackdowns on drug use and underage drinking, left the students feeling their social lives were being limited. The *Catalyst* printed:

"C.C. has nearly everything a student needs to survive independently from society. We have our own bookstore, our own parties, our own President, our own paper, our own condoms, and our own fabricated problems. But let's face it, the administration and the faculty, with the help of the Colorado Springs Police, is systematically peeling our social life away. The Worner Center is steadily becoming the only social outlet aside from aborted [beer parties] highlighted by friendly chats with [police] officers and their pets [police dogs]. C.C. needs a retreat; a place to eat, meet friends and relieve the stress of the Block Plan—legally!"[54]

---

[54]Bret Bishop, "Wooglin's Deli Coming Soon; C.C. Grads Provide Alternative Fare," *Catalyst*, 22 September 1989, 5. Also see "Wooglin's Opens," *Catalyst*, 17 November 1989, 6.

Apparently Wooglin's Deli met that need very well. It rapidly became a most popular place for students, faculty, and administrators to get together, eat, and, upon occasion, relax.

THE JERRY CARLE WEIGHT ROOM

Following a fund-raising drive, particularly among former football players, Colorado College added a weight room to El Pomar Sports Center. The new weight room was named in honor of Jerry Carle, who was retiring after 33 years as the football coach at the College.[55] It was located in the west end of the basement of El Pomar next to the turf room.

George Lyon, a member of the Board of Trustees from Minneapolis-St. Paul, Minnesota, took the lead in raising the necessary funds.[56] The Jerry Carle Weight Room included many kinds of exercise machines as well as weight lifting paraphernalia. There were exercise bicycles, cross-country skiing machines, and a wide variety of weights and dumbbells.[57] In subsequent years stair-climbing machines and treadmills for running and walking exercise were added.

The weight room was an instant hit with faculty and administrators as well as students. Faculty and administrators were more likely to work out in the weight room at lunchtime and in the early afternoon. Late in the day the students took over, with members of intercollegiate sports teams having priority in the late afternoon.

A plaque on the wall in the new weight room noted coach Carle's contribution to sports history at Colorado College and listed the names of those who gave money to help build the weight room. There also was a framed drawing of coach Carle in his coaching shirt with his coach's whistle hanging around his neck.

COLLEGE RANKINGS

By the late 1980s something new and controversial had been added to college and university rankings in the United States. A weekly newsmagazine, *U.S. News & World Report*, began publishing its own rankings in an annual guide entitled "America's Best Colleges." Because *U.S. News* was widely read

---

[55]Ed Pells, "Coach Carle Retires," *Catalyst*, 1 December 1989, 1. Ed Pells, "Carle: A Permanent Fixture At C.C.," *Catalyst*, 1 December 1989, 17.

[56]Gresham Riley oral history, 27 May 1992, 23.

[57]Ed Pells, "Jerry Carle Weight Room Opens," *Catalyst*, 6 October 1989, 21.

and copies of the magazine were found in thousands of homes throughout the nation, colleges and universities became sensitive to how they fared in the magazine's annual evaluations.

Colorado College did very well in the first years of the *U.S. News* rankings of liberal arts colleges. For three years the College placed in the top 25 in the United States, according to *U.S. News*, and one year was noted as an "Up-and-Comer" among the best liberal arts institutions. *U.S. News* also occasionally noted the College's unique Block Plan and the unusual opportunities it provided for closer student-faculty relationships.

In the fall of 1989 Colorado College dropped out of the "Top 25" in the *U.S. News & World Report* rankings. President Gresham Riley was quick to point out that the evaluation system used by *U.S. News* was constantly being changed and that it was very difficult for anyone, no matter how well informed, to arbitrarily establish that one college was better than another. "I would have preferred that we had maintained our position on that [Top 25] list," President Riley said, "but on the other hand I do not conclude from our absence that we are any less of an institution than we were in previous years."[58]

Nonetheless, the annual rankings of liberal arts colleges by *U.S. News & World Report* became a significant annual event for the students, faculty, administrators, and alumni of Colorado College. The College community was elated when the ranking of Colorado College went up and sad and concerned when it went down.[59]

THE CARTER HERBARIUM

In the spring of 1990 the College named its 10,000 specimen plant collection for Professor of Biology Jack L. Carter. The Carter Herbarium

---

[58]Jeremy Treister, "C.C. Drops From Top 25," *Catalyst*, 3 November 1989, 1.

[59]Julie Bohl, "C.C. Drops In Rankings," *Catalyst*, 9 October 1992, 1. Kathryn Mohrman, President of the College, "Mohrman Claims Magazine Poll Lacks Proper Focus; C.C. Cracks Coveted *U.S. News & World Report* Top Twenty List," *Catalyst*, 23 September 1994, 7. Sarah Newton, "College Holds Steady At Number 28," *Catalyst*, 20 September 1996, 1. "C.C. Among The Best," *Access*, September 1997, 1. In the "1998 Annual Guide to America's Best Colleges," *U.S. News* rated Colorado College 31st among the top 40 liberal arts colleges (tied for 30th with Kenyon College in Ohio). See "Best National Liberal Arts Colleges," *U.S. News & World Report*, 1 September 1997, 106. In 1999 Colorado College tied for 24th with Barnard College, Connecticut College, Macalester College, Oberlin College, and the University of the South. See "National Liberal Arts Colleges," *U.S. News and World Report*, 31 August 1998, 90.

was located on the Biology floor of the new Barnes Science Center and the collection was made readily available for student use.

Jack Lee Carter earned his B.S. and M.S. degrees at Emporia State College in Kansas and his Ph.D. at the University of Iowa. He joined the Colorado College Biology Department in 1968. He greatly expanded the herbarium at the College, creating the finest collection of southern Colorado flora in the nation. One result of opening the collection to student use was that students began contributing significant plants to the collection. Through an international network of herbariums set up to share specimens, Professor Carter also greatly expanded the non-Colorado portion of the collection.[60]

MEN'S AND WOMEN'S CROSS COUNTRY GOES TO NATIONALS

In the fall of 1990 the men's cross country team, for the first time in the College's history, qualified for the National competition, which was held at Grinnell College in Iowa. More than 180 runners, representing 21 college teams, entered the race. "It was an incredible field," said cross country coach Ted Castaneda. "[It was] somewhat intimidating, but all teams deserved to be there, and we were no different!"

When the long run over a hilly and rolling course was completed, Colorado College ranked 15th out of the 21 teams. The top cross country runner for the College was Torre Pena, who finished 52nd. Pat Judge crossed the line close behind Pena in 67th place.[61]

In 1996 the College had outstanding men's and women's cross country teams. Both teams qualified to go to the Division III National Cross Country Championships held in Rock Island, Illinois. The women's team finished eighteenth in the nation. The men's team placed nineteenth.[62]

STUDENTS PROTEST WAR PREPARATIONS

Approximately 150 students and faculty rallied in front of Worner Center in the late fall of 1990 to protest United States Government preparations

---

[60]Timothy Van Luven, "Herbarium Dedicated To Jack L. Carter," *Catalyst*, 23 March 1990, 2.

[61]"C.C. Cross Country Team Finishes 15th At Nationals; First National Ranking In C.C. History," *Catalyst*, 30 November 1990, 23.

[62]Sally Wurtzler, "Cross Country Makes History; Team Advances To Nationals After Meet In Claremont," *Catalyst*, 15 November 1996, 17. Eric Coe, "Harriers Set Personal Records In Championship Meet; Cross Country A Success At Nationals," *Catalyst*, 6 December 1996, 17.

for a possible war in the Middle East. Following the Iraq invasion of the independent nation of Kuwait in August of 1990, U.S. President George Bush ordered a major buildup of U.S. military forces in Saudi Arabia along the Iraq border. President Bush made it clear he would use those military forces if necessary to liberate Kuwait from Iraqi rule.

The protest leaders emphasized the point that, if the military draft were reinstituted to provide recruits to fight a war with Iraq, a significant number of Colorado College students would be drafted and sent to the battlefront. A list of all 20-year-old male students, allegedly the first group to be subject to a revived draft, was read aloud. Later in the day the war protesters staged an informal march along the sidewalks of downtown Colorado Springs. They carried a homemade banner tie-dyed with the words: "No War: There Are Alternatives."

Not everyone who attended the rally was opposed to U.S. military action against Iraq. Chuck Kole, a Colorado College student and a member of the U.S. Army reserves, commented: "I really don't think you guys are helping. We're missing a big issue. We're not going to let heinous aggression go unchecked anywhere in the world." He was joined by sophomore Kristin Thomas, who said the protest was aimed at the wrong people. She explained: "We can't blame the soldiers. And if we pull out it's going to be slaughter in the Middle East."[63]

Early in 1991 President Bush, with the full support of the United Nations, launched the long-anticipated U.S. invasion of Iraq. The military campaign went so swiftly and the war ended so quickly—with a United Nations victory—that there was little opportunity for protest. The nation of Kuwait was freed from Iraqi rule, and the United States then withdrew its military forces without overthrowing the existing government in Iraq. United Nations military casualties were unusually light. Although the student and faculty protests of the Iraq war were sincere and very intense, they quickly ended when victory was achieved.[64]

---

[63]Robert A. Neer, "Members Of C.C. Community Rally Against War," *Catalyst*, 14 December 1990, 1.

[64]Robert A. Neer, "Community Protests War," *Catalyst*, 25 January 1991, 1. Justin Blum, "War Protestors March To Military Recruiting Center," *Catalyst*, 22 February 1991, 1.

DICK WOOD RETIRES

The man who presided over the admission of three decades of college students to Colorado College retired in the spring of 1991. Richard E. Wood stopped reading applicant files and put more time into sailing his 24-foot Black Watch sailboat.

Dick Wood served in the Navy during World War Two. When the war was over, he went to Dickinson College in Pennsylvania, earning his undergraduate degree in 1952. After getting a Master's degree at Columbia University in New York, he moved to Colorado and raised funds for Denver University. He came to Colorado College as a fund-raiser in 1959 and, two years later in 1961, took charge of the Admissions office.

One of the major achievements of Dick Wood's tenure as Director of Admissions was the abandonment of the 60 percent male, 40 percent female admissions ratio. Wood noted that basing admission solely on merit produced an almost equal male-to-female ratio at the College.

Dick Wood recalled that, when he first came to Colorado College in the 1960s, the Admissions office operated "by the seat of [its] pants" and on "charm and energy." Later on, Wood said, the College added more pizzazz to admission operations by distributing action-packed videos about student life and colorful view books of the major features of the campus.

Minority enrollment increased to about 10 percent of the student body during Dick Wood's years as Admissions Director. He encouraged the College to increase diversity on the campus by recruiting Hispanic and Native American students as well as African-Americans. At the time he retired, over half of the Native American students attending Associated Colleges of the Midwest (ACM) colleges were at Colorado College.

Upon the occasion of Dick Wood's retirement, President Gresham Riley congratulated him for his "ambassadorial role" when representing the College on recruiting trips across the nation. Riley also praised Wood for the "stature, dignity, [and] professionalism he has brought to the whole admissions process."[65]

---

[65]Jason Jarvis, "Search Begins For Admissions Director As Wood Sails Into The Sunset Of September," *Catalyst*, 25 January 1991, 3. For a retrospective view of Dick Wood's years at Colorado College, see Richard E. Wood oral history, 11 December 1991.

CHAPTER 13

Two Years of Transition

In the fall of 1991 College President Gresham Riley took a one-semester sabbatical from his presidential duties and, with his wife Pamela, took up temporary residence in London, England. Using their London accommodations as a base of operations, the Rileys periodically toured on the European continent.

During President Riley's absence, Professor of Political Science Thomas Cronin became the Acting President of Colorado College. A widely published scholar on the subject of the United States presidency, Cronin had taught at the College since 1979 and occupied the McHugh Family Distinguished Chair in American Institutions and Leadership. Shortly after he was appointed Acting President, Cronin announced the publication of his latest book, an in-depth study of Colorado state government and politics coauthored with his close friend and colleague, Political Science Professor Robert Loevy.[1]

The Cronin Administration

In his new role of Acting President, Thomas Cronin sought to have a consensual impact on the Colorado College community. He frequently went on walking tours of the campus, visiting with students and faculty and acquainting himself with the inner-workings of the institution. He made a particular effort to reach out to the staff employees of the College and make certain their concerns were heard and acted upon.

The major change at the College during Thomas Cronin's acting presidency was the construction of tasteful stone signs in the medians of

[1]Cheri Gette, "Loevy And Cronin Write For Political Series," *Catalyst*, 22 February 1991, 3.

Cascade and Nevada avenues that identified the name of the College and the year of its founding—1874. The signs were heavily landscaped with shrubbery and, in the summer months, were surrounded by blooming flowers. But Tom Cronin was quick to point out that the decision to build these attractive new signs had been made the previous semester while Gresham Riley was occupying the presidential office.[2]

Anxious to show off the accomplishments of Colorado College students, Acting President Cronin arranged for a display of student designed and printed posters that had advertised major campus events over the years. The posters, printed by students working under the direction of Professor of Art James Trissel, were framed and hung in the Coburn Gallery in Worner Center for one month. The display was entitled *A Visual Diary of Colorado College* and featured posters advertising everything from poetry readings to major lectures to dance and music performances.[3] The framed posters later were used to permanently decorate the walls in Gaylord Hall in Worner Center and in the west wing of Armstrong Hall near the President's office.

Thomas Cronin's time as Acting President of Colorado College turned out to be excellent preparation for his academic future. One year later, in the spring of 1993, he was named President of Whitman College in Walla Walla, Washington. Similar to Colorado College, Whitman was a small liberal arts college (1,200 students) with a strong teaching tradition. "I love C.C.," Cronin told the *Catalyst,* and he said the thought of teaching his final class at the College was "saddening."[4]

GRESHAM RILEY RESIGNS

In January of 1992 the student newspaper, the *Catalyst,* reported that President Gresham Riley had announced his resignation as President of Colorado College. The resignation was to take effect on June 30, 1992. Riley and his wife, Pamela Riley, had returned from sabbatical in England at the end of the 1991–1992 fall semester. Riley carried out his duties as

---

[2]Recollection of the author of a conversation with Thomas Cronin, Acting President of Colorado College, 1 July 1991 to 31 December 1991.

[3]Betsey Russell, "Experience 'A Visual Diary Of Colorado College,' " *Catalyst,* 11 October 1991, 15.

[4]John Anthony, "Cronin Moves On; Professor Heads For Walla Walla," *Catalyst,* 14 May 1993, 1.

President throughout the following spring semester. He presided at the 1992 graduation ceremonies.[5]

THE STRUGGLE OVER PREEMINENCE

Gresham Riley's tenure in office included the most successful fund-raising drive in Colorado College history, the Colorado College Campaign, which eventually raised $53 million. He increased the endowment from $40 million to $175 million. He oversaw the construction of two of the College's most admired new buildings—the Worner Campus Center and the Barnes Science Center. He enlarged and professionalized the administration of the College to make it more informed and effective. He brought in national consultants in an effort to get the College the best professional advice available. And he involved the entire campus community in the decision-making process more than any previous President of the College ever had done.

Gresham Riley was committed to making Colorado College one of the preeminent liberal arts colleges in the United States. To accomplish this task, President Riley was willing to continually raise the College's tuition as well as its faculty salaries. To keep and attract competent faculty, Riley strongly supported the Eight Block Year so that the Block Plan would lose some of its reputation for creating heavy faculty workloads. Riley thus was willing to propose rapid increases in the College budget and use the money to undertake new programs that enhanced the College's growing academic reputation.[6]

But there was another viewpoint in the Colorado College community. This other viewpoint held that the time had come to *downsize* both the budget and the academic ambitions of the College. This view held that the 1990s were going to be tough times for liberal arts colleges such as Colorado College. The applicant pool of available high school graduates was going to be so small that observers were referring to the *Baby Bust* generation, a term of contrast to the large *Baby Boom* generation that entered colleges and universities from the 1960s to the 1980s. Prudence dictated that tuition increases and faculty salaries be kept under strict control. The

---

[5]Mark Glaze, "Board Moves To Find Riley's Successor," *Catalyst*, 31 January 1992, 1.

[6]For Gresham Riley's view of his activities and accomplishments as President of Colorado College, see Gresham Riley oral history, 27 May 1992, 38–43.

sentiment was frequently heard that the College needed to be run in the manner that many business corporations were being run at the time, with a general philosophy of cutting back and controlling expenses. It was not the time to be emphasizing high educational attainment.

Supporters of downsizing the College pointed to the mild recession that gripped the United States during 1990 and 1991. This recession was serious enough to become a major issue in the 1992 election for President of the United States. George Bush, the incumbent Republican President, was defeated by his Democratic challenger, William Clinton, mainly on the issue of the faltering economy.

And there were a number of voices, some of them on the faculty, that did not want to see the College change very much. These persons believed that the drive for preeminence would leave behind "our kind of student," the highly qualified but not exceptional student who could not get into a prestige college or university but who could get into Colorado College and get a quality education. If Colorado College became a prestige institution itself, it was argued, such students would no longer be able to get accepted at Colorado College, and part of the College's tradition would be lost.[7]

President Riley not only pressed forward with his goal of making Colorado College a preeminent liberal arts institution, he was willing to argue strongly and publicly that was the direction in which he wanted the College to go. He also staunchly and outspokenly defended the principle of freedom of speech in academia, even when that speech took the form of aggressive and confrontational protests against the College's investments in racially-segregated South Africa.

David Finley, Dean of the College at the time Riley left the presidency, noted: "[A number of people] thought of Colorado College as a good, strong regional college best served by having limited ambitions. They wanted to consolidate recent financial and enrollment gains and not press too strenuously forward. They did not see Colorado College as the prestigious national college that Gresham Riley was pressing for."[8]

As for Gresham Riley, he gave this view of his years at Colorado College:

---

[7]Recollection of the author.

[8]Author's notes, interview with David D. Finley, former Dean of Colorado College, 4 December 1997.

"I knew all along I was *not* going to retire from academic life as the President of Colorado College. If I had retired from the presidency at age 65 in the year 2003, I would have been President 22 years. That would have been too long. I had already seen the need to 'repot' myself someday at another institution. When the Colorado College Campaign was successfully completed and the $53 million raised, I even conversed with a number of people about it."[9]

"But differences with [various groups] at the College contributed to my leaving when I did. I had high aspirations for the College, and I believed there was no danger of high tuition increases pricing us out of the market. I believed we could afford to strive to be one of the finest liberal arts colleges in the nation. I believed we had the financial resources and the people who could do it."

"I tried to convince [people] that controversy is a sign of health in an educational institution. I called for a more open and inclusive decision-making style that encouraged lively discussions and a degree of conflict. Such conflicts emerged on the campus over South African investments, outlawing discrimination based on sexual preferences, and the adoption of the Eight Block Year."

"Encouraging discussion and controversy the way I did made [life on the Colorado College campus] more challenging during my presidency. It made it more challenging for me, too."

Five years after his departure from Colorado College, Gresham Riley looked back with pleasure and accomplishment on his tenure as the College's President. "Not many people," he said, "get the opportunity to shape a quality educational institution for 11 years."[10] He also noted that he had been part of a continuum of Colorado College presidents, those serving after World War II, who had sought to restore the College to the achievement and reputation of the earlier years under President William F. Slocum. Riley concluded: "I hope future historians will write . . . that I . . . helped an institution that *did* have a glorious past return to that past."[11]

---

[9]One of the persons who recalled such a conversation was David D. Finley, Dean of Colorado College 1987–1992. Author's notes, interview with David D. Finley, former Dean of Colorado College, 4 December 1997.

[10]Author's notes, interview with Gresham Riley, 11 June 1997.

[11]Gresham Riley oral history, 27 May 1992, 46.

Although the Riley presidency was over, Gresham and Pamela Riley remained an occasional part of the Colorado College scene. Gresham Riley returned to the campus to help celebrate the inauguration of his successor, and he periodically visited the College, socializing with old friends and lunching with the general faculty in Gates Common Room.[12] Pamela Riley returned now and then to teach a course for the Drama and Dance Department and direct a play.[13]

Two years after leaving Colorado College, Gresham Riley was appointed the President of the Pennsylvania Academy of Fine Arts in Philadelphia. He served in that position for four years, from 1994 to 1998. This premier school of the arts was founded in 1805 by renowned artist Charles Wilson Peale, who had been inspired by U.S. President Thomas Jefferson to attempt to create an "American School of Art." Riley took over an institution of 250 undergraduate students, 50 graduate students, and 1,000 part time non-degree students. He also took charge of a museum housing one of the nation's finest collections of historic and contemporary works by American artists.[14]

Gresham and Pamela Riley entered happily into the social, educational, and intellectual life of the city of Philadelphia. They purchased and moved into a four-story Colonial row house, built in 1769, located in the newly-fashionable Old City section of downtown Philadelphia. "Pamela and I succeeded in being 'repotted,'" Gresham Riley said. "It was rewarding to move on and do something enriching in an exciting community."[15]

A New Mountain Cabin

During the 1991–1992 school year, the College began the process of rebuilding the Colorado College Cabin, a foothill retreat located in the mountains west of Divide, Colorado. The rustic Cabin, built mainly with

---

[12]Recollection of the author.

[13]For instance, Pamela Riley taught *American Women Playwrights* during Block 3, 1997–1998. *Colorado College Catalog 1997–1998*, 95. Also see Tim Farrell, "Musical Production 'Alice' Shows Feminine Life," *Catalyst*, 12 December 1997, 3B.

[14]"Former C.C. President Elected To Another," *Catalyst*, 11 February 1994, 2.

[15]Author's notes, interview with Gresham Riley, 11 June 1997.

student labor, had burned down in a fire on May 18, 1991. There was no one from the College at the Cabin at the time it burned down, so the exact cause of the fire was never discovered.

The Cabin was built in 1980 on mountain land given to the College by alumnus Donald Cameron. Less than an hour's drive from the campus, the Cabin proved to be a relaxing close-in retreat for getting away from the urban atmosphere and hurried pace of the College itself. Student groups often went up to the Cabin for extended meetings, and occasionally a professor would take his or her class up to the Cabin for a few days or a weekend of study in a more natural environment.

The new Cabin was built by a professional construction company rather than students. It had complete kitchen facilities and enough bunks in a sleeping loft to house an entire Block Plan class of students overnight. There were large outdoor porches for sitting out in the sunshine and gazing at the scenery. The new Cabin sat on a high hilltop and, like the old cabin that burned, had a spectacular view of the surrounding mountains.[16]

John Sheridan, the College Librarian, and his wife, Dindy Sheridan, started a popular tradition at the new Cabin. Every Thanksgiving the Sheridans invited new members of the faculty and support staff to join them at the Cabin for a big Thanksgiving dinner. Any students who were staying on campus with no place to go for Thanksgiving also were invited. International students, in particular, took advantage of this opportunity to enjoy a unique United States holiday in a cozy and attractive Rocky Mountain setting.

The College Chaplain, Bruce Coriell, joined John and Dindy Sheridan in sponsoring this happy event. "It is a friendly place to be for those who can't be home for whatever reason," Coriell explained. "It is better than eating Thanksgiving dinner out of a microwave." Melissa Gilbert, a student who took advantage of the Thanksgiving hospitality at the Cabin, added: "It is a non-traditional, 90s kind of Thanksgiving—friends, family, friends of friends, semi-strangers, complete strangers—and everyone has a good time."

---

[16]Marcy McDermott, "C.C. Cabin II Resurrection In Progress," *Catalyst*, 13 September 1991, 2. Stephanie Bailey, "C.C. Cabin Nears Completion," *Catalyst*, 8 May 1992, 2.

The Sheridans and Chaplain Coriell said they would continue the Thanksgiving tradition at the Cabin as long as there were members of the College community who needed a substitute family on Thanksgiving Day. And John Sheridan pointed out that not having television at the Cabin was a plus rather than a minus. "For all we know," Sheridan said, "all the football games could have been cancelled. Just going for a crisp walk following the meal was good enough for us."[17]

ROLLERBLADING AND SKATEBOARDING

Every fad that swept the United States tended to find its way to the students at Colorado College. In the early 1990s rollerblading became popular on the campus. Students would put on the expensive rollerblades, which were actually the latest version of sidewalk rollerskates, and glide quickly and effortlessly about the campus. The major drawback appeared to be the many scrapes and bruises rollerbladers received when they lost their balance and fell down while skating at high speed. The well-equipped student rollerblader sported a helmet, knee pads, and elbow pads to minimize the damage from the occasional "wipe out."[18]

Although it was not a new fad, a number of students used skateboards to get themselves more quickly from place to place at the College. The flat boards with roller wheels on the bottom were propelled by the student putting one foot on the board and pushing-off with the other foot on the sidewalk or street. The major advantage of a skate board over a bicycle was that the student, upon arriving at his or her destination, could take a skate board into the dormitory room or the classroom. A bicycle had to be locked up outdoors where, despite the lock, it might be stolen. One of the bigger thrills in skateboarding at Colorado College appeared to be rolling at high speed down the ramped underpass that tunneled under Tutt Library and gliding up the other side.[19]

---

[17]Anne Gatchel, "Trip To C.C. Cabin Provides Thanksgiving Away From Home," *Catalyst*, 10 November 1995, 13. Bret Bell, "Thanksgiving At The C.C. Cabin; [Administrators] Help Those Who Cannot Go Home For The Holiday," *Catalyst*, 1 December 1995, 2.

[18]Photo by Robin Rosenberg, "Sophomore Matt Moyer is one of the many C.C. students who have taken up rollerblading," *Catalyst*, 13 September 1991, 5. Chris Hildebraud, "Rollerbladers Finally Get The Street Respect They Deserve," *Catalyst*, 3 May 1996, 17.

[19]Andrea Godsman, "Skateboarders Voice Opinion About On-Campus Rights," *Catalyst*, 14 November 1997, 5.

THE COLORADO PRESIDENTIAL PRIMARY

On March 3, 1992, the state of Colorado held its first-ever presidential primary. The Colorado presidential primary was very much a "Made At Colorado College" product because the initial push for the primary came from Political Science Professor Robert Loevy. The successful bill to create the Colorado presidential primary was carried at the state legislature in Denver by state Senator Mike Bird, a Professor of Economics at Colorado College. Professors Loevy and Bird teamed together to co-chair the political committee that won approval of the state's electorate for the Colorado presidential primary at the November 1990 general election.[20]

The new Colorado presidential primary gave Colorado College students who wished to do so the opportunity to register to vote in Colorado and thereby participate directly in the presidential nominating process. Any student who was a U.S. citizen and 18-years-old or older could register in Colorado and then vote in either the Republican or the Democratic presidential primary.

Because the Colorado presidential primary was scheduled so early in the primary calendar, all the major candidates for both the Democratic and Republican presidential nominations campaigned in the state, and most made at least one campaign swing through Colorado Springs. The excitement came directly to the Colorado College campus when former California Governor Jerry Brown, one of the three leading competitors for the Democratic nomination, gave a standing-room-only speech in Gates Common Room in Palmer Hall.

A liberal Democrat, Jerry Brown called for an immediate cut of 50 percent in the United States military budget. The money saved, the former California Governor said, should be spent on high speed intercity trains and harnessing solar and wind power. He supported a national health care program and a conservation corps to put unemployed youths to work improving public parks and recreation areas. He particularly attacked nuclear facilities, particularly the one at Rocky Flats on the outskirts of Denver. Considerable numbers of Colorado College students

---

[20]For a detailed description of the creation of the Colorado presidential primary, see Robert D. Loevy, *The Flawed Path To The Presidency 1992: Unfairness And Inequality In The Presidential Selection Process* (Albany, NY: State University of New York Press, 1994), 46–50.

and faculty had participated in protest demonstrations at Rocky Flats over the years.[21]

Jerry Brown's campaign speech at Colorado College, and those given at other colleges and universities around the state, appeared to work with Colorado Democrats. Jerry Brown narrowly won the Colorado Democratic presidential primary, and the surprise victory gave a big boost to his campaign. Brown was defeated, however, in subsequent primaries in other states, and Arkansas Governor Bill Clinton won the 1992 Democratic nomination and was elected U.S. President the following November.

A New Dean

Prior to his departure from Colorado College, outgoing President Gresham Riley appointed Political Science Professor Timothy Fuller to be the Dean of the College. Fuller replaced David Finley, also a Professor of Political Science, who resigned after serving five years as Dean. Once again there were raised eyebrows—but no formal complaints—when the third Political Science professor in a row (Brooks, Finley, Fuller) was named to the deanship.

Professor Finley returned to the classroom and his students. As a specialist in Soviet-American relations, he had his work cut out for him. During the five years he served as Dean, the Berlin Wall was torn down, the former Eastern Europe was democratized, and the Soviet Union broke up into a number of independent states. Professor Finley had to review and prepare a great deal of new material in order to keep his classes current with the massive recent changes in the world situation.

In appointing Professor Timothy Fuller the new Dean, President Riley said his choice was influenced by Fuller's well-known commitment to the liberal arts college ideal. "I am confident that Tim Fuller is the right person for this assignment," Riley said. "In these days of criticism of higher education, I was looking for someone who had thought carefully about the lib-

[21]Stephanie Van Auken, "Presidential Candidate Jerry Brown Speaks To Students; Former California Governor, On The Stump For The Colorado Primary, Calls For Ouster Of The 'Corrupt Political System,'" *Catalyst*, 28 February 1992, 1. For a lengthier account of Jerry Brown's visit to Colorado College, see Loevy, *The Flawed Path To The Presidency 1992*, 59–62.

eral arts and sciences education, its role within American society, and the appropriate relationship between teaching and scholarship."[22]

A story that circulated on campus told about an evening when Professor Fuller was addressing a group of Colorado College alumni on the merits of the College and its academic program. When Fuller was finished speaking, a member of the College administration came up to Fuller and said: "You really believe all this liberal arts [propaganda], don't you?" Professor Fuller acknowledged that he "really" did, and the administrator later apologized to Fuller for making such an inappropriate remark.[23]

Timothy Fuller possessed a background that was very similar to a number of the early founders of Colorado College. Although he was born in Chicago, Illinois, on January 15, 1940, both his mother's and his father's families were from the Boston area in Massachusetts. In addition, his father's family had attended the Elliott Street Congregational Church in Newton, Massachusetts, for several generations.

Fuller graduated from New Trier High School in Winnetka, Illinois, in 1957. He went on to Kenyon College in Gambier, Ohio, graduating in 1961, and from there to Johns Hopkins University, where he did graduate work in Political Science, specializing in the political philosophy of John Stuart Mill. He came to Colorado College in 1965 to teach Political Theory. In 1971 Johns Hopkins awarded him the Ph.D. degree "with distinction."

Professor Fuller had the unique honor of being present at the precise moment when the basic idea behind the Block Plan was first suggested. Fuller had joined Glenn Brooks, the designer of the Block Plan, and Don Shearn, a Professor in the Psychology Department, for a beer at Murphy's Tavern on North Nevada Avenue. It was during this particular strategy session that Professor Shearn made his famous comment: "Why don't you just give me 15 students and let me work with them."

During the 1969–1970 academic year, Timothy Fuller served on the faculty Academic Program Committee, which adopted the detailed rules for the day-to-day operation of the Block Plan. Twenty years later Fuller

---

[22]Stephanie Van Auken, "Riley Appoints Professor Tim Fuller Dean Of The College," *Catalyst*, 27 March 1992, 1.

[23]Recollection of the author from a conversation with Timothy Fuller.

chaired the faculty committee which came up with the Half-Block proposal as the best way to alleviate the scheduling problems connected with the Eight Block Year. Fuller later commented that the addition of Half-Block courses "solved virtually all the problems associated with the Eight Block Year."

Timothy Fuller was well aware that he was taking charge of the Dean's office at a delicate moment in the College's history. It would be his job to help provide as smooth a transition as possible from Gresham Riley's presidency to that of Riley's as yet unnamed successor. It also would be part of Fuller's responsibility to help rekindle friendly relationships among various groups in the College community—relationships which had been sorely tested over the previous years at the College.[24]

ANOTHER ACTING PRESIDENT

On July 1, 1992, Professor of Music Michael Grace became the Acting President of Colorado College. The Presidential Selection Committee searching for a permanent successor to outgoing President Gresham Riley decided to take extra time to interview candidates and make a final choice. As a result, the Board of Trustees appointed Michael Grace to take the presidency of the College for a period of one year.

The College had recruited one of its own graduates for Acting President. A native of Philadelphia, Michael Grace was a member of the Colorado College Class of 1963. He also received one of the last graduate degrees in Music awarded by the College, earning a Master of Arts in Music in 1964. From there it was on to Yale University, where he was awarded a Ph.D. in Music in 1974. Michael Grace joined the Colorado College faculty in 1967 while still working for his Ph.D.

While an undergraduate at Colorado College, Michael Grace had been a full-fledged member of the protest generation of the early 1960s. He played the guitar and sang folk songs protesting war and economic inequality. As a young faculty member at the College, he joined the peaceful protests against the Vietnam War, one time going down to the Colorado Springs Draft Board and quietly reading the names of United

---

[24]Author's notes, interview with Timothy Fuller, Dean of Colorado College, 12 January 1998.

States military personnel killed in Vietnam. "There was a period," Michael Grace later recalled, "when I was always having to choose between spending all my time protesting the war or completing my doctoral dissertation." The doctoral dissertation was eventually completed.

Although a committed teacher who had every intention of returning to the classroom once his one-year stint in the President's office was completed, Michael Grace did have administrative credentials. He served as Dean of the Summer Session from 1987 to 1990, and he had been Chairman of the Board of Trustees at the Colorado Springs School, the local private preparatory school that used an academic calendar based on the Colorado College Block Plan. "I know it was important that I had been a Trustee of the Colorado Springs School," Michael Grace later explained. "The Colorado College Board of Trustees knew I had a 'Trustee perspective' on educational issues."[25]

Michael Grace was well aware of the delicate and challenging job that lay ahead of him. He was the College's second Acting President within a period of one year, Thomas Cronin having held the position the first semester one year earlier. Gresham Riley had returned to the presidency for only one semester before departing. The College needed a stabilizing hand on the throttle during the year a new, permanent President was being chosen.

"I thought it would be somebody more political than I am," Michael Grace told the student newspaper, the *Catalyst*. "[But] that could have been one of the reasons [I was chosen]. There was a feeling that they didn't want somebody who might pursue too strongly a specific political agenda. . . ."

Michael Grace made it clear that one of his goals as Acting President would be to restore an atmosphere of civility and cooperation to the campus. He told the student newspaper: "There have been certain areas where one group might not completely trust or agree with another group. If nothing else, I want to make sure that there are good, open, trustful, and candid communications taking place between various constituen-

[25]Author's notes, interview with Michael Grace, Acting President of Colorado College 1992–1993, 26 January 1998.

cies. . . . That would be the right kind of environment to welcome the new President into."[26]

In an effort to start building up confidence and esprit de corps among the faculty, Acting President Grace joined with the new Dean, Timothy Fuller, in hosting a series of Sunday night dinners for small groups of faculty at the President's House. These dinners had no other purpose than to get conversations going between the various members of the faculty and generate an atmosphere of friendliness and conviviality.[27]

THE PENROSE PAPERS

One of the most valued collections in Tutt Library at Colorado College was the Penrose Papers. These were the personal papers of Spencer Penrose, the man who had come to Colorado from Philadelphia and made millions of dollars in various mining ventures. Penrose also built the Broadmoor Hotel, and he created El Pomar Foundation, which had given millions of dollars to Colorado College over the years.

Acting President Michael Grace had been in the President's office only five days when he received a very interesting telephone call. A high-ranking executive at El Pomar Foundation requested that the Penrose Papers be removed from Tutt Library at Colorado College and henceforth housed at the Foundation's El Pomar Center in the Broadmoor area of Colorado Springs. El Pomar Center was a conference center, owned and operated by El Pomar Foundation, that had been the former home of Spencer Penrose and his wife Julie.

The College administration had qualms about relinquishing its ownership of the Penrose Papers. John Sheridan, the Head Librarian at Tutt Library, feared that the Penrose Papers would not be as well-protected at the Foundation as they were in Tutt Library. If they remained at Tutt Library, the Penrose papers would be in a climate-controlled environment and would be cared for in perpetuity by trained librarians. But, on the

[26]Robert A. Neer, "Grace Assumes Presidency," *Catalyst*, 11 September 1992, 1.

[27]Author's notes, interview with Timothy Fuller, Dean of Colorado College, 12 January 1998.

Michael Grace
A Professor of Music at Colorado College, Grace served as Acting President of the College during the 1992–1993 academic year.

other hand, the College wanted to cooperate with the Foundation that had been one of the College's principal financial benefactors.

A major accomplishment of Michael Grace's acting presidency and Timothy Fuller's first year as Dean was finding a successful solution to the problem of the Penrose Papers. The College loaned the original papers to El Pomar Foundation but did not give up actual ownership. A complete set of copies of the papers was retained in Tutt Library in case anything unfortunate happened to the original documents while at El Pomar. And an agreement was signed that the Penrose Papers would automatically be returned to Colorado College if, at a future date, El Pomar Foundation no longer wanted them or was unable to adequately house them.[28]

"The Penrose Papers situation got my acting presidency off to a challenging start," Michael Grace later pointed out. "But I learned a valuable lesson. Establishing and nurturing peaceful relations with the various organizations that support the College is vital. Maintaining 'institutional good will' is a big part of the College President's job."[29]

A New Hockey Coach

At the end of the 1992–1993 academic year, Colorado College needed a new men's ice hockey coach. Suddenly Acting President Michael Grace was faced with a difficult decision. A number of members of the faculty were staunchly opposed to NCAA Division I men's ice hockey at Colorado College and urged Acting President Grace to only name an interim men's ice hockey coach to replace the outgoing head hockey coach. These faculty members were hoping that the permanent President of the College, scheduled to take office on July 1, 1993, could be persuaded to have the College withdraw from Division I men's ice hockey. That decision would be easier to make if Colorado College only had an interim men's ice hockey coach rather than a permanent coach.[30]

---

[28]Author's notes, interview with Timothy Fuller, Dean of Colorado College, 12 January 1998.

[29]Author's notes, interview with Michael Grace, Acting President of Colorado College 1992–1993, 26 January 1998.

[30]For faculty criticism of Division I men's ice hockey, see "Reactions," *Catalyst*, 5 February 1993, 1. Also see Paul Kutsche, "Has The Time Come For Division I Hockey To Go," *Catalyst*, 12 February 1993, 9.

"I resisted just hiring an interim coach," Acting President Michael Grace later explained. "I thought it would demoralize the men's ice hockey team and make it very difficult to recruit the high quality players that are absolutely necessary to maintain a competitive Division I team. In other words, I would be making the decision to downgrade the men's ice hockey team rather than leaving that decision to my permanent successor. I decided not to take an action that would have such a negative impact on the men's ice hockey program. I worked to not let the program die—or start to die."[31]

Michael Grace ordered a search committee formed to hire a permanent, full-time men's ice hockey coach for Colorado College. After considering a number of highly qualified candidates from throughout the nation, the College hired Don Lucia and put him to work trying to develop the men's ice hockey team as a top NCAA Division I competitor.

OUTREACH TO JAPAN

In the fall of 1992 Acting President Michael Grace joined a group of college presidents from the midwestern United States that took a ten-day goodwill tour of Japan. The purpose of the trip was to promote international studies and arrange international student exchanges between Japan and the United States. While on the tour Acting President Michael Grace visited with civic officials and businesspersons in Fujiyoshida, the Japanese sister city of Colorado Springs. As a result of that contact, community leaders in Fujiyoshida raised more than $80,000 and contributed it to Colorado College for making improvements in the Japan theme house on the campus.[32]

While in Tokyo, Michael Grace hosted a Colorado College alumni dinner. More than 45 persons, all of them connected to the College in one way or another, came from all over Japan to hear the Acting President speak and to renew their Colorado College contacts. Among the more interesting guests were three women graduates, all of them former Division I women soccer players at the College, who were playing professional soccer in Japan.[33]

---

[31]Author's notes, interview with Michael Grace, Acting President of Colorado College 1992–1993, 26 January 1998.

[32]Vicki Southern, "Grace Focuses On Budget," *Catalyst*, 30 October 1992, 1.

[33]Author's notes, interview with Michael Grace, Acting President of Colorado College 1992–1993, 26 January 1998.

THE CHARLES LEAMING TUTT, JR., STATUE

In the early fall of 1992 the College erected and dedicated a full-size statue of Charles Leaming Tutt, Jr., one of the leading benefactors of Colorado College. The statue was placed outside the entrance of Tutt Library, which was named for Charles Leaming Tutt, Jr. The statue featured Tutt dressed in a business suit holding a western-style businessman's hat. The bronze statue was sculpted by Cloyd Barnes of Denver.

Charles Leaming Tutt, Jr., was the scion of one of the leading families of Colorado Springs. His father was the business partner of Spencer Penrose, and the older Tutt and Penrose made millions from gold mines at Cripple Creek and other mining ventures. Charles Leaming Tutt, Jr., was born in 1891 and passed away in 1961. He was a leader of El Pomar Foundation, which donated funds to build Tutt Library and El Pomar Sports Center and helped with a number of other projects at Colorado College.

The bronze statue of Charles Leaming Tutt, Jr., cost approximately $30,000 and was partly donated by Ed Honnen, a member of the Colorado College Class of 1921 and a friend of Tutt's. El Pomar Foundation also contributed to the memorial statue.[34]

The statue of Charles Leaming Tutt, Jr., quickly became a part of campus life at Colorado College. For instance, prior to important men's ice hockey games, the statue often was clothed in a Colorado College men's ice hockey uniform.

CHEERLEADING RETURNS

Was the famous "school spirit" of the 1950s about to reemerge at Colorado College? Were pep rallies, large crowds at football games, and even cheerleading about to stage a comeback? There were signs this was happening in the early 1990s when a 24 member cheerleading team organized at Colorado College and began performing at home sporting events.

The team, which was not financially supported by the College, consisted of a performance group of ten women and a stunt group of seven women and seven men. The performance group was captained by Sarah Davidson, Class of 1994, and the stunt group was led by David Hewell,

---

[34]Diana Zipeto, "C.C. Unveils Tutt Memorial," *Catalyst*, 11 September 1992, 4.

Class of 1993. In order to avoid the objectification of women traditionally associated with cheerleading, the team emphasized athletic skills and quality performance rather than attractive appearance.

Barbara Yalich, Vice President of Development and College Relations, served as an ad hoc adviser and coordinator for the cheerleading team. She noted that cheerleading and other aspects of school spirit had faded in the late 1960s and early 1970s when students became more concerned with anti-Vietnam War protests and the Women's Movement. The costs of reviving a cheerleading team at Colorado College—for such things as uniforms, equipment, and training camp fees—came out of the team members' pockets and from contributions from friends of the College.

Skill levels were high on the new cheerleading team. At a Universal Cheerleading Association training camp during the summer of 1992, the Colorado College team finished in first place in the cheer leading competition at the camp.[35]

COACH JERRY LEAR RETIRES

In the spring of 1993 swimming coach Jerry Lear retired. He stepped down with a career record of 199 wins, 119 losses, and 1 tie in dual swimming meets. In his final year of coaching, Jerry Lear was named Coach of the Year by the Intermountain Swim League.

Jerry Lear was a native of La Junta, Colorado. He attended La Junta High School and, as a high school athlete, helped La Junta win Colorado state championships in three sports—football, basketball, and track—in a single academic year. Lear served as an officer in the U.S. Marine Corps, and he earned his B.A. degree from the University of Denver in 1954. He coached at Paonia High School in Paonia, Colorado, and Palmer High School in Colorado Springs before joining the Colorado College coaching staff in 1963.

Lear served 30 years as the swim coach at Colorado College. He also was an assistant football coach for 27 seasons. Although his coaching days

---

[35]Amy Maurer, "Cheerleaders Set Hopes Higher For The Future," *Catalyst*, 16 October 1992, 2.

were ending, he stayed on at the College as Director of Schlessman Pool and as a life guarding and water safety instructor.[36]

THE CENTER FOR COMMUNITY SERVICE

An increasingly important focus of student activity was the Center for Community Service, the office located in Worner Center where students could go to get information about community service projects. Name a social problem—and the Center would find a way for a student to participate in solving it. Internships and work projects were available that enabled students to help reduce problems of homelessness, child abuse, children's education, care of the elderly, etc. Volunteer organizations with which students could do community service included the local AIDS Task Force, the Differently Abled Awareness Coalition (DAAC), Environmental Action, Habitat for Humanity, and Kare Enough about Elderly People (KEEP).

Lynn Rhodes, the Director of Community Service at the College in the early 1990s, worked to structure the program so that students experienced both service and *learning*. Students were encouraged to think about what they learned from their service experience and how it was affecting their lives and their values.[37]

One of the most popular and successful community service projects was the Colorado College soup kitchen. Every Sunday at noon, Colorado College students served a hot meal to the homeless and other needy citizens of Colorado Springs. It was the only free meal served to the destitute on that day at that time.

The soup kitchen operated out of the basement of Shove Chapel. It had the unique distinction of being the first soup kitchen in the United States run exclusively by college students.

The Colorado College student who initiated and organized the soup kitchen was Becky Manchester. Mainly on the strength of her successful efforts in behalf of the soup kitchen, Becky Manchester was awarded a national Harry S. Truman Fellowship to help pay for undergraduate and graduate studies leading to a career in public service.

---

[36]"Lear Named Coach Of The Year," *Catalyst*, 26 February 1993, 17.

[37]Mel Berwin, "Rhodes And Lutze Help Community Service Happen," *Catalyst*, 7 May 1993, 7. Melody Schmid, "Bursting The Bubble: Community Extends Beyond Campus," *Catalyst*, 14 November 1997, 6.

Another popular community service project was "Help The Holidays Happen," an effort by the students to collect food, toys, and clothing in order to provide a nice Christmastime holiday for needy families in Colorado Springs.[39]

A CHANGED ATMOSPHERE

As the 1992–1993 academic year drew to a close, there was a real sense that an atmosphere of calm and quiet had returned to the Colorado College community. Acting President Michael Grace was being praised for the manner in which he had steered the College to a state of cooperation and mutual purpose. In fact, as Michael Grace prepared to turn the presidential office over to his successor, there were those who suggested that other liberal arts colleges similar to Colorado College should be considering him as presidential timber.[40]

But external factors to the College were contributing to this feeling of well-being at the College. The fall of the Berlin Wall in 1989 and the breakup of the Soviet Union in 1991 had greatly altered the world situation. Revolutionary movements in Central America that had been supported by the old Soviet government lost their momentum and ceased to have broad appeal to students and faculty at Colorado College. The decision by the United States to greatly cut back its arsenal of nuclear weapons ended the protest demonstrations at places such as the Rocky Flats nuclear weapons plant outside Denver.

Another international event contributed to the new atmosphere of peace and cooperation on the Colorado College campus. The White government in South Africa abandoned its policy of strict racial segregation and prepared to grant full political power to that nation's Black majority. Divestment in South Africa, an issue which had divided the Colorado College community for more than a decade, was no longer relevant as South Africa advanced rapidly toward becoming a racially integrated society.

---

[39]Joseph Sharman, "Soup Kitchen Receives Grant," *Catalyst*, 17 September 1993, 4. Ayesha Nawaz, "Community Kitchen Volunteers Help Those Less Fortunate," *Catalyst*, 20 October 1995, 1. Chara Armon and Joseph Sharman, "Holidays Benefit Starting," *Catalyst*, 12 November 1993, 3. Megan McKee, "C.C. Helps The Holidays Happen," *Catalyst*, 18 November 1994, 1.

[40]Recollection of the author.

And, by the spring of 1993, the United States economy had begun to improve. The national economy clearly was entering a robust period of economic growth and low unemployment. The gloomy economic outlook of 1991 and 1992 had faded completely. The voices which had called for tight budgets and downsized operations at Colorado College were no longer heard.

A NEW PRESIDENT

One of the most important activities at Colorado College during the 1992–1993 academic year was the selection of a President to succeed Gresham Riley. The process was both elaborate and public. A Presidential Selection Committee, composed of Trustees, faculty members, and administrators, interviewed the top 13 contenders out of the 202 persons who applied for the job. The list of 13 was then narrowed to a final four contenders, all of whom were brought to the campus for two days of interviews and meetings with the various members of the College community.[41]

Students were given access to the finalists, and the student newspaper, the *Catalyst*, conducted interviews and wrote frank evaluations of the various candidates.[42] It was a sign of the changing times in academia that two of the finalists were men and two were women. The merits of the candidates, both positive and negative, were discussed publicly at a fall faculty meeting.[43]

The final decision rested with the College's Board of Trustees. Midway through the 1992–1993 academic year, the Board announced that Kathryn Mohrman, the Dean of Undergraduate Studies at the University of Maryland at College Park, was going to be the next President of Colorado College.[44] The Board's selection corresponded with what many observers said was the clear choice of the students and faculty of Colorado College.

---

[41]Amy Maurer, "Presidential Search Narrowed To Four; Candidates Speak To Campus And Answer Questions," *Catalyst*, 11 September 1992.

[42]Mac McDonald, "Elliot Addresses Gay Issues," *Catalyst*, 18 September 1992, 1. Justin Lippard, "Sullivan Plans To Cut Costs," *Catalyst*, 18 September 1992, 1. Jud Lohnes, "Ellis Outlines Ideas," *Catalyst*, 2 October 1992, 2.

[43]Sean McLaughlin, "Faculty Debates Candidates," *Catalyst*, 2 October 1992, 1.

[44]Justin Blum, "Trustees Select Mohrman To Lead College," *Catalyst*, 4 December 1992, 1.

CHAPTER 14

KATHRYN MOHRMAN TAKES THE HELM

Kathryn Jagow Mohrman was born on September 23, 1945, in Oak Park, Illinois. When she was in junior high school, her father became the chief financial officer at Knox College in Galesburg, Illinois. As a result, Kathryn Mohrman spent her junior high and high school years close by Knox College, a small liberal arts college very similar to Colorado College. She thus became familiar with the values and intellectual style of a liberal arts college several years before she went to college herself.

"When it came time for me to apply to college," Mohrman later explained, "it was made clear to me that I was to select a liberal arts college. One of the colleges I looked at—I remember touring the campus—was Colorado College. But I ended up at Grinnell College [in Grinnell, Iowa,] partly because Knox and Grinnell had a tuition-exchange program for faculty children."[1]

At Grinnell College Kathryn Mohrman majored in History. She wrote her senior thesis on Grinnell graduates who had become important leaders in U.S. President Franklin D. Roosevelt's administration. A number of these Grinnellians, most notably Harry Hopkins, played key roles in the successful development of the New Deal, President Roosevelt's program for using government spending and government aid to end the

---

[1]This and subsequent quotes from Kathryn Mohrman are from the author's notes, interview with Kathryn Mohrman, President of Colorado College, 30 January 1998. Also see Memorandum on College History, Kathryn Mohrman to author, 4 February 1998.

Great Depression of the 1930s. "Public service is a strong theme at Grinnell," Mohrman pointed out, "and these Grinnell graduates who so strongly influenced the New Deal played a major role in building the public service tradition at Grinnell."

Mohrman graduated from Grinnell College in 1967 and went directly to graduate study in History at the University of Wisconsin at Madison. She wrote her master's thesis on the educational backgrounds of New Deal administrators. She detailed how intellectually strong colleges and universities—such as Harvard University, the University of Wisconsin, and Grinnell College—produced a disproportionate number of the important New Deal functionaries. "I learned from this study," Mohrman noted, "that good colleges and universities have powerful and lasting effects on people. The gospel of social service at Grinnell, the tradition of progressivism at Wisconsin—it was the values imparted at these institutions that inspired their graduates to want to work in the New Deal."

While in graduate school Kathryn Mohrman married William Mohrman, who was earning his law degree at Wisconsin. After Wisconsin, they moved to Washington, D.C., where Kathryn Mohrman held a variety of jobs in educational lobbying offices. She studied for her Ph.D. degree in Public Policy by attending night school at George Washington University. Her doctoral dissertation was on U.S. Government policy toward "life long learning," i.e., adult education. The major conclusion of her dissertation was that the government should only subsidize adult education programs that create badly needed job skills for the national economy. "Knitting and weaving courses for adults are nice," Mohrman said, "but they represent consumption, not investment, and should not be paid for by the government." Mohrman received her Ph.D. degree in 1982.

Most of Kathryn Mohrman's professional career was spent in college and university administration. From 1980 to 1993 she was a member of the Board of Trustees at Grinnell College. She was an Associate Dean at Brown University in Providence, Rhode Island, and she was a guest scholar at the prestigious Brookings Institution in Washington, D.C. Prior to assuming the presidency of Colorado College, she was Dean of Undergraduate Studies at the University of Maryland at College Park.

It was at the University of Maryland that Kathryn Mohrman saw "the other side" of higher education in the United States. Maryland had an enrollment of 37,000 students, and those students came from a wide variety of social and economic backgrounds. While at Maryland, Kathryn Mohrman worked to institute an honors program for talented students, strongly emphasized improved academic advising, and put in a teaching and learning center where both students and faculty could study and practice advanced teaching techniques. "For someone like me, with an undergraduate liberal arts background," Mohrman said, "working at the University of Maryland was an extraordinary education."

"But much of my educational and professional life has been at small colleges," Mohrman concluded. "I spent my high school years close to Knox, I attended Grinnell, and I was a Grinnell Trustee [for 13 years].... Clearly, I am completely connected to the ideals and realities of small liberal arts colleges."

And college administration could be said to have been a family tradition for Kathryn Mohrman. Her father, Elmer Jagow, later left Knox College to become the President of Hiram College in Ohio. Elmer Jagow and Kathryn Mohrman had the unusual honor of being a father-daughter team in terms of serving as college presidents.[2]

Kathryn Mohrman was more than pleased with her new assignment as President of Colorado College. "If my fairy godmother had created the perfect job for me," Mohrman later wrote, "she could not have done much better!"[3]

THE NEW PRESIDENT ON CAMPUS

Prior to officially taking over the presidency of the College on July 1, 1993, Kathryn Mohrman taught a course in the Political Science Department on the political aspects of educational administration. "I was delighted to have

---

[2]Joseph Sharman, "C.C. To Inaugurate Mohrman Saturday," *Catalyst*, 10 September 1993, 1.

[3]Memorandum, Kathryn Mohrman to author, 4 February 1998, 1.

a chance to teach . . . ," Mohrman told the *Catalyst*, "because I had a chance to see the Block Plan firsthand. I think I will be able to explain it much better in the future to parents, donors, and others based on that personal experience. I found it to be both exhilarating and exhausting but, for me, the intensity made the class experience much more rewarding."

President Mohrman saw setting priorities as her most important task in her first year in the presidential office. "We are fortunate to be in sound financial shape," Mohrman said, "but there will never be enough money to do everything we want to do. We can't expect to make all our decisions right away. . . . But I hope we can work together this year to build consensus about our top priorities for time, energy, and funding."

The new President noted that she often was asked how Colorado College compared to the other institutions, such as Brown University and the University of Maryland at College Park, where she had worked. She said the big difference at Colorado College was its small size and the clarity of its mission as a teaching institution. The new President explained: "This is a great place because it is small enough that people are individuals, that students know everyone in their classes, that faculty members are human beings—and not just lecturers in the front of a huge room. . . . [Colorado College] has a clearly focused mission on undergraduate education in the liberal arts and sciences. There is no question what the first priority should be. The commitment to learning and discovery here is clear."[4]

Kathryn Mohrman was the first woman ever to hold the presidency of Colorado College. "I encountered no problems concerning my gender when I arrived at the College," Mohrman later commented. "Very quickly I saw that it was going to be no big deal that I was the first woman to lead the institution."

THREE ISSUES

Shortly after her arrival on campus, Kathryn Mohrman learned there were three immediate issues that she should deal with as President. These

---

[4]Kathryn Mohrman, "The President Answers Common Questions," *Catalyst*, 10 September 1993.

Kathryn Mohrman
The first woman to be selected as President of Colorado College, Mohrman launched an $83 million fund-raising drive in the spring of 1998.

issues were not set before her by direct order of the Board of Trustees. They were implied in a large number of conversations she held with students, faculty members, and Trustees. The three issues were:

1. Bring the "Strategic Planning" process to a satisfactory conclusion.
2. Clarify the status of Division I sports. If Division I sports were to be retained at the College, find a way to reinvigorate them.
3. Resolve the issue of fraternities and sororities. These social units were to be removed from the campus or, if they were retained, a satisfactory role was to be found for them in the student social life at the College.[5]

ISSUE 1: STRATEGIC PLANNING

The first issue President Mohrman had to deal with was "Strategic Planning." At the behest of the Board of Trustees, Colorado College began in the early 1990s to evaluate its position in the academic world and take steps to guarantee its future survival, both in terms of economic solvency and educational advancement. Glenn Brooks, the designer of the Colorado College Block Plan, was hired to do the early studies and gather the basic statistics that would get the Strategic Planning process started.

In the fall of 1993 Kathryn Mohrman, acting in her capacity as the College's new President, issued the first Strategic Planning report. The document, issued mainly to invite input from the entire College community, quietly but firmly recommitted the College to its traditional goals. Among the report's major statements were the following principles:

- The College, with a student body of slightly less than 2,000 students, should be no larger and maybe a bit smaller.

[5]Author's notes, interview with Kathryn Mohrman, President of Colorado College, 30 January 1998.

- The College should remain focused on undergraduate education.
- The College should remain committed to the liberal arts and sciences.
- The College should do more to capitalize on its distinctive features, such as the Block Plan and its location in the American West.
- The College should reaffirm its commitment to academic freedom.
- The College should continue to award financial aid on the basis of need.[6]

The following spring President Mohrman issued the final recommendations of the Strategic Planning process. The document was renamed *The Interim Report On The Future Of Colorado College.* Major goals stated in this document included:

- The College should increase student diversity by recruiting and retaining ethnic minorities as well as attracting international students.
- The College should create more housing options for students centered around academic themes, i.e., designate more theme houses.
- The College should continue to bring sports programs into conformity with National Collegiate Athletic Association (NCAA) rules concerning gender equity, i.e., more emphasis on women's sports.
- The College should honor and diversify its faculty by increasing the number of endowed chairs, distinguished professorships, and Minority Scholars in Residence.
- The College should expand the number of interdisciplinary courses, with particular emphasis on American Ethnic Studies, Women's Studies, and Environmental Studies.

[6]Kathryn Mohrman, "Strategic Planning Report Given," *Catalyst*, 3 December 1993, 1.

There were a number of individuals and organizations on the Colorado College campus that had hoped the Strategic Planning report would recommend eliminating the fraternities and sororities and would call for the College to withdraw the men's ice hockey team and the women's soccer team from Division I competition. President Mohrman told the *Catalyst* those two issues were left out of the Strategic Planning report so that the College could first deal with its academic concerns. She said the Strategic Planning process would address social and athletic concerns on the campus at a future date.[7]

President Mohrman summed up her role in the shaping of the final Strategic Planning report. "When I arrived at Colorado College, I found the Strategic Planning process was focused on many important issues but *not* on the fundamental activity of the College—academics. I pushed for the document to make clear that, as Colorado College strategically planned for the future, our commitment to academic values and student needs was clearly spelled out."[8]

President Mohrman began a strong and steady push to shift a higher proportion of the College budget to academic purposes. "The percentage change isn't great," she noted, "but it means we are putting our money where our [stated goals are]."[9]

ISSUE 2: DIVISION I SPORTS

President Mohrman made two major decisions in the area of College athletics. The first decision was to more completely balance the men's sports program with the women's sports program at the NCAA Division III level. This meant making the tough decision to eliminate men's baseball and golf and institute women's lacrosse and softball. Other decisions leading to greater gender equity in sports at Colorado College included hiring more women coaches, paying them salaries commensurate with their men

---

[7]Justin Blum, "Strategic Planning Report Given: Mohrman," *Catalyst*, 11 March 1994, 1.

[8]Author's notes, interview with Kathryn Mohrman, President of Colorado College, 30 January 1998.

[9]Memorandum, Kathryn Mohrman to author, 4 February 1998, 2.

counterparts, and reassigning a portion of the locker and shower space in El Pomar Sports Center from men's sports to women's sports.[10]

The second decision by President Mohrman concerning College athletics was to retain NCAA Division I sports. Gender equity was not a problem with this decision, because the College already had a Division I men's ice hockey team and a Division I women's soccer team. This decision by President Mohrman to keep and enhance Division I sports was greatly abetted by the fact that, at the time the decision was made, a movement was afoot in the Colorado Springs community to build a brand new sports arena which could serve as a grand new home for the Colorado College men's ice hockey team.

A NEW WORLD ARENA

In March of 1994 the Broadmoor Hotel tore down the Broadmoor World Arena. The marvelous old ice rink, which had hosted Colorado College men's ice hockey throughout the entire history of the hockey program, was dismantled to make way for expansion of the hotel.

A brand-new sports arena was proposed for Colorado Springs. It was to be a multi-purpose non-profit facility paid for entirely by voluntary contributions. One of the College's largest financial contributors, El Pomar Foundation, got this latest arena project rolling with an initial contribution of $15 million. Peter Susemihl, a Colorado Springs attorney who was a Colorado College graduate of the Class of 1966 and a College Trustee, headed up the fund-raising drive.

Although Colorado College was not going to own this new facility, the College played an important role in its financing. On October 16, 1994, President Kathryn Mohrman reaffirmed the College's commitment to Division I sports for men's ice hockey and women's soccer. She also noted that construction of a new ice arena, with a larger number of seats than the old Broadmoor World Arena, would greatly increase the College's income from ticket sales for men's ice hockey. This added income would

[10]Josie Henjum, "Committee On Gender Equity In Athletics Submits Recommendations To President," *Catalyst*, 13 May 1994, 14. Also see Sarabecka Mullen, "Women's Softball: New To C.C. Sports," *Catalyst*, 2 February 1996, 17. Sonja Hovey, "Lady Tigers Get Win; Varsity Softball Attains First Victory Of Season," *Catalyst*, 5 April 1996, 17.

help to reduce the cost to the College of Division I sports. In addition, because the Colorado College men's ice hockey team was going to be one of the principal permanent performers in the new arena, President Mohrman asked "a few selected alumni and friends to donate to the arena project in recognition of its importance to the College."[11]

This campaign to get alumni, trustees, and friends of the College to donate to the new arena on behalf of the College was a success. In September of 1995 President Mohrman announced that the College had arranged for a $1 million contribution to the new arena. Of that total, $750,000 was being contributed by alumni, trustees, and friends of the College and $250,000 from College funds. President Mohrman emphasized that the College's $250,000 contribution came from current funds and was not paid from either the endowment or existing academic programs.[12]

Shortly thereafter Edith Gaylord Harper, a Colorado College Trustee, contributed $500,000 to the new arena on behalf of the College. She made the gift in honor of Milo Yalich, captain of the 1950 Colorado College men's ice hockey team that won the NCAA Championship. Edith Harper's gift also honored Peggy Fleming, who won a gold medal in women's figure skating at the 1968 Olympics. Peggy Fleming was a Colorado College student at the time she was training for the Olympics.[13]

The new facility was named the Colorado Springs World Arena and was constructed at the intersection of Interstate Highway 25 and Circle Drive in south Colorado Springs. The 7,000 seat facility featured an ice rink, but the ice could be covered when necessary and other sports, such as basketball, played. The new World Arena also could be configured for conventions, trade shows, or musical and dramatic presentations.

[11]Joseph Sharman, "Division I Sports Survive Review," *Catalyst*, 21 October 1994, 1. The Board of Trustees subsequently approved President Mohrman's endorsement of Division I sports. Julie Gordon, "Board Of Trustees Evaluates Division I Proposal, Financial Aid Policy And Cost," *Catalyst*, 18 November 1994, 2.

[12]Julie Gordon, "$1 Million Contribution To World Arena Announced; Future Tiger Hockey Home Should Be Completed In 1997," *Catalyst*, 22 September 1995, 3.

[13]Sally Wurtzler, "Trustee Gift Pushes World Arena Project Forward," *Catalyst*, 2 February 1996, 1.

Permanent, year-round practice ice rinks were constructed adjacent to but as an integral part of the new facility.[14]

During the three-and-one-half-year gap between the time the Broadmoor World Arena was torn down and the new Colorado Springs World Arena was completed, the Colorado College men's ice hockey team played its home games at the ice rink in the field house at the United States Air Force Academy. Although the Academy rink was located some distance north of Colorado Springs, it was a comfortable facility with good visibility from almost every seat.

A Men's Ice Hockey Revival

The 1993–1994 season was the last year that the men's ice hockey team played at the Broadmoor World Arena. The team went out of the famous old ice rink in style by winning games. The team quickly climbed into first place in the Western Collegiate Hockey Association (WCHA). Under the skilled direction of new coach Don Lucia, the Colorado College team won the WCHA Championship.[15]

But this glorious final season in the Broadmoor World Arena had a bittersweet ending. Colorado College lost to Michigan Tech in the WCHA playoffs. The men's ice hockey team was not one of the 12 teams invited to play in the NCAA tournament to determine a national champion.[16]

The following season, 1994–1995, the men's ice hockey team did better. Colorado College repeated as WCHA Champions, won in the WCHA playoffs, and was invited to play in the NCAA tournament. The team lost the first tournament game to the University of Minnesota by a score of 5 to 2 and thus was eliminated.[17]

But the best was yet to come. In the 1995–1996 season, the men's ice hockey team repeated for the third straight year as WCHA Champions.[18]

---

[14]Julie Gordon, "Broadmoor Ice Rink To Go; Colorado College Worries The Change Might Discontinue Home Hockey Games Played There," *Catalyst*, 1 October 1993, 1. "World Arena Forms; The Organization Exists to Oversee Arena's Construction," *Catalyst*, 8 April 1994, 2.

[15]Mike Rabinovitch, "WCHA Champions," *Catalyst*, 11 March 1994, 17.

[16]"WCHA League Champion C.C. Tigers Fail To Get NCCA Bid," *Catalyst*, 1 April 1994, 18.

[17]Mike Rabinovitch, "Tigers End Season, Lose To Minnesota," *Catalyst*, 31 March 1995, 20.

[18]Karen Heasley, "3-Peat: Tigers Claim WCHA Championship Title, Continue To Lead Nation," *Catalyst*, 23 February 1996, 19.

It was on to the NCAA tournament in Cincinnati, Ohio, where Colorado College advanced to the final championship game against the University of Michigan. The game was tied at the end of three periods and went into sudden-death overtime. One of the most exciting athletic contests in Colorado College history ended when a Michigan player slipped the puck past Ryan Bach, Colorado College's All American goalie. The Colorado College men's ice hockey team had to settle for second best in the nation.[19]

But the success of the 1995–1996 men's ice hockey team united the College community. Over 500 students and faculty gathered around the various television sets in Worner Center to watch the championship game and cheer on the Colorado College team. "The [campus] was at first devastated when the team lost," commented the *Catalyst*. "The silence was chilling. There were more than a few wet cheeks in the crowd. But when the shock wore off and everyone thought about the whole picture, they realized that being associated with the second best hockey team in the nation was nothing to scoff at. . . . Pride replaced all other emotions as the [campus] realized what thirty men had accomplished in six months."[20]

One of the most important things the resurgent men's ice hockey teams of the mid–1990s accomplished was to stir up interest in Colorado College ice hockey just at the time money was being raised to build the new World Arena. As the men's ice hockey team won game after game, it helped to stimulate more contributions to pay the cost of building the team's new home. "Colorado College was one of the major contributors to the World Arena financially," noted Marty Scarano, the Athletic Director at the College. "It's not an exaggeration to say that the World Arena is here in large part because of the strength of our hockey program."[21]

---

[19]Jonathan Erwin, "Tigers Ready To Return To Final Four Next Year," *Catalyst*, 5 April 1996, 16.

[20]"C.C. Unites For Hockey," *Catalyst*, 5 April 1996, 5. Also see Autumn Klinikowski, "Tiger Hockey: The Year That Almost Was," *Catalyst*, 10 May 1996, 18.

[21]Eric Martens, "A Multi-Million Dollar Playground," *Catalyst*, 30 January 1998, 6. Dave Moross, "New Home Ice Of Worldly Proportion," *Access*, December 1997, 1. Also see Todd Harman and Angie Reese, "C.C. Hockey Finally Has A Home; El Pomar Donates Millions," *Colorado Springs Gazette*, 14 January 1998, ARENA6. The *Gazette* published a special 8 page section on 14 January 1998 celebrating the opening of the new World Arena.

The Arena Opens

On January 23, 1998, the Colorado College men's ice hockey team played its first home game in the new Colorado Springs World Arena. President Kathryn Mohrman dropped the ceremonial first puck, after which the Colorado College team played the University of Wisconsin. A number of men's ice hockey alumni returned to the campus for a reunion and to see the historic first game. Sadly for Colorado College, the hockey team lost a thrilling game to Wisconsin in overtime by a 6–5 score.[22]

One of those who found the new World Arena truly rewarding was Music Professor Michael Grace, the Acting President during the 1992–1993 academic year. "When I looked around at almost 8,000 people at that first Colorado College hockey game in the new World Arena," Grace commented, "I was very glad I had not hired an interim coach and downgraded the hockey program back when I was Acting President. I realized I was part of the Division I hockey program going a long, long way."[23]

In having one of its intercollegiate sports team play at a public facility in Colorado Springs, the College simply was continuing one of its longest and finest traditions. Prior to the construction of El Pomar Sports Center, the men's basketball team had played some of its home games in the Colorado Springs City Auditorium. During the many years the College had a men's baseball team, that team practiced and played its home games at the municipal baseball field in the city's Memorial Park. Before it was torn down, the Burns Theater downtown was the site of the College's intercollegiate public speaking contests and an occasional College assembly. By making the men's ice hockey team the major attraction at the new Colorado Springs World Arena, Colorado College was continuing its role of having its sports teams use the facilities of the larger community and thereby enhance those facilities.

---

[22]Eric Yin, "Tigers Unable To Stop Wisconsin," *Catalyst*, 30 January 1998, 16. Photograph labeled "President Kathryn Mohrman drops the ceremonial first puck at the new World Arena," *Access*, February 1998, 1. Also see Angie Reese, "C.C.'s Arena Debut Turns Sauer In OT; Ex-C.C. Coach's Club Downs Tigers 6–5," *Colorado Springs Gazette*, 24 January 1998, SP1.

[23]Author's notes, interview with Michael Grace, Interim President of Colorado College 1992–1993, 26 January 1998.

COLORADO SPRINGS WORLD ARENA

The Colorado College men's ice hockey team lined up for the playing of the Star Spangled Banner at the first-ever ice hockey game played at the brand new World Arena. The date was January 23, 1998. K.J. Voorhees was the team member at left.

ISSUE 3: FRATERNITIES AND SORORITIES

In the ten years from 1985 to 1995, fraternity and sorority membership at Colorado College dropped from 30 percent of the student body to only 15 percent of the student body. There also was increasing concern that these quasi-independent social units placed too much emphasis on alcohol as an essential component of student social life at the College.

President Mohrman decided to retain the fraternities and sororities at Colorado College but removed their "houses" to a "student organization quad" being constructed east of Nevada Avenue. The fraternities could either build a new structure for their house or could refurbish one of the former residences owned by the College in that east Nevada area. The sororities could build a new structure or move one of their existing lodges over from the existing sorority lodge area north and west of Loomis Hall. The idea was to keep the fraternities and sororities but relocate their houses and lodges away from the main campus west of Nevada Avenue.

There was grumbling from some of the student officers of the fraternities about this plan, particularly moving all the fraternity houses to east of Nevada Avenue. Despite the clamor, the Board of Trustees adopted the plan and made it the official policy of the College. But there were fraternity and sorority leaders who were pleased that President Mohrman had retained a role for these social units at the College. "Some of the bad sentiment has been forgotten," said Kent Van Vleet, a fraternity leader, "because we know [the fraternities and sororities are] going to continue."[24]

ALUMNI PARTICIPATION CHALLENGE

In the fall of 1993 the College successfully completed a three-year drive to increase alumni contributions. During the drive the number of alumni giving money each year increased from 32 percent of the College's total graduates to 65 percent. The program was so successful the College moved from last place to first place among a selected group of 11 national liberal arts colleges. The average private liberal arts institution has an

---

[24]Sally Wurtzler, "Greeks, College At Odds Over Campus Plan; Implementation Of Trustee Decision Hindered By Details, Questions," *Catalyst*, 13 December 1996, 1.

alumni participation rate of 34 percent, so at 65 percent Colorado College had almost doubled the average rate.[25]

These record numbers of alumni contributors enabled the College to qualify for $200,000 in matching money from the Adolph Coors Foundation in Denver. One half of the Coors money was used to build a new all-weather running track circling the football gridiron at Washburn Field. The other half was used to improve computer technology at Tutt Library, particularly to make it easier for students and faculty to have computer access to off-campus computer networks and data bases.[26]

Alumni contributions provided a significant portion of the College's total budget in the early 1990s. Tuition paid only about 70 percent of the cost of educating a student at Colorado College. The remaining 30 percent was paid by grants, income from the College's endowment, and gifts—including gifts from the alumni.[27]

THE MAX KADE FOREIGN LANGUAGE THEATER

Armstrong 300, the old audio-visual room on the top floor of Armstrong Hall, had long been a popular place to show films on the Colorado College campus. The small but functional theater was equipped with a giant movie screen that covered the entire western wall of the room. It also featured an enclosed projection booth and an excellent sound system.

In the fall of 1993, thanks to a grant of $60,000 from the Max Kade Foundation, Armstrong 300 was refurbished as a foreign language theater. The seating was upgraded, and the decor of the theater was styled after turn-of-the-20th-Century Vienna. A theatrical control room was added as well as a large size video projection system. Student theatrical productions in German, Spanish, French, and other foreign languages were to be held in the newly restyled facility.

---

[25]In subsequent years, when a special drive was no longer in effect, the alumni participation rate at Colorado College dropped to around 50 percent, still a high figure compared to most other colleges and universities. Author's notes, interview with Diane Benninghoff, Director of Alumni Relations at Colorado College, 24 June 1998.

[26]For an update on technological change at Tutt Library in the mid-1990s, see Sarah Parmley, "Tutt Library Installs The TIGER Database," *Catalyst*, 16 September 1994, 4.

[27]College Relations, "Percentage Of Alumni Donations Double," *Catalyst*, 17 September 1993, 3.

Previously foreign language productions at Colorado College were staged at a variety of locations on campus, none of them very satisfactory. With the opening of this new theater, foreign language theater had a permanent home. The lighting and sound systems installed were specially designed for a small theater environment.

Thanks mainly to the efforts of Professor of German Horst Richardson, Colorado College had a strong tradition of putting on a play in the German language every academic year. Professor Richardson's colleague, Professor of German Armin Wishard, explained: "Colorado College has the most active German theater tradition of any college in the United States, and that includes big universities."[28]

The new dramatic facility was named the Max Kade Foreign Language Theater in honor of the man who established the foundation that donated the money to pay for it.

DORMITORY RENOVATION

Meeting in November of 1993, the Board of Trustees voted to renovate the three major residence halls at the College. Mathias Hall was to get its face-lift during the summer of 1994, Slocum Hall was to be redone during the summer of 1995, and Loomis Hall was to be made-over during the summer of 1996.

The renovations, costing a total of $10.2 million for all three dormitories, were designed to ready the buildings for another 20 years of student use. Plans called for installing new bathrooms, new carpeting, fresh interior paint, improved computer facilities, and new furniture. The lighting was to be upgraded in both the dormitory rooms and the hallways. In addition, the infrastructure of the buildings—the plumbing, heating, and electrical systems—were to be reconditioned or replaced.

All three residence halls were designed and constructed prior to the adoption of coeducational dormitory living at Colorado College. The renovations, particularly the bathroom renovations, were being undertaken in such a way as to make the three dorms as compatible as possible for coed living.

---

[28]Libby Hruska, "Language Theater Opens," *Catalyst*, 12 November 1993, 2.

Traditionally college and university dormitories are built with borrowed money and the loans are paid off with room charges collected from the students. An additional reason for deciding to rehabilitate the major dormitories in 1993 was that an attractive long term interest rate, 5.36 percent for a 20-year loan, was available to the College. The money was raised by selling general revenue bonds through the city of Colorado Springs.[29]

Colleges and universities are not only educational institutions. They also carry out what is often called the "Hotel Function," the housing and feeding of the residential students. In committing to upgrade its three major dormitories, Colorado College was committing to running as excellent a "Hotel" for the students as reasonably possible.[30]

A NEW WING FOR SLOCUM HALL

In the mid–1990s increasing numbers of students were electing to live on campus in residence halls rather than off campus in rented houses and apartments. To accommodate this increased demand for dormitory space, the College expanded its residence hall capacity by adding a fourth wing on to Slocum Hall. The new wing, constructed in the spring and summer of 1995, was three stories high. It ran in a southerly direction from the west end of the west wing of Slocum Hall. The top two floors contained standard dormitory rooms accommodating 38 students. The first story was reserved for a multi-purpose room and a kitchen. The multi-purpose room, named "Slocum Commons," quickly became a popular place for meetings and social receptions on the campus.[31]

HISPANIC LITERARY HERITAGE

During the 1990s Colorado College was the headquarters for a major scholarly effort to preserve and index Hispanic literary works published in

---

[29]Julie Gordon, "Board Of Trustees Makes Major Decisions," *Catalyst*, 10 December 1993, 1. Joseph Sharman, "Mathias Renovations Completed—Almost," *Catalyst*, 16 September 1994, 1. Libby Hruska, "Loomis Newly Renovated," *Catalyst*, 15 September 1995, 5.

[30]James Stauss, Provost of Colorado College during the early 1970s, frequently referred to the dormitories and the dining halls as the "Hotel Function" of the College.

[31]Julie Gordon, "New Wing To Be Added To Slocum," *Catalyst*, 10 March 1995, 3. Stephanie Grimme, "Slocum Addition Leaves No Room For Improvement," *Catalyst*, 22 September 1995, 3.

newspapers and magazines. Professor of Romance Languages Clara Lomas headed up the project and used both paid assistants and student volunteers to find and catalog works of fiction, non-fiction, poetry, and commentary written by Hispanic authors. Because Hispanic peoples first entered the territory that is now the United States in the 1600s, Professor Lomas and her fellow workers were searching through more than 300 years of Hispanic literary effort.

The project was known as the [Hispanic] Annotated Periodical Literature Project. It was part of a larger study, "Recovering the United States Hispanic Literary Heritage," based at the University of Houston in Texas.[32]

COPYRIGHT REGULATION

In the early 1990s there was increased national attention to the problem of copyright violations on college and university campuses. Authors and publishers complained loud and long about the financial loss they suffered when professors made multiple copies of scholarly articles or book chapters and distributed them to students free of charge.[33]

That practice essentially came to an end at Colorado College after the administration issued a number of memoranda to the faculty detailing the exact situations in which copy machines could and could not be used. To be on the safe side, the College hired a copyright specialist to advise faculty on copyright law and aid faculty in obtaining the required permissions when distributing copied materials. More often than not such permission required the payment of a fee, and the various academic departments began allocating money to pay such fees.

A NEW MASCOT?

In the spring of 1994 Andy Brown, the President of the student government at Colorado College, arranged for the student body to vote on chang-

---

[32]Katherine C. Eastman, "C.C. Helps Nationwide Hispanic Literary Project," *Catalyst*, 11 February 1994, 6. Jean Lyle, "History In The Making; Grads, Undergrads Research Mexican-American Literature, Rewrite History Books," *Catalyst*, 29 March 1996, 5.

[33]Julie Gordon, "Copyright Reg[ulation]s Strengthened," *Catalyst*, 25 February 1994, 1.

ing the mascot from the "Tiger" to the "Greenback Cutthroat Trout." The question was to be voted on at the same time the student body elected new members of the student government. "A unique [College] needs something unique," Brown said. "A lot of high schools and colleges around the nation have the 'Tiger' as their mascot. And the 'Greenback Cutthroat Trout' is something native to Colorado, whereas 'Tigers' aren't."

As the date of the election drew near, it began to appear there was substantial support to adopt the "Trout" as the College mascot. People began speculating as to just what the change would mean. Would automobile bumper stickers reading "Tiger Hockey" be replaced with ones labeled "Trout Hockey?" Would the four bronze "Tigers" at the base of the Earle Flagpole have to be removed and replaced with four sculpted "Trout?" And would the College have to remove the "Tiger" images and the word "Tigers" from the uniforms of the College's 18 athletic teams, replacing them with a "Trout" image and the word "Trout?"

The movement gained so much momentum that the College Bookstore began selling "Trout" T-shirts even before the election was held.[34] The opposition mounted a "Squish-The-Fish" campaign.

Fortunately for traditionalists and "Tiger" lovers, the student body narrowly voted to keep the "Tiger" as the school mascot. The vote was 468 (53 percent) for the "Tiger" and 423 (47 percent) for the "Greenback Cutthroat Trout."[35] But the issue did not end there. At the 1994 graduation ceremonies, President Kathryn Mohrman handed "Trout" lover Andy Brown a large frozen trout to go with his College diploma.

DOUBLE MAJORS

Starting with the 1994–1995 academic year, students were permitted to take a double major. That meant that, within the normal course of a four-year Colorado College career, students could take two majors at the same time. A student thus could graduate as a French/Political Science

---

[34]Julie Gordon, "Mascot Vote Sparks Debate," *Catalyst*, 1 April 1994, 2. Andy Brown and Thomas Quinlen, "The Cutthroat Trout Debate Continues," *Catalyst*, 8 April 1994, 13. Josie Henjum, "Cutthroat Trout: A Bad Idea," *Catalyst*, 8 April 1994, 18.

[35]"C.C.C.A. Election Results," *Catalyst*, 15 April 1994, 1.

double major or as a Physics/Philosophy double major. The new rules even permitted students to double up with a straight major and an interdisciplinary major. An example of this was an English/History-Political Science major.

Students taking a double major had to meet all the requirements of both majors. This produced some concern that students who double majored would miss out on one of the most important goals of a liberal arts education—knowing about and being able to discourse upon a wide variety of subjects. It was feared that students with double majors would only have time to take courses in their two fields of specialization and would miss out on the broader aspects of a liberal arts education.

Despite these reservations, the faculty adopted the double major and made it available to those students who wanted it. But Dean Timothy Fuller made it clear the College was not urging students to double major. Taking a single major in conjunction with a wide variety of courses in many fields remained the preferred alternative.[36]

A PROFESSOR RUNS FOR GOVERNOR

Professor of Economics Mike Bird, who served in the Colorado state legislature from 1982 to 1994, decided to run for the 1994 Republican nomination for the Colorado governorship. With his twelve years of state legislative experience, Professor Bird was by far the most qualified candidate in the field, and his campaign got off to a strong start. At the last minute, however, a millionaire Denver oilman with no experience in elected public office entered the Republican primary.

The primary election came down to a battle of the dollars. Mike Bird raised more than $250,000, mostly in small contributions, for the campaign. His millionaire opponent, however, spent ten times as much, $2.5 million, most of it the millionaire's own money. The Denver oilman proceeded to flood the television airwaves with slick commercials. On election night in early August of 1994, the millionaire candidate easily won the Republican primary, and Professor Bird's quest for the Colorado governorship was over.

---

[36]Julie Gordon, "Double Major A Go," *Catalyst*, 16 September 1994, 2.

Mike Bird ended his political career, at least for the moment, and returned to teaching Economics full-time at Colorado College. As for the millionaire who won the Republican primary, he was soundly defeated by incumbent Democratic Governor Roy Romer in the November general election.[37]

A PROFESSOR PUBLISHES

Professor of History Douglas Monroy published a book on the experiences of Mexican immigrants in California. The book took both an interdisciplinary and multicultural approach, detailing the manner in which the Spanish, Mexicans, Euro-Americans, and Native Americans interacted to form the unique cultural mix that was frontier California. The book was entitled *Thrown Among Strangers: The Making Of Mexican Culture In Frontier California*. It was awarded the James A. Rawley Prize of the Organization of American Historians for 1990.[38]

A second prodigious publishing faculty member in the History Department was Professor Dennis Showalter. He was from Minnesota and received his B.A. from St. John's University and his Ph.D. from the University of Minnesota. He published extensively in the fields of Military History and Modern German History. Among his better known books were *The Wars of Frederick The Great* and *Voices From The Third Reich: An Oral History.*

FACULTY MILESTONES

In the fall of 1994 the College lost one of its most venerable Natural Science professors. William C. Champion, Professor of Chemistry, died from breathing complications associated with an asthmatic condition.

Bill Champion was born March 12, 1930, in Illinois. He attended the University of Illinois on an American Legion scholarship, earning a Bachelor of Science degree in Chemistry. Following two years of military service in Korea, he went to Cornell University in New York to get a Ph.D. He joined the Colorado College Chemistry Department in 1959.

---

[37]For a book on the 1994 governor's race in Colorado and Mike Bird's role in it, see Robert D. Loevy, *The Flawed Path To The Governorship 1994: The Nationalization Of A Colorado Statewide Election* (Lanham, MD: University Press Of America, 1996).

[38]Kristopher Lindbloom, "An Author In Our Midst: Douglas Monroy," *Catalyst*, 18 November 1994, 15.

As a result of a laboratory accident while he was in graduate school, Professor Champion had only limited vision (10 percent vision in one eye). He was famous for spending hours grading student examinations with a magnifying glass. His teaching was said by the students to be as concentrated and highly focused as his vision.[39]

Professor Douglas Freed, a member of the Psychology Department for 38 years, retired in the spring of 1995. He received both his B.A. and his Ph.D degrees from the University of Minnesota. Similar to many retired professors, Doug Freed continued to teach a block or two at the College. For instance, in the fall of 1995, he taught the popular interdisciplinary course, *Freedom And Authority*. In an effort to explain why he was not teaching a Psychology course, Freed said: "I have never primarily identified myself with a [specific] field."[40]

During the Vietnam War, Douglas Freed donated many hours of his personal time to counseling young men at Colorado College on legal methods of avoiding the military draft by attaining conscientious objector status.

Douglas Fox, Professor of Religion, was named the 1995 Colorado Professor of the Year by the Carnegie Foundation for the Advancement of Teaching. A native of Sydney, Australia, Professor Fox received his B.A. from the University of Sydney and his Ph.D. from the Pacific School of Religion in Berkeley, California. A published scholar, his many books included *Dispelling Illusion*, published in 1993, and *Direct Awareness of Self*, which came out in 1995.

Professor Fox was properly modest when he learned he had been named Colorado Professor of the Year. "When I first heard that I had received the award," Fox said, "I was delighted but then moderately embarrassed because there are a lot of other professors who are just as deserving of the award." He said he hoped his award would "increase awareness of Colorado College and its programs and faculty."[41]

Bill Champion, Doug Freed, and Doug Fox were among the last of that famous group of professors who were hired in the 1950s and 1960s and, at the end of lengthy teaching careers, retired in the 1990s. As a

---

[39]Mike Smith, "Campus Remembers A True Champion," *Catalyst*, 2 December 1994, 9.

[40]Stephen Raher, "Professor Doug Freed Retires," *Catalyst*, 20 October 1995, 2.

[41]Julie Gordon, "Religion Professor Given Prestigious Award," *Catalyst*, 3 November 1995, 2.

group, these professors were celebrated for their deep devotion to teaching. Some of them published books and articles, but the major focus of their professional careers always was on their students.

ART IN NEW YORK CITY

One of the great features of majoring in Art at Colorado College was the senior trip to visit art museums and galleries in New York City. Each year about 30 senior Art Studio and Art History majors spent one week in the city said by many to be the "art capital" of the United States. Costs of the student trip were paid for by the Berg Fund through the Getty Foundation.

Professor of Art Gale Murray was one of the faculty members who obtained financing and set up this senior trip for Art majors. "The excitement of seeing real works of art and of being in direct contact with the contemporary art scene is important for the students," she said. "New York is a central place for innovative art as well as the traditional." The senior trip also gave the students the opportunity to be in a large, invigorating, and supportive art community in contrast to the somewhat limited and isolated art environment in Colorado Springs.[42]

THE FINAL JANUARY SYMPOSIUM

In January of 1995 the College held its last major Symposium, at least for a while. President Mohrman decided that, in view of low student attendance, the January Symposium no longer merited the approximately $65,000 required each year to continue it. Mohrman said she made the decision after "watching how students vote[d] with their feet." Only 300 of the College's 1,900 or so students attended the final January Symposium, which was on the topic of *Sexuality and Gender.*[43]

In some ways, the January Symposium was a victim of the new Half-Block courses. With the advent of the Half-Block, the Symposium had to be scheduled over just three days—the three days between the end of

---

[42]Libby Hruska, "New York Provides Unique Experience For Art Majors," *Catalyst*, 3 November 1995, 1.

[43]Joseph Sharman, "Symposium Likely To Face Budgetary Ax," *Catalyst*, 3 February 1995, 2. Allison Bonner, "Students React: Cancellation Of Symposium Unpopular Decision," *Catalyst*, 3 February 1995, 9. Also see Tracy Fantle, "Sexuality And Gender Issues To Seize Spotlight In January," *Catalyst*, 2 December 1994, 10.

Half-Block and the beginning of Block 5. Students taking Half-Block were just ending nine-days of course work when Symposium began, and many felt they needed a break rather than three more days of intense intellectual and scholastic activity.

The real loss was to the faculty and to the friends of the College in Colorado Springs. They were the most faithful attenders of the January Symposium, and many of them remarked on how much they would miss it.

A FRATERNITY DEPARTS

In February of 1995 the College withdrew its official recognition of one of the fraternities. The fraternity members were given two weeks to vacate the fraternity house and find other living quarters for the remainder of the semester. "The reason our charter was revoked," one member of the fraternity said, "was . . . about 15 years of probation and probation violations." It was the second fraternity in six years to exit the campus because of severe disciplinary problems.[44]

THE GLASS HOUSE

The vacated fraternity house, located in the fraternity quadrangle north of Palmer Hall, became an additional residence hall at the College. As a result of the efforts of student Ryan Paul Haygood, the building was turned into a multicultural dormitory. It was open to members of minority groups and non-minority students interested in furthering the goals of ethnic diversity on the campus. It was called the Glass House because the students living in it knew they would be watched carefully by those wondering if a multicultural dormitory could work well at Colorado College.[45]

---

[44]Jennie Randall, "And Then There Were Three . . . ; Fraternity Dissolved," *Catalyst*, 3 March 1995, 1. Jennie Randall, ". . . Lose Appeal, Face Eviction Deadline," *Catalyst*, 10 March 1995, 1. Amber Anderson, ". . . Decision Evokes Emotion," *Catalyst*, 10 March 1995, 10.

[45]Amber Anderson, "New House Seen As A Benefit To Entire Campus; New Theme House Seeks To Improve Diversity," *Catalyst*, 12 May 1995, 13. Diane Cochran, "Glass House To Continue Through 1996–1997 School Year," *Catalyst*, 26 April 1996, 1. Ryan Paul Haygood, "Minority Students Demand Accommodation," *Catalyst*, 31 January 1997, 6. Ryan Paul Haygood, "Small Numbers Of Minorities In Dorms Not Multi-Cultural Arrangement; Glass House Does Foster Campus Diversity," *Catalyst*, 12 December 1997, 19.

A Sorority Closes

There was another setback to the social system at Colorado College when a sorority, one that had been on campus for over sixty years, closed its doors. There were only 15 active members and, following an unsuccessful rush in the fall of 1995, the remaining women in the chapter voted to dissolve.

With the loss of two fraternities and the demise of one sorority, Colorado College was left with three fraternities and three sororities. Some observers believed, however, that the fraternities and sororities would be stronger with a smaller number of social units competing for members.[46]

Computer Registration

The technological revolution continued at Colorado College in the spring of 1995 when, for the first time in the College's history, students registered for upcoming classes completely by computer. Instead of writing their proposed class schedules down on a piece of paper and turning it in, all students were required to go to a computer terminal and type in their course selections. There were some reports of long lines waiting to use computer terminals, but the Registrar's Office promised to fix that problem by making more terminals available for future course registrations. Electronic registration appeared to be a big success. Margaret Van Horn, the College Registrar, said the next step would be having students "drop" and "add" individual courses by computer. That would bring an end to one of the more famous pieces of paper in Colorado College history—the Registrar's "Drop-Add Slip" for changing a course.[47]

Men's Lacrosse

NCAA Division I men's ice hockey and NCAA Division I women's soccer traditionally made most of the sports news at Colorado College, but in the mid 1990s the NCAA Division III men's lacrosse team attracted major interest. In 1995–1996 the men's lacrosse team won its third consecutive Rocky Mountain Intercollegiate Lacrosse League (RMILL) title. The men

---

[46]Bert Bell, "… Closes Chapter In C.C. History," *Catalyst*, 17 November 1995, 3.

[47]"Preregistration Deemed Success," *Catalyst*, 14 April 1995, 4.

stickers capped the season with a final victory over the University of Denver by a blowout score of 15–9.[48]

WOMEN'S STUDIES

In the fall of 1995 the College created a Women's Studies major. The new major was composed of courses taught by faculty members in other academic departments, and many of the Women's Studies courses were cross-listed with those departments. The new major made Women's Studies a recognized part of the curriculum.[49]

25 YEARS OF THE BLOCK PLAN

At the start of the 1995–1996 academic year, the Colorado College Block Plan marked its 25th anniversary. A quarter of a century had gone by since Block 1, 1970–1971, when the faculty and the students at the College had hesitantly but bravely embarked on an adventurous new calendar.

A Block Plan Advisory Committee evaluated the Block Plan as it finished year 25 and began year 26. The study found the Block Plan functioning well and recommended no changes. The Block Plan was particularly praised for increasing students' abilities to master and retain academic knowledge, for focusing classes on student discussion rather than faculty lectures, and for providing unique opportunities for field study away from the campus.[50]

MAJOR GIFTS

Computer manufacturing millionaire David Packard, who made the major gift to the College that resulted in the construction of Packard Hall, made another gift to the College of $4 million. This gift was used as a challenge grant. The College decided to try to raise the additional funds to match Packard's donation four to one, thereby hoping to garner an additional $16 million.[51]

---

[48]"LAX Ends Season As RMILL Champs; 4 Named All-League," *Catalyst*, 3 May 1996, 16.

[49]Lisa Gesson, "Women Studies Now An Official Major," *Catalyst*, 1 December 1995, 14.

[50]Libby Hruska, "Block Plan Celebrates 25 Years Of Excellence," *Catalyst*, 13 October 1995, 1.

[51]Julie Gordon, "Packard Challenge Nearing Completion," *Catalyst*, 13 October 1995, 3. David Packard passed away shortly after making this final gift to the College. See Jonathan Irwin, "College Benefactor Packard Dies At 83," *Catalyst*, 29 March 1996, 1.

Another major gift to Colorado College came from Trustee Patricia Crown-Tapper and her family. They donated $1 million to help improve teaching at Colorado College. The Crown-Tapper Teaching and Learning Center (TLC) was set up in the basement of the Tutt Library Addition under the direction of Robert D. Lee, Professor of Political Science and the College's resident expert on the Middle East. The Crown-Tapper Center brought in visiting lecturers on the subject of college teaching and held a variety of forums and discussion groups to enable faculty to share and evaluate various teaching methods and ideas. "In its first years," President Kathryn Mohrman noted, "it has had a low-keyed but positive impact on faculty work."[52]

ENTER THE *LEW*

Rastall Center was the old student center which in 1987 was enlarged into Worner Campus Center. Rastall Center had Benny's Basement, a student pub located in the basement that functioned effectively as a place for students to congregate, hang out, relax, and listen to both live and recorded entertainment. "Benny's was dark, smoky, loud, pungent and crowded (usually)," a former student noted. It was a place to get "3.2 beer, soft drinks, and burnt boiled coffee, . . . and sometimes there was even popcorn. It was the only late-night hangout for groups of students larger than [what] could fit into the wing lounges. . . ."[53]

Benny's ceased to exist when Rastall Center became Worner Center, and a number of groups on campus tried to find a way to create a pub-style, night club-like place for Colorado College students to find entertainment, relaxation, and collegiality. Hindering this process was the fact that the drinking age in Colorado had been raised to age 21, so the majority of the students who came to a new campus pub would not be old enough to imbibe alcohol.

---

[52]Memorandum on College History, Kathryn Mohrman to author, 4 February 1998, 2. Also see Julie Gordon, "Packard Challenge Nearing Completion," *Catalyst*, 13 October 1995, 3.

[53]John DeLaHunt, Class of 1987, "Alumnus Reflects On The Predecessor To The LEW: Benny's Basement," *Catalyst*, 17 October 1997, 2.

There was an unsuccessful effort to at least partly revive Benny's Basement by creating the Tiger Pit. Some rooms in the basement of Worner Center were equipped with video games and other forms of entertainment, but the Tiger Pit somehow just never worked out as a student after-hours gathering place.

In the fall of 1997 the student government and Marriott, the College food service, made a major effort to open a successful student pub and night club. The result was the LEW, which took over the area in Worner basement previously occupied by the Tiger Pit. The space was extensively remodeled and equipped with a bar, tables and chairs, etc. Both food and drink were served in the LEW, with careful checking of identification cards required to make sure alcohol was not served to underage students. The LEW was to be open every night of the week but Sunday from 4 P.M. to 12 Midnight. There was a 1 A.M. closing time on Saturday night.[54]

The LEW was named, obviously, for the initials and nickname of Lloyd Edson Worner, the former President of Colorado College for whom Worner Center was named.

THE RETURN OF THE D GRADE

In the fall of 1997 the faculty voted to reinstitute the grades of D and D+. Colorado College had not used the D grade since 1969, when the short lived Honors (H), High Pass (HP), Credit (C), and No Credit (NC) grading system was adopted. After 1971 the College went back to the traditional A, B, and C grades but did not include the D grade. The grade scale was A-B-C-NC (No Credit).

Students and faculty alike were aware that, with no D grade to register a poor performance in a class, the C grade became a "bad" grade. A senior Education major, Carl Nowlin, explained how this logic worked: "An A is for people who know what they're doing, a B is for people who at least show up [for class], and a C is for when you [really antagonize the professor]."

Grade inflation was the major reason given for bringing back the D and D+ grades. The all-campus Grade Point Average (GPA) climbed from 3.080 (B) in 1986–1987 to 3.309 (B+) in 1996–1997. It was argued

[54]Jody Snee, "Police Called To LEW Grand Opening Party," *Catalyst*, 17 October 1997, 4.

that students who were doing poorly in a course were getting C- grades that should have been D or D+ grades. The all-campus Grade Point Average would start to fall, so the logic went, if weaker students were getting Ds instead of low Cs on their transcripts.

Supporters of the D grade were trying to give a good name to the grade of C. They pointed out that a C- was barely passing under the A-B-C system, but if the D grade returned the C grade would become more respectable and no longer be associated with near failure.

The new D and D+ grades took effect at the start of the 1998–1999 academic year.[55]

THE CAMPUS MASTER PLAN

In 1994 the College began the development of a new Campus Master Plan. The Colorado College Campus Planning Study, which had been conducted by Campus Planner Richard Dober in 1982–1983, was more than ten years old. The time had come to once again gather data, take surveys, initiate discourse with various groups in the campus community, and thereby come up with a rational plan for meeting the future physical needs of the College.

Phil Rector, the Physical Plant Director, was the project manager for the Campus Master Plan. He was ably aided by a committee of faculty, administrators, and trustees chaired by Michael Grace, Professor of Music and the recent Acting President of the College. To provide professional expertise, the Campus Master Plan Committee hired Thompson and Rose Architects of Cambridge, Massachusetts.[56]

This Campus Master Plan, undertaken in the 1990s, differed somewhat from the Campus Planning Study of 1983. The earlier study was more specific, carefully defining new buildings and their uses and locating them at definite spots on the Colorado College campus. The Campus Master Plan of the 1990s was broader in scope, more oriented to aes-

[55]Holly Benner and Diane Cochran, "Making the GraDe," *Catalyst*, 7 November 1997, 6.

[56]Sarah Parmley, "Campus Planning Hires Massachusetts Architectural Firm To Finish," *Catalyst*, 23 September 1994, 3.

thetics, sought to take a longer look into the future, and came up with more generalized recommendations.[57]

An Aesthetic Critique

The Campus Master Plan process began with Thompson and Rose making an evaluation of the aesthetics of the existing campus. They pointed out that the Tutt Library addition invaded the central portion of the main campus quadrangle and suggested the Tutt addition might be "phased out" over the next 20 years. They praised Armstrong Hall for its "tough, modernistic aesthetic" but noted that it was "somewhat of a failure as an inhabitable building." And they called for preservation of the former private residences surrounding the campus, most of them College owned, that were being used as small dormitories and theme houses.[58]

A Vision of the Future

In November of 1995 the Board of Trustees adopted Phase One of the Campus Master Plan, which provided a blueprint of the College's physical needs through the year 2005. This ambitious list of campus improvements included:

- Construction of a new Geology/Psychology/Environmental Science building, close to Palmer Hall and Barnes Science Center, to house the Geology and Psychology Departments, previously housed in Palmer Hall. Space released in Palmer Hall by Geology and Psychology would be used to expand the Social Science departments and the Math Department in Palmer Hall. The new building would also contain the College's Environmental Science program.
- Construction of a Performing Arts Center with a small theater seating 350 to 500 persons. This theater would be par-

[57]Author's notes, interview with Michael Grace, Professor of Music and Chairman of the Campus Master Plan Committee, 26 January 1998.

[58]Joseph Sharman, "Master Plan Decides Campus Future," *Catalyst*, 11 November 1994, 1. A number of Thompson and Rose recommendations were described in the text under the photographs accompanying this article.

ticularly designed for student production of plays. The building would be located East of Armstrong Hall and would include office space for the Drama and Dance Department.

- Renovation of Armstrong Hall to make the building more attractive and add additional space. The first floor would be reconfigured for administrative offices, the second floor for classrooms, and the third floor for faculty offices.
- Development of an "Academic Village" along Wood Avenue by creating seven dormitories, each one housing 50 students. The theme houses and language houses would remain in this area, along with some faculty housing. A new food service facility would be constructed for this campus residential area. The purpose of the Academic Village would be to create on campus the apartment-style living that students seek when moving off campus.
- Construction of two new intramural athletic fields on College-owned land east of Nevada Avenue.

These were the major short-term goals recommended in Phase One of the Master Plan. Other recommendations, set forth in Phase Two and Phase Three of the Master Plan, were to be implemented between 2005 and 2025. These recommendations included renovating Armstrong Theater in Armstrong Hall, adding a north addition to Tutt Library, and relocating Honnen Ice Rink so that once again the Cossitt Amphitheater could be used for outdoor meetings, dramatic productions, and rallies. Another longterm future project was to construct a student recreation center to go with the proposed new intramural athletic fields east of Nevada Avenue.

One minor recommendation in the plan was implemented immediately. That was the elimination of all vehicle parking on Cascade Avenue where it passes through the Colorado College campus. By removing all the parked cars and trucks from Cascade, the College made it easier for motorists to see pedestrians—most of them students—as they crossed Cascade Avenue at the various crosswalks.[59]

[59]Author's notes, interview with Michael Grace, Professor of Music and Chairman of the Campus Master Plan Committee, 26 January 1998. Also see Julie Gordon, "Vision Plan Approved By

This final version of the Colorado College Master Plan caught the imagination of both the College community and opinion leaders in Colorado Springs. Early in 1998 this ambitious and exciting plan for the physical future of the campus received an award from the Partnership for Community Design, an organization of local residents interested in furthering good planning and aesthetic enhancement in Colorado Springs.[60]

"A Course of Distinction"

The Master Plan for the future of Colorado College would have been meaningless if the money were not raised to pay for the many programs and projects included in the plan. The fall of 1997 found the College preparing for a major fund-raising campaign to garner the financial capital to turn the dreams in the Master Plan into reality. The amount of money to be raised was set at $83 million. A major goal of the campaign was to expand financial aid to students in an effort to keep the College accessible to those with limited financial resources.

The fund-raising campaign was named "The Campaign For Colorado College: A Course Of Distinction." The double meaning of the word "Course" was intended. It referred to both the "course" of the future and an academic "course," such as those taught at the College. El Pomar Foundation gave its support to the fund-raising campaign by contributing $5 million for the new Geology/Psychology/Environmental Science building.[61]

The 1997–1998 Reaccreditation

In the fall of 1997 Colorado College came up for recertification by the North Central Association Of Colleges And Schools. Libby Rittenberg,

---

Trustees," *Catalyst*, 17 November 1995, 3. Noel Sullivan, "The Academic Village; Master Plan's Residential Life Scheme Will Attempt To Join Academics With Student Life," *Catalyst*, 8 March 1996, 3. Julie Gordon, "Master Plan In Action; East Campus Changes Planned," *Catalyst*, 7 March 1997, 3. Todd Wilson, "City Approves Master, East Campus Plans," *Access*, October 1997, 1. Jody Snee, "Master Plan Begins With Construction On Yampa Street," *Catalyst*, 12 December 1997, 4.

[60]"Designers, Planners Get Yearly Awards; Group Honors Projects That Enhance Local Area," *Colorado Springs Gazette*, 25 January 1998, NEWS2.

[61]Ovetta Sampson, "El Pomar's $5 Million Helps Fund CC Building," *Colorado Springs Gazette*, 4 September 1998, NEWS1.

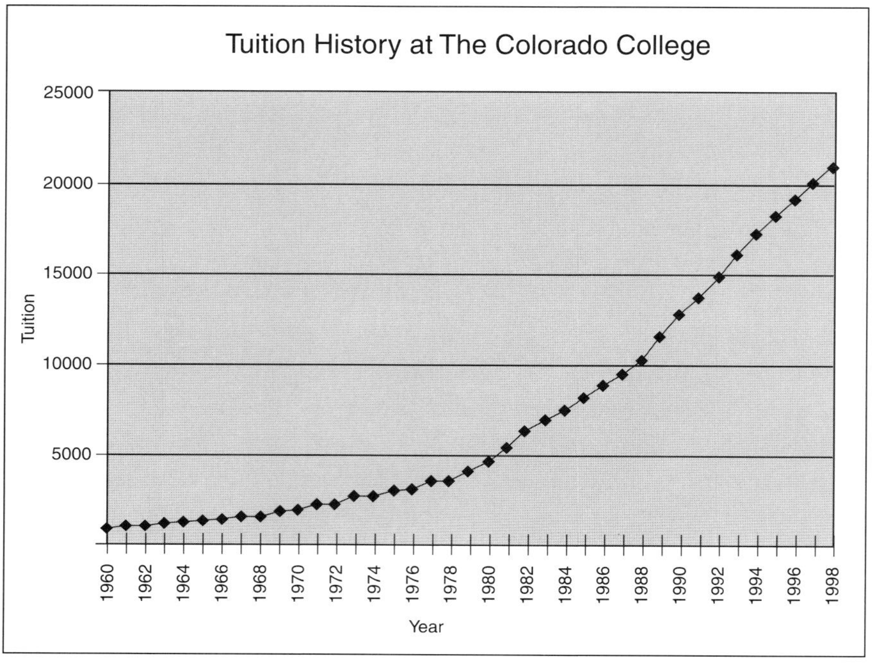

TUITION IN CONSTANT DOLLARS
Tuition at Colorado College increased from less than $1,000 per year in 1960 to more than $20,000 per year in 1998. Substantial increases in financial aid helped to keep Colorado College affordable for many middle class families.

Professor of Economics, chaired the Reaccreditation Steering Committee. Following an in-depth visit to the campus, a delegation from the North Central Association reported they would recommend the reaccreditation of Colorado College with considerable enthusiasm. Both President Kathryn Mohrman and Professor of Psychology John Horner, the Chair of the faculty governing body at Colorado College, noted the high praise from the North Central visiting committee for the condition of the College, particularly the quality of the students.[62]

---

[62]Conversations with the author. The 1997–1998 Reaccreditation Report was entitled: "Implementing Our Strategic Priorities: How Far Have We Come?"

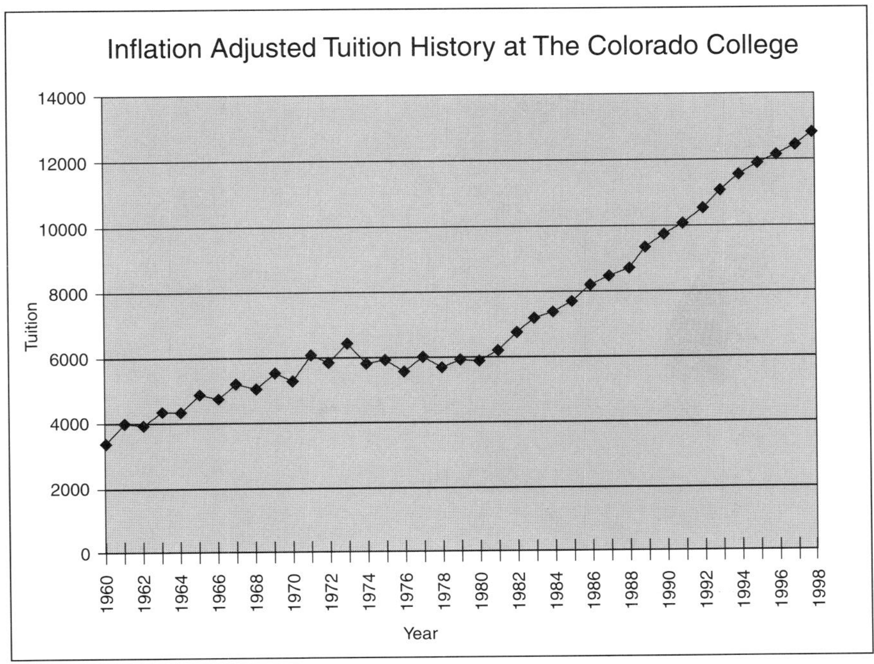

TUITION IN 1982 DOLLARS

When adjusted for inflation, tuition at Colorado College rose from $3,000 per year in 1960 to more than $12,000 per year in 1998. Despite these faster-than-inflation increases, tuition at Colorado College in 1998 was still less than what was being charged at many other prestige colleges and universities.

Clearly Colorado College was providing a superior product, but many observers noted that it also was becoming an expensive product. Tuition for the 1998–1999 academic year was set at $20,880. Room and board added another $5,328. But, to keep a Colorado College education available to students with limited finances, the College was devoting approximately 20 percent of its 1998–1999 operating budget to financial aid programs.[63]

[63]Form letter, President Kathryn Mohrman to the Students of Colorado College, 4 March 1998.

THE 125TH ANNIVERSARY CELEBRATION

During the 1998–1999 academic year, Colorado College marked its 125th anniversary. A special Symposium was scheduled on the topic of *Cultures in the 21st Century: Conflicts and Convergences.* Lief Carter, the McHugh Family Distinguished Professor of American Institutions and Leadership, was hard at work lining up speakers for this major campus intellectual event. Professor of Music Donald Jenkins was leading the Colorado College Chorale as it prepared to sing Bach's Mass in B Minor. Maxwell Taylor, the former Vice President for Student Life at the College, was busy editing a book of memoirs by key figures in the recent history of the College.

THE BLOCK PLAN YEARS

Colorado College enjoyed a long and distinguished history throughout all of its 125 years, but the 31 years from 1968 to 1999 were particularly notable. It was during that period that the College developed, adopted, and implemented an unusual academic calendar—the Block Plan. In fact, it could be argued that the name of Colorado College became synonymous with the Block Plan. When asked if they had heard of Colorado College, many people would say, "Yes—that's the Block Plan college."[64]

The distinguishing characteristic of the Block Plan was that it attracted a faculty that wanted to teach. The result was that Colorado College was solidified as a teaching college, much more so than most other liberal arts colleges and universities. The reputation of the Block Plan for demanding additional faculty commitment to teaching had two interesting effects. (1) It attracted dedicated teachers to the College and put off those potential faculty members who were not prepared to place teaching at the center of their academic careers. (2) The reputation of the Block Plan as demanding of faculty time and effort discouraged most other college faculties from adopting the Block Plan, thus keeping Colorado College a "unique" place, for the most part, on the academic landscape.

---

[64]Observation of the author.

One of the big surprises of the Block Plan at Colorado College was that it turned out to be a good merchandising tool as well as an inspired way of organizing a college calendar. "At the time the Block Plan was adopted," President Kathryn Mohrman pointed out, "the faculty was thinking only of its potential as a better way to teach the liberal arts and get students to participate more actively in their own educations. It was only later that the College discovered the Block Plan was also a marketing tool—a way of attracting more academically committed and intellectually adventurous students. The College soon was in the position where, if the Block Plan were dropped, the College would lose many of its best and most exciting applicants."[65]

Through the years from 1968 to 1999, Colorado College periodically set new goals. But the institution never strayed from its main goal—to provide a high quality undergraduate liberal arts education to motivated and inquiring students.

A SECOND GOLDEN AGE

From the perspective of the 1998–1999 academic year, the historically-minded observer could look back and see that Colorado College was in its Second Golden Age. From the early 1950s to the late 1990s, the College experienced an outstanding period of enrollment growth, financial development, and academic improvement. Four of the College's presidents—William Gill, Louis Benezet, Lloyd Worner, and Gresham Riley—presided over this exciting and beneficial period in the College's history. And this Second Golden Age showed no sign of ending as the presidency of Kathryn Mohrman got underway and up to full throttle.

The First Golden Age of Colorado College had occurred under legendary President William Frederick Slocum. It was Slocum who gave the College a great national reputation and, during an intense period of fund-raising and building construction, gave the campus its basic shape and form. The turmoil following Slocum's departure from the College, coupled with the financial problems of the Great Depression and the disrup-

---

[65]Author's notes, interview with Kathryn Mohrman, President of Colorado College, 30 January 1998.

tion of World War II, replaced the First Golden Age with a period of enduring stability rather than notable progress.

But starting in the early 1950s, expansion and progress and achievement once again became the watchwords at Colorado College. External factors played an important part. The College benefitted greatly from the rapid population growth and increased economic activity that characterized the state of Colorado in the post-World War II period. The Baby Boom generation that went to college in the late 1960s and early 1970s provided Colorado College with an unusually large and talented applicant pool from which to choose students. Also important was the generosity of major benefactors—such as El Pomar Foundation and David Packard—that brought a substantial increase in monetary gifts to the College.

But factors internal to Colorado College also helped to create and sustain this Second Golden Age. The faculty, supported strongly by both the students and the Board of Trustees, was unusually inventive where the academic program at the College was concerned. Adoption of such teaching innovations as the Adviser Plan, and the willingness to experiment with exciting new courses such as *Renaissance Culture* and *Patterns In Nature*, revealed an institution that in no way was intellectually standing still. Then, in 1968, with the creative development and successful implementation of the Block Plan, Colorado College gave itself a totally unique and extremely interesting academic calendar. The Block Plan clearly was the academic and intellectual cornerstone of Colorado College's Second Golden Age.

ON TO THE FUTURE

Although the 125th Anniversary of Colorado College found the institution well into its Second Golden Age, the College was preparing to continue to move forward. The Strategic Planning report, issued as the *Interim Report On The Future Of Colorado College*, had reaffirmed the College's commitment to undergraduate liberal arts education. The Campus Master Plan had identified the physical needs, both immediate and future, of the College's physical plant. A major fund-raising campaign, *The Campaign For Colorado College: A Course Of Distinction*, was underway to bring in $83 million. That amount of money was thought to be required to tend to both the academic and the physical needs of the College.

Once again, as it turned 125 years old, Colorado College was preparing to move forward with new ideas and new programs—and ever remain the same committed liberal arts college it had always been. Colorado College was, indeed, "A Place Of Learning."

BIBLIOGRAPHY

Books:

Abbott, Carl, Stephen J. Leonard, and David McComb. *Colorado: A History Of The Centennial State*, 3rd ed. Niwot, CO: University Press of Colorado, 1994.

Anderson, George L. *General William J. Palmer: A Decade Of Colorado Railroad Building 1870–1880*. Colorado Springs, CO: Colorado College, 1936.

Athearn, Robert G. *Rebel Of The Rockies: A History Of The Denver And Rio Grande Western Railroad*. New Haven, CT: Yale University Press, 1962.

Bates, Samuel P. *History of Pennsylvania Volunteers, 1861–1865*. Harrisburg, PA: B. Singerly, State Printer, 1869–71.

Beach, Arthur G. *A Pioneer College: The Story of Marietta*. Privately printed, 1935.

Benezet, Louis T. *General Education In The Progressive College*. New York, NY: Arno Press, 1971. First published New York, NY: Columbia University Teachers College, 1943.

Buckley, Louise. *The History Of Colorado College, 1874–1904*. M.A. Thesis in History, Colorado College, 1935.

Burgess, Mary Elizabeth, and Wanetta W. Draper. *The First Congregational Church of Colorado Springs, Colorado: The First One Hundred Years, 1874–1974*. Colorado Springs, CO: First Congregational Church, 1974.

Cronin, Thomas E., and Robert D. Loevy. *Colorado Politics And Government: Governing The Centennial State*. Lincoln, NE: University of Nebraska Press, 1993.

Finley, Judith Reid. *Time Capsule 1900: Colorado Springs A Century Ago*. Colorado Springs, CO: Pastwords Publications, 1998.

Fisher, John S. *A Builder Of The West: The Life Of General William Jackson Palmer*. Caldwell, ID: Caxton Printers, 1939.

Fletcher, Robert S. *A History Of Oberlin College*, v. I, v. II. Oberlin, OH: Oberlin College, 1943.

Fuess, Claude Moore. *Amherst: The Story Of A New England College*. Boston, MA: Little, Brown, and Company, 1935.

Fuller, Timothy, ed. *Something Of Great Constancy: Essays In Honor Of The Memory Of J. Glenn Gray, 1913–1977*. Colorado Springs, CO: Colorado College, 1979.

Fuller, Timothy. *This Glorious And Transcendant Place*. Colorado Springs, CO: Colorado College, 1981.

Hale, Horace M. *Education In Colorado*. Denver, CO: News Printing Company, 1885.

Havighurst, Walter. *The Miami Years, 1809–1984*, 175th Anniversary ed. New York, NY: Putnam's, 1984.

Hawkins, Hugh. *Pioneer: A History Of The Johns Hopkins University, 1874–1889*. Ithaca, NY: Cornell University Press, 1960.

Hershey, Charlie Brown. *Colorado College: 1874–1949*. Colorado Springs, CO: Colorado College, 1952.

Howbert, Irving. *Memories Of A Lifetime In The Pike's Peak Region*. Glorietta, NM: Rio Grande Press, 1970. First published Corpus Christi, TX: Louis V. Boling Books, 1925.

Kirk, Charles E., ed. *History of the Fifteenth Pennsylvania Volunteer Cavalry*. Philadelphia, PA: 1906.

Lanner, Max. *Historical Notes On The Music Department Of Colorado College, 1874–1959* (Additional Notes by Richard J. Agee, 1959–1994). 1994. Available at Colorado College Archives.

Lipsey, John J. *The Lives Of John J. Hagerman: Builder Of The Colorado Midland Railway*. Denver, CO: Golden Bell Press, 1968.

Loevy, Robert D. *The Flawed Path To The Governorship 1994*. Lanham, MD: University Press of America, 1996.

Loevy, Robert D. *The Flawed Path To The Presidency 1992*. Albany, NY: State University of New York Press, 1995.

Michel, Lester A. *111 Years Of Chemistry At Colorado College*. 1988. Available at Colorado College Archives.

Oakeshott, Michael. *A Place Of Learning*. Colorado Springs, CO: Colorado College, 1975.

Rastall, B. M. *The Cripple Creek Strike Of 1893*. Colorado Springs, CO: Colorado College, 1905.

Reid, J. Juan. *Colorado College: The First Century, 1874–1974*. Colorado Springs, CO: Colorado College, 1979.

Schneider, James G. *The Navy V–12 Program: Leadership For A Lifetime*. Boston, MA: Houghton-Mifflin, 1987.

Sprague, Marshall. *Colorado: A History*. New York, NY: Norton, 1984.

Sprague, Marshall. *Newport In The Rockies: The Life And Good Times Of Colorado Springs*, Centennial ed. Chicago, IL: Sage Books, 1971.

Street, Gary. *A History Of Colorado College Football*. Publication, Colorado College Book Store.

Tenney, Edward Payson. *Looking Forward Into The Past.* Nahant, MA: Rumford Press, 1910.

Tenney, Edward Payson. *The New West: As Related To The Christian College*, 3rd ed. Cambridge, MA: Riverside Press, 1878.

Ubbelohde, Carl, Maxine Benson, and Duane A. Smith. *A Colorado History*, 7th ed. Boulder, CO: Pruett Publishing, 1995.

Wilson, Suzanne C. *Column South, With The 15th Pensylvania Cavalry. . . .* Flagstaff, AZ: J.F. Colton, 1960.

Articles:

"Address By President Slocum." *Colorado College Tiger*, 19 March 1909, 7.

Arnest, Barbara M. "Montgomery Hall's 100th Anniversary Also Celebrates National Historic Dedication." *Colorado College Catalyst*, 19 April 1991, 9.

Arnest, Barbara M. "The Other Seven Presidents." *Colorado College Bulletin*, February 1975, 19.

Arnest, Barbara M. "The St. Matthew Passion And A Community Of Singers." *Colorado College Bulletin*, May 1975, 31–37.

Benezet, Louis T. "Some Passing Thoughts About Change." *Colorado College Bulletin*, February 1975, 17–18.

Carne-Ross, D. S. "The Nipping Of Our Cultural December." *Colorado College Bulletin*, May 1975, 11–20.

"Colorado College." *Mecca*, no date, 7–11. Photograph Files: Buildings – Campus Views – Collections. Colorado College Archives.

"Death Of General Palmer." *Colorado College Tiger*, 19 March 1901, 1.

Dougherty, James G. "The Beginnings Of Colorado College." *Colorado College Bulletin*, Feburary 1975, 10–15.

Finley, Judith Reid. "Colorado College Oral History Project," a series of recorded interviews with important persons associated with Colorado College. Colorado College Archives.

Freed, Doublas W., and Carl L. Roberts. "Mirror Of New England: The Early Years Of Psychology At Colorado College." *Journal Of The History Of The Behavioral Sciences*, January 1988, 46.

Kerr, James Hutchison. "Colorado College: After Dinner Paper." 12 June 1907. Colorado College Archives.

Kerr, James Hutchison. "The Pioneer Days of Colorado College." *El Paso County Democrat*, Pioneer ed., December 1908.

Kerr, James Hutchison. "When Colorado College Was Not In Flower." 24 October 1904. Colorado College Archives.

Lee, Mabel Barbee. "Stormy Young Rebels." *Denver Post*, Empire Magazine, 30 December 1951, 8–9.

Loomis, Ruth. Letter to "Mr. Ormes," 25 February 1928. Colorado College Archives.

"Memorial Statue To General Palmer Will Be Erected." *Colorado Springs Gazette Telegraph*, Annual Edition, 1925.

"Men Of Note Affiliated With Mining And Mining Interests In The Cripple Creek District." No publisher cited, 1905. Colorado College Archives.

"Midnight Scholars." *Newsweek*, 30 December 1974.

"President Slocum." *Congregationalist*, 22 February 1900, 259.

"President Slocum's Lectures At Andover." *Congregationalist*, 25 April 1903, 581.

"Students Gave The Slocums Big Send-Off Tuesday Night: Marched To The Station Where Many Cheers Were Given." *Colorado College Tiger*, 13 October 1916, 1.

"The Colorado College Plan," *Critique*, Center for the Study of Higher Education, University of Toledo, Toledo, Ohio, March 1973.

"The Plan Still Loved." *Colorado College Bulletin*, May 1975, 39–42.

"Tribute To First Citizen." *Colorado College Tiger*, 19 March 1909, 1.

"W. F. Slocum Resigns From C.C. Presidency: Goes East Soon In Interests Of Endowment Fund." *Colorado College Tiger*, 15 September 1916, 1.

Worner, Lloyd. "College Community Should Ponder Goals." *Colorado College Catalyst*, 4 October 1975, 5.

INDEX

Colorado College: A Place of Learning 1874–1999

Designed by Sally Hegarty
Photographs: Tutt Library Special Collections
Composed by Rachel Hegarty in BaskervilleMT with QuarkXPress
on Apple Macintosh systems
Printed by Fittje Brothers Printing Company, Colorado Springs
on 70lb Luna Matte Finish
Bound by Mountain States Bindery, Salt Lake City
in Lexotone, Marine Blue in an edition numbering 2,500 copies
One hundred of this title and companion book, *Colorado College: Memories and Reflections* collected by Maxwell Taylor, were bound in boxed sets by Karen Pardue, White River Studio, Colorado Springs in Campanetta Acid-free Cloth